THE MONGOLS

THE MONGOLS
A History

Jeremiah Curtin

With a foreword by
THEODORE ROOSEVELT

DA CAPO PRESS
A Member of the Perseus Books Group

Cataloging-in-Publication data for this book is available from the Library of Congress.

Originally published by Little, Brown and Company, Boston, in 1908
First Da Capo Press edition 2003
ISBN 0–306–81243–6

Published by Da Capo Press
A Member of the Perseus Books Group
http://www.dacapopress.com

Da Capo Press books are available at special discounts for bulk purchases in the U.S. by corporations, institutions, and other organizations. For more information, please contact the Special Markets Department at the Perseus Books Group, 11 Cambridge Center, Cambridge, MA 02142, or call (800) 255-1514 or (617) 252-5298, or e-mail j.mccrary@perseusbooks.com.

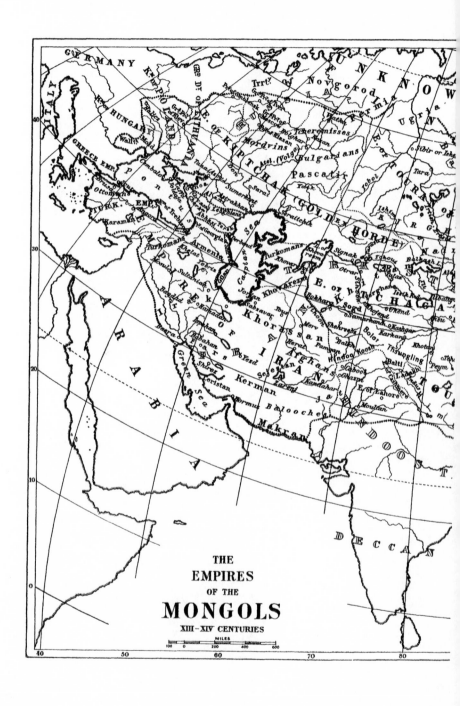

THE
EMPIRES
OF THE
MONGOLS
XIII–XIV CENTURIES

MILES
100   0   200   400   600

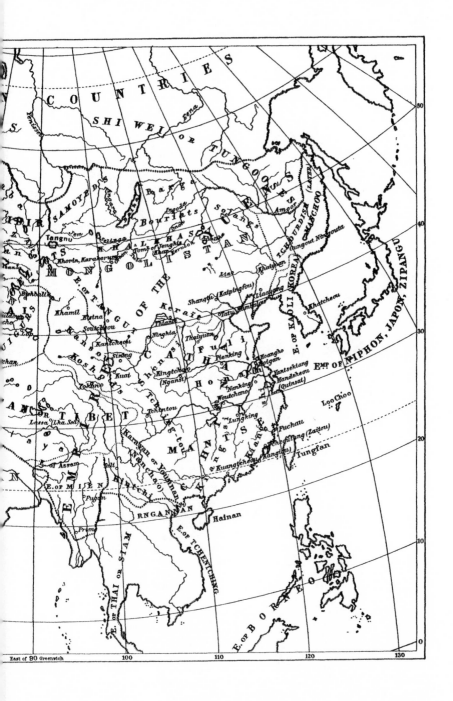

East of 90 Greenwich

FOREWORD

THE death of Jeremiah Curtin robbed America of
one of her two or three foremost scholars. Mr. Curtin,
who was by birth a native of Wisconsin, at one time
was in the diplomatic service of the Government;
but his chief work was in literature. The extraordinary
facility with which he learned any language, his gift
of style in his own language, his industry, his restless
activity and desire to see strange nations and out of
the way peoples, and his great gift of imagination
which enabled him to appreciate the epic sweep of
vital historical events, all combined to render his work
of peculiar value. His extraordinary translations of
the Polish novels of Sienkiewicz, especially of those
dealing with medieval Poland and her struggles with
the Tartar, the Swede and the German, would in themselves have been enough to establish a first class reputation for any man. In addition he did remarkable
work in connection with Indian, Celtic and other
folk tales. But nothing that he did was more important
than his studies of the rise of the mighty Mongol
Empire and its decadence. In this particular field no
other American or English scholar has ever approached
him.

Indeed, it is extraordinary to see how ignorant even

the best scholars of America and England are of the tremendous importance in world history of the nation-shattering Mongol invasions. A noted Englishman of letters not many years ago wrote a charming essay on the Thirteenth Century — an essay showing his wide learning, his grasp of historical events, and the length of time that he had devoted to the study of the century. Yet the essayist not only never mentioned but was evidently ignorant of the most stupendous fact of the century — the rise of Genghis Khan and the spread of the Mongol power from the Yellow Sea to the Adriatic and the Persian Gulf. Ignorance like this is partly due to the natural tendency among men whose culture is that of Western Europe to think of history as only European history and of European history as only the history of Latin and Teutonic Europe. But this does not entirely excuse ignorance of such an event as the Mongol-Tartar invasion, which affected half of Europe far more profoundly than the Crusades. It is this ignorance, of course accentuated among those who are not scholars, which accounts for the possibility of such comically absurd remarks as the one not infrequently made at the time of the Japanese-Russian war, that for the first time since Salamis Asia had conquered Europe. As a matter of fact the recent military supremacy of the white or European races is a matter of only some three centuries. For the four preceding centuries, that is, from the beginning of the thirteenth to the seventeenth, the Mongol and Turkish armies generally had the upper hand in any contest with European foes, appearing in Europe always as invaders and often as conquerors; while no ruler of Europe of their days had to his credit such mighty feats of arms, such wide conquests, as Genghis Khan, as Timour the Limper, as Bajazet, Selim and Amurath, as Baber and Akbar.

The rise of the Mongol power under Genghis Khan was unheralded and unforeseen, and it took the world as completely by surprise as the rise of the Arab power six centuries before. When the thirteenth century opened Genghis Khan was merely one among a number of other obscure Mongol chiefs and neither he nor his tribe had any reputation whatever outside of the barren plains of Central Asia, where they and their fellow-barbarians lived on horseback among their flocks and herds. Neither in civilized nor semi-civilized Europe, nor in civilized nor semi-civilized Asia, was he known or feared, any more, for instance, than the civilized world of today knows or fears the Senoussi, or any obscure black mahdi in the region south of the Sahara. At the moment, Europe had lost fear of aggression from either Asia or Africa. In Spain the power of the Moors had just been reduced to insignificance. The crusading spirit, it is true, had been thoroughly discredited by the wicked Fourth Crusade, when the Franks and Venetians took Constantinople and destroyed the old bulwark of Europe against the Infidel. But in the crusade in which he himself lost his life the Emperor Barbarossa had completely broken the power of the Seljouk Turks in Asia-Minor, and tho Jerusalem had been lost it was about to be regained by that strange and brilliant man, the Emperor Frederick II, " the wonder of the world." The Slavs of Russia were organized into a kind of loose confederacy, and were slowly extending themselves eastward, making settlements like Moscow in the midst of various Finnish

peoples. Hungary and Poland were great warrior
kingdoms, tho a couple of centuries were to pass before
Poland would come to her full power. The Caliphs
still ruled at Bagdad. In India Mohammedan warred
with Rajput; and the Chinese Empire was probably
superior in civilization and in military strength to any
nation of Europe.

Into this world burst the Mongol. All his early
years Genghis Khan spent in obtaining first the control
of his own tribe, and then in establishing the absolute
supremacy of this tribe over all its neighbors. In
the first decade of the thirteenth century this work
was accomplished. His supremacy over the wild
mounted herdsmen was absolute and unquestioned.
Every formidable competitor, every man who would
not bow with unquestioning obedience to his will,
had been ruthlessly slain, and he had developed a
number of able men who were willing to be his devoted
slaves, and to carry out his every command with un-
hesitating obedience and dreadful prowess. Out of
the Mongol horse-bowmen and horse-swordsmen he
speedily made the most formidable troops then in
existence. East, west and south he sent his armies,
and under him and his immediate successors the area of
conquest widened by leaps and bounds; while two
generations went by before any troops were found in
Asia or Europe who on any stricken field could hold
their own with the terrible Mongol horsemen, and
their subject-allies and remote kinsmen, the Turko-
Tartars who served with and under them. Few conquests have ever been so hideous and on the whole so
noxious to mankind. The Mongols were savages as
cruel as they were brave and hardy. There were Nes-

torian Christians among them, as in most parts of Asia
at that time, but the great bulk of them were Shaman-
ists; that is, their creed and ethical culture were about
on a par with those of the Comanches and Apaches
of the nineteenth century. They differed from Com-
anche and Apache in that capacity for military
organization which gave them such terrible efficiency;
but otherwise they were not much more advanced, and
the civilized peoples who fell under their sway experienced a fate as dreadful as would be the case if
nowadays a civilized people were suddenly conquered
by a great horde of Apaches. The ruthless cruelty of
the Mongol was practised on a scale greater than ever
before or since. The Moslems feared them as much
as the Christians. They put to death the Caliph, and
sacked Bagdad, just as they sacked the cities of Russia
and Hungary. They destroyed the Turkish tribes which
ventured to resist them with the merciless thoroness
which they showed in dealing with any resistance in
Europe. They were inconceivably formidable in battle,
tireless in campaign and on the march, utterly indifferent to fatigue and hardship, of extraordinary prowess
with bow and sword. To the Europeans who cowered
in horror before them, the squat, slit-eyed, brawny
horsemen, " with faces like the snouts of dogs," seemed
as hideous and fearsome as demons, and as irresistible
by ordinary mortals. They conquered China and set
on the throne a Mongol dynasty. India also their
descendants conquered, and there likewise erected
a great Mongol empire. Persia in the same way fell
into their hands. Their armies, every soldier on horseback, marched incredible distances and overthrew
whatever opposed them. They struck down the

Russians at a blow and trampled the land into bloody
mire beneath their horses' feet. They crushed the
Magyars in a single battle and drew a broad red furrow
straight across Hungary, driving the Hungarian King
in panic flight from his realm. They overran Poland
and destroyed the banded knighthood of North Germany in Silesia. Western Europe could have made
no adequate defense; but fortunately by this time the
Mongol attack had spent itself, simply because the
distance from the central point had become so great. It
was no Christian or European military power which
first by force set bounds to the Mongol conquests;
but the Turkish Mamelukes of Egypt in the West,
and in the East, some two score years later, the armies
of Japan.

In a couple of generations the Mongols as a whole
became Buddhists in the East and Moslems in the
West; and in the West the true Mongols gradually
disappeared, being lost among the Turkish tribes
whom they had conquered and led to victory. It was
these Turkish tribes, known as Tartars, who for over
two centuries kept Russia in a servitude so terrible,
so bloody, so abject, as to leave deep permanent marks
on the national character. The Russians did not
finally throw off this squalid yoke until thirty years
after the conquest of Constantinople by the Ottoman
Turks, the power of the Tartars waning as that of the
Ottomans approached its zenith. Poland was now rising
high. Its vast territory extended from the Baltic to
the Black Sea. It was far more important than Mus-
covy. In the " Itinerary " of that widely travelled
Elizabethan, Fynes Morrison, we learn that the Turks
dreaded the Polish armies more than those of Germany,.

or of any other nation; this was after the Hungarians had been conquered.

The scourge of the Mongol conquests was terrible beyond belief, so that even where a land was flooded but for a moment, the memory long remained. It is not long since in certain churches in Eastern Europe the litany still contained the prayer, " From the fury of the Mongols, good Lord deliver us." The Mongol armies developed a certain ant-like or bee-like power of joint action which enabled them to win without much regard to the personality of the leader; a French writer has well contrasted the great " anonymous victories " of the Mongols with the purely personal triumphs of that grim Turkish conqueror whom we know best as Timour the Tartar, or Tamerlane. The civil administration the Mongols established in a conquered country was borrowed from China, and where they settled as conquerors the conduct of the Chinese bureaucracy maddened the subject peoples almost as much as the wild and lawless brutality of the Mongol soldiers themselves. Gradually their empire, after splitting up, past away and left little direct influence in any country; but it was at the time so prodigious a phenomenon, fraught with such vast and dire possibilities, that a full knowledge of the history of the Mongol people is imperatively necessary to all who would understand the development of Asia and of Eastern Europe. No other writer of English was so well fitted to tell this history as Jeremiah Curtin.

THEODORE ROOSEVELT.

SAGAMORE HILL, *September 1, 1907.*

CONTENTS

CHAPTER I

PAGE

Geographical spread of the word Mongol. — Beginning of the Mongol career. — Mythical account of Temudjin's origin. — Kaidu, ancestor of the great historical Mongols. — Origin of the Urudai and Manhudai tribes. — Family of Kaidu. — Origin of the Taidjuts. — Bartan, grandfather of Temudjin. — Yessugai, father of Temudjin. — Kabul's visit to China. — Capture and escape of Kabul. — Shaman killed for the death of a patient. — Death of Ambagai. — Death of Okin Barka. — March of Kutula against China. — Kaidan, Tuda and Yessugai hold a council. — Attack of the Durbans. — Bartan, the father of Yessugai, dies. — Triumph of Yessugai 1

CHAPTER II

Rivalry between descendants of Kabul and Ambagai. — Kidnapping of Hoelun by Yessugai. — Birth and naming of Temudjin. — Yessugai finds a wife for Temudjin. — Death of Yessugai, 1175. — Neglect of Hoelun. — Targutai draws away Yessugai's people. — Temudjin begins his career by the murder of his half-brother. — Capture of Temudjin by the Taidjuts. — Temudjin's escape from captivity. — Assistance rendered by Sorgan Shira. — Marriage of Temudjin to Bortai. — Friendship of Temudjin and Boörchu. — Alliance of Togrul and Temudjin. — Chelmai, son of Charchiutai. — Capture of Bortai by the Merkits. — Pursuit of Temudjin. — Origin of the worship of Mount Burham. — Assistance of Togrul in recovering Bortai. — Ancestors of Jamuka. — Temudjin made Khan. — Appointment of officers. — Temudjin's first victory in battle. — Temudjin's brutal punishment of prisoners. — Juriats join Temudjin's forces. — Marriage of Temudjin's sister to Podu. — Marriage of Temudjin's mother to Munlik. — Barins withdraw from alliance. — Efforts of Temudjin to win the friendship of Jamuka 16

CHAPTER III

Attack of Temudjin and Togrul upon the Lake Buyur Tartars. — Togrul is given the title of Wang Khan. — Attack of Temudjin upon the Churkis. — Origin of the Churkis. — Death of Buri Buga. — Adopted sons of Hoelun, mother of Temudjin. — Temudjin and Wang Khan attack the Merkits, 1197. — Desertion of Wang Khan. — Wang Khan's men routed by Naimans. — Rescue of Wang Khan by Temudjin. —

PAGE

Second defeat of the Naimans. — Temudjin and Wang Khan become
as father and son to each other. — Wang Khan and Temudjin march
against the Taidjuts, 1200. — Taidjuts are joined by several neighboring tribes. — Offering made by Taidjuts and their allies when
taking oath. — Defeat of Taidjuts and Merkits by Temudjin. —
Jamuka is made Khan. — Effort of Jamuka to surprise and kill
Temudjin, 1201. — Shamans cause wind and rain to strike Temudjin. —
Defeat of Jamuka. — Punishment of Temudjin's brother, Belgutai, for
exposing plans. — Temudjin marches against the Tartars. — Marriage
of Temudjin to Aisugan. — Defeat of Tukta Bijhi, a Merkit chief. —
Temudjin asks for Wang Khan's granddaughter for Juchi. — Efforts
of Jamuka to rouse the jealousy of Sengun, son of Wang Khan. —
Sengun tries to break the alliance between his father and Temudjin.
— Discovery of a plot to kill Temudjin. — Attack of Wang Khan and
Sengun upon Temudjin. — Victory of Temudjin. — Death of Huildar.
— Message of Temudjin to Wang Khan. — Message of Temudjin to
Sengun. — Message of Temudjin to Jamuka. — Attack of Temudjin
upon Wang Khan. — Defeat of Wang Khan and Sengun. — Temudjin
rewards his warriors. — Temudjin takes as wife the daughter of
Jaganbo, Wang Khan's brother. — Death of Wang Khan and Sengun,
1203 37

CHAPTER IV

Attack upon Temudjin by Baibuga, his father-in-law. — Council held by
Temudjin, 1204. — Battle with the Naimans, autumn of 1204. —
Capture of Kurbassu, the wife of Baibuga. — Surrender to Temudjin
of tribes allied to Jamuka. — Subjection of the Merkits. — Marriage
of Temudjin to the daughter of Dair Usun. — Revolt and pursuit of
the Merkits. — Death of Tohtoa. — Defeat and capture of Jamuka. —
Death of Jamuka. — Temudjin is made Grand Khan, takes the title
Jinghis. — Temudjin rewards his officers. — Temudjin gives his wife
to Churchadai. — Temudjin distrusts his brother, Kassar. — Defence
of Kassar by his mother, Hoelun. — Death of Hoelun. — Temudjin
alarmed at the power of Taibtengeri, a Shaman. — Murder of Taibtengeri. — Jinghis Khan's (Temudjin) campaign against Tanguts. —
Jinghis Khan's position secured in Northeastern Asia. — Kara Kitai,
geographically. — The Uigurs. — Triumphs of Jinghis alarm China. —
Mission of Jinghis' envoys to the Uigurs. — Indignation of the Uigurs.
— Mongols invade Tangut, 1207. — Tangut King gives his daughter in
marriage to Jinghis. — Return of Jinghis. — Arslan Khan of the Karluks gives homage to Jinghis. — Marriage of Arslan to Altun Bijhi,
Jinghis' daughter. 62

CHAPTER V

China, 618 to 907, A. D. — Fall of Tang dynasty. — The Kitans. — Parin
proclaims himself Emperor, 916. — House of Sung unites nearly all
China, 960. — Tribute paid by the Sung Emperor to the Kitans, 1004.
— Victory over the Kitans by Aguta in 1114. — Founding of a new
State, Kin kwe, by Aguta. — Death of Aguta. — Invasion of North
China by Kin Emperor, 1125. — Kin Emperor besieges Kai fong
fu, 1126. — Sung Emperor seized and sent to Manchuria. — Message of Jinghis Khan to the sovereign of China. — Jinghis sets out
to subdue the Chinese Empire, 1211. — Sons of Jinghis. — Army
equipment. — Advance of 1,200 miles to the Great Wall of China.
— Friendship of the Onguts. — Insurrection of the Kitans. — Chong
tu invested. — Jinghis sends Subotai against the Merkits. — Jin-

Contents

ghis resumes activity in China, 1213. — Attack of Tangut on China, 1213. — Mongols attack lands bordering on the Hoang Ho, 1214. — Defence of Chong tu. — Mongols attack Nan king. — Defeat of the Merkits. — Corea's submission to Jinghis, 1218. — Death of Boroul, 1217. — Origin of Mukuli, one of Jinghis' greatest generals. — Jinghis' fourth attack on the Tanguts, 1218. — Origin of Kara Kitai. — Victory of Yeliu over Kashgar. — Invasion of Kwaresm by Yeliu. — Treachery of Gutchluk. — Execution of Gutchluk by Chepe. — Kara Kitai attacked by Shah Mohammed. — The World-Shaking Limper (Tamerlane). — Attack of Kara Kitans by Mongols. — Death of the Gurkhan of Kara Kitai, 1136 79

CHAPTER VI

Addition of Kara Kitai to Mongol domains. — End of Seljuk rule. — Kutb ud din Mohammed made Kwaresmian Shah. — Mohammed seizes Balk and Herat. — Invasion of the lands of the Gurkhan by Mohammed, 1208. — Defeat and capture of Shah Mohammed. — Mohammed and Osman make an attack on the Gurkhan. — Success of the Kwaresmian Shah. — Mohammed gives his daughter in marriage to Osman, ruler of Samarkand. — Kwaresmians killed by Osman. — Storming of Samarkand by Mohammed. — Death of Osman. — Seizure of a part of the Gur Kingdom. — Assassination of Ali Shir by command of Mohammed, his brother, 1213. — Winning of Ghazni by Mohammed, 1216. — Discovery of letters from the Kalif warning the Gurs against Mohammed. — Efforts of Nassir the Kalif to stop Kwaresmian growth. — Limited power of the Kalif. — Envoy sent by Mohammed to the Kalif. — Ali ul Muluk is recognized as Kalif. — Murder of Ogulmush by command of the Kalif. — Annexation of Irak by Mohammed. — Mohammed advances on Bagdad. — Retreat of Mohammed. — Mohammed alarmed by Mongol movements. — Mohammed receives envoys from Jinghis Khan, 1216-17. — Sunnites and Shiites. — Determination of the Kalif to ask Jinghis to defend the Sunnites. — Invitation to Jinghis branded on the head of the envoy. — Message of Jinghis to Shah Mohammed. — Arrest of Mongolian merchants. — Second message from Jinghis to Mohammed. — Murder of Bajra, Jinghis Khan's envoy. — Turkan Khatun, the mother of Shah Mohammed. — Trouble caused by Turkan Khatun. — A Mongol tempest. — Conspiracy of Bedr ud din. — Arrangement of the Mongol army. — Investment of Otrar, November, 1218. — Capture of Otrar, April, 1219. — Slaughter of the Turk garrison at Benakit. — Escape of Melik Timur. — Investment of Bokhara, June, 1219. — Surrender of Bokhara. — Feeding of Mongol horses in the Grand Mosque. — Storming of the fortress. — March of Jinghis on Samarkand. — Surrender of Samarkand. — Pursuit of the Kwaresmian ruler 93

CHAPTER VII

Indecision of Shah Mohammed. — Escape of Mohammed to Nishapur. — Submission of Balkh. — Proclamation of the Shah to Nishapur. — Pursuit of Mohammed. — Withdrawal of Mohammed from Nishapur. — Sack of Nishapur. — Flight of Mohammed to an island in the Caspian. — Death of Shah Mohammed January 10, 1221. — Escape of Turkan Khatun to the mountains. — Succession of Jelal ud din. — Surrender of Ilak and of Turkan Khatun. — Siege and capture of the Kwaresmian capital. — Attack made on the Talekan district by Jinghis. — Siege of Ghazni. — March of Tului against Khorassan, 1220. — Attack on Nessa. — Attack and capture of Merv. — Revenge of

PAGE

Togachar's widow. — March of the Mongols against Herat. — Turk-
mans near Nerv escape and form the nucleus of the Ottoman Empire.
— Jelal ud din at Ghazni, 1221. — Death of a grandson of Jinghis. —
Revenge of Jinghis. — Retreat of Jelal from Ghazni. — Pursuit of
Jelal by Jinghis. — Battle at the Indus between Jelal and Jinghis. —
Leap of Jelal into the Indus. — Siege of Herat, 1222. — Mongol army
marches on Herat a second time 113

CHAPTER VIII

Jinghis passes the winter near the Indus, 1222-23. — Resolve of Jinghis
to return to Mongolia, 1223. — Myths regarding this resolution. —
Command of Jinghis to kill useless prisoners. — March of Chepe Noyon
to Tiflis. — Command of Jinghis to Chepe Noyon to exterminate the
Polovtsi. — March of Chepe to Tiflis. — Chepe's alliance with the
Polovtsi. — Betrayal of the Polovtsi, their flight to Russia. — Mystislav
aids the Polovtsi against the Mongols. — Defeat of the Russians on the
Kalka, 1224. — Terror of Southern Russia. — Jinghis at his home on
the Kerulon, 1225. — Mukuli's conquest of lands belonging to the Kin
dynasty, 1216. — Death of Mukuli, 1223. — Jinghis enters Tangut, 1226.
— Siege of Ling chau. — Submission of Ling chau. — Death of Jinghis
Khan, 1227. — Burial of Jinghis. — Jinghis Khan's disposal of his
Empire. — Kurultai of election held on the Kerulon, 1229. — Accession
of Ogotai. His plans of expeditions. — Offerings made to the shade
of Jinghis. — First work of Ogotai 131

CHAPTER IX

Condition of Persian Irak at the time of Jinghis Khan's death. — Flight
of Jelal ud din to Delhi. — Marriage of Jelal to the daughter of
Iletmish. — Effort of Jelal to take possession of his inheritance. —
Founding of the Kara Kitan dynasty of Kerman. — Marriage of Jelal
to the daughter of Borak. — Advance of Jelal into Fars. — Marriage
of Jelal to the daughter of the Atabeg of Shiraz. — Effort of Jelal to
overcome his brother, Ghiath. — Jelal marches against Nassir, Kalif
of Islam. — Capture of Dakuka by Jelal, 1225. — Possession of Tebriz
by Jelal. — Expedition against Georgia, 1225. — Second march of Jelal
to Tiflis, 1226. — Conquest of Georgia. — Jelal attacks Kars. — Defeat
of a Mongol division by Jelal. — Attack of the Mongols on Jelal in
Ispahan, 1227. — Murder of Mohammed, a favorite of Jelal. — Ghiath
ud din strangled by Borak. — Jelal demands tribute from the Shirvan
Shah. — Attack of Jelal on the combined armies of Georgia and
Armenia. — Second siege of Khelat by Jelal. — Death of Nassir the
Kalif, 1225. — Succession of Zahir as Kalif and then of Mostansir. —
Jelal invested with the title of Shah in Shah. — Capture of Khelat by
Jelal, 1230. — Defeat of Jelal at Kharpert. — March of Jelal on
Khelat. — March of Jelal on Gandja. — Attack and defeat of Jelal by
Mongols. — Death of Jelal, 1231. — End of Kwaresmian dynasty . 145

CHAPTER X

Ravage of Amid and Mayafarkin by Mongols. — Devastation of Azerbaidjan. — Capture of Erbil by Mongols. — Mongols in Arabian Irak, 1238.
— Capture of Gandja by Mongols, 1235. — Capture of Tiflis by Mongols,
1239. — Mongols advance to the Tigris. — Visit of Prince Avak and
his sister, Tamara, to Ogotai, 1240. — Mongols in Syria, 1244. —

Contents

Capture of regions north of Lake Van. — Sheherzur sacked by
Mongols. — The Mongols driven off from Yakuba by Bagdad troops. —
Refusal of Queen Rusudan to leave Usaneth. — Death of Rusudan.
— Installation of Kuyuk, 1246. — Death of Kei Kosru, 1245. — Struggle
of Rokn ud din for rule in Rūm. — Death of Alai ud din. —
Mangu Grand Khan of the Mongols, 1251. — Visit of Rokn ud din to
Sarai. — Entrance of Baidju into Rūm. — Great ruin effected by
Mongols in Asia Minor. — Appointment by Juchi of Chin Timur as
Governor of Kwaresm. — Ravaging by Kwaresmian bands in Khoras-
san. — Attack upon the Kankalis by Chin Timur. — Visit of the Prince
of Iran to Ogotai. — Authority transferred from Chin Timur to Sari
Bahadar. — Reinstatement of Chin Timur. — Chin Timur's choice of
Kurguz as chancellor. — Death of Chin Timur, 1235. — Visit of Kurguz
to Ogotai. — Kurguz appointed to collect taxes. — Residence of Kurguz
at Tus. — Command of Ogotai to raise up Khorassan, and repeople
Herat. — Struggle between Sherif and Kurguz. — Death of Kurguz. —
Succession of Sherif. — Sherif's oppression of the people of Tebriz.
— Death of Sherif, 1244. — Visit of Argun to the Kurultai which
elected Kuyuk, 1251. — Election of Mangu, 1251. — Argun's reception
in Merv. — Shems ud din's reign in Herat. — Death of Rokn ud din. —
Death of Shems ud din, 1244. — Death of Kutb ud din, 1258. — Position of Persia in 1254 172

CHAPTER XI

The Ismailian known in Europe as Assassins. — Death of Mohammed, 632.
— Omar made Kalif, 634. — Murder of Aly, 661. — Election of Muavia
in Damascus. — Winning of Egypt by Muavia. — Yezid, son of Muavia,
named heir. — Death of Muavia. Succession of Yezid, 680. — Death of
Muslim. — Hussein camps on the plain of Kerbala. — Death of Hussein,
October, 680. — Babek, 816. — Seizure of Babek by Motassim, 835. —
Execution of Babek. — Origin of Abdallah. — Spread of the peculiar
beliefs of Abdallah. — Amed, son of Abdallah. — Rise of Karmath. —
Fights in the East and West. — Obeidallah, first Fatimed Kalif, 909.
— Winning of Egypt and Southern Syria by descendants of Obeidallah,
967. — Addition of Aleppo to the Fatimed Empire, 991. — Founding of
the Eastern Ismailians, or Assassins, by Hassan Ben Sabah. — Omar
Khayyam and Nizam ul Mulk. — Death of Alp Arslan. — Seizure of the
fortress of Alamut by Hassan Sabah, 1090. — Rivalry of Hassan and
Nizam ul Mulk. — Death of Nizam ul Mulk and Melik Shah,
1092. — Peculiar belief of Hassan Sabah. — Assassins in Syria.
— Friendship of Risvan, Prince of Aleppo, for the Order. —
Assassination of the Prince of Mosul, 1113. — Death of Risvan. —
Akhras attempts to exterminate the Assassins. — Revenge of the
Assassins. — Surrender of the fortress of Sherif, 1120. — Death of
Hassan Sabah, 1124. — Kia Busurgomid succeeds Hassan Sabah. —
Possession of Banias by Assassins. — Hugo De Payens, Grand Master
of the Templars in Jerusalem, 1129. — Death of Togteghin. — Succession
of his son, Tajulmuluk. — Efforts to murder Tajulmuluk. — Execution
of the Assassins 197

CHAPTER XII

Murder of Aksonkor Burshi, Prince of Mosul, 1126. — Murder of Busi,
Prince of Damascus. — Murder of Sindjar's vizir by Assassins, 1127. —
Vengeance of Assassins. — Death of a Fatimid Kalif by the daggers of
the Assassins, 1134. — Death of Kia Busugomid, 1138. — Appointment
of Mohammed to succeed his father. — Murder of Mostereshed. — Death

PAGE

of Rashid, his successor. — Assassin doctrine as delivered to Sindjar.
— Succession of Mohammed, 1138. — Nur ed din in Syria. — Attack
against Damascus, 1154. — Friendship of Nur ed din for the
Abbasids. — Triumph of Nur ed din in Haram. — Arrival of
Shawer in Damascus. — Shawer's request for aid against the
Crusaders. — Plot of Shawer to destroy Shirkuh. — Death of Shirkuh,
1169. — Saladin's origin. — Saladin first vizir of the Kalif. — Exposure
of the secrets of the Assassins by Hassan II. — Efforts of Hassan to
established his descent from Kalifs of Egypt. — Death of Hassan. —
Death of Nur ed din, 1174. — Egypt governed by Saladin in the name
of Salih. — Defeat of the troops of Aleppo, by Saladin, 1175. — End
of the Fatimid Kalifat. — Saladin attacked by Assassins. — Attack
of Massiat by Saladin. — Compromise of Sinan. — Death of Mohammed
II. — Succession of Jelal ud din Hassan, son of Mohammed, 1213. —
Jelal's return to the true faith. — Death of Jelal ud din, 1225. — Succes-
sion of his son, Alai ed din. — Death of Alai ed din. — Succession of
Rokn ud din. — Attack of Hulagu upon the Assassins. — Surrender of
Rokn ud din. — Visit of Rokn ud din to the court of Mangu, 1257. —
Death of Rokn ud din 222

                       CHAPTER XIII

Message of Hulagu to Kalif of Bagdad, 1257. — Kalif rebukes Hulagu. —
Hulagu's envoys insulted by the people. — Second message of the
Kalif to Hulagu to warn him against making war on the Abbasids.
— Attempted treason of Aké, commandant of Daritang. — Possession
of the Daritang road by Hulagu. — Prediction of the astrologer. —
Capture of Luristan by the Mongols. — Advance of Feth ud din to
meet the Mongol division. — Opening of canals from the Tigris by the
Mongols. — Triumph of Hulagu. — Submission of the Kalif of Bagdad.
— Bagdad sacked by the Mongols. — Death of Kalif of Bagdad, 1258.
— Appointment of Ben Amran as prefect. — Alb Argun's accession to
the throne of Luristan. — Summons of Hulagu to Bedr ud din, Prince
of Mosul. — Presents given by the Prince of Mosul to Hulagu. — Death
of Salih, 1249. — Death of Turan Shah, successor of Salih. — Accession
of Eibeg to the throne of Egypt. — Attempt of Nassir to drive Eibeg
from the throne. — Message of Hulagu to Nassir. — Advance of
Hulagu's army into Syria. — Accusation of Hulagu against Kamil,
the Eyubite prince. — Summons sent by Hulagu to the Prince of
Mardin. — Message of Nassir to Mogith. — Succession of Mensur, son
of Eibeg. — Kutuz becomes Sultan. — Siege of El Biret. — Mongols
camp near Aleppo. — Assault and capture of Aleppo, January 25, 1260.
— Damascus left defenceless by Nassir 247

                       CHAPTER XIV

News of the death of Mangu, 1259. — Desire of Kutuz to take the field
against the Mongols. — Imprisonment of Hulagu's envoy. — Meeting
of the two armies on the plain of Ain Jalut, 1260. — Defeat of the
Mongols by Kutuz. — Arrival of Kutuz in Damascus. — Pursuit of
the Mongols by Beibars. — Death of Kutuz, 1260. — Enthronement of
Beibars. — Youth of Beibars. — Yshmut, son of Hulagu, demands the
surrender of Mayafarkin. — Death of Kamil. — Attack of Yshmut on
Mardin. — Kalif's investiture of Beibars with the sovereignty. — Departure from Cairo of the Sultan and the Kalif, 1262. — Entrance of
Mostansir into Hitt. — Attack of Sanjar on the Mongols who were

moving against Mosul. — Death of Sanjar. — Siege of Mosul. —
Slaughter of the inhabitants of Mosul. — Death of Prince of Mosul. —
Death of Salih. — Visit of Salih, the Melik of Mosul, to Beibars in
Egypt. — Enthronement of Beibars. — Berkai's criticism of Hulagu. —
Defeat of Hulagu by Nogai. — Return of Hulagu to Tebriz. — Letter
of Beibars to Berkai. — Detention of envoys by Michael Palaelogus. —
Desire of Berkai for an alliance against Hulagu. — Attack of Hayton,
King of Cilicia, on Egyptian territory. — Death of Seif ud din Bitikdji,
1263. — Troubles in Fars. — Reception of Seljuk Shah at the Oxus, by
Hulagu. — Death of Abu Bekr, 1260. — Accession of Mohammed Shah
to the throne of Fars, 1262. — Death of Seljuk Shah. — Uns Khatun
placed on the throne of Fars, 1264. — Sherif ud din claims to be the
Mahdi promised by the Shiites. — March of the Mongols against Sherif
ud din. — Siege of El Biret, 1264. — Death of Hulagu, 1265. — Death
of Hulagu's wife Dokuz Khatun. — Berkai's second campaign to the
Caucasus, 1264. — Death of Berkai, 1266. — Nogai's army retreats on
Shirvan 267

CHAPTER XV

Kin Emperor sends offerings to the spirit of Jinghis Khan, 1229. —
Mongols continue warfare in China. — Siege of Li ho chin by Mongols,
1227. — King Yang attacked by Mongols, 1229. — Defeat of the Mongols by Yra buka, 1230. — Advance of Ogotai and Tului on China. —
Ogotai anxious to seize Honan. — Surrender of Fong tsiang. — Arrival
of Yra buka, the Kin general at Teng chu, 1234. — Tului's report to
Ogotai of the situation in Honan. — Siege of Yiu chin by Tului. — Cap-
ture and death of Yra buka. — Ogotai visits Tului. — Ogotai asks the
Kin Emperor to submit. — Advance of Mongols on Shan chiu. — Fall of
Honan. — Siege of Nan King. — Appearance of the plague. — Flight of
the Emperor from his capital. — Attack of the capital by Subotai. —
Defence of Pian king. — Surrender of Pian king. — Execution of
Baksan. — Appearance of Mongols near Tsai chiu. — Attack of Tsai
chiu by Tatchar, son of Boroul. — Nin kia su yields the throne to
Ching lin. — Death of Nin kia su. — Death of Ching lin. — Death of
Tului, October, 1232. — End of dominion of the Kins in China, 1234 . 295

CHAPTER XVI

Kurultai summoned by Ogotai at Talantepe, 1234. — Kurultai summoned
by Ogotai at Kara Kurum, 1235. — Batu marches West. — An army sent
to Cashmir and India. — Expedition against China. — Assassination of
Tsui li. — Recall of Subotai. — Reoccupation of Ching tu by the
Chinese 1239. — Sack of Ching tu by Mongols. — Entrance into Hu
kuang of Kutchu, 1236. — Death of Kutchu. — Attack on Liu chiu by
Chagan, a Mongol general, 1238. — Withdrawal of Chagan. — Three
victories of Meng kong over Mongols, 1239. — Offers of peace by Wang
tsie, a Mongol envoy. — Death of Ogotai, 1241. — Influence of Abd ur
Rahman over the widow of Ogotai. — Delay of Batu in coming to the
Kurultai. — Election of Kuyuk as Emperor. — Death of Turakina,
Ogotai's widow. — Death of Fatima, a favorite of Turakina. — Batu
learns of the death of Kuyuk, 1248. — Kurultai called by Batu. —
Mangu, son of Tului, saluted as Emperor, 1251. — Refusal of Ogotai's sons to recognize the legality of the Kurultai which appointed
Mangu. — Discovery of a plot to assassinate Mangu. — Death
of Siurkukteni, mother of Mangu, 1252. — Desire of Mangu to

PAGE

kill the partisans of Ogotai's sons. — Removal of all Uigurs favorable to Ogotai's descendants by Mangu. — Mangu gives Honan to Kubilai, 1252. — Tali the capital of Nan chao under Mongol rule. — Return of Kubilai to Mongolia. — Journey of Uriang Kadai to Mangu's court to report on work done in the South, beyond China. — Return of Uriang Kadai, 1254. — Summons of Uriang Kadai to Chen chi kung, sovereign of Tung king (Gan nan), to own himself tributary to Mangu. — Surrender of Kiao chi, the Gan nan capital, to Uriang Kadai. — Chen chi kung resigns in favor of his son, 1253. — Popularity of Kubilai in China. — Jealousy of Mangu. — Recall of Kubilai, 1257. — March of Mangu to the Sung Empire. — March of Mangu against Ku chu yai, a fortress west of Pao ning. — Mangu's conquest of Western Su chuan. — Death of Mangu, 1259. — Kubilai at Ju in Honan, 1259. — Effort of Arik Buga, master at Kara Kurum, to usurp power. — Treaty of Kia se tao and Kubilai. — Encampment of Kubilai outside the walls of Pekin. — Election and enthronement of Kubilai. — Battle between Kubilai and Arik Buga. — Defeat of Arik Buga . . 310

CHAPTER XVII

March of Arik Buga to Kara Kurum. — Attack of Arik Buga on Kubilai northeast of Shang tu. — Defeat of Arik Buga. — Reverses of Arik Buga. — Appeal of Arik Buga to the mercy of his brother, 1264. — Death of Arik Buga, 1266. — Claim of Kaidu, grandson of Ogotai, to headship of the Mongols. — Decision of Kubilai to conquer all China. — Revolt of Litan, one of Kubilai's generals. — Death of Litan. — Kubilai moves against Southern China, 1267. — Kubilai's command to At chu to besiege Siang yang, 1268. — Attack of Mongols on Fan ching, 1273. — The Emperor's discovery of the siege of Siang yang by the Mongols. — Control of Fan ching by the Mongols. — Surrender of Siang yang by Liu wen hwan. — Death of Tu tsong, the Emperor, August, 1274. — Surrender of many cities to Bayan. — Surrender of Su chuan, 1278. — Bayan advises Kubilai to continue operations in China. — Arrival of the Emperor and Empress at Kubilai's court. — March of Bayan against Lin ngan. — Election of Y wang as governor of the Empire. — Command obtained from the Emperor, by Bayan, ordering Sung subjects to submit to the Mongols. — Chinese defections follow Mongol successes. — Effort of Alihaiya to bribe Ma ki to surrender Kwe lin fu, the capital of Kiang se. — Defeat and capture of Ma ki. — Death of Toan tsong, 1278. — Kuang Wang is made Emperor under the name Ti ping. — Destruction of the army of the Sung Emperor. — Blocking of Chinese vessels by Mongol barges. — Capture of more than 800 Chinese vessels. — Death of Chang shi kie. — Kubilai finds himself master of China, January 31, 1279 336

CHAPTER XVIII

Struggle of Kubilai with Kaidu lasting from the death of Arik Buga to the death of Kubilai. — End of the Sung dynasty. — Departure of troops for Corea. — Mongol fleet encounters a storm. — Return of the fleet. — Attack and defeat of the King of Burma. — Death of Sutu, a distinguished Mongol general. — Kubilai plans a second Japanese expedition. — Victory of Kubilai's forces over the Tung king men in seventeen engagements. — Visit of Yang ting pie to the islands south of China, 1285. — Arrival of the ships of ten kingdoms in Tsinan chiu. — Desire of Tok Timur to put Shireki, son of Mangu, on the throne,

Contents

1277. — Tok Timur attacked by Bayan. — Flight of Tok Timur. — Tok Timur asks aid of Shireki; failing to get it he sets up Sarban. — Forming of a new league against Kubilai by Kaidan with Nayan as leader. — Capture and death of Nayan. — Gift of Kara Kurum to Bayan, as headquarters. — Kubilai's departure from Shang tu for the West. — Recall of Bayan. — Kubilai sends a thousand ships to attack Java. — Effort of Wang chu to free the Chinese Empire. — Death of Ahmed, Kubilai's Minister of Finance. — Execution of Wang chu. — Execution of Sanga. — Death of Kubilai, February, 1294. — Election of Timur. — Death of Bayan at the age of fifty-nine. — Treaty of Timur with the King of Tung king. — Spread of revolt. — Death of Kaidu, 1301. — Daughter of Kaidu. — Homage rendered Chabar as Kaidu's successor. — Timur acknowledged as overlord. — War between Chabar and Dua, 1306. — Death of Dua. — Gebek, son of Dua, proclaimed successor. — Attack of Chabar on Gebek. — Defeat of Chabar 361

CHAPTER XIX

Accession of Ananda, grandson of Kubilai. — Removal of Ananda. — Succession of Khaishan, under the name of Kuluk. — Death of Khaishan, 1311. — Batra is proclaimed under the name Bayantu. — Cause and beginning of the ruin of Mongol power in China. — Appointment of Shudi Bala as successor of Bayantu. — Death of Bayantu in 1320. — Assassination of Shudi Bala. The first death by assassination in the Imperial family. — Succession of Yissun Timur. — Appointment of Asukeba as heir. — Death of Yissun Timur. — The widow of Yissun Timur proclaims Asukeba. — Effort of Tob Timur to secure the throne for his brother, Kushala. — Defeat of the partisans of Asukeba. — Exile of the Empress. — Sudden death of Kushala while feasting, 1329. — Tob Timur is made Emperor. — Death of Tob Timur. — Death of the young son of Kushala. — Accession of Togan Timur, Kushala's eldest son. — Revolt in Honan, Su chuan and Kwang tung. — Removal of Tob Timur's tablet from the hall of Imperial ancestors, 1340. — Completion of the annals of the Liao, the Kin, and the Sung dynasties. — Insurrection in South China, 1341. — Fang kwe chin, a pirate, harries the coast of Che kiang. — Declaration of Han chan tong of the appearance of Buddha to free China from the Mongol yoke. — Death of Han chan tong. — Departure of Mongols from the Yang tse region. — Capture of Han yang and Wu chang in Hu kwang by Siu chiu hwei. — Recapture of Hang chiu by the Mongol general, Tong pu. — Appearance of Chang se ching in Kiang nan. — Siu chiu hwei proclaims himself Emperor. — Defeat of a Mongol general by Ni wen tsiun. — Appearance of Chu yuan chang, the man destined to destroy Mongol rule, and found the Ming dynasty. — Capture of Nan king, Yang chiu and Chin kiang by Chu. — Defeat of adherents of Ming wang, the pseudo Sung Emperor, by Chagan Timur, a Mongol general. — Control of Hu kwang and Kiang si by Siu chiu hwei. — Chin proclaims himself Emperor. — Plans of Chagan Timur to capture Nan king. — Aiyuchelitala named as heir by Togan Timur. — Invitation of Ali hwei to Togan Timur to yield what is left of Mongol power. — Defeat of Tukien Timur. — Assassination of Chagan Timur by Wang se ching. — Appearance of Ming yu chin as Emperor. — March of Chu, the coming Emperor of China, against Chin yiu liang. — Defeat of Chin yiu liang. — Surrender of cities to Chu. — Effort of Polo Timur to capture Tsin ki. — Defeat of Polo Timur by Ku ku Timur. — The heir of the Mongol throne acts against the Grand

Contents

PAGE

Khan, his father. — Polo Timur made commander-in-chief by Togan
Timur. — News of the capture of Shang tu. — Death of Ming yu chin,
1366. — Disappearance of Han lin ulh. — Efforts of Chu to liberate
China. — Surrender of all cities to Chu's generals. — Terror of Togan
Timur caused by conquests of Chu. — Chu proclaimed Emperor, the
name Ming is given to his dynasty. — Entrance of Chu into Ta tu,
1368. — Death of Togan Timur. — Capture of Togan Timur's grandson by Ming forces. — Advance of Su tu, the Ming general, to the
Kerulon. — Death of the Mongol heir. Succession of his son Tukus
Timur, 1378. — Defeat of Tukus Timur by Chu forces. — Assassination
of Tukus Timur. — Civil war roused by Yissudar. — Invitation of the
Emperor of China to Buin Shara to declare himself vassal. — Invasion
of Mongolia by a Chinese army. — Yung lo's advance to the Kerulon.
— Defeat of the Mongols. — Death of Buin Shara, 1412. — The Manchu
dynasty. — End of Mongol power 384

THE MONGOLS

THE MONGOLS

CHAPTER I

CLASSIFICATION, MYTH AND REALITY

FROM an obscure and uncertain beginning the word Mongol has gone on increasing in significance and spreading geographically during more than ten centuries until it has filled the whole earth with its presence. From the time when men used it at first until our day this word has been known in three senses especially. In the first sense it refers to some small groups of hunters and herdsmen living north of the great Gobi desert; in the second it denotes certain peoples in Asia and Eastern Europe; in the third and most recent, a worldwide extension has been given it. In this third and the broad sense the word Mongol has been made to include in one category all yellow skinned nations, or peoples, including those too with a reddish-brown, or dark tinge in the yellow, having also straight hair, always black, and dark eyes of various degrees of intensity. In this sense the word Mongol co-ordinates vast numbers of people, immense groups of men who are like one another in some traits, and widely dissimilar in others. It embraces the Chinese, the Coreans, the Japanese, the Manchus, the original Mongols with their near relatives the Tartar, or Turkish tribes which hold Central Asia, or most of it. Moving westward from China this term covers the Tibetans and with them all the non-Aryan nations and tribes until we reach India and Persia.

In India, whose most striking history in modern ages is Mongol, nearly all populations save Aryans and Semites are classified with Mongols. In Persia where the dynasty is Mongol that race is preponderant in places and important throughout the whole kingdom,

1

though in a minority. In Asia Minor the Mongol is master, for the Turk is still sovereign, and will be till a great rearrangement is effected.

Five groups of Mongols have made themselves famous in Europe: the Huns with their mighty chief Attila, the Bulgars, the Magyars, the Turks or Osmanli, and the Mongol invaders of Russia. All these five will have their due places later on in this history.

In Africa there have been and are still Mongol people. The Mamelukes and their forces at Cairo were in their time remarkable, and Turkish dominion exists till the present, at least theoretically, in Egypt, and west of it.

Not restricted to the Eastern hemisphere the word Mongol is still further used to include aboriginal man in America.

Thus this great aggregation of people is found in each part of both hemispheres, and we cannot consider the Mongols historically in a wide sense unless we consider all mankind.

In the first, that is the original and narrowest sense of the word it applies to those Mongols alone who during twelve centuries or longer have inhabited the country just south of Lake Baikal, and north of the great Gobi desert. It is from these Mongols proper that the name has at last been extended to the whole yellow race in both hemispheres.

The word Mongol began, it is said, with the Chinese, but this is not certain. It is certain, however, that the Chinese made it known to the great world outside, and thus opened the way to that immense application now given it. The Tang dynasty lasted from 618 to 907 and left its own history. In that history the term Mongol appears as Mong-ku, and in the annals of the Kitan dynasty which followed the Tang Mong-ku-li is the form which is given us. The Kitans were succeeded by the Golden Khans, or Kin Emperors, and in the annals of their line the Mong-ku are mentioned very often.

The Mongols began their career somewhat south of Lake Baikal where six rivers rise in a very remarkable mountain land. The Onon, the Ingoda and the Kerulon are the main western sources of that immense stream the Amoor, which enters the Sea of Okhotsk and thus finds the Pacific. The second three rivers: the Tula, Orhon, and Selinga flow into Lake Baikal, and thence, through the

Lower Angara and Yenissei, are merged in Arctic waters directly in front of Nova Zembla.

These two water systems begin in the Kentei Khan mountains which have as their chief elevation Mount Burhan. The six rivers while flowing toward the Amoor and Lake Baikal water the whole stretch of country where the Mongols began their activity as known to us. There they moved about with their large and small cattle, fought, robbed, and hunted, ate and drank and slew one another during ages without reckoning. In that region of forest and grass land, of mountains and valleys, of great and small rivers the air is wholesome though piercingly cold during winter, and exceedingly hot in the summer months. There was subsistence enough for a primitive life in that country, but men had to fight for it savagely. Flocks and herds when grown numerous need immense spaces to feed in, and those spaces of land caused unending struggle and bloodshed. The flocks and herds were also objects of struggle, not flocks and herds only, but women. The desirable woman was snatched away, kidnapped; the good herd of cattle was stolen, and afterward fought for; the grass covered mountain or valley, or the forest with grass or good branches, or shrubbery for browsing was seized and then kept by the men who were able to hold it.

This stealing of cattle, this grabbing of pasture and forest, this fighting, this killing, this capture of women continued for ages with no apparent results except those which were personal, local, and transient till Temudjin the great Mongol appeared in that harsh mountain country. This man summed up in himself, and intensified to the utmost the ideas, strength, temper and spirit of his race as presented in action and life up to his day. He placed the Mongols on the stage of the world with a skill and a power that were simply colossal and all-conquering. The results which he won were immediate and terrifying. No man born of woman has had thus far in history a success so peculiar, so thorough and perfect, so completely acknowledged by mankind as the success won by Temudjin. There is in his career an unconquerable sequence, a finish, a oneness of character that sets it apart among all the careers of those mighty ones in history who worked for this life and no other, and strove for no object save that which is tangible, material and present; success of such kind and success so enormous that a common intelligence might yearn for it, but have no more chance of winning than of reaching the stars, or of seeing the sun during night hours.

The career of this Mongol is unique in the world, unapproachable, since its object was unmixed and immediate and his success in attaining it was so great that it seems, we might say, superhuman.

The account which is given us of Temudjin's origin is a myth tale, excepting a few generations directly preceding him. Genealogy in the form of a myth tale is no exception in the case of any people, — no wonder. It is the rule and inevitable, the one method used by each primitive folk to explain its own origin. All early men in their own accounts are descended from gods who are either divine mythic animals, or elements, or forces, or phenomena which become later on the progenitors of nations, or their totems.

The first mythic parents or founders of Temudjin's family were a blue wolf and a gray doe. These two swam across a lake, reached the river Onon near its sources and settled down permanently at the foot of Mount Burhan, where a son called Batachi was born to them. Ninth in descent from Batachi were Duva Sohor, and Doben. The former had only one eye which was fixed in the middle of his forehead, but with that eye he saw beyond three mountain ranges. Once these two brothers climbed up Mount Burhan, and were gazing at the world from the top of it when Duva Sohor beheld many people moving down the Tungeli. "There is the wife for my brother, unless she is married," thought Duva. "Go and see her," said he then to Doben. Doben went to the new people straightway and learned that the woman was single and that her name was Alan Goa. The moving people were dependents of one Horilartai.

In time before that Bargudai, who owned Bargudjin on Lake Baikal, had a daughter whom he gave to Horilartai of Horntumadun. From this marriage came Alan Goa, born at Alih Usun. They had left their old place since the hunting of ermine and squirrels had been stopped there. Horilartai removed to Mount Burhan, where game was abundant. He joined Shinchi Boyan, the master of Mount Burhan, and began the clan Horilar. Thus Doben found Alan Goa, who bore him two sons, Bugundai and Bailgun Etai.

Duva the one-eyed had four sons. The two brothers and their

six sons lived in one company till Duva's death; after that Duva's four sons deserted their uncle, and founded the clan known as Dorbian.

One day while Doben was hunting he found in the forest a man roasting vension and straightway asked meat of him. The man kept one flank and the lungs, and gave the remainder to Doben who tied what he got to his saddle, and started off homeward. He met on the road a poor man and a small boy. " Who art thou ? " inquired Doben. " I am of the Malish Boyandai," said the poor man, " I am in need, give me venison, I pray thee, I will give thee my son in return for it." Doben gave the man a deer leg, took the boy home, and made him his attendant.

Some years passed, the boy grew, and Doben died. The boy, now a man, served the widow. While a widow Alan Goa bore three sons; the eldest was Buga Hatagi, the second Tusalchi, the third Boduanchar. The two sons born of Doben said once to each other: " Our mother has no husband, no brother of our father has ever been in this yurta, still she has three sons. There is only one man in the house, he has lived with us always; is he not their father ? "

Alan Goa learned that the two elder brothers were curious concerning the other three, so one day she called in her five sons and seating them together gave each one an arrow and told him to break it. Each broke his arrow. She then bound five arrows firmly together and commanded to break them — not one of the brothers could break the five arrows when tied in a bundle.

" Ye are in doubt," said she then to her eldest and second son, " as to who is the father of my third, fourth and fifth sons. Ye wonder, and with reason, for ye know not that a golden hued man makes his way to this yurta. He enters through the door by which light comes, he enters in through the smoke hole like sunshine. The brightness which comes from him fills me when I look at him. Going off on the rays of the sun or the moon he runs like a swift yellow dog till he vanishes. Cease talking idly. Your three youngest brothers are children of Heaven, and no one may liken them to common men. When they are khans ye will know this."

Alan Goa instructed her sons then, and said to them: " Ye all are my children, ye are all sons of mine. If ye stand apart like those five broken arrows it will be very easy to break you, but if ye keep one mind and one spirit no man on earth will be able to injure you, ye will be like those five arrows in the bundle."

Alan Goa died soon after this talk with her children. Four of the brothers took what belonged to all five of them, counting the youngest a weakling and simple they gave him no property whatever. He, seeing that they would not treat him with justice, said in his own mind: "I will go from this place, I will leave them." Then mounting a sorry roan horse with galled back and mangy tail he left his four brothers and rode away up the Onon to live at some new spot in freedom. When he reached Baljunala he built a small yurta, or hut at the place which seemed best to him and lived in it. One day he saw a falcon swoop down on a woodcock and seize it there near his yurta; he plucked hairs from the mangy tail of his horse, made a snare, caught the falcon, and trained it. When the wolves drove wild beasts toward the yurta in hunting he killed them with arrows, or took for himself and the falcon what the wolves left uneaten. Thus he lived the first winter. When spring came the falcon caught ducks and geese in great numbers.

Beyond the ridge of Mount Duilyan, which was there near his yurta, flowed the Tungeli, and at the river lived a new people. Boduanchar, who went to hunt daily with his falcon, discovered this people and drank in their yurtas, mare's milk which they gave him. They knew not whence he had come, and he asked not who they were, though they met every day with good feeling.

At last Boduanchar's eldest brother, Hatagi, set out to find him if possible and reached the Tungeli, where he saw the new people with whom Boduanchar was in friendship.

"Have ye seen a young man with a mangy tailed horse?" asked he. "On the horse's back are white spots which are marks of old gall sores." "We have seen the young man with that horse — he has also a falcon. He comes here each day to drink mare's milk, but we know not the place of his yurta. Whenever wind blows from the northwest it drives hither as many duck and goose feathers as there are flakes in a snowstorm. He must live with his falcon northwest of us. But wait here a while and thou wilt see him." Soon they saw the young man coming. Boduanchar became reconciled and went home with Hatagi.

"A man is complete who has a head on his body," said Boduanchar to himself. And aloud he said as they traveled, " A coat is complete when a collar is sewed to it." The brother said nothing on hearing these words for the first time; Boduanchar repeated the saying. " What dost thou mean ? " asked Hatagi. " Those men on the river," said Boduanchar, " have no head in their company; great and small are all one to them. We might take their ulus [1] very easily." " Well," replied Hatagi, " when we reach home we will talk of this; if we agree we will take the place."

The five brothers talked over the plan and were willing. Boduanchar led them back to the village. The first person seized by him was a woman. " Of what stock art thou ? " asked Boduanchar. " I am of the Charchiuts," answered the woman. The five brothers led all the people to their own place; after that they had cattle; they had also attendants to wait on them, when eating. Boduanchar took his first captive as wife and she bore him a son from whom the Balin clan was descended. Boduanchar took another wife and by her begat Habichi, who in time had a son Mainyan Todan who took as wife Monalun, from whom seven sons were born to him; the eldest of these was Katchi Kyuluk, and the youngest, Nachin.

Monalun loved command; she was harsh in her household and severe to all people. With her Mainyan Todan gained great wealth of all kinds, and lived at Nush Argi. Though there was no forest land near his yurta he had so many cattle when the herds were driven home, that not five ells of ground within eyesight could be found with no beast on it.

Mainyan Todan departed from life while his seventh son was an infant. At this time the Jelairs, that is, some descendants of Doben and Alan Goa, who had settled on the Kerulon near the Golden Khan's border, warred with his people very often. On a time the Golden Khan sent his forces against them; the Jelairs thinking the river impassable sneered at the enemy, and taking their caps off fell to mocking and shouting: " Would ye not like to come over and take all our horses and families ? " Roused by this ridicule and banter the enemy made rafts under cover, and crossed the Kerulon quickly. They rushed forward and defeated the Jelairs. They slew all whom they met or could find, not sparing even children. Most of the Jelairs were slain, except some who

[1] A village or community.

had camped in a place where the enemy did not reach them. These survivors found refuge at Monalun's settlement, where they fell to digging roots for subsistence, and spoiled a large space used in training young horses.

The widow was enraged at this trespass. She was riding in a cart when she saw it. Rushing in with attendants she trampled down some of the people, and dispersed them. Soon after this those same Jelairs stole from the sons of the widow a large herd of horses. When they heard of this robbery those sons hurried off to recover the animals. In their great haste they forgot to take armor. Monalun sent their wives on in carts with the armor, and she herself followed. Her sons were lying dead when their wives brought the armor. The Jelairs then slew the women, and when she came up they killed Monalun also.

The descendants of Katchi Kyuluk were all dead now except the youngest son, who was living apart from the others at Bargudjin on the eastern shore of Lake Baikal, and Kaidu his eldest son's only offspring, a small boy who was saved by his nurse, who hid with the child under firewood.

When news came to Nachin that his family had been slaughtered he hurried on to Nush Argi and found there some wretched old women with the little boy Kaidu, and the nurse who had saved him. Nachin was anxious to examine the Jelair country, recover some part of his brothers' lost property, and take a stern vengeance on the Jelairs, but he had no horse to ride on this journey. Just then a sorrel stallion from the herd that had been stolen by the Jelairs wandered back to Nush Argi. Nachin took this beast and set out alone to reconnoitre. The first men to meet him were two hunters on horseback, a son and his father, who were riding apart from each other. Each had a hawk on his wrist, and Nachin saw that both birds had belonged to his brothers.

" Hast thou seen a brown stallion, with mares, going eastward ? " asked he of the younger man. " I have not," said the stranger, " but hast thou seen ducks or geese on thy journey ? " " I have seen many;" replied Nachin; "come, I will show them to thee." The man followed Nachin, who at his own time well selected turned on this Jelair and killed him. He fettered the horse, tied the hawk to the saddle, turned and rode toward the second man ; upon reaching him he asked if he had seen a brown stallion, and mares going eastward. "No," said the man, "but hast thou seen my son who is hawking here near us?" "I have seen him," said Nachin. "He is bleeding from the nose and that delays him." Nachin then killed the second man and rode along farther, taking with him the hawks and the horses. He came at last to a valley where many horses were grazing; some boys were herding the beasts, and throwing stones for amusement. Nachin from a high place examined the country and since there was no one in sight he went into the valley, killed the boys and urged on the herd to Nush Argi, leading the two hunters' horses and bringing the hawks with him. Nachin then took his nephew, and the old women with the nurse, and drove all the horses to Bargudjin. There he lived for some years, and reared and trained his young nephew, who when old enough was made chief over two groups of Mongols; later on other groups were connected with these two. The Jelairs were crushed and enslaved by Kaidu and Nachin, who returned at the right time to Nush Argi. In that chief place of his family he acquired many cattle, and laid the foundation of Mongol dominion.

Nachin, as Mongol story depicts him, is one of the few men in history who were not self-seeking. He saved the small remnant of his family which escaped from the Jelairs, and was for some time the real guardian of the Mongols. He saved the boy Kaidu, and, seeking no power for himself, turned every effort to strengthening his nephew.

From that nephew, Kaidu, are descended the greatest historical men of his people, men without whom the name Mongol might not have risen from obscurity to be known and renowned as it now is.

Nachin had two sons, Urudai and Manhudai, from whom are descended the Uruts and Manhuts, two tribes which under Kuildar and Churchadai saved the fortune of Temudjin in his most desperate battle at Kalanchin.

Kaidu had three sons; the eldest was Boshin Kordokshin, the second Charaha Lingu, the third Chao Jinortaidji. Kaidu's eldest son had one son named Tumbinai, and died soon after the birth of that single descendant. Kaidu's second son had a son named Sengun Bilghe, who had a son Ambagai, and from this strong son, Ambagai, were descended the Taidjuts.

Kaidu's second son took his eldest brother's widow, and from her had a son, Baisutai, from whom came the Baisuts. Kaidu's third son had six sons, who were the founders of six clans among Mongols. Tumbinai, son of Boshin, Kaidu's eldest son, had two sons, Kabul and Sinsaichilai. Kabul had seven sons; the second of these, Bartan, had four sons; the third of these four sons was Yessugai.

Kabul was made khan, and though he had seven sons he did not wish to give rule to any one of them. So he gave it to Sengun Bilghe, the father of Ambagai. Kabul the Khan, son of Tumbinai, was renouned for great courage. His fame reached the Emperor of China, who had such regard for this chief that he sent envoys inviting him to the court as an evidence of friendship, and with the concealed hope of making a treaty through which the Mongols might act with North China. Kabul made the journey. The Emperor received him with honor, and entertained him with the best food and drink in the country. But, since the Chinese were given to deceit very greatly, as Kabul thought, and attacked each opponent from an ambush, he feared wiles and most of all poison; hence he avoided food and drink and withdrew from a feast under pretexts, but returned later on when relieved of suspicion, and fell to eating and drinking with very great relish. The Chinese were astounded at sight of his thirst and his hunger. " High Heaven must have made him to rule," exclaimed they, " else how could he drink and eat so enormously, and still have an appetite and be sober." But after a time he seemed tipsy, clapped his hands, reeled toward the Emperor, seized his beard and stroked his ear, to the horror of ministers, who cried out at once, and were ready to rush at the Mongol.

The Khan turned then to the Emperor and smiled very coolly. " If the Golden Khan holds me guilty," said he, " let him know that the will of my hand is to blame, not my own will. My hand has done that which displeases my own will and I condemn my hand's action."

The Emperor was calm and deliberate; at that time he wished above all things to wheedle his visitor, so he reasoned in his mind as follows: " If I punish this man his adherents, who are many, may rise and begin a long war with me." Hence he kept down his anger, and commanded to bring from his treasure house silken robes, embroidered in gold, of right size for the Mongol. A crown and a gold girdle were brought with them. He put these on Kabul, and showing marks of high honor dismissed him with friendship when the time came for parting.

When Kabul had set out for home the ministers insisted that it would not be possible to leave the man's conduct unnoticed. Roused at last by these speeches the Emperor sent off an envoy requesting Kabul to return to him. Kabul replied harshly, and kept on his journey. The Emperor was enraged now in earnest and sent men a second time not to request but to summon, and with them a good force of warriors to bring in the Mongol by violence if need be. Kabul had gone far on his journey, and, since the Golden Khan's messengers took a new road by mere hazard, they missed him. They went all the way to his yurta, and as he had not yet returned his wives said on hearing the message: "He will follow the Golden Khan's wishes." The messengers turned from the yurta and after a while met Kabul hastening homeward; they seized him and led him off quickly for delivery to their master. On the journey they halted at the house of a Saljut, who was friendly to the captive.

"These men are taking thee to death O Kabul," said the Saljut, "I must save thee. I have a horse which outstrips every wind, and is swifter than lightning. If thou sit on this beast thou canst save thyself — thou wilt escape at the first chance." Kabul mounted that horse, but his foot was made fast to the chief envoy's stirrup. In the night he unbound it, however, and shot away in the darkness. They pursued and hunted him with all speed, but only at Kabul's own yurta were they able to come up with him. There he received them with all hospitality, and gave his enemies a splendid new tent which belonged to a wife whom he had just taken; he gave also the best entertainment. Soon after, he summoned his servants (his sons were not with him). "These people," said he, "wish to take me to the Golden Khan to be killed by him with terrible torture. Ye must save me."

The servants fell unawares on the Golden Khan's messengers, and killed every man of them. Kabul was saved that time, but soon after he fell ill and died — very likely of poison — thus leaving the world to his seven sons, who were very ambitious. These sons were so great through their valor and courage that no combination of enemies could meet them successfully. They were all of one mother, Kulku Goa, a Kunkurat woman, whose younger brother, Saïn Tegin, was the cause of involving the family in a terrible blood feud.

Saïn Tegin fell ill and they called in a shaman of the Taidjuts to cure him. He died notwithstanding the art of this shaman, who was slain either on his way home or soon after, by the relatives of the dead man. This caused a great battle between the Taidjuts and Saïn Tegin's adherents and relatives, joined now by Kabul's sons, who favored the cause of their uncle. In this battle Kaidan met a Taidjut in single encounter, split open his saddle, swept him down from his horse, and wounded him dreadfully. The Taidjut, who recovered only after a twelve month of suffering, began a new struggle as soon as strength came to him. Kaidan brought horse and rider to the earth, each wounded grievously; though ten mounted men rushed at the victor, he so used spear and sword on them that he came out in triumph. Thus began the great blood feud which later on Temudjin used with such deadly effect on the Taidjuts and Tartars.

Between Lake Buyur and Lake Kulon is a river, on this river a large group of Tartar tribes lived at that period. Ambagai, son of Sengun, went to find a new wife at Lake Buyur but was seized by some Tartars and sent to the Kin Emperor, who took his life very cruelly. Before his captors had set out with Ambagai he sent home this message: " Tell Kutula, fourth son of my cousin Kabul, who has seven sons, and Kaidan, one of my ten sons, that I, who ruled men, am a prisoner and must die in great suffering. And remember these words of mine, all of you: Though ye were to wear every nail from the fingers of each hand, and lose the ten fingers on both hands, ye must avenge me."

The Golden Khan in return for offenses committed against him by Ambagai's relatives, had him nailed to a wooden ass, flayed alive, and then chopped into small pieces slowly, beginning with his fingers and toes, till his whole body was finished.

Okin Barka, Kabul's eldest son and a brother of Kutula, had been captured by the Tartars, sent to the Golden Khan, and put to death in the same way as Ambagai. This was done because Kabul had killed the Golden Khan's messengers.

Before Ambagai was tortured he sent Bulgadji, his slave, to the Golden Khan with this warning: " It is shameful to kill me. I was seized most perfidiously, I am here without reason. If thou kill me all chiefs among Mongols will rise and avenge the injustice." The Golden Khan paid no heed to the message, but after the hideous execution he sent Bulgadji on courier horses to Mongolia with the command to tell all there that Ambagai had been nailed to the wooden ass, his skin stripped from him while living, and his body then chopped into pieces bit by bit. On the way Bulgadji passed through the land of the Durbans, who would not give horses, and no matter what he said they took no note of him. When his horses were so weary that they could go no farther he left them, went home on foot and told all to Kaidan, whose son, Tuda, told the whole tale to Katula and Yessugai, his nephew. Kaidan, Tuda and Yessugai held a council immediately and resolved with many Mongols to avenge Okin Barka and Ambagai. Kutula was chosen khan then to lead the expedition. They held a great feast when the election was over, and all became grandly excited. They danced round a wide-spreading tree with great energy, and stamped out a ditch of such depth that they were hidden to their knees in it.

Kutula assembled all warriors who were willing to go, and marched against China. The Golden Khan's forces were defeated, and routed with terrible slaughter. The Mongols took booty of unspeakable value, took all that men could bear with them, or that horses could carry. They came home filled with delight, bringing woven stuffs of all species, every kind of rich furniture, weapons and implements, and driving before them immense herds of horses, and large and small cattle.

While on the way home Kutula when passing through the land of the Durbans went to hunt with a small force of followers. On seeing these people the Durbans assembled a numerous party and attacked them; they killed some, and scattered the others. Kutula left alone saved himself by fleeing, and drove his swift horse through a swamp to the opposite edge of the soft place. The beast stopped and stuck fast there; Kutula stood on the saddle and sprang to firm ground from it. The Durbans seeing him on foot, were well satisfied. " Oh let him go," said they, " of what use is a man when his horse is gone." Then, while they stood looking, he pulled his horse out of the quagmire, mounted and rode away in their presence. The swamp extended so far on either hand that they cared not to follow.

Kutula's surviving attendants returned to the army, spread news of his death, and declared that the Durbans had killed him. His warriors reached home somewhat earlier than the Khan and since he had not appeared on the road and his attendants said that he had been killed by the Durbans Yessugai made a funeral feast for their leader and went to Kutula's wife to announce her husband's death and with her drink the cup to his memory. On appearing before her he began to lament, and weep bitterly. " Why hast thou come ? " asked she, " and why art thou weeping ? " He told the cause of his grief and his coming. " I believe not a word of all thou hast told me," said the woman. " Would Kutula let Durbans kill him, Kutula whose voice is like thunder in the mountains, a voice which reaches high heaven, would Kutula let common men kill him ? He would not, his delay has another cause. He is living. He has stopped for some work of importance, he will come later on."

But the warriors and Kutula's attendants felt sure that the Khan had been murdered.

When Kutula had pulled his horse out of the quagmire, and ridden away safely, he was savagely angry. " How have those vile, wretched Durbans brought me to such trouble," raged he, " and driven off all my servants ? Must I go home empty-handed ? No, I will not leave these places unplundered." Then he rode till he found a brown stallion, also a great herd of mares and their colts with them. He mounted the stallion, let out his own horse which ran forward, then drove the mares which followed the saddle beast. Riding farther in the steppes he found nests of wild geese; dismounting he took off his boots, filled the great legs of them with goose eggs, remounted and rode away home on the stallion, holding the boots and driving the mares and their colts to his yurta.

A vast crowd of people had assembled to lament and show honor to the memory of Kutula, and now, astonished at his sudden arrival, they rejoiced beyond measure, and turned all their sorrow and wailing into a feast of triumph and gladness. " Ha ! " said the wife then to Yessugai, " did I not tell thee that no Durbans, or other men could bring down Kutula ? "

After his great success against China, Kutula moved on the Tartars and punished them unsparingly for sending Okin Barka, his brother, to the Golden Khan for destruction.

But now broke out afresh the great hatred of the ten sons of Ambagai for Kutula and his brothers. Those ten Taidjut brothers fell on the six surviving sons of Kabul and killed five of them, killed all except Bartan, who burst his way out of the murderous encounter with three serious wounds in his body, and fled with four attendants. His son Yessugai, who had been hurled to the earth from his saddle, sprang up quickly and, though only thirteen years of age, sent his spear through the body of a Taidjut who was mounted, brought him down dying, sprang to the empty saddle, rushed away and caught up with his father. Through this wonderful promptness and skill he was able to save himself.

Bartan's wife, Maral Kayak, fled on foot from her yurta with three other sons, Mangutu, Naigun and Daritai, and reached her wounded husband.

The Taidjut triumph was perfect for a season. Bartan's power had departed, he died soon and gave place to his son, a young hero. This son was Yessugai, the name means number nine, his full name was Yessugai Bahadur, the ninth hero. He was ninth too in descent from that youngest son of Alan Goa, Boduanchar, who rode off alone from injustice.

At this time the tendency had increased very greatly among chiefs of Mongol clans to make other chiefs subordinates, or assistants. This was true specially of men descended from Kabul and from Ambagai. If rival or smaller chiefs would not accept the position a conflict resulted, attacks were made by small parties or larger ones, or through war or poison; the weaker men when ambitious were swept from existence. The continual interference of China by intrigue or by arms, or by bribery through titles or presents, through rewards to individuals, or dire ghastly punishments where punishment seemed more effective, did something also to strengthen and consolidate the loosely coherent society of the Mongols, and thus helped unwittingly the work of strong men seeking power north of China.

Yessugai, through activity and keenness succeeded in winning co-operation sufficient to undo the great Taidjut triumph. Kabul's sons again got the primacy.

CHAPTER II

THIS intense rivalry between the descendants of Kabul and Ambagai was the great ruling fact among Mongols at this epoch. Kabul and Ambagai were second cousins, both being third in descent from Kaidu, that little boy saved by his nurse from the Jelairs; the Kaidu whose descendants were the great ruling Mongols of history. Kabul and Ambagai are remarkable themselves, and are notable also as fathers of men who sought power by all means which they could imagine and bring into practice.

Yessugai with his brothers was now triumphant and prosperous. He was terribly hostile to the Buyur Lake Tartars; he was ever watching the Taidjut opposition, which though resting at times never slumbered. Once in the days of his power Yessugai while hawking along the Onon saw a Merkit named Yeke Chilaidu taking home with him a wife from the Olkonots. Seeing that the woman was a beauty Yessugai hurried back to his yurta and returned with his eldest and youngest brothers to help him. When Yeke saw the three brothers coming he grew frightened, struck his horse and rushed away to find some good hiding place, but found none and rode back to the cart where his wife was. " Those men are very hostile," said the woman. " Hurry off, or they will kill thee. If thou survive find a wife such as I am, if thou remember me call her by my name." Then she drew off her shift and gave it to Yeke. He took it, mounted quickly and, seeing Yessugai approaching with his brothers, galloped up the river.

The three men rushed after Yeke, but did not overtake him, so they rode back to the woman, whose name was Hoelun. She was weeping. Her screams when they seized her " raised waves on the river, and shook trees in the valley."

" The husband has crossed many ridges already, and many

waters," said Daritai, Yessugai's youngest brother, " no matter
how thou scream he will not come to thee, if thou look for his
trail thou wilt not find it. Stop screaming !" Thus they took
Hoelun, and she became a wife then to Yessugai.

Some months after the capture of Hoelun, Yessugai made attacks
on the Tartars, and among other captives took Temudjin Uge, a
chieftain. Hoelun gave birth to a son at that period [1] near the
hill Dailiun Baldak. The boy was born grasping a lump of dark
blood in his fist very firmly, and since he was born when Temudjin
Uge was taken they called the child Temudjin. After that Hoelun
had three other sons: Kassar, Hochiun and Taimuge, and one
daughter, Taimulun.

When this first son had passed his thirteenth year Yessugai set
out with the lad on a visit to Hoelun's brothers to find among them
a wife for him. When between the two mountains Cihurga and
Cheksar he met one Desaichan, a man of the Ungirs. " Whither
art thou going O Yessugai ? " asked Desaichan. " I am going
with my son to his uncles to look out a bride for him among them."
" Thy son has a clear face and bright eyes," said Desaichan.
" Last night I dreamed that a white falcon holding the sun and the
moon in its talons flew down to my wrist, and perched on it. ' We
only know the sun and the moon through our eyesight,' said I to
some friends of mine, ' but now a white falcon has brought them
both down to me in his talons, this must be an omen of greatness.'
At the right time hast thou come hither Yessugai with thy son and
shown what my dream means. It presages high fortune un-
doubtedly. I have a daughter at home, she is small yet but come
and look at her."

Then he conducted the father and son to his yurta. Yessugai
rejoiced in his heart very greatly at sight of the girl, who in truth
was a beauty. She was ten years of age, and named Bortai. Next
day Yessugai asked Bortai of Desaichan as a bride for young
Temudjin. " Will it show more importance if I give her only after
much begging," asked the father, " or will it show slight esteem
if I give her in answer to few words ? We know that a girl is not
born to remain in the household forever. I yield her to marry thy
son, and do thou leave him here for a time with me."

The agreement was finished and Yessugai went away without

[1] 1161.

Temudjin. On the road home he stopped at Cheksar and met
Tartars who arranged there a feast for him. Being hungry and
thirsty from traveling he halted. His hosts, who knew well that he
had captured and killed very many of their people, Temudjin Uge
with others, had poison made ready, and gave it in drink to him.
Yessugai rode away and reached home in three days, but fell ill
on the journey, and his trouble increased as he traveled. " There
is pain in my heart," said he, " who is near me? " At that time
Munlik, a son of Charaha, happened in at the yurta, and Yessugai
called him. " My children are young," said he, " I went to find a
bride for my son Temudjin, and have found her. On the way home
I was poisoned by enemies. My heart is very sore in me, so go
thou to my brothers and see them, see their wives also. I give
thee this as a duty; tell them all that has happened. But first
bring me Temudjin very quickly. "

Yessugai died[1] shortly after without seeing Temudjin.

Munlik went with all haste to Desaichan. " Yessugai," said he,
" wants to see Temudjin, he has sent me to bring the boy." " If
Yessugai is grieving let Temudjin go, and return to me afterward."
Munlik took Temudjin home as instructed. In the spring following when Ambagai's widows were preparing the offerings to
ancestors before moving to the summer place they refused to share
sacrificed meats with Hoelun, and thus shut her out from their
ruling circle and relationship. " Better leave this woman here with
her children, she must not go with us," said the widows. Targutai
Kurultuk, who was then in authority, went from the winter place
without turning to Hoelun, or speaking. He with Todoyan
Jirisha his brother had enticed away Yessugai's people. Munlik's
father, Charáha, an old man, strove to persuade Targutai and his
brother to take Hoelun, but they would not listen to him or to any
man. " The deep water is gone, the bright stone is broken," said
Todoyan, " we cannot restore them, we have nothing to do with
that woman, and her children." And when Targutai with his
brother was starting, a warrior of his thrust a spear into Charáha's
back and the old man fell down mortally wounded.

Temudjin went to talk with Charáha and take advice from
him. " Targutai and his brother," said the old man, " have
led away all the people assembled by thy father, and our relatives."

[1] 1175.

Temudjin wept then and turned to his mother for assistance. Hoelun resolved quickly; she mounted, and, directing her attendants to take lances, set out at the head of them. She overtook the deserting people and stopped one half of them, but even that half would not go back with her. So Targutai and Todoyan had defeated Hoelun with her children, and taken one half of Yessugai's people; the second half joined other leaders. But Hoelun, a strong, resolute woman, protected her family and found means to support it. Her children lived in poor, harsh conditions, and grew up in the midst of hostility and hatred. To assist and give help to their mother they made hooks out of needles and fished in the river Onon which was close to their dwelling. Once Temudjin and Kassar went to fish with their half brothers, Baiktar and Belgutai, Yessugai's children by another wife. Temudjin caught a golden hued trout and his half brothers took it from him. He went then with Kassar to Hoelun. "We caught a golden hued fish," said they, "but Baiktar and Belgutai took it." "Why do ye quarrel?" asked the mother, "we have no friends at present; all have deserted us; nothing sticks to us now but our shadows. We have no power yet to punish the Taidjuts. Why do ye act like the sons of Alan Goa, and quarrel? Why not agree and gain strength against enemies?"

Temudjin was dissatisfied; he wished Hoelun to take his side and go against Baiktar. "The other day," said he, "I shot a bird and Baiktar took this bird also. He and his brother to-day snatched my fish from me. If they act always in this way how can I live with them?" And he turned from his mother very quickly. Both brothers rushed out, slammed the door flap behind them and vanished.

When they were out they saw Baiktar on a hill herding horses. Temudjin stole up from behind, and Kassar in front; they had taken arrows and were aiming when Baiktar turned and saw them. "Why treat me like a splinter in the mouth, or a hair on the eyeball?" asked he. "Though ye kill me spare my brother, do not kill Belgutai." Then he bent his legs under him, and waited.

Temudjin from behind and Kassar in front killed Baiktar with arrows. When they went home Hoelun knew by their faces what had happened. "Thou wert born," said she to Temudjin, "grasping blood in thy fingers. Thou and thy brother are like dogs when devouring a village, or serpents which swallow alive what they spring upon, or wolves hunting prey in a snow storm. The injuries done us by the Taidjuts are terrible, ye might plan to grow strong and then punish the Taidjuts. But what are ye doing ? "

Well might she ask, for she did not know then her wonderful son Temudjin, for whom it was as natural to remove a half brother, or even a brother, by killing him as to set aside any other obstacle. He who worked all his life till its end to eliminate opponents was that day beginning his mighty career, and his first real work was the murder of his half brother Baiktar, whose father was his own father, Yessugai.

No matter who Temudjin's enemies were he removed them as coolly as a teacher in his classroom rubs figures from a black board. He struck down the Taidjuts as soon as he felt himself strong enough, but before he could do that his task was to weed out and train his own family. The first work before him was the empire of his household. Neither mother, nor brother, nor anyone must stand between Temudjin and his object; in that he showed his great singleness of purpose, his invincible will power, his wisdom in winning the success which his mind saw. The wisdom of Temudjin in building up empire was an unerring clear instinct like the instinct of a bee in constructing its honeycomb, or the judgment and skill of a bird in finding the proper material, and weaving the round perfect nest for its eggs and its little ones.

Temudjin began his career in real practice by killing his half brother mainly through the hand of his full brother Kassar, who was famed later on as the unerring strong archer, and who in time tried unsuccessfully to rival the invincible Temudjin.

Temudjin was now master in a very small region, but he was master. His mother and brothers did not dominate, or interfere, they assisted him. The family lived for a time in seclusion and uninjured till at last Targutai roused up his followers to action. " Temudjin and his brothers have grown," said he, " they are stronger." Taking with him some comrades he rode away quickly to find Temudjin with his family. From afar Hoelun and her children saw the men coming and were frightened. Temudjin seized his horse quickly, and fled before others to the mountain. Belgutai hid his half brothers and sister in a cliff, after that he felled trees to stop the horsemen. Kassar sent arrows to hinder

the Taidjuts. " We want only Temudjin, we want no one else,"
said they. Temudjin had fled to Mount Targunai and hidden
there in dense thickets whither they could not follow. They surrounded Targunai and watched closely.

He spent three days in secret places, and then led his horse out
to flee from the mountain. When near the edge of the forest the
saddle fell. He saw that breast strap and girth were both fixed
securely " A saddle may fall," thought he, " though the girth
be well fastened, but how can it fall when the breast strap is holding
it ? I see now that Heaven is protecting me."

He turned back and passed three other days hiding; then he
tried to go out a second time — a great rock fell in front of him,
blocked the road and stopped his passage. " Heaven wills that I
stay here still longer," said Temudjin. He went back and spent
three other days on the mountain, nine days in all without eating.
" Must I die here alone and unheard of ? " thought he despair-
ingly. " Better go at all hazards." He cut a way near the rock
and led his horse down the mountain side.

The Taidjuts, who were watching outside very carefully, seized
Temudjin and took him to Targutai, who commanded that a
kang be put on him, and also fetters, and that he live one day and
night in each tent. So he passed from one family to another in
succession. During these changes he gained the close friendship
of one Sorgan Shira, and of an old woman. The old woman was
kind and put rags on the kang at the points where his shoulders
were galled by it.

Once the Taidjuts made a feast near the Onon and went home
after sunset, appointing a boy to watch over the captive. Temudjin
had been able to break his own fetters, and seeing that all had gone
home felled the boy with the kang in which his own head and both
hands were fastened. Then he ran to a forest along the Onon
and lay down there, but, fearing lest they might find him, he rose,
hurried on to the river and sank in it, leaving only his face above
water.

The boy soon recovered and screamed that the captive had fled
from him. Some Taidjuts rushed quickly together on hearing
him, and searched around everywhere. There was moonlight
that evening and Sorgan Shira of the Sulduts, who was searching
with others, and had gone quite a distance ahead, found Temudjin,

but did not call out. " The Taidjuts hate thee because thou hast wisdom," said he to the captive, " thou wilt die if they find thee. Stay where thou art for the present, and be careful, I will not betray thee to any one."

The pursuers went some distance while searching. " This man escaped during daylight," said Sorgan Shira, when he overtook them. " It is night now and difficult to find him. Better search nearer places, we can hunt here to-morrow. He has not come thus far, — how could he run such a distance with a kang on his shoulders ? "

On the way back Sorgan Shira went to Temudjin a second time. " We shall come hither to-morrow to search for thee," said he. " Hurry off now to thy mother and brothers. Shouldst thou meet any man tell him not that I saw thee." When Sorgan Shira had gone, Termudjin fell to thinking and thought in this manner: " While stopping at each tent I passed a day with Sorgan Shira; Chila and Chinbo his sons showed me pity. They took off the kang in the dark from my shoulders and let me lie down then in freedom. He saw me to-day, I cannot escape till this kang is taken off, he will do that, I will go to him. He will save me."

So Temudjin went and when he entered the yurta Sorgan Shira was frightened. " Why come now to me ? " inquired he. " I told thee to go to thy mother and brothers." " When a bird is pursued by a falcon," said Temudjin, " it hides in thick grass and thus saves itself."

" We should be of less value than grass were we not to help this poor youth, who thus begs us," said to himself Sorgan Shira. The boys took the kang from the captive and burned it, then they hid Timudjin in a cart which they piled high with wool packs and told Kadan, their sister, to guard the wool carefully, and not speak of Temudjin to any living person.

The Taidjuts appeared on the third day. " Has no one here seen that runaway ? " asked they of Sorgan. " Search where ye will," was the answer. They searched the whole yurta, then they searched around the house in all places, and threw out the wool till they came to the cart box. They were going to empty this also when Sorgan laughed at them, saying, " How could any man live in a cart load of wool this hot weather ? " They prodded the wool then with lances; one of these entered Temudjin's leg, but he was silent and moved not. The Taidjuts were satisfied, and went away without emptying the cart box.

" Thou hast come very near killing me," said Sorgan to Temudjin. " The smoke of my house would have vanished, and my fire would have died out forever had they found thee. Go now to thy mother and brothers."

He gave Temudjin a white-nosed, sorrel mare without a saddle, gave him a boiled lamb which was fat because reared by two mothers, gave him a skin of mare's milk, a bow and two arrows, but no flint lest he strike fire on the way, and betray himself.

Temudjin went to the ruins of his first house and then higher up the Onon till he reached the Kimurha. He saw tracks near that river and followed them on to Mount Baitar. In front of that mountain is a smaller one, Horchukin; there he found all his brothers and Hoelun his mother. Temudjin moved now with them to Mount Burhan. Near Burhan is the high land Gulyalgu, through this land runs the river Sangur, on the bank of that river is a hill called Kara Jiruge and a green colored lake near the foot of it. At this lake Temudjin fixed his yurta, trapped marmots and field mice, and thus they lived on for a season. At last some Taidjut thieves drove off eight horses from Temudjin, leaving only the white-nosed sorrel mare which Sorgan had given him, and on which Belgutai had gone to hunt marmots. He came back that evening with a load of them.

" The horses have been stolen," said Temudjin. " I will go for them," said Belgutai. " Thou couldst not find them," answered Kassar, " I will go. " Ye could not find them, and if ye found them ye could not bring them back," called out Temudjin, " I will go."

Temudjin set his brothers aside as useless at that juncture, their authority and worth were to him as nothing. Temudjin's is the only, the genuine authority. He rode off on the white-nosed sorrel mare, and followed the trail of the eight stolen horses. He traveled three days and on the fourth morning early he saw near the road a young man who had led up a mare and was milking her. " Hast thou seen eight gray horses ? " asked Temudjin. " Before sunrise eight horses went past me, I will show thee the trail over which they were driven." Temudjin's weary beast was let out then to pasture; a white horse with a black stripe on its spine was led in to go farther. The youth hid his leather pail and his bag in the grass very carefully. "Thou art tired," said he to Temudjin, "and art anxious. My name is Boörchu, I will go with thee for thy horses. Nahu Boyan is my father, I am his one son and he loves me."

So they set out together and traveled three days in company. On the third day toward evening they came to a camp ground and saw the eight horses. "Stay at this place O my comrade," said Temudjin, "I will go and drive off those horses."

"If I have come hither to help thee why should I stay alone and do nothing?" asked Boörchu. So they went on together and drove off the horses. The thieves hurried after them promptly and one, who rode a white stallion, had a lasso and was gaining on the comrades. "Give me thy quiver and bow," said Boörchu," I will meet him with an arrow." "Let me use the bow," answered Temudjin, "those enemies might wound thee." The man on the white horse was directing his lasso and ready to hurl it when Temudjin's arrow put an end to his action. That night Temudjin and Boörchu made a journey which would have taken three days for any other men, and saw the yurta of Nahu Boyan in the distance at daybreak.

"Without thy help," said Temudjin, "I could not have brought back these horses. Without thee I could have done nothing, so let us divide now these eight beasts between us." "I decided to help thee," answered Boörchu, "because I saw thee weighed down and weary from sorrow and loneliness, why should I take what is thine from thee? I am my father's one son, his wealth is enough for me, more is not needed. If I should take thine how couldst thou call me thy comrade?"

When they entered the yurta of Nahu Boyan they found the old man grieving bitterly for Boörchu. On seeing them he shed tears and reproached his son sharply. "I know not," said Boörchu in answer, "how I thought of assisting this comrade, but when I saw him worn and anxious I had to go with him. Things are now well again, for I am with thee, my father." Nahu Boyan became satisfied when he heard the whole story. Boörchu rode off then and brought the leather milk pail, killed a lamb, filled a bag with mare's milk, and tying it to the horse like a pack gave Temudjin all to sustain him. "Ye are young," said Nahu Boyan, "be ye friends, and be faithful." Temudjin took farewell of Boörchu and his father. Three days after that he had reached home with his horses. No words could describe the delight of his mother and brothers when they saw him.

Temudjin had passed his thirteenth year when he parted from Bortai. He went down the Kerulon now with his half brother, Belgutai, to get her. Several years had passed and he had a wish to marry. Bortai's father rejoiced at seeing Temudjin. "I grieved," said he, "greatly and lost hope of seeing thee when I heard of Taidjut hatred."

Both parents escorted their daughter and her husband. Desai-chan after going some distance turned homeward, as was usual for fathers, but Bortai's mother, Sotan, went on to Temudjin's yurta.

Temudjin wished now to have Boörchu, wished him as a comrade forever, and sent Belgutai to bring him. Boörchu said nothing to his father or to any one; he took simply a humpbacked sorrel horse, saddled him, strapped a coat of black fur to the saddle and rode away quickly to Temudjin's yurta; after that he never left him.

Temudjin removed from the Sangur to the springs of the Kerulon and fixed his yurta at the foot of the slope known as Burji. Bortai had brought with her a black sable cloak as a present to Hoelun. "In former days," said Temudjin to his brothers, "our father, Yessugai, became a sworn friend, an 'anda,' to Togrul of the Keraïts, hence Togrul is to me in the place of my father, we will go now and show Togrul honor."

Temudjin and two of his brothers took the cloak to Togrul in the Black Forest on the Tula. "In former days," said Temudjin as he stood before Togrul, "thou didst become anda to Yessugai, hence thou art to me in the place of my father. I bring thee to-day, my father, a gift brought by my wife to my mother." With these words he gave the black sable to Togrul, who was pleased very greatly with the offering.

"I will bring back to thee thy people who are scattered," said Togrul in answer, "and join them again to thee, I will keep this in mind very firmly, and not forget it."

When Temudjin returned home the old man Charchiutai came from Mount Burhan with the bellows of a blacksmith on his shoulders, and brought also Chelmai, his son, with him. "When thou wert born," said Charchiutai to Temudjin, "I gave thee a lined sable wrap, I gave thee too my son Chelmai, but as he was very little at that time, I kept the boy with me and trained him, but now when he is grown up and skilful I bring him. Let him saddle thy horse and open doors to thee." With that he gave his son Chelmai to Temudjin.

Some short time after this, just before daybreak one morning, Hoakchin, an old woman, Hoelun's faithful servant, who slept on the ground, sprang up quickly and called to her mistress: "O mother, rise, I hear the earth tremble! O mother, the Taidjuts are coming, our terrible destroyers! Hasten, O mother!" "Rouse up the children," said Hoelun, "wake them all quickly!" Hoelun rose to her feet as she was speaking. Temudjin and his brothers sprang up and ran to their horses. Hoelun carried her daughter Taimulun. Temudjin had only one saddle beast ready. There was no horse for Bortai, so he galloped off with his brothers. Thus showing that self-preservation was his one thought.

Hoakchin, the old woman, hid Bortai, she stowed her away in a small black kibitka (cart), attached a pied cow to it and drove along the river Tungela. As the night darkness cleared and light was approaching some mounted men overtook the old woman. "Who art thou?" asked they, riding up to her. "I go around and shear sheep for rich people, I am on my way home now," said Hoakchin. "Is Temudjin at his yurta?" asked a horseman. "Where is it?" "His yurta is not far, but I know not where he is at this moment," answered Hoakchin.

When the men had ridden off the old woman urged on the cow, but just then the axle broke. Hoakchin wished to hurry on foot to the mountain with Bortai, but the horsemen had turned back already and came to her. "Who is in there?" asked a man as he pointed at the kibitka. "I have wool there," replied the old woman. "Let us look at this wool, brothers," said one of the mounted men. They dragged Bortai out, and then put her on horseback with Hoakchin. Next they followed on Temudjin's tracks to Mount Burhan, but could not come up with him. Wishing to enter the mountain land straightway they tried one and another place, but found no road of any kind open. In one part a sticky morass, in another a dense growth of forest and thicket. They did not find the secret road and could not break in at any point. These horsemen were from three clans of Merkits. The first had been sent by Tukta Bijhi of the Uduts; the second by Dair Usun of the Uasits; the third by Haätai Darmala of the Haäts. They had come to wreak vengeance on Temudjin because Yessugai, his father, had snatched away Hoelun from Chilaidu, and this Hoelun was Temudjin's mother. They now carried off Bortai, Temudjin's wife, who was thus taken in vengeance, as they said, for the stealing of Hoelun.

Temudjin, fearing lest they might be in ambush, sent his half brother, Belgutai, and Boörchu, with Chelmai to examine and discover. In three days when these men were well satisfied that the Merkits had gone from the mountain, Temudjin left his hiding place. He stood, struck his breast and cried looking heavenward: " Thanks to the ears of a skunk, and the eyes of an ermine in the head of old Hoakchin, I escaped capture. Besides that Mount Burhan has saved me, and from this day I will make offering to the mountain, and leave to my children and their children this duty of sacrifice." Then he turned toward the sun, put his girdle on his back, took his cap in his hand, and striking his breast bent his knees nine times in homage; he made next a libation of tarasun, a liquor distilled out of mare's milk.

After that Temudjin with Kassar and Belgutai went to Togrul on the Tula and implored him, " O father and sovereign," said Temudjin, " three clans of Merkits fell on us suddenly, and stole my wife, Bortai. Is it not possible to save her ? "

" Last year," said Togrul, " when the cloak of black sable was brought to me, I promised to lead back thy people who deserted, and those who were scattered. I remember this well, and because of my promise I will root out the Merkits, I will rescue and return to thee Bortai. Inform Jamuka that thy wife has been stolen. Two tumans[1] of warriors will go with me, let Jamuka lead out the same number."

Jamuka, chief of the Juriats at that time, was descended from a brother of Kabul Khan, and was third cousin therefore to Temudjin. Temudjin sent his brothers to Jamuka with this message: " The Merkits have stolen my wife, thou and I have the same origin; can we not avenge this great insult ? " He sent Togrul's statement also. " I have heard," said Jamuka, " that

[1] A tuman is ten thousand.

Temudjin's wife has been stolen, I am grieved very greatly at his trouble and will help him." He told where the three clans were camping, and promised to aid in bringing back Bortai.

"Tell Temudjin and Togrul," said he, "that my army is ready. With me are some people belonging to Temudjin; from them I will gather one tuman of warriors and take the same number of my own folk with them, I will go up to Butohan Borchi on the Onon where Togrul will meet me." They took back the answer to Temudjin, and went to Togrul with the words from Jamuka.

Togrul set out with two tumans of warriors toward the Kerulon and met Temudjin at the river Kimurha. One tuman of Togrul's men was led by Jaganbo, his brother. Jamuka waited three days at Butohan Borchi for Togrul and Jaganbo; he was angry and full of reproaches when he met them. "When conditions are made between allies," said he, "though wind and rain come to hinder, men should meet at the season appointed. The time of our meeting was settled, a given word is the same as an oath, if the word is not to be kept no ally should be invited."

"I have come three days late," said Togrul. "Blame, and punish me, Jamuka, my brother, until thou art satisfied."

The warriors went on now, crossed the Kilho to Buura where they seized all the people and with them the wife of the Merkit, Tukta Bijhi. Tukta Bijhi, who was sleeping, would have been captured had not his hunters and fishermen hurried on in the night time and warned him. He and Dair Usun, his brother, rushed away down the river to Bargudjin. When the Merkits were fleeing at night down along the Selinga, Togrul's men hunted on fiercely and were seizing them. In that rushing crowd Temudjin shouted: "Bortai! O Bortai!" She was with the fleeing people; she knew Temudjin's voice and sprang from a small covered cart with Hoakchin, the old woman. Running up, she caught Temudjin's horse by the bridle. The moon broke through clouds that same moment, and each knew the other.

Temudjin sent to Togrul without waiting. "I have found," said he, "those whom I was seeking; let us camp now and go on no farther to-night." They camped there. When the Merkits with three hundred men attacked Temudjin to take vengeance for snatching off Chilaidu's wife, Hoelun, Tukta Bijhi, the brother of Chilaidu, with two other leaders rode three times round Mount Burhan, but could not find Temudjin, and only took Bortai. They gave her as wife to Chilger, a younger brother of Chilaidu, the first husband of Hoelun, Temudjin's mother. (This Chilaidu was perhaps Temudjin's father.) Now, when a great army was led in by Togrul and Jamuka, Chilger was cruelly frightened. " I have been doomed like a crow," said he, " to eat wretched scraps of old skin, but I should like greatly the taste of some wild goose. By my offenses against Bortai I have brought evil suffering on the Merkits; the harm which now has befallen them may crush me also. To save my life I must hide in some small and dark corner." Having said this he vanished. Haätai Darmala was the only man captured; they put a kang on his neck and went straight toward Mount Burhan.

Those three hundred Merkits who rode thrice round Mount Burhan were slain every man of them. Their wives, who were fit to continue as wives, were given to new husbands; those who should only be slaves were delivered to slavery.

" Thou, O my father, and thou my anda," said Temudjin to Togrul and Jamuka, " Heaven through the aid which ye gave me has strengthened my hands to avenge a great insult. The Merkits who attacked me are extinguished, their wives are taken captive, the work is now ended." That same year Bortai gave birth to her first son, Juchi, and because of her captivity the real father of Juchi was always a question in the mind of Temudjin.

The Uduts had left in their camp a beautiful small boy, Kuichu. He had splendid bright eyes, was dressed in river sable, and on his feet were boots made of deer hoofs. When the warriors took the camp they seized Kuichi and gave him to Hoelun. Temudjin, Togrul and Jamuka destroyed all the dwellings of the Merkits and captured the women left in them. Togrul returned then to the Tula. Temudjin and Jamuka went to Hórho Nachúbur and fixed a camp there. The two men renewed former times and the origin of their friendship; each promised now to love the other more firmly than aforetime, if possible. Temudjin was in his boyhood, eleven years of age, when they made themselves " andas " the first day; both were guests of Togrul at that period. Now they swore friendship again, — became andas a second time. They discussed friendship with each other: "Old people," said Temudjin,

" declare that when men become andas both have one life as it were; neither abandons the other, and each guards the life of his anda. Now we strengthen our friendship anew, and refresh it." At these words Temudjin girded Jamuka, with a golden belt, which he had taken from the Merkits, and Jamuka gave him a rich girdle, and a splendid white stallion, which he had captured. They arranged a feast under a broad spreading tree near the cliff known as Huldah, and at night they slept under one blanket together.

Temudjin and Jamuka, from love, as it were, of each other, lived eighteen months in glad, careless company, but really each of the two men was studying and watching his anda and working against him with all the power possible as was shown very clearly in the sequel. At last during April, while moving, the two friends spurred on ahead of the kibitkas and were talking as usual: " If we camp near that mountain in front," said Jamuka all at once, " the horseherds will get our yurtas. If we camp near the river the shepherds will have food for their gullets." Temudjin made no answer to words which seemed dark and fateful, so he halted to wait for his wife and his mother; Jamuka rode farther and left him. When Hoelun had come up to him Temudjin told her the words of Jamuka, and said, " I knew not what they could signify, hence I gave him no answer. I have come to ask thy opinion, mother." Hoelun had not time to reply because Bortai was quicker. " People say," declared Bortai, " that thy friend seeks the new and despises the old; I think that he is tired of us. Is there not some trick in these words which he has given thee? Is there not some danger behind them? We ought not to halt, let us go on all night by a new road, and not stop until daybreak. It is better to part in good health from Jamuka." " Bortai talks wisdom," said Temudjin. He went on then by his own road, aside from Jamuka, and passed near one camp of the Taidjuts who were frightened when they saw him; they rose up and hurried away that same night to Jamuka. Those Taidjuts left in their camp a small boy, Kokochu. Temudjin's men found the lad and gave him as a present to Hoelun.

After this swift, all night's journey when day came Temudjin's party was joined by many Jelairs. Horchi of the Barin clan came then to Temudjin after daybreak and spoke to him as follows: " I know through a revelation of the spirit what will happen, and to thee I now tell it: In a vision I saw a pied cow coming up to Jamuka; she stopped, looked at him, dug the earth near his yurta and broke off one horn as she was digging. Then she bellowed very loudly, and cried: ' Give back my horn, O Jamuka. After that a strong hornless bull came drawing the pins of a great ruler's tent behind Temudjin's kibitka. This great bull lowed as he traveled, and said: ' Heaven appoints Temudjin to be lord of dominion, I am taking his power to him.' This is what the spirit revealed in my vision. What delight wilt thou give me for this revelation?" "When I become lord of dominion, I will make thee commander of ten thousand," said Temudjin. "I have told thee much of high value," said Horchi. "If thou make me merely commander of ten thousand what great delight can I get from the office? Make me that, and let me choose also as wives thirty beautiful maidens wherever I find them, and give me besides what I ask of thee." Temudjin nodded, and Horchi was satisfied.

Next came a number of men from four other clans. These had all left Jamuka for Temudjin, and joined him at the river Kimurha. And then was completed a work of great moment: Altan, Huchar and Sachai Baiki took counsel with all their own kinsmen, and when they had finished they stood before Temudjin and spoke to him as follows: "We wish to proclaim thee," said they. "When thou art Khan we shall be in the front of every battle against all thy enemies. When we capture beautiful women and take splendid stallions and mares we will bring all to thee surely, and when at the hunt thou art beating in wild beasts we will go in advance of others and give thee the game taken by us. If in battles we transgress thy commands, or in peace we work harm to thee in any way, take from us everything, take wives and property and leave us out then in wild, barren places to perish." Having sworn thus they proclaimed Temudjin, and made him Khan over all of them.

Temudjin, now Khan in the land of the four upper rivers, commanded his comrade Boörchu, whom he called "youngest brother," together with Ogelayu, Hochiun, Chedai and Tokolku to carry his bows and his quiver. Vanguru and Kadan Daldur to dispense food and drink, to be masters of nourishment. Dagai was made master of shepherds, Guchugur was made master of kibitkas. Dodai became master of servants. After that he commanded Kubilai, Chilgutai and Karkaito Kuraun with Kassar his brother to be swordbearers; his half brother Belgutai with Karal Daito Kuraun to be masters of horse training. Daichu, Daihut, Morichi and Muthalhu were to be masters of horseherds. Then he commanded Arkai Kassar, Tagai and Sukagai Chaurhan to be like near and distant arrows, that is, messengers to near and distant places. Subotai the Valiant spoke up then and said: " I will be like an old mouse in snatching, I will be like a jackdaw in speed, I will be like a saddlecloth to hide things, I will ward off every enemy, as felt wards off wind, that is what I shall be for thee."

Temudjin turned then to Boörchu and Chelmai. " When I was alone," said he, " ye two before other men came to me as comrades. I have not forgotten this. Be ye first in all this assembly." Then he spoke further, and said to other men: " To you who have gathered in here after leaving Jamuka, and have joined me, I declare that if Heaven keeps and upholds me as hitherto, ye will all be my fortunate helpers and stand in high honor before me; " then he instructed them how to perform their new duties.

Temudjin sent Tagai and Sukagai to announce his accession to Togrul of the Keraits. " It is well," said Togrul, " that Temudjin is made Khan; how could ye live even to this time without a commander? Be not false to the Khan whom ye have chosen."

Temudjin sent Arkai Kassar and Belgutai with similar tidings to Jamuka who answered: " Tell Altan and Huchar, Temudjin's uncle and cousin, that they by calumnies have parted me now from my anda, and ask them why they did not proclaim Temudjin when he and I were one person in spirit? Be ye all active assistants to Temudjin. Let his heart be at rest through your faithfulness."

This was the formal official reply, Jamuka's real answer was given soon after.

Taichar, a younger brother of Jamuka, was living not far from Mount Chalma, and a slave of Temudjin, named Darmala, was stopping for a season at Sari Keher — a slave was considered in the customs of that age and people as a brother, hence was as a brother in considering a vendetta and dealing with it — Taichar stole a herd of horses from Darmala whose assistants feared to follow and restore them, Darmala rushed alone in pursuit and came up with his herd in the night time; bending forward to the neck of his horse he sent an arrow into Taichar; the arrow struck his spine and killed the man straightway. Darmala then drove back his horses. Jamuka to take vengeance for his brother put himself at the head of his own and some other clans; with these he allied himself straightway with Temudjin's mortal enemies, the Taidjuts. Three tumans of warriors (30,000) were assembled by Targutai and Jamuka. They had planned to attack their opponent unexpectedly and crossed the ridge Alaut Turhau for this purpose. Temudjin, in Gulyalgu at that time, was informed of this movement by Mulketokah and by Boldai who were both of them Ikirats. His warriors all told were thirteen thousand in number and with these he marched forth to meet Targutai and Jamuka. He was able to choose his own time and he struck the invaders as suited him. He fought with these enemies at Dalandaljut and gained his first triumph, a bloody victory, and immense in its value as results proved.

Targutai and Jamuka were repulsed with great loss. Their army was broken and scattered, and many were taken prisoners. After this fierce encounter Temudjin led his men to a forest not far from the battleground where he ranged all his prisoners, and selected the main ones for punishment. Beyond doubt there were many among them of those who had enticed away people after the poisoning of Yessugai, Temudjin's father, men who had left the orphan and acted with Targutai his bitterest enemy. In seventy, or, as some state, in eighty large caldrons, he boiled alive those of them who were worthiest of punishment. The boiling continued each day till he had tortured to death the most powerful and vindictive among his opponents. This execution spread terror on all sides, and since Temudjin showed the greatest kindness to his friends not only during those days, but at all times and rewarded them to the utmost, hope and fear brought him many adherents.

The Uruts and Manhuts, the first led by Churchadai, and the second by Kuyuldar, drew away from Jamuka and joined Temudjin, the new victor. Munlik of the clan Kuanhotan came also, bringing with him his seven mighty sons who were immensely great fighters, and venomous. This Munlik, a son of that Charaha whom one of Targutai's followers had wounded to death with a spear thrust, was the man who had brought home Temudjin from the house of Desaichan his father-in-law when his own father, Yessugai, was dying.

Soon after the boiling to death of those captives in the forest a division of the Juriats, that is Jamuka's own clansmen, came and joined Temudjin for the following reason: The Juriat lands touched those of Temudjin's people, and on a certain day men of both sides were hunting and the parties met by pure chance in the evening. " Let us pass the night here with Temudjin," said some of the Juriats. Others would not consent, and one half of the party, made up altogether of four hundred, went home; the other two hundred remained in the forest. Temudjin gave these men all the meat needed, and kettles in which they could boil it, he treated them generously and with friendship.

These Juriats halted still longer and hunted with Temudjin's party. They received every evening somewhat more of the game than was due them; at parting they were satisfied with Temudjin's kindness and thanked him sincerely. At heart they felt sad, for their position was painful. They wished greatly to join Temudjin, but desired not to leave their own people; and on the way home they said to one another as they traveled: "The Taidjuts are gone, they will not think of us in future. Temudjin cares for his people and does everything to defend them." On reaching home they talked with their elders. " Let us settle still nearer to Temudjin," said they, " and obey him, give him service." " What harm have the Taidjuts done you ? " was the answer. " They are kinsfolk; how could we become one with their enemy, and leave them ? " Notwithstanding this answer Ulug Bahadur and Tugai Talu with their kinsmen and dependents went away in a body to Temudjin.

" We have come," said they, " like a woman bereft of her husband, or a herd without a master, or a flock without a shepherd. In friendship and agreement we would live with thee, we would draw our swords to defend thee, and cut down thy enemies."

" I was like a sleeping man when ye came to me," said Temudjin, " ye pulled me by the forelock and roused me. I was sitting here in sadness, and ye cheered me, I will do what I can now to satisfy your wishes." He made various rules and arrangements which pleased them, and they were satisfied perfectly, at least for a season.

Temudjin wished to strengthen his position still further, and desired to win to his alliance Podu who was chief of the Kurulats, whose lands were adjacent to the Argun. This chief was renowned as an archer and a warrior. Temudjin offered him his sister in marriage. The offer was accepted with gladness. Podu was ready to give Temudjin half his horses, and proffered them.

" Oh," said Temudjin, " thou and I will not mention either taking or giving; we two are brothers and allies, not traffickers or traders. Men in the old time have said that one heart and one soul cannot be in two bodies, but this is just what in our case I shall show to all people as existing. I desire nothing of thee and thy people, but friendship. I wish to extend my dominion and only ask faithful help from my sister's husband and his tribesmen." The marriage took place and Podu was his ally.

Soon after this first group of Juriats had joined Temudjin, some more of their people discussed at a meeting as follows: " The Taidjuts torment us unreasonably, they give us nothing whatever, while Temudjin takes the coat from his back and presents it. He comes down from the horse which he has mounted and gives that same horse to the needy. He is a genuine leader, he is to all as a father. His is the best governed country." This fraction also joined Temudjin.

Another marriage to be mentioned was that of Temudjin's mother to Munlik, son of Charáha, and father of the seven brothers — the great fighters. All these accessions of power, and his victory so strengthened Temudjin and rejoiced him that he made for his mother and step-mothers and kinsfolk, with all the new people, a feast near the river Onon, in a forest. At this feast feminine jealousy touching position, and the stealing of a bridle, brought about a dispute and an outbreak. In spite of Temudjin's power and authority an encounter took place at the feast which caused one chief, Sidje Bijhi of the Barins, to withdraw with his party. He withdrew not from the feast alone, but from his alliance with Temudjin.

The quarrel began in this way: Temudjin sent a jar of mare's milk first of all to his mother, to Kassar and to Sachai Baiki. Thereupon Holichin and Hurchin, his two step-mothers grew angry. " Why not give milk to us before those people, why not give milk to us at the same time with Temudjin's mother ? " asked they as they struck Shikiur who was master of provisions. This striking brought on a disturbance. Thereupon Temudjin commanded his half brother, Belgutai, to mount his horse and keep order and take Buri Buga on the part of the Churkis to help him. A man of the Hadjin clan and connected with the Churkis stole a bridle and was discovered by Belgutai who stopped him. Buri Buga, feeling bound to defend this man, cut through Belgutai's shoulder piece, wounding him badly.

Belgutai made no complaint when his blood flowed. Temudjin, who was under a tree looking on, noted everything. "Why suffer such treatment?" inquired he of Belgutai. "I am wounded," said Belgutai, "but the wound is not serious; cousins should not quarrel because of me." Temudjin broke a branch from the tree, seized a milk paddle, sprang himself at the Churkis and beat them; then seizing his step-mothers he brought them back to their places, and to reason.

The two Juriat parties which had joined Temudjin grew cool in allegiance soon after that feast at the river. They were brought to this state of mind beyond doubt by intrigues of Jamuka; next they fought with each other, and finally deserted.

Jamuka was a man of immense power in plotting, and one who never ceased to pursue his object. Temudjin tried to win some show of kindness from Jamuka. In other words he made every effort to subdue him by deep subtle cunning, but all efforts proved fruitless. These men were bound to win power. Without power life was no life for either one of the two master tricksters. Whatever his action or seeming at any time Jamuka was Temudjin's mortal enemy always. He kept undying hatred in his heart, and was ever planning some blow at his rival. When the Juriats were at their best he was plotting, when they were scattered and weak and had in part gone to Temudjin he was none the less active and made common cause with the enemies of his opponent wherever he could find them. Temudjin cared for no man or woman, and for no thing on earth if opposed to his plans of dominion.

CHAPTER III

A FRESH opportunity came now to Temudjin to beat down an enemy and strengthen himself at the same time. The Kin Emperor sent Wang Kin, his minister, with an army against the Lake Buyur Tartars since they would neither do what he wished, nor pay tribute. Not having strength to resist, they moved to new places, higher up on the Ulcha. Temudjin acted now in a double manner; on the one hand he seemed as if helping the Kin sovereign and represented his action to the Golden Khan's minister in that way. Meanwhile when assembling his intimates he said: " Those Buyur men killed both my father and uncle; now is the time to attack them, not to help the Kin sovereign, but to avenge our own people." To Togrul he sent in great haste this statement: " The Golden Khan is pursuing the Lake Buyur Tartars; those men are thy enemies and mine, so do thou help me, my father."

Togrul came with aid quickly. Temudjin sent to Sachai Baiki and Daichu of the Churkis and asked help of them also. He waited six days for reinforcements, but no man appeared from the Churkis. Thereupon he with Togrul marched down the Ulcha and fell on the Tartars. He was on one bank, and Togrul on the other. The Tartars could not retreat since the Golden Khan's men were pursuing, so they raised a strong fortress against them. Temudjin and Togrul broke into this fortress; many Tartars were slain, and many captured, among them their leader. Temudjin put this man to death in revenge for his father. Immense booty was taken by Temudjin and his ally in captives, in cattle and property of all sorts; among other things taken was a silver cradle and a cloth of gold which lay over it. Temudjin received praise for his action. Without striking a blow the Kin minister had accomplished his mission, and later he took to himself, before his sovereign, the merit of making Togrul and Temudjin do his work for him. He gave Temudjin the title Chao Huri, and to Togrul the title of Wang Khan was given. "I am thankful," said the minister. "When I return I will report all to my sovereign, and win for you a still higher title." Then he departed.

Temudjin, and Togrul now Wang Khan, and thus we shall call him hereafter, went to their own places also.

In the captured Tartar camp a boy was discovered; he had a gold ring in his nose, around his waist was a belt edged with sable and it had golden tassels. They took the lad straightway to Hoelun, who made him her sixth son, and named him. He was known ever after as Shigi Kutuku. Temudjin had left at Halil Lake many people; while he was absent the Churkis stripped fifty of these men, tore their clothes off, and slew ten of them. Temudjin was enraged at this action.

"Why endure deeds of this kind from the Churkis?" exclaimed he. "At our feast in the forest they cut Belgutai in the shoulder. When I was avenging my father and uncle they would not give aid to us, they went to our enemies and helped them, now I will punish those people befittingly."

So he led out his men to ruin the Churkis. At Dolon Boldau on the Kerulon he captured every Churki warrior except Sachai Baiki, and Daichu who rushed away empty-handed. Temudjin hunted these two men untiringly till he caught them. "We have not done what we promised," said they in reply to his questions. They stretched out their necks as they said this, and Temudjin cut their heads off. He returned after that to Dolon Boldau and led off into slavery what remained of the Churkis.

The origin of the Churkis was as follows: Kabul Khan, Temudjin's great grandfather, had seven sons. Of these the eldest was Okin Barka. Kabul chose strong, daring, skilled archers and gave them as attendants to Okin Barka. No matter where they went those attendants vanquished all who opposed them, and at last no man dared vie with such champions, hence they received the name Churki.

Kabul Khan's second son, Bartan, was father of Yessugai, Temudjin's supposed father. Kabul's grandson, child of his third son Munlair, was Buri Buga the comrade of the grandsons of Okin Barka. Buri Buga had given his adhesion to the Khan much earlier than others, but he remained independent in feeling, hence Temudjin did not trust him.

Though no man among Mongols could equal Buri Buga in strength or in wrestling he did not escape a cruel death. Sometime after the reduction of the Churkis Temudjin commanded Belgutai and Buri Buga to wrestle in his presence. Whenever Belgutai wrestled with Buri Buga the latter was able with one leg and one hand to hold him as still as if lifeless. This time Buri Buga, who feigned to be beaten, fell with his face to the earth under Belgutai, who having him down turned toward Temudjin for direction. Temudjin bit his lower lip; Belgutai knew what this sign meant, and putting his knee to the spine of Buri Buga seized his neck with both hands, and broke the backbone of his opponent.

" I could not lose in this struggle," said the dying Buri Buga, " but, fearing the Khan, I feigned defeat, and then yielded, and now thou hast taken my life from me."

At this time Talaigutu, a man of the Jelairs who had three sons, commanded the eldest, named Gunua with his two sons, Mukuli and Buga to go to Temudjin and say to him: " These sons of mine will serve thee forever. If they leave thy doors draw from their legs all the sinews within them, after that cut their hearts out, and also their livers." Then Talaigutu commanded Chilaun, his second son, to present himself with Tunge and Hashi his own two sons, and speak as follows: " Let these my sons guard thy golden doors carefully. If they fail take their lives from them." After that Talaigutu gave Chebke his third son to Temudjin's brother, Kassar. Chebke had found in the camp of the Churki a boy, Boroul, whom he gave to Hoelun. Hoelun having placed the four boys: Kuichu, Kokochu, Shigi Kutuku, and Boroul with her own children, watched over all with her eyes during daylight, and listened to them with her ears in the night time; thus did she rear them.

Who was Togrul of the Keraits, known better as Wang Khan ? This is a question of deep interest in the history of the Mongols, for this man had great transactions with Temudjin, he had much to do also with Yessugai, Temudjin's father. Markuz

Buyuruk, Togrul's grandfather, who ruled in his day, was captured by Naur, a Tartar chieftain, and sent to the Kin emperor who had him nailed to a wooden ass, and then chopped into pieces. His widow resolved to take vengeance on Naur for this dreadful death of her husband. She set out some time later on to give a feigned homage to Naur and to marry him if possible, as was stated in confidence by some of her servitors. She brought to Naur a hundred sheep and ten mares, besides a hundred large cow-skins holding, as was said, distilled mare's milk, but each skin held in fact a well armed living warrior.

A feast was given straightway by Naur during which the hundred men were set free from the cowskins, and, aided by attendants of the widow, they slew the Khan and his household.

Markuz left four sons, the two most distinguished were Kurja Kuz and Gurkhan. Kurja Kuz succeeded his father. Togrul succeeded Kurja Kuz his own father by slaying two uncles, besides a number of cousins. Gurkhan, his remaining uncle, fled and found asylum with Inanji, Taiyang of the neighboring Naimans, whom he roused to assist him. Gurkhan then with the Naiman troops drove out Togrul and made himself ruler. Togrul, attended by a hundred men, went to Yessugai and implored aid of him. Yessugai reinstated Togrul, and forced Gurkhan to flee to Tangut.

Togrul vowed endless friendship to his ally and became to him a sworn friend or " anda." When Yessugai was poisoned by Tartars, Temudjin his son, a boy at that time, lost authority and suffered for years from the Taidjuts. Togrul gave help and harbored him. After that, as has been already related, when Temudjin had married and the Merkits stole his wife, Togrul assisted in restoring her, and with her a part of Temudjin's people. In 1194 he was given the title Wang Khan. Later his brother expelled him, and this time he fled to the Uigurs, but sought aid in vain from the Idikut, or ruler, of that people. He led a wretched life for some time without resource or property, and lived, as is stated, on milk from a small herd of goats, his sole sustenance. He learned at last that Temudjin had grown in power, hence he begged aid from him, and got it.

Temudjin gave Wang Khan cattle and in the autumn of that year, 1196, made a feast for this his old benefactor, and promised to consider him thenceforth as a father, and to help him as an ally.

In 1197 the two allies defeated the Barins, seizing Sidje Bijhi and Taidju their leader. That same year they fell upon the Merkits, a nation of four tribes ruled then by Tukta Bijhi. One of these tribes was defeated near the Selinga. Temudjin let Wang Khan keep all the booty taken. Wang Khan in 1198, the year following, undertook unassisted a war against the Merkits, captured Jilaun, the son of Tukta Bijhi, and slew Tugun, another son. He took also Kutu, Tukta's brother. He seized all Jilaun's herds and people, but gave no part of this booty to Temudjin.

In 1199 the two allies marched to attack the Naimans, a people strong and famous while under Buga Khan, an able ruler, but when this Khan died his two sons, to gain a certain concubine left by their father, began a murderous quarrel, which brought about the division of the country. The elder man, Baibuga, called Taiyang,[1] by his subjects and his neighbors, retained the level country, while Buiruk, his brother, took mountain places. Each ruled alone, and each was an enemy of the other. Wang Khan and Temudjin, remembering former robberies by the Naimans, and wishing too to add wealth and power to what they themselves had, attacked Buiruk at Kizil Bash near the Altai. They seized many captives and much precious booty. Buiruk then moved westward followed closely by the allies and fighting with great vigor. One of his leaders, Edetukluk, who brought up the rear guard, fought till his men were all slain, or made prisoners. He struggled alone then till his saddle girth burst, and he was captured.

After this the allies came in contact with Gugsu Seirak, another of the Naiman commanders, who had much greater forces and had chosen his position. This man had plundered Wang Khan's brother somewhat earlier and a portion of his kinsfolk. The allies had met him already, and hoped now to crush him. They would have attacked him immediately, but since evening was near they chose to wait till next morning for battle. Jamuka, ever ready to injure Temudjin, went to Wang Khan and made him believe that he was on the eve of betrayal, and would be ruined by Temudjin and the Naimans. Wang Khan set out for home that

[1] Great King in Chinese.

night. Temudjin thus deserted was forced to withdraw which he did unobserved.

Gugsu Seirak followed Wang Khan in hot haste and overtook his two brothers. He captured their families, as well as their property and cattle. Then he entered Wang Khan's land and found there rich booty of all kinds. Wang Khan sent Sengun, his son, to meet Seirak; meanwhile he hurried off messengers to Temudjin, and begged of him assistance. Temudjin considering the plight of his ally, but still more his own peril should Wang Khan's men be routed and captured by the Naimans, sent his four ablest chiefs to assist him. These were Boorchu, Mukuli, Boroul and Jilaun. These four led their men by hurried marches, and had just reached the battle-ground when Wang Khan's force was broken, his best leaders killed and Sengun, his son, on a lame wounded stallion, was fleeing. All the Khan's property had been taken by the Naimans. Boorchu dashed up with all speed to Sengun, gave him the horse on which he himself had ridden up to that moment and sat then on the gray steed which Temudjin had given him as a mark of great favor. He was not to strike this horse for any reason; he had merely to rub the whip along his mane to make him rush with lightning speed during action.

Boorchu sent forward his fresh troops, chosen warriors, and next he rallied Sengun's scattered forces to help them against the Naimans. The Naimans, drunk with victory and not thinking of defeat, were soon brought to their senses. Temudjin's heroes recovered everything snatched from Wang Khan's people, both horses and property. Wang Khan on the field there thanked his firm ally and thanked the four splendid leaders in the warmest words possible. He gave Boorchu ten golden goblets and a mantle of honor; he rewarded others with very great bounty, and said as they were leaving him: " Once I appeared as a fugitive, naked and hungry; Temudjin received me, he nourished and clothed me. How can I thank my magnificent son for his goodness? In former days Yessugai brought back my people, and now Temudjin has sent his four heroes; with Heaven's help they have vanquished the Naimans, and saved me; I will think of these benefits, and never forget them."

When the old Khan had gone back to his yurta and all had grown quiet on every side Temudjin went to visit his " father " and " anda." At the Black Forest the two men expressed to each other their feelings, and at last Temudjin described with much truth, and very carefully, though with few words, the real position:

" I cannot live on in safety without thy assistance, my father. The Naimans on one side and my false, plotting relatives on the other, afflict me. My relatives rouse up the Taidjuts and every enemy against me, but seeing thy love for me they know that while thou art alive and unchanged, and art ruling they cannot destroy me. Thou too, O my father, canst not live on in safety without my firm friendship. Without me thy false brothers and cousins, assisted by their allies, would split up thy people and snatch thy dominion. They would kill thee unless by swift flight thou wert able to save thyself from ruin. Sengun, thy son, would gain nothing, he too would be swept both from power and existence, though he does not see this at present. I am his best stay, as well as thine, O my father. Thou art my greatest stay too and support. Without thee all my enemies would rise up at once to overwhelm me, but were I gone, and my power in their hands thy power would pass soon to thy deadliest enemies, thy relatives. Our one way to keep power and live on in safety is through a friendship which nothing can shatter. That friendship exists now, and we need only proclaim it. Were I thy elder son all would be quiet and settled for both of us."

When Wang Khan was alone he spoke thus to himself and considered: " I am old, to whom shall I leave the direction of my people? My younger brothers are without lofty qualities; my brother Jaganbo is also unable to stand against enemies. Sengun is the only man left me, but whatever Sengun's merits may be I will make Temudjin his elder brother. With these two sons to help me I may live on securely."

At the Black Forest Temudjin became elder son to Wang Khan. Up to that time he had called the old chieftain his father through friendship, because he and Yessugai had both been his " andas " and allies. Now Wang Khan and Temudjin used the words " son " and " father " in conversing and with their real value. This adoption of Temudjin excluded Sengun in reality from the earliest inheritance, and Temudjin knew well, of course, that immense opposition would come from Sengun and Jamuka.

" We shall fight side by side in war against enemies," said Wang

Khan to his new elder son. " In going against wild beasts we are
to hunt with common forces. If men try to raise quarrels between
us we will lend no ear to anyone, and believe only when we have
met and talked carefully together over everything, and proved it."
Thus they decided, and their friendship on that day was perfect.

The crushing defeat of the Naimans, which lowered them much,
immediately raised Temudjin above every rival. Jamuka's
plotting had turned against himself most completely, and if he
had planned to help Temudjin he could not have helped better.
Somewhat later Juchi Kassar snatched another victory from the
Naimans, and weakened them further. Tukta Bijhi, the Merkit
chief, sent Ordjank and Kutu, his brothers, to rouse up the Taidjuts afresh against Temudjin. Ongku and Hakadju took arms
and made ready to help Targutai, the Taidjut chief, with Kudodar and Kurul.

Temudjin and Wang Khan marched in the spring of 1200
and met those opponents at the edge of the great Gobi desert,
where they crushed them completely. Targutai and Kudodar
were both slain. Targutai was the man who had acted so bitterly
against Temudjin after his father was poisoned. This Taidjut
leader fell now at the hand of Jilaun, a son of that same Sorhan
Shira, who had rescued Temudjin from the river Onon, taken the
kang from his neck and hidden him under wool racks. Hakadju
and Ongku, who had helped on this war by enabling Tukta Bijhi
to rouse up the Taidjuts fled now to Bargudjin with Tukta
Bijhi's two brothers, while Kurul found a refuge with the Naimans. Still this defeat did not end Taidjut rancor. The Katkins and Saljuts shared also this hatred. Temudjin strove
however, to win them, and sent an envoy with this message:
" Each Mongol clan should support me, I then could protect all
without exception." This envoy was insulted; some snatched
entrails from a pot and slapped his face with them; they struck
him right and left and drove him off amid jeers, and loud howling.

These people knew clearly, of course, that after insults of that
kind they were in great danger. The Taidjuts had been crushed,
and still earlier the Naimans. The blow which was sure to come
soon would strike them unsparingly, hence they formed a league
quickly and met at Arabulak with some of the Jelairs, the Durbans,
the Kunkurats, and Tartars. These five peoples killed with swords

a stallion, a bull, a dog, a ram and a he goat. " O Heaven and earth hear our words and bear witness," cried they at the sacrifice: " We swear by the blood of these victims, themselves chiefs of races, that we deserve death in this same manner if we keep not the promise made here to-day." They vowed then to guard each secret faithfully, and attack the allies without warning or mercy.

Temudjin was advised of the pact and the oath by Dayin Noyon a Kunkurat chieftain, hence he had time to meet those confederates near Buyar Lake, where he dispersed them after fighting a fierce, stubborn battle. Somewhat later he met a detachment of Taidjuts and some Merkits near the Timurha and crushed them also. Meanwhile the Kunkurats ceased their resistance, and set out to join Temudjin, but Kassar, his brother, not knowing their purpose, attacked and defeated them. They turned thereupon to Jamuka and joined his forces.

In 1201 the Katkins and Saljuts with Kunkurats, Juriats, Ikirats, Kurulats, Durbans and Tartars met at Alhuibula and chose Jamuka for their Khan. They went after that to the Tula and took this oath in assembly: " Should any man disclose these our plans may he fall as this earth falls, and be cut off as these branches are cut off." With that they pushed down a part of the river bank, and hacked off with their sabres the branches of a tree. They made plans then to surprise Temudjin when unguarded, and slay him.

A certain man named Kuridai, who had been present at the oath taking, slipped away home and told the whole tale to his brother-in-law, Mergitai, a Kurulat, who happened in at the yurta. Mergitai insisted that Kuridai should gallop off swiftly to Gulyalgu and explain the plot to Temudjin since he, Kuridai, with his own ears had heard it. " Take my gray horse with stumpy ears, he will bear thee in safety," said Mergitai. Kuridai mounted and rode away swiftly. On the road he was captured by a sentry, but that sentry, a Kurulat also, was devoted soul and body in secret to Temudjin, so not only did he free Kuridai when he heard of his errand, but he gave him his own splendid stallion. " On this horse," said the Kurulat, " thou canst overtake any man, but no man on another beast could overtake thee."

Kuridai hurried off. On the way he saw warriors bearing a splendid white tent for Jamuka. Some attendants of these men pursued him, but soon he was swept out of sight by the stallion. In due time he found Temudjin, who on hearing the tidings sprang quickly to action. He sent men to Wang Khan who brought his army with promptness and the two allies marched down the Kerulon against their opponent.

Jamuka who intended to fall unawares on his rival was caught himself at a place called Edekurgan. While he was marshalling his forces Buiruk and Kuduk, his two shamans, raised a wind and made rain fall to strike in the face Temudjin and his allies, but the wind and rain turned on Jamuka. The air became dark and the men tumbled into ravines, and over rough places. "Heaven is not gracious to-day," said Jamuka, "that is why this misfortune is meeting us." His army was scattered. The Naimans and others then left him, and, taking those who had proclaimed him, Jamuka withdrew down the river.

Wang Khan pursued Jamuka while Temudjin followed Autchu of the Taidjuts, and those who went with him. Autchu escaped, hurried home, rallied his people, crossed the Onon and began action. After many encounters there was a fierce all day battle with Temudjin, then both sides promised to hold their places that night on the battle-ground. Temudjin had been wounded in the neck and had fainted from blood loss. Chelmai, his attendant and comrade, sucked out the blood which was stiffening, and likely to choke him. The chief regained consciousness at midnight. Chelmai had stripped himself naked, to escape the more easily if captured, and stolen into the enemy's camp to find mare's milk, but found only cream which he took with such deftness that no one noted him either while coming or going. He went then for water, mixed the thick cream with it, and had a drink ready. Temudjin drank with much eagerness, drawing three breaths very deeply, and stopped only after the third one. "My eyes have gained sight," said he, "my soul is now clear again."

With these words he rose to a sitting position. While he was sitting there day dawned, and he saw a great patch of stiff blood there by his bedside. "What is this?" asked he, "why is that blood so near me?" "I did not think of far or near," answered Chelmai, "I feared to go from thee, even as matters were I both spat blood and swallowed it — Not a little of thy blood has gone into my stomach in spite of me."

" When I was in those great straits," asked Temudjin, who now
understood what had taken place, " how hadst thou courage to
steal to the enemy all naked? If they had caught thee wouldst
thou not have said that I was here wounded? " " If they had
caught me I should have told them that I had surrendered to
them, but that thou hadst then seized me, and learning that I had
surrendered hadst stripped me and wert just ready to cut off my
head when I sprang away, and ran to them for refuge. They would
have believed every word, given me clothes, and sent me to labor.
I should have stolen a horse soon and ridden back to thee."
" When the Merkits were seeking my life on Mount Burhan," said
Temudjin, " thou didst defend it, now thou hast sucked stiffened
blood from my neck and saved me. When I was dying of thirst
thou didst risk thy own life to get drink and restore me, I shall not
forget while I live these great services."

Temudjin saw next day that Jamuka's men had scattered in
the night while his own men were still on the battle-ground. He
hunted after the enemy then for some distance; all at once
on a hill a woman dressed in red was heard shouting: " Temudjin! Temudjin! " very loudly. He sent to learn who she was,
and why she was shouting. " I am Kadan, the daughter of Sorgan
Shira," said the woman. " The people have tried to cut down
my husband, and I was calling Temudjin to defend him."

Temudjin sent quickly to save Kadan's husband, but he was
dead when they found him. Temudjin then called Kadan to sit at
his side, because of the time when she guarded him under wood-
packs at her father's. One day later Sorgan Shira himself came
to Temudjin. " Why come so late? " inquired Temudjin. " I
have been always on thy side," replied Sorgan, " and anxious to
join thee, but if I had come earlier the Taidjuts would have
killed all my relatives."

Temudjin pursued farther, and when he had killed Autchu's
children and grandchildren he passed with his warriors to Hubahai
where he spent that winter. In 1202 Temudjin moved in spring
against those strong Tartars east of him. That people inhabited
the region surrounding Buyur Lake and east of it, hence they
were neighbors of the Juichis of that day, known as Manchus in
our time. Those Tartars had seventy thousand yurtas and
formed six divisions. Their conflicts with each other were frequent,

and each tribe plundered every other. Between these Buyur Tartars and the Mongols bitter feuds raged at all times. Temudjin fell on two tribes called Iltchi and Chagan. Before the encounter he instructed his warriors very strictly: " Hunt down those people, when ye conquer slay without pity, sparing no man. Touch no booty till the action is over; after that all will be honestly divided." He heard later on that Kudjeir and Daritai his two uncles, with Altan his cousin had disregarded this order and seized what they came upon. He deprived these men straightway of all that they had taken, and when a division was made at the end of the struggle no part was given them. Through this strictness and punishment Temudjin lost the goodwill of those chiefs who opposed him in secret and confirmed later on the great rupture made between him and Wang Khan by Jamuka.

Temudjin had slain many Tartars in this conflict and captured most of the survivors, now he counseled with his relatives as to what should be done with those captives. " They deserve punishment," said he; " they killed our grand uncle and our father. Let us slay every male who is higher than the hub of a cart wheel. When that is done we must make slaves of the others and divide them between us." All who were present accepted this method. The question being settled in that way Belgutai went from the council.

" What have ye fixed on to-day?" inquired Aike Cheran, a Tartar captive belonging to Belgutai. " To kill every male of you, who is higher than the hub of a cart wheel," said Belgutai. The other prisoners on learning this broke out and fled, never stopping till they reached a strong place in the mountains and seized it.

" Go and capture their stronghold," commanded Temudjin. This was done with much trouble and bloodshed. The Tartars fought with desperation and were slain to the last one, but many of Temudjin's choicest warriors were lost in the slaughter. "Belgutai told the enemy our secrets," said Temudjin, " many good men have perished because of this. Belgutai is excluded from council, hereafter let him stay out of doors and guard against thefts, fights and quarrels. Belgutai and Daritai may come to us only when counsels are ended."

When Temudjin had killed all the male Tartars who were

higher than the hub of a cart wheel he took as wife Aisugan, a daughter of that same Aike Cheran who had put the question to Belgutai. Aisugan gained Temudjin's confidence quickly; she pleased him and soon she said to him: " I have an elder sister, Aisui, a beauty; she ought to be the Khan's consort. Though she is just married I cannot tell where she is but we might find her."

" If she is a beauty," said Temudjin, " I will find her. Wilt thou give then thy place to thy sister? " " I will give it as soon as I see her," said Aisugan. Temudjin sent men to search out Aisui. They found her in a forest where she was hiding with her husband. The husband fled, and Aisui was taken to Temudjin. Aisugan gave her place to her sister. One day Temudjin was sitting near the door of his tent with these sisters, and drinking. Noting that Aisui sighed deeply suspicion sprang up in him. He commanded Mukuli, and others in attendance, to arrange the people present according to the places which they occupied. When all were reckoned one young man was found unconnected with any ulus, or community. " What man art thou? " inquired Temudjin. " I am Aisui's husband," replied the young stranger. " When they took her I fled, now all is settled and ended, I came hither thinking that no man would note me in a great throng of people."

" Thou art a son of my enemy," said Temudjin. " Thou hast come to spy out and discover. I killed thy people and find no cause to spare thee more than others." Temudjin had the man's head cut off.

The Merkit chief, Tukta Bijhi, came back from Lake Baikal and attacked Temudjin, but was baffled. He turned then to Buiruk of the Naimans who joined a confederacy of Katkins, Durbans, Saljuts and Uirats together with Merkits and moved in 1202, near the autumn, with a strong force to strike Temudjin who was supported by Wang Khan, his old ally. Because of the season Temudjin retired to mountain lands near the Kitan (North Chinese) border, his plan being to lure on the enemy to dangerous high passes where attacks and bad weather might ruin them. The confederates followed fast through the mountains and skirmished, but before they could fight a real battle, wind and snow with dense fog, brought on, as was said, by magicians, struck them all and stopped action. The confederates were forced to retreat greatly weakened; they lost men and horses killed by falling in the fog over precipices, while multitudes perished in wild places from frost and bitter cold. Jamuka was moving on to join the Naimans, but when he saw the sad plight of the confederates he fell to plundering a part of them, and after he had taken good booty from the Saljuts and the Katkins he encamped near Temudjin and his ally, observed very closely what was happening, and waited.

Temudjin and Wang Khan passed the winter on level land near the mountains where snow served as water. While there he asked in marriage Wang Khan's granddaughter, Chaur Bijhi, for his own eldest son, Juchi, and Wang Khan mentioned Temudjin's daughter, Kutchin Bijhi, for Sengun's son Kush Buga. These two marriage contracts, agreed on at first, were broken later for various not well explained reasons. Jamuka was beyond doubt the great cause in this matter, and raised the whole quarrel. This rupture was followed by wrangling and coolness between the two allies, thus giving a still further chance to Jamuka. As he had never been able to estrange Wang Khan thoroughly from Temudjin he turned now in firm confidence to Sengun. He conquered Wang Khan's son and heir with the following statements: " Temudjin has grown strong, and desires to be the greatest among men. He has determined to be the one ruler, he cannot be this unless he destroys thy whole family, he has resolved to destroy it, and he will do so unless thou prevent him. Temudjin has made a firm pact with thy enemy Baibuga, Taiyang of the Naimans; he is to get help from Baibuga, and is only waiting for the moment to ruin thy father, that done he will seize and kill thee, he will take thy whole country, and keep it."

In this way Jamuka filled Sengun's heart with great fear and keen hatred, feelings strengthened immensely by Temudjin's uncles, Daritai and Kudjeir, who, with Altan, his cousin, were enraged at the loss of their booty, and for other reasons. These men declared that every word uttered by Jamuka was true. A great plot was formed, and directed by Jamuka, to surprise Temudjin and kill him. Jamuka, who was watching events and working keenly, took with him Altan and others, at the end of 1202, and went again to Sengun, who was then living north of Checheher, and while attacking Temudjin spoke as follows: "Envoys are moving continually between Temudjin and the Naimans; those envoys are fixing the conditions of thy ruin. All this time Temudjin is talking of the ties between himself and thy father whom he calls his 'father' also. Thy father has made Temudjin his elder son. Thou art now Temudjin's younger brother, and hast lost thy inheritance, soon thou wilt lose thy life also. Unless thou destroy this man, very quickly he will kill thee. Dost thou not see this?"

When Jamuka had finished, Sengun went at once to his friends to explain and take counsel. "If we are to end him, I myself will fall on his flank. Say the word, I will do so immediately. For thee we will slay Hoelun's children to the last one," said Altan and Kudjeir. "I will destroy him hand and foot," said Ebugechin. "No, take his people," said another, "what can he do without people? Whatever thy wish be, Sengun, I will climb to the highest top with thee, and go to the lowest bottom when needed."

Sengun listened to his comrades and Jamuka. He sent Saihan Todai to report their discourses to his father. "Why think thus of my elder son, Temudjin?" asked Wang Khan as an answer. "We have trusted him thus far. If we hold unjust, evil thoughts touching him, Heaven will turn from us. Jamuka has been thousand tongued always and is unworthy of credit." Thus Wang Khan rejected all the words sent him. Sengun again sent a message: "Every man who has a mouth with a tongue in it speaks even as I do, why not believe what is evident?"

Again Wang Khan answered that he could not agree with them. Sengun then went himself to his father: "To-day thou art living," said he, "but still this Temudjin accounts thee as nothing. When thou art dead will he let me rule the people assembled by thee and thy father with such effort? Will he even leave life to me?" "My son," said Wang Khan, "how am I to renounce my own promise and counsel? We have trusted Temudjin up to this time. If without cause we think evil now of him, how can Heaven favor us?" Sengun turned in anger from his father. Wang Khan called him back to remonstrate. "It is clear, O my son," said he, "that Heaven does not favor us. Thou wilt reject Temudjin no matter what I tell thee, thou wilt act in thy own way, I see that, but victory, if thou win it, must be thine through thy own work and fortune."

Sengun turned to his father for the last time: "Think on this scourge risen against us," said he. "If thou stop not this Temudjin we are lost, thou and I, without hope; if thou spare him, we shall both die very soon. We must put an end to the man, or be ruined. He will kill thee first of all, and then my turn will come very quickly."

Wang Khan would hear nothing of this murder; he would at least have no part in it. But strongly pressed by his son he said finally: "If ye do such a deed ye must be alone in it. Keep away from me strictly."

Temudjin's death was the great object now for Sengun and Jamuka. Temudjin's uncles and one of his cousins were in the plot also. Sengun himself formed the plan and described it in these words very clearly: "Some time ago," said he, "Temudjin asked our daughter for his eldest son, Juchi; we did not give her at that time, but now we will send to him saying that we accept his proposal. We will make a great feast of betrothal and invite him. If he comes to it we will seize the vile traitor and kill him."

When they had settled on this plan Sengun sent envoys to Temudjin accepting the marriage proposals, and inviting him to the feast of betrothal. Temudjin accepted and set out with attendants. On the way he stopped at the house of Munlik his step-father, the husband of Hoelun. Munlik became thoughtful and serious as he heard of the invitation. "When we asked for their maiden," said he, "they were haughty and refused her; why invite now to a feast of betrothal? Better not go to them; excuse thyself saying that thou hast no beast fit to travel, that it is spring and thy horses are all out at pasture."

Temudjin agreed with Munlik and instead of going himself sent Bugatai with Kilatai to the festival, and returned home very quickly. When Sengun saw the two men sent as substitutes he knew at once that Temudjin had seen through his stratagem. He called a council immediately. "We must act quickly now," said he. "We will move with all force against Temudjin to-morrow, but send, meanwhile, a strong party to seize him while south of Mount Mao." Aike Charan, who was Altan's youngest brother and one of Wang Khan's chosen leaders, had been at the council. He hastened home that same evening and told his wife, Alikai, Sengun's entire stratagem. "They have settled at last to capture the Khan," said he, " and to-morrow they will seize him. If some man to-night would warn Temudjin his reward would be enormous." " Speak not idle words," said the woman. " Our servants may hear thee, and think thy talk serious."

Badai, a horseherd who had just brought in mare's milk, over-heard Aike Charan and the answer of Alikai. He turned at once and told Kishlik. " I too will listen," said Kishlik who was his comrade. Kishlik went in then and saw Aike Charan's son, Narinkeyan, whittling arrows and looking at his parents. " Which of our servants," asked he, " should lose his tongue lest he tell what ye have said to each other? " Kishlik heard these words, though Narinkeyan did not know it. " Oh Kishlik," said Narin-keyan, turning to the horseherd, " Bring me in the white horse and the gray one, I will go riding to-morrow."

Kishlik went out quickly. " Thou hast told the truth," said he to Badai. " We must ride now tremendously, thou and I, we must ride to-night to Temudjin and save him, tell him everything." They ran to the pasture, caught both horses and rode off without seeing Narinkeyan. They reported all to Temudjin, told him Aike Charan's whole story and the words of Narinkeyan.

Temudjin summoned his trustiest servants immediately and hurried off to the northern side of Mount Mao. Chelmai he com-manded to follow and watch every movement of the on-marching enemy. At noon the next day Temudjin halted briefly and two horseherds, Alchidai and Chidai, brought in tidings that the enemy was advancing very swiftly. A great dust cloud was rising up from them and was visible on the south of Mount Mao. Temud-jin hurried on till he reached Kalanchin, a place selected by him for battle. There he stopped, disposed all his forces, and assem-bled his leaders.

Meanwhile Sengun with Wang Khan, who had at last by much urging been persuaded to join this expedition, were advancing at all the speed possible, and soon men could see them. They halted at once for battle. " Who are the best men among Temud-jin's warriors? " asked Wang Khan of Jamuka. " The Uruts and Manhuts are best," said Jamuka, " they are never disordered; they have used swords and spears from their boyhood. When they strike thou wilt see dreadful fighting." " Well," said Wang Khan, " let our hero Hadakji fall on them first with his Jirkins;

after him will go Achik Shilun with the Omans, and Tunkaits, and Shilaimun, with a strong force of our body guards. If these do not finish them our own special warriors will give them the death blow."

While Wang Khan was thus making dispositions, Temudjin on his side spoke to the Urut commander: "Uncle Churchadai, I would give thee the vanguard, what is thy own wish?" Churchadai was just ready to answer when Huildar spoke up: "O Khan, my dear friend (he was Temudjin's anda), I will mount my strong steed and break, with my Manhuts, through all who oppose us. I will plant thy tail standard on Gubtan, that hill at the rear and left flank of the enemy. From that hill I will show thee my firmness and valor. If I fall, thou wilt nourish my children, thou wilt rear them. Relying on Heaven it is all one to me when my fate comes." "Go thou," said Temudjin, "and take Gubtan."

Huildar fixed the tail standard on Gubtan. Churchadai spoke when his turn came. "I will fight," said he, "in front of the Khan, I will be in the vanguard with my Uruts." And he arranged his strong warriors in position. Barely were they ready when Hadakgi and the Jirkins made the first onrush and opened the battle. They were met by the Uruts, who not only received their attack with all firmness, but drove them back in disorder. While the Uruts were following this broken vanguard Wang Khan sent Achik Shilun and his Omans to strike on the Uruts. Huildar attacked from Gubtan this new reinforcement and broke it, but being thrown from his horse by a spear cast, the Omans rallied, and were sent with the Tunkaits against Churchadai. Both forces were hurled back by the Uruts, strengthened greatly by Temudjin. Shilaimun attacked next with Wang Khan's own body-guards. These also were broken by Churchadai reinforced this time by Temudjin. Sengun now, without leave from his father, rushed into the struggle taking with him Wang Khan's special warriors. The battle raged to the utmost and Sengun had some chance of victory when an arrow from Churchadai's bow pierced his cheek and he fell badly wounded.

When the Keraits saw their chief down, and night already on them, they stopped fighting. Sengun had not carried his point, and Temudjin held the field, hence the victory was on his side although very slightly. It was late in the evening and dark, so he brought together his men and was careful to seek out and save Huildar. Temudjin during that night withdrew from the battle-ground, and at daybreak discovered that Ogotai, his son, with Boroul and Boorchu were all three of them missing. " Those two faithful men," said Temudjin, " have lived with my son, and now they have died with him." He grieved that day greatly. The next night he feared an attack, and held all his people in readiness to receive it. At daybreak he saw a man riding in from the battle-ground, and recognized Boorchu; he turned his face heavenward, struck his breast, and was grateful.

" My horse," said Boorchu, when he had ridden up to Temudjin, " was killed by the enemy; while escaping on foot I saw a pack horse that had wandered far from the Keraits. He had a leaning burden. I cut the straps, let the pack fall, then mounted the beast and rode hither."

A second horseman appeared somewhat later. When he had drawn near it was seen that besides his legs two others were hanging down near them. Ogotai and Boroul were on that horse. Boroul's mouth was all blood besmeared; he had sucked stiffened blood from Ogotai's neck wound; Temudjin wept when he saw this. He burned the wound with fire straightway, and gave Ogotai a drink to revive him.

" A great dust has risen near the enemy," said Boroul, " they are moving southward as it seems toward Mount Mao."

Temudjin marched now to Dalan Naimurgas where Kadan Daldur brought him tidings: " When Sengun was wounded," said Kadan, " Wang Khan said to his counsellor: ' We have attacked a man with whom we should not have quarreled. It is sad to see what a nail has been driven into Sengun, but he is living and can make a new trial immediately.' Achik Shilun spoke up then: ' When thou hadst no son,' said he, ' thou wert praying to receive one, now when thou hast a son thou shouldst spare him.' Wang Khan yielded and gave up further thought of battle. ' Carry my son back with care,' said he to his attendants, ' do not shake him.' Father and son then turned homeward."

Temudjin marched toward the East. Before starting he reviewed the remnant of his army and found only five thousand men altogether. On the way his men hunted. While beating in game Temudjin tried to restrain Huildar whose wound had not healed, but he rushed quickly at a wild boar, his wound opened, and he died shortly after. They buried him on Ornéü, a hill near the Kalka. At the place where that river falls into Lake Buyur lived the Ungirats; Temudjin sent Churchadai with the Uruts and Manguts to talk with that people. "Remember our blood bond," said he to them in Temudjin's name, "and submit to me; if not, be ye ready immediately for battle." After this declaration they submitted, hence Temudjin did not harm them. When he had thus won the Ungirats he went to the eastern bank of the Tugeli, and thence sent Arkai Kassar and Siwege Chauni to Wang Khan with the following message: "We are now east of the Tugeli, grass here is good, and our horses are satisfied. Why wert thou angry with me, O my father, why didst thou bring such great fear on me? If thou hadst the wish to blame, why not give the blame reasonably, why destroy all my property? People divided us, but thou knowest well our agreement, that if men should talk to either one of us to the harm of the other we would not believe what was said till we, thou and I, should explain questions personally. But my father, have we had any personal explanation? Though small, I am worth many large men, though ugly I am worth many men of much beauty. Moreover thou and I are two shafts of a single kibitka, if one shaft is broken an ox cannot draw the kibitka. We are like two wheels of that kibitka; if one wheel is broken the kibitka cannot travel. May I not be likened to the shaft, or the wheel of a kibitka? Thy father had forty sons; thou wert the eldest, therefore thou wert made Khan. After that thou didst kill Tai Timur and Buga Timur; these were two of thy uncles; thou hadst the wish also to kill Erke Kara, thy brother, but he fled to the Naimans. A third uncle, in avenging his brother, went against thee with an army, and thou didst flee with one century of men to the Haraun defile. At that time thy daughter was given by thee to Tukta Bijhi the Merkit, and from him thou didst come to my father with a prayer for assistance. My father drove out thy uncle who fled then to Kashin, and my father brought back thy people. In the Black Forest of Tula thou didst make thyself an anda to my father. And moved in those days by gratitude, thy words to him were of this kind: 'For thy benefactions to me

I will make return not only to thee, but thy children and grand-children. I swear by High Heaven that I will do so.' After that thy brother Erke Kara got troops from the Naimans, made war on thee a second time, and drove thee to the lands of the Gurkhan. In less than a year thou didst weary of the Gurkhan and leave him. Passing through the Uigur country thou wert brought to such straits as to nourish thyself with the milk of five sheep that went with thee, and with blood from the camel on which thou wert riding. At last thou didst come to me on a gray, old, blind, wretched horse. Because of thy friendship for my father I sent men to meet thee and bring thee with honor to my camp ground. I collected what I could from my people, and gave thee provisions. Later on, when thou hadst conquered the Merkits I let thee keep all their property and cattle. After that when thou and I were pursuing Buiruk of the Naimans, and fighting with Gugsu Seirak, thou didst make fires in the night time, deceitfully withdraw, and forsake me. As Gugsu Seirak missed seeing my forces he followed after thee swiftly. He captured the wives of thy brothers, and their warriors; he captured half thy people. Again thou didst ask me for aid and I gave it. I sent my four heroes who saved thee, and restored what the Naimans had taken. Thou didst thank me at that time most heartily. Why attack now without cause, why attack when I have not done any evil to thee or to Sengun, or harmed either one of you?"

When the men gave these words to Wang Khan he sighed deeply and answered: "I should not have quarreled with Temudjin, I should have stayed with him." Then he cut his middle finger and putting the blood from it into a small horn, he said: "If I harm Temudjin may I be cut as this finger is cut." He gave the horn then to Temudjin's messenger.

To Jamuka Temudjin sent this message: "Through envy and hatred thou hast parted me from my father. In former days when we lived, thou and I, at his yurta, that one of us two who rose earlier took mare's milk from the dark drinking cup kept by my father. I rose early always, and thou didst conceive toward me hatred at that time. Drink now from my father's dark drinking cup, much loss there will not be to anyone from thy drinking." Temudjin then commanded to say to Altan and to Huchar: "I know not why ye resolved to desert me, O Huchar. We wished first to make thee khan since thou art the son of Naigun, but thou wert unwilling. Thy father, O Altan, ruled as khan once, hence we wished to choose thee to rule over us; thou wouldst not yield to our wishes. Sachai Baiki and Taichu, sons of Bartan had still higher claims, but both men rejected our offer. After that ye and with you the whole people proclaimed me as khan, though, as ye know, I was unwilling. Ye have withdrawn from me now and are helping Wang Khan. But ye have begun what ye never can finish. I advise you to meet me with confidence for without me ye are powerless. Work well with me to hold the headwaters of our rivers; let no stranger come in to snatch them from our people."

Temudjin commanded to say to a slave named Togrul: " I have called thee my brother for the following reason: On a time Tumbinai and his brother Charaha had a slave known as Okda. This slave had a son Subaigai and he a son Kirsan Kokocho, and he a son Aiga Huantohar, this last man begat thee. Why dost thou flatter Wang Khan and adhere to him? Altan and Huchar would never let other men rule over my flock. Thou art my slave by inheritance, hence I address thee as brother."

To Sengun Temudjin sent this message: " I am a son of thy father born with my clothes on; thou art his son born in nakedness. Once our father showed equal kindness to both of us, but dark suspicion attacked thee, and thou, fearing lest I might trick thee in some way, conceived a great hatred and expelled me unjustly. Cease causing grief to thy father, go to him now and drive out his sorrow. Unless thou expel from my heart that old envy against me it will be clear that thou hast the wish to be Khan ere thy father dies naturally. Shouldst thou wish to confer with me, and come to agreement send hither two men for that purpose." Arkai Kassar and Suge Gaichaun gave these words to Sengun, and he answered:

" When Temudjin spoke of my father as Khan he called him old murderer while he did so, and when he called me his sworn friend he jeered at me touching the Merkits, and said that I came to this world to handle rams' tails and remnants. I know the hidden sense of his speeches, I know what his plans are. Battle is my first and last answer to Temudjin. Bilge Baiki and Todoyan raise ye the great standard; feed our steeds carefully."

When Arkai Kassar returned he told everything. Temudjin

went to the lake called Baljuna where many of the Kurulats came
to him. Juchi Kassar had disobeyed Temudjin his elder brother,
he had in fact been disloyal and had tampered with the enemy.
Not present at the great Kalanchin battle he had either favored
Wang Khan, or been captured with his children, his wife and his
followers. After that he escaped with two servants and searched
in hardship and hunger for Temudjin till finally he found him at
Lake Tunga. Kassar turned now to his brother's side thoroughly,
and the two men examined how best they might fall on Wang
Khan unexpectedly. They worked out their stratagem and sent
Haliutar and Chaurhan as if going to Wang Khan with this message
from Kassar: " I have seen not a shadow of my brother; I have
gone over all roads without finding him; I called him, but he
heard me not. I sleep at night with my face toward the stars and
my head on a hillock. My children and wife are with thee, O
Khan, my father. If thou send a trusty person I will go to thee.
I will return and be faithful." " Go," said Temudjin to the
messengers, " we will leave this place straightway, when ye return
come to Arhalgougi on the Kerulon." Temudjin then commanded
Churchadai and Arkai Kassar to lead the vanguard.

Kassar's two servants appeared before Wang Khan and gave
him the message as if coming from their master. Wang Khan
had set up a golden tent and arranged a great feast in it. When
he heard the words, he said: " If that is true, let Kassar come
to us." He sent with the two messengers Iturgyan, a trusted
warrior. When not far from Arhalgougi Iturgyan judged by
various signs that a camp must be near them, so he turned and
rushed away. Haliutar, whose horse was far swifter, spurred on
ahead of him, but not venturing to seize the man, blocked the road
to his stallion. Chaurhan, who followed, struck Iturgyan's horse
in the spine with an arrow, brought him down to his haunches,
and stopped him. They seized Iturgyan then and took him to
Temudjin, who sent him to Kassar, who killed him.

The two messengers then said: " Wang Khan has made a rich
golden tent; he is careless and is feasting. This is the time to
attack him." " Very well," said Temudjin, " let us hasten."
When they arrived at the place they surrounded Wang Khan, and
a fierce battle followed. On the third day of this battle the Keraits
had not strength to fight longer. Wang Khan and Sengun had

both vanished, no one knew by what road they had saved themselves, or when they had fled from the battle-ground.

"I could not let you kill my sovereign," said Hadak, the chief leader to Temudjin, "and I fought long to give Wang Khan and Sengun time to save themselves. If thou command I shall die, but if thou give life I will serve thee." "A man fighting as thou hast to rescue his lord is a hero," said Temudjin, "be one among mine and stay with me." So he made Hadak a commander of one hundred, and bestowed him on Huildar's widow. Since Huildar had planted the standard on Gubtan and fought with such valor his descendants had received for all time rewards assigned widows and orphans. Temudjin now divided the Keraits among his comrades, and assistants.

Wang Khan's brother, Jaganbo, had two daughters, the elder of these was Ibaha. Temudjin himself took Ibaha, and Sorkaktani, the younger, he gave to Tului, his son. Because of these daughters, Jaganbo's inheritance was not given to other men. To Kishlik and Badai, the two horseherds who had warned him, he gave Wang Khan's golden tent with all the gold dishes set out in it, and the men who had served at the tables. Kishlik and Badai with their children and grandchildren were to keep everything won by them in battle, and all the game taken in hunting.

"These two men," said Temudjin, as he gave their rights to them, "saved my life from Sengun and his father, and by Heaven's help and protection I have crushed all the Kerait forces and won my dominion. Let my descendants remember the measure of this service. My enemies, not knowing Heaven's will, wished to kill me. Kishlik who brought warning of their treachery, was in that hour Heaven's envoy; hence I have given him Wang Khan's golden tent with utensils and music, as I might to a prince of my family."

Wang Khan and Sengun had fled almost unattended toward the land of the Naimans. At Didik, a ford on the Naikun, Wang Khan, who was tortured with thirst, stopped to drink from the river. A Naiman watch, guarding the passage, seized the old Khan, and killed him (1203). Wang Khan told who he was, but the guard would not credit his story. He cut his head off immediately, and sent it to Baibuga. Sengun, being at some distance, did not rush up to rescue his father, but went with Ko-

kocha, his attendant, and Kokocha's wife, farther west past the
Naimans. He stopped to drink somewhat later and seeing a wild
horse which flies were tormenting, he stole up to kill him. Kokocha wished now to desert and take Sengun's saddle horse; he
intended to tell Temudjin where Sengun was, but his wife was
indignant. "How leave thy master, who gave thee food and good
clothing, how desert him?" She refused to advance and was
very angry. "Thou wilt not go with me? Dost wish to be wife
to Sengun, perhaps?" asked Kokocha. "If thou go, O Kokocha,
leave that gold cup behind. Let Sengun have even something
to drink from." Kokocha threw down the cup, and hurried off
to find Temudjin.

"How receive service from any man of this kind?" asked
Temudjin when he heard how Kokocha had treated his master.
The deserter told his tale, and was put to death straightway.
But his wife was rewarded for her loyalty to Sengun.

When Wang Khan's head was brought to Baibuga his mother,
Gurbaisu, had music before it with an offering. In the time of
this ceremony the face seemed to smile at the honor. Baibuga,
who thought the smile mockery, was offended and made the skull
into a drinking cup rimmed and ornamented with silver.

"In the East," said Baibuga, "is that man Temudjin who
drove out Wang Khan and brought him to ruin. This man
may be thinking to make himself lord over all of us. There is
only one sun in the heavens; how can two real lords be on earth
at the same time? I will go to the East and seize this Temudjin,
I will take all his people."

Sengun when deserted by Kokocha fled toward the Tibetan
border and subsisted for a season by plundering, but was captured
some time later and slain by Kilidj Arslan, the ruler of that region,
who sent Sengun's children and wives back to Temudjin, and
submitted to his sovereignty.

Thus perished the Khan of the Keraits and his son, and with
them the separate existence of their people.

CHAPTER IV

ONE more great struggle was in store now for Temudjin, that with Baibuga, the Naiman, his father-in-law. Baibuga, alarmed at the rising power of his own daughter's husband, sent an envoy to Ala Kush Tegin, the Ongut chief, to get aid. "Thou knowest," said Baibuga, "that two swords cannot be in one scabbard, or two souls in one body. Two eyes cannot be in one socket, or two sovereigns in one region. Make haste then to seize the horn of empire which this upstart is seeking."

Ala Kush and the Onguts lived next the Great Wall of China, and guarded it, at least, during intervals, for the emperor of China. This Ongut chief was sagacious; he was near Temudjin and remote from Baibuga; he judged that the former was rising and the latter declining; hence after some thought he neglected Baibuga, left his message unanswered, and sent an envoy to explain the whole matter to Temudjin. Baibuga found other allies, however.

Knowing clearly his father-in-law's intention, Temudjin did not fail to be first on the battle-ground. As the spring of 1204 was beginning he held a great council of his leaders. Some thought their horses too weak after winter, but others preferred to move promptly. Action pleased Temudjin, hence he set out immediately, but halted before he reached the Naiman boundary. It was autumn when he entered the enemy's country, and found arrayed there against him men from the Merkits, the Keraits, Uirats, Durbans, Katkins, Tartars, and Saljuts. In fact, forces from each hostile people were ready before him in the hope of destroying, or at least undermining his primacy. There was also Jamuka, his irrepressible enemy. Temudjin ranged his army for action.

To Juchi Kassar, his brother, he confided the center. Overseeing himself the entire army, he reserved a certain part for his own use.

When Jamuka saw this arrangement he said to his officers: " My friends, Temudjin knows how to range men for battle much better than Baibuga." And foreseeing an evil end to Baibuga in that action Jamuka fled from the field of battle quickly.

The two armies met and fought desperately from sunrise to sunset. Many times the great issue seemed doubtful, but when all was wavering like two even scales of a balance Temudjin came with new forces at the perilous moment and gave greater weight to his own side. Just after sunset the Naiman force broke and fled in confusion, sweeping with it Baibuga, badly wounded. The Taiyang fled on foot, first to a neighboring mountain where Kurbassu, his wife was. Later on he was hurried to a place of more safety, where he died soon of wounds and of blood loss. Temudjin, ever swift to pursue, hunted down his fleeing father-in-law; his men captured Kurbassu, who was joined to his household. They captured also Baibuka's seal keeper, Tatungo, an Uigur of learning. Brought before Temudjin he explained what a seal is. " Remain with me," said the conqueror, " use the seal in my name, and teach my sons the language, and lore of the wise Uigurs."

All allies of the Naimans submitted, except the Merkits and the Tartars, who fled from the battlefield. Gutchluk, Baibuga's son, sought safety with Buiruk his uncle.

At this time the Chatalans, the Katkins, and all others who had followed Jemuka, surrendered to Temudjin. Temudjin now hurried in pursuit of Tukta Bijhi, the chief of the Merkits. He hunted him to Sari Keher, and captured many of his people; but Tukta Bijhi fled farther with Chilaun and Katu, and a few attendants.

At the beginning of the Merkit subjection, Dair Usun, chief of the Uasit Merkits, gave Kulan Khatun, his daughter, to Temudjin. When he was taking the girl to the conqueror the road was impassable through disorder. He met on the way a man, Naya of the Barins. " I am giving my daughter to Temudjin," said Dair Usun to Naya. " Come with me," answered Naya. " If thou go alone, wandering warriors will kill thee and do what they like with thy daughter." So he and Dair Usun traveled three

days together, and after that Kulan was given to Temudjin, who
on learning that she had been three days in company with Naya,
was angry.

"Torture this Naya," said Temudjin, "learn all his secrets
and kill him." When they set about torturing Naya, Kulan
spoke up to save him. "On the road Naya met us; he said that
he was one of the Khan's men, and since on the way there were
many disorderly warriors he offered to help us. My father and
I were three days in his company. Without Naya's help I know
not what would have happened. Torture him not, but if the
Khan will be merciful examine my innocence."

"I serve my lord faithfully," said Naya. "I hold it my duty
to bring to him beautiful women, and the best of all horses. If
there are thoughts beyond this in me, I am ready to die at any
moment."

"Kulan speaks with wisdom," said Temudjin. That same day
the girl was examined. Temudjin grew convinced that she was
truthful and liked her the more for her wisdom. He dismissed
Naya, saying: "This man is not false, we may trust him with
tasks of importance."

After the subjection of the Merkits Kuda, the wife of Tukta
Bijhi was given to Temudjin's son, Ogotai. Later on one-half of
the Merkits revolted, retired and took Taikal a fortress in the
mountains. The son of Sorgan Shira was sent to attack them
Temudjin himself went to the Altai, and there passed the winter.
In the spring he crossed the mountains in search of Tukta
Bijhi. At that time Gutchluk joined Tukta Bijhi; they drew
up their army at the Irtish near its sources, and there
Temudjin found and attacked them. Tukta Bijhi was
killed in a very fierce battle, his sons were unable to bear
off the body, so they cut his head from the trunk and thus
saved it. The Merkits fled from the battlefield, and more than
half of those warriors were drowned in the Irtish, the rest
scattered and saved their lives as best they could. Gutchluk fled
to the land of the Karluks, and still farther westward to the Gurkhan. Kutu and Chilaun fled through Kanli and Kincha.

While all this was happening Sorgan Shira's son captured the
fortress at Taikal and killed or seized all the Merkits. Those
who had not left their own home land revolted as well as the

others, but were captured through men sent by Temudjin to quell
them.

" If we let those people remain in one land," declared Temudjin,
" they will rise again, surely." And he had them conducted in
small bands to various new places. That same year Temudjin
made an iron kibitka for Subotai, and sent him to hunt down
and seize all the other sons of Tukta Bijhi. " Those men,"
said Temudjin, " though defeated in battle, tore away recently, like
wounded wild deer, or like wanton young stallions; and now thou
must find them. If they fly on wings to the sky, become thou a
falcon and catch them; if like mice they bore into the earth, be
a strong iron spade and dig them out of it; if they hide as fish in
the sea, be a net and enclose them. To cross deep ravines and
high mountains choose the time when thy horses are not weary.
Spare thy warriors on the road, and hunt not at all save when
need comes. When thou must hunt, hunt very carefully. Let not
thy warriors use croupers, or breast straps, lest their horses rush
feebly. Should any man refuse thee obedience bring him hither, if
I know him, if not do thou kill him on the place of refusal. If
with Heaven's aid and protection thou seize Tukta Bijhi's sons, slay
them straightway." Then he added: " When I was young three
bands of Merkits pursued me, and thrice did they ride round Mount
Burhan. These men have fled now with loud insolent speeches, but
do thou hunt them down to the uttermost limits if need be. I
have made a kibitka of iron to convey and protect thee. Though
far away thou wilt ever be near me. Heaven will keep thee most
surely while traveling, and will give thee assistance."

When the Naimans and Merkits were captured by Temudjin,
Jamuka had lost all his people, and was left in the land of the
Naimans deprived of property, and attended by only five servitors.
He went then to the mountain Tanlu and lived there by robbery
and hunting. One day those five servitors seized him and took
him to his enemy. Jamuka sent these words then to Temudjin.
" Slaves had the insolence to seize their own master, and betray
him. Mistake not, O Khan, my friend, these words which I
send thee."

" Is it possible to leave men unpunished who betray ? " asked
Temudjin. " Give them to death with their children and grand-
children ! " Then he commanded to slay those five traitors

before the eyes of Jamuka to whom he sent at the same time this message: " Once I made thee a shaft of my kibitka, but thou didst desert me. Thou hast joined me again, so now be my comrade. Should one of us forget, the other will remind him. If one falls asleep the other will rouse him. Though thou didst leave me, thou wert still in reality my assistant. Though thou didst oppose I got no harm in the end from that action. When thou and I had a battle thy heart was regretful, apparently. When I warred with Wang Khan thou didst send me his discourses. That was the earliest service. When I was battling with the Naimans thy words made their hearts shake; that was another good service."

These words were taken to Jamuka and he answered: " When we became andas in boyhood we ate food too strong for our stomachs; we gave words to each other which nothing can take from our memory. People roused us to quarrel and we parted. I blush when I think of my speeches uttered once to my anda, and I dare not look now at thee. It is thy wish that I be for the future thy comrade. I might call myself thy comrade, but I could be no comrade to thee in reality. Thou hast joined peoples together, thou hast built up dominion, no man on earth can now be thy comrade. Unless thou kill me I shall be for thee henceforth like a louse on thy collar outside, or a thorn in thy inner neck-band. Thou wouldst not be at rest in the daytime, while at night thou wouldst sleep with alarm in thy bosom were I to be near thee. Thy mother is prudent, thou thyself art a hero, thy brothers are gifted, thy comrades are champions, thou hast seventy-three leaders, but from childhood I have had neither father nor mother, I have no brothers, my wife is a babbler, my comrades are traitors, hence, O my anda, whom Heaven has preferred, give me death the more quickly that thy heart may be quiet. If thou let me die without blood loss I, after death and for ages, will help thy descendants and protect them."

On hearing this answer Temudjin said: " Jamuka, my anda, went his own way in life, but his words have in fact never harmed me. He is a man who might change even now, but he has not the wish to live longer. I have tried divination to search out good reasons to kill him, but have not discovered them thus far. What must I do? He is a man of distinction, and we may not take his life without reasons. Ah, now I have found the right reason! Say this to him: ' Because of horse stealing and quarrels between Taichar, my slave, and Darmala, thy brother, thou didst attack me and fight at Baljuna; thou didst frighten me dreadfully. I wish now to forgive thee, and make thee my comrade, but thou art unwilling. I am sorry that thy life should be taken, but thou wilt not permit me to save it; hence we must do what thou wishest."

Temudjin then commanded to take life from Jamuka without blood loss, and bury him with honor. Altan and Huchar were put to death also at that time.

When Temudjin had subdued to his own undivided dominion the various peoples opposed to him he raised on the Upper Onon, in 1206, his great standard of nine white tails and took the title Jinghis (Mighty) to distinguish him from all other Khans. After that he rewarded Munlik, Boörchu, Mukuli and others who had helped him in building the Empire, and those who had shown special service. " Thou hast been to me a comrade," said Jinghis (as we shall now call Temudjin), to Munlik his step-father, " thou hast helped me very often, but above all when Wang Khan and his son were enticing me to a false feast to kill me. If I had not halted that day I should have dropped into hot fire and deep water. I remember this service of thine, and will not let my descendants forget it. Henceforth thou wilt sit first in thy order. As I reward thee by the year, or the month, so will that reward be continued to all thy descendants unbrokenly."

" In my youth," said Jinghis to Boörchu, " Taidjut thieves stole my eight horses; I had chased three days and nights after them when I met thee; thou didst become then my comrade and ride three days and nights with me to find and restore those eight horses. Why did it happen that Nahu Boyan, thy rich father, who had only one son, let that son be my comrade? Because in thee traits of high justice were evident. After that when I called thee to help me thou didst not refuse and wert prompt in thy coming. When the three Merkit clans drove me into the forests of Mount Burhan thou didst not desert me; thou didst share my great suffering. When I spent a night before the enemy at Talan and a great blinding rain came thou didst give me rest, and spread out thy felt robe above me, and stand there and hold it, and not let that rain touch me. Thou didst stand in that painful position

until daybreak, resting first on one leg and then on the other.
This proves thy unbounded devotion. It would not be possible
to recount all the good deeds which thou hast done since I saw
thee the first day. Besides thou and Mukuli advised me to that
which was proper, and stopped me from that which should be
omitted. Through doing the right thing in every great trial I
have reached my high power and dominion. Sit thou now with
a few men above all others. I free thee from punishment for
nine death offenses. Be a commander of ten thousand, and rule
the land westward till thou touch the Golden Mountains." [1]

Then he turned to Mukuli and said to him: "When we were
at Hórho Nachubur at the thick spreading tree under which
Khan Kutula made merry and was dancing, Heaven bestowed
wisdom and tidings which became clear to thee. I remember
the words given then by thy keen father, Gunua, and I make thee
prince now because of those words, and thy conduct ever after.
Sit thou above other men in society, be a commander of ten thous-
and on the left wing, and govern on the east to the Haraün mountains. Thy descendants will inherit thy dignity."

"In youth," said Jinghis to Horchi, "thou didst prophesy
touching me; thou didst share with me toils after that and wert
to me a true comrade. Now when thy words of fore-knowledge
are verified and proven, I give thee what thou didst ask for at that
time: I give thee the right to choose for thyself thirty beautiful
maidens and women among all conquered nations. Bring together three thousand of the Bali, the Adarki and other clans ruled
by Achik and by Togai, and when thou hast ten thousand assembled command them and govern those people. Put up thy camps
as may please thee among forest nations on the Irtish, and guard
well that region. Let all affairs there be under thy management,
thou hast now thy heart's wish."

Jinghis turned then to Churchadai: "Thy greatest service," said he, "was in that dreadful battle at Kalanchin
against the strong Khan of the Keraits. When Huildar declared that he would seize and hold Gubtan thou didst
take the vanguard. Success in that desperate encounter came
from thee beyond any man. Thou didst break and hurl back
the Jirkins, the strongest of the enemy, and after them came still

[1] The Altai.

others who broke the line of my own chosen body-guard, who held the strong central position. Thou didst wound with thy own hand Sengun in the cheek while he was making the last fearful onrush. Hadst thou not struck him then, it is unknown what would have followed. Later on, when we were moving down the Kalka, I relied upon thee as I might on a lofty immovable mountain. On arriving at Baljuna thou didst fight in the vanguard again, and with Heaven's great assistance we crushed the Keraits at last, and because of that triumph the Naimans and the Merkits could not resist us, and were scattered. When they were scattered, Jaganbo gave me his daughters and thus saved his people, but later on he revolted; then thou didst think out a plan to entrap him and capture his people. That is thy second great service."

With these words Jinghis gave Churchadai his own wife, Ibaha, the daughter of Jaganbo, to whom he spoke then as follows: " Ibaha, I do this not because I have ceased to love thee, not because thou hast an evil temper of mind, or art lacking in beauty. I give thee to Churchadai to reward him in the highest way possible. I give thee to Churchadai because of his inestimable service, and I desire those of my sons and descendants who shall receive the throne after me to honor the dignity and fame of Ibaha. Now thou wilt grant me a favor: Thy father gave with thee Ashi Timur, who is master of thy kitchen and two hundred men to work under him. In going leave with me one hundred of those men, and leave also Ashi." Then Jinghis said to Churchadai: " I command thee to govern four thousand of the Uruts. Thou didst tame the wild, and bring down the rebellious, thou and Chelmai with Chepé and Subotai. Ye have been like four raging watch-dogs in swiftness. If I sent you to any place ye crushed hard immense stones into gravel, ye overturned cliffs, and stopped the great rush of deep waters, hence I command you to be in the battle front. The four heroes: Boörchu, Mukuli, Boroul and Chilaun I command to be behind me. Churchadai to be in front, and thus make my heart free to be fearless. Kubilai be the elder in all warlike matters and decisions." Then he added: " Because of disobedience I do not make Baidun a commander apart and independent; I join him to thy person, that is better. Let him act with thee, and see thou what will come of it."

After that Jinghis said to Boörchu and others: " Hunán is like a fearless wolf in the night time, in the day he is like a black raven. He joined me and never would act with bad people. In every affair take ye counsel with Hunán and Kokosi. Let Hunán be commander of ten thousand under my eldest son, Juchi. No matter what Hunán and Kokosi and Daigai and Usun heard and saw they kept back no word, and never distorted a word which they told me."

" When I was born at the river Onon," said Jinghis to Chelmai, " thy father came from Mount Burhan with the bellows of a blacksmith on his shoulders, and brought a sable wrap to put around me. Thou wert in swaddling clothes that day, O Chelmai, and he gave thee to serve me for life and inseparably. Thou hast grown up with me, and shown immense service. Thou art my fortunate comrade. I release thee from nine death penalties and reward thee."

" In former times," said Jinghis to Vanguru, the master of nourishment, " thou with three yurtas of the Tokuruts, and five yurtas of Torguts, and with the Chanshikits and the Baiyuts made one single camp with me. In darkness and fog thou hast never lost thy way marching. In scattering and disorder thou hast never lost thy head, thou hast endured cold and wet with me always and nothing could shake or discourage thee. What reward dost thou wish of me this day ? "

" If thou in thy favor command me to choose," said Vanguru, " I should wish to collect all the Baiyuts who are scattered."

Jinghis consented. " Collect them, be their commander and govern them," was his answer. And he continued : " Vanguru and Boroul while managing on the right and the left as masters of nourishment, and dispensing food justly, ye have pleased my heart well, so henceforth sit ye on horseback when food and drink are dispensed to great gatherings in the open. While feasting in tents take your places on the right and the left at the door on the south side, and send food and drink to all present."

" My mother took you," said Jinghis to Shigi Kutuku and Boroul and Kuichu and Kokochu, " from camps where men left you, she made you her sons, she reared and prepared you to be comrades to us, her own children. Ye have paid her well for this benefaction. Boroul was my comrade in the perils of battle, in nights of snow and of rain and of tempest. When exposed to the enemy he never let me lack drink or food. On a time when we had destroyed nearly all of the Tartars, one of them, Hargil Shila, while fleeing for his life felt great hunger and turned to get food from my mother. ' If thou desire food,' said she to the Tartar, ' sit on that side of the entrance.' He sat at the west of the door and there waited. Just then Tului, my son, who was five years of age, came in and was going out soon after when the Tartar caught him, thrust him under his arm and snatched a knife quickly. ' He will kill the child! ' screamed my mother. Altani, Boroul's wife, who was sitting east of the door, rushed at the Tartar, caught his hair with one hand and pulled his knife with the other so vigorously that she and the knife fell together. Now Chedai and Chelmai, who had just killed a cow a little north of the yurta, heard Altani screaming. They ran, one with a knife, the other with an axe and killed the stranger. Altani, Chedai and Chelmai disputed then as to who had shown the greatest service. ' If we had not run up,' said Chedai and Chelmai, ' thou couldst not have managed the Tartar, O woman, and he would have finished Tului.' ' If I had not screamed,' said Altani, ' ye would not have run up, and if I had not seized his hair and snatched the knife from him, Tului would have perished ere ye could have saved him.' Boroul's wife won the word battle. In the struggle with Wang Khan at Kalanchin, Ogotai was wounded in the neck with an arrow. Boroul sucked the blood from the wound, and thus saved him from stifling. He has repaid very richly the trouble of rearing him by saving two sons of mine. In the most difficult places he was never neglectful, hence nine times will I save him from suffering the death penalty."

Jinghis spoke next to Sorgan Shira: " When I was young," said he, " Targutai Kurultuk, with his brethren the Taidjuts, captured me. Thou, with thy son, hid me at thy yurta and commanded Kadan, thy daughter, to serve me, and ye then gave me freedom. Day and night I remember this service, but ye came to me late and only now am I able to reward you. What may your wish be ? " " We should like," answered they, "to make a camp in the Merkit land, at Sailyange, and whatever other reward may be possible, let the Khan give it." "Let it be as ye wish; make your camp in that country. Besides, let all your descendants bear arrows and bows, and drink a cup of wine in the camp of the

Khan when ye come to it. Nine death offenses will be forgiven you." To Chilaun and Chinbo, sons of Sorgan Shira, he said: "How could I forget the words spoken once on a time by you, and the deeds done when ye spoke thus. Now should anything fail you come yourselves and inform me," and he said further: "Sorgan Shira, Badai and Kishlik, ye are free. Keep all the booty which ye may take during warfare at any time, and whatever game ye kill in hunting. Sorgan Shira, once thou wert Todayan's servant. Badai and Kishlik, ye were horseherds to Aike Cheran; live with me henceforth and be happy."

"When thou with thy father seized Targutai," said Jinghis to Naya, "thou didst say: 'How could we yield up our master?' Ye let him go then and came to me as subjects. For that reason I said: 'Those people understand lofty duty, I will trust them.' Boörchu is now commander of ten thousand on the right hand. Mukuli is commander of ten thousand on the left, be thou a commander in the center."

Jinghis then directed Daigai, his shepherd, to collect homeless people and command them. When all who had labored to build up the Empire had received their rewards and offices Jinghis Khan's step-father, Munlik, brought his seven sons to the assembly and received for them good recognition. The fourth man of these was a shaman, Kokochu, a man of boundless ambition. Taibtengeri was his second name. No one could tell who among these seven brothers was the most self-willed and bitter. One day they attacked Juchi Kassar and beat him. Kassar complained to Jinghis of this treatment; Jinghis became angry. "Thou hast boasted," said he, "that no man is thy equal in valor and skill. If that be true why let those fellows beat thee?" Kassar shed tears from vexation, went out, and for three days after that made no visit to his brother. Meanwhile Taibtengeri went to Jinghis to incense him against Kassar. "The spirit has given me a sacred command from High Heaven," said the shaman, "Jinghis will rule people at first, and then will come Kassar. If thou set not Kassar aside thy rule will be short-lived."

When Jinghis heard these words he went that same night to seize Kassar. Kuichu and others informed Hoelun, who set out that night also in a kibitka drawn by a swift going camel. She reached Kassar's yurta at sunrise, just as Jinghis, having tied

Kassar's sleeves, had taken cap and girdle from him and was asking him questions. When Jinghis saw his mother he was wonderfully astonished, and alarmed also. Hoelun was very angry. Stepping out of her kibitka, she untied Kassar, gave him back cap and girdle, then sitting down, she put her feet under her, bared her bosom and addressed the two brothers: " See these breasts of mine both of you? Ye two have drunk from them. What crime has Kassar committed that thou, Temudjin, art destroying thy own kindred flesh in this brother? When thou wert an infant thou didst drink from this breast; neither thou, Temudjin nor Temugu could draw my breasts thoroughly; only Kassar could empty both sides and relieve me. Temudjin, thou hast gifts, but Kassar alone has the strength and the art to shoot arrows. Whenever men have risen in rebellion he has brought them down with his arrows, and tamed them. Every enemy now is destroyed, and Kassar is needed no longer."

Jinghis waited till Hoelun's anger had subsided. Then he said: " I was frightened when I acted. I am ashamed at this moment." He went out after these words, but later, unknown to his mother, he took away Kassar's people, for the most part, leaving only fourteen hundred yurtas. At first he had given him four thousand. When Hoelun learned of this action she grieved much, and died shortly after. Chebke was placed then with Kassar to guard him.

After this many men gathered to the shaman, Taibtengeri, among others people who belonged to Temugu, Jinghis's youngest brother. Temugu sent Sokor to lead back those people, but Taibtengeri beat him, put a saddle on his back, and sent him to his mother. Next day Temugu went himself to Taibtengeri. The seven brothers surrounded him. " How didst thou dare to send men to take people from us?" roared the brothers, and they were ready to beat him. " I ought not to have sent men to you," said Temugu, much frightened. " As thou art to blame, then beg pardon." And they forced him to kneel to them straightway.

The next day, very early, while Jinghis was in bed, Temugu fell on his knees before him and told how Taibtengeri and his brothers had treated him. He wept while relating the details. Jinghis had said no word yet, when Bortai came from her bed with a blanket around her and, shedding tears meanwhile, spoke as follows: " This man has beaten Kassar, and now he has forced Temugu to his knees to beg pardon. What kind of order is this in thy dominion? If while thou art living they ruin thy brothers, majestic as cedars, when thou art dead the people, who are like grass blown by wind, or a mere flock of birds, will not obey thy small, helpless children."

" Taibtengeri will come to-day," said Jinghis to Temugu. " Deal with him as thou pleasest." Temugu went out and agreed with three very strong wrestlers. Munlik came later with his seven sons, and when Taibtengeri sat near the door on the west side, Temugu, as he passed, seized him roughly by the collar. " Yesterday," said he, " thou didst force me to my knees; I will try strength to-day with thee." While Temugu was struggling with him the cap fell from the head of the shaman; Munlik took the cap and put it under his arm. " Wrestle not here!" cried Jinghis, " go outside." When the two men stepped forth from the yurta Taibtengeri was seized by the wrestlers who broke his spine and threw him aside to the left where he fell near the wheel of a kibitka. " Taibtengeri," said Temugu to Jinghis, " forced me to my knees yesterday to beg pardon; now when I wish to try strength with him, he lies down and refuses to rise. It is clear that he is a coward."

Munlik understood and began to weep bitterly. " O Khan," said he, " I was thy assistant before thou wert even at the beginning of thy greatness, and I have continued to serve thee till this day." While he was speaking his six sons stood near the center of the yurta and watched the door. They began to put up their sleeves as if for a struggle. Jinghis rose. He was frightened, but shouted with sternness and authority, " Aside, I wish to go out!" He went out, and his body-guard of archers surrounded him. Seeing that Taibtengeri was dead, Jinghis commanded to pitch his own tent above the shaman's body, and then he went to another place. In the tent put over the body the door and upper aperture were fastened, and at first a guard was placed around it. On the third day at dawn the upper aperture opened, and the body of the wizard was lifted out through it. When inquiries were made, all learned that the body had vanished through the upper aperture, or smoke hole.

" Taibtengeri calumniated my brothers and beat them," said

Jinghis, "hence Heaven looked on him with anger, and snatched away both his life and his body." After that he reproached Munlik sharply: "Thou hast failed," said he, "to teach thy sons what was needed very greatly in their case — obedience. This one tried to equal me, hence I extinguished him. Had I known thee earlier I should have put an end to thee, as I have to Jamuka, to Altan and Kudjeir. But if a man gives a word in the morning and breaks it ere night comes, or gives it in the evening and breaks it in the morning, the judgment of people will shame him. I have promised to save thee from death, so let us now end this matter."

After these words Jinghis Khan's anger was diminished. When Taibtengeri was dead the vanity of Munlik and his sons decreased greatly and soon disappeared altogether.

In 1207 a new and victorious campaign was begun against Tangut which had failed to pay tribute, but was brought down now, thoroughly, at least, for a season. The subjection of the Kirghis and this new victory over Tangut secured the position of Jinghis in Northeastern Asia. There was not one man now to challenge his dominion. Groups of people, or tribes, might rebel, but there was no power to stop him or modify his policy. He was preparing to meet foreign nations. The first turn was for China.

Kara Kitai (Black Cathay) was at that time a very large Empire composed of many nations. The ruler of each of these nations acknowledged the overlordship of the Gurkhan or sovereign. In length Kara Kitai extended westward from Tangut to the Kwaresmian Empire, and in width from the Upper Irtish to the Pamir highlands. Within its borders were the lakes now known as Balkash, Issikkul and Lob Nor. Of cities now existing, Kuldja would be close to the center, Kashgar and Yarkend a good distance from its western border, while Khotan would be well removed from its southernmost limit.

Nearly all Central Asia was included in this Empire, while vassal states extended far beyond its western and southwestern borders. The Uigurs, whose chief city was Bish Calik, lived in the northeast corner of the Empire and touched on the Naimans. These Uigurs are famous, at least among scholars, as having been the most devoted to learning of all Turkish nations; from them it was that the Mongols received an alphabet and their earliest instruction.

The Idikut, or ruler, of the Uigurs acknowledged the Gurkhan as overlord, but the yearly tribute which he paid, and the daily tyranny of the agent near his court, so annoyed him that he took this official's life at a place known as Kara Kodja. He resolved thereupon to seek the protection of Jinghis, whose triumphs and whose power were threatening even China, and filling all Asia with amazement and terror. Bardjuk, the watchful Idikut, had appointed an embassy to the conqueror, but events had delayed its departure.

When the three sons of Tukta Bijhi and their uncle fled taking their father's head, which they had cut with all haste from his body on the battlefield, they despatched an envoy in advance to the Idikut to beg a refuge for themselves, and protection. The Idikut, seeing danger in their visit, slew the envoy, took the field against the brothers, and scattered all their forces. But later on he was troubled greatly by this act; for these new opponents might side with the Mongols, or they might join the Gurkhan; they might rouse either party to move against him. The Idikut's delight was great, therefore, and genuine when Mongol envoys appeared before him. Jinghis had heard of the Idikut's resolve, and, knowing well what good might rise from it, had taken action very promptly, and despatched as envoys Alp Utug and Durbai to the ruler of the Uigurs.

The Idikut showed the highest honor to these envoys, and dismissed them with every mark of courtesy and friendship, associating two envoys of his own to bear to Jinghis Khan the following message: " The fame of the world-conquering sovereign has come to me. I have agreed till very recently with the Gurkhan, and was just preparing to explain through an embassy a change in my position, and to yield myself with upright heart to thee, all conquering and mighty sovereign. While thinking over this I saw thy envoys coming toward me, and then I beheld a blue heaven through the clouds around me. I beheld a bright sun in the sky. I saw besides a blue shining river where just before the ice had hidden everything. I was filled with delight to my innermost being. I yield to thee the land of the Uigurs. I myself am the servant and son of Jinghis Khan the Immovable."

At first sight it might seem that the Mongol Khan would be satisfied with a statement of this kind, but he was far from satisfaction, for just then came four envoys from the sons of Tukta Bijhi, declaring their subjection.

The Uigur envoys were received with every honor, but since he doubted the Idikut's sincerity, Jinghis sent envoys a second time with this message: " If the Idikut has the honest wish to subject himself let him come to us in person, and present us with what there is of greatest value in his treasure house."

On hearing this message the Idikut went to his treasure house and took from it the best of gold, silver, pearls, and other precious objects. These were sent to Jinghis Khan that same summer, but the Idikut excused himself from offering them in person, and added various reasons to explain his own absence.

Fresh disorders broke out in Tangut, which caused new campaigning. The Mongols invaded that country a third time, routed its warriors, captured the city of Uiraka and the fortress of Imen. A second Tangut army was scattered, and Chong sing, the chief capital, was invested. During this siege peace was concluded and the Tangut king gave his daughter to Jinghis in marriage.

During 1209 the Mongol sovereign returned home in triumph and found Arslan Khan of the Karluks and the Idikut of the Uigurs waiting to render him homage. Arslan Khan had till then ruled conjointly with an agent of the Gurkhan, his suzerain. But, as the power of the Gurkhan had diminished in recent days very sensibly, many princes, who had recognized him up to that time, revolted. Among these was the Sultan of Khotan, who marched against him with an army, and persuaded Arslan Khan to drop allegiance. Arslan made haste to help the Sultan all the more, since at that time he was advised of the Gurkhan's plans by that sovereign's deceitful Emir, Tanigu. This traitor so represented Arslan to his overlord, the Gurkhan, that the latter gave him the title " son," and appointed for him the agent whom Tanigu recommended. But when Mongol victories sent panic throughout Northern Asia, Arslan acted quickly. He slew the agent of the Gurkhan, joined Jinghis Khan very promptly, and waited for his favor.

Arslan said that if he received a golden girdle, and a high position

in the Mongol service he would have one wish alone ungratified:
to be the fifth son of the great Khan.　Jinghis, divining this wish
of his, or learning of it, had it gratified.　He gave Arslan his
daughter, Altun Bighi, in marriage, and with her the title of fifth
son was added.

Thus Jinghis Khan was intrenched in Kara Kitai very firmly.
His next move was on Kitai itself, the great North China Empire.
He was now master of mighty legions drawn from all tribes whose
leaders and chiefs he had driven from existence in that fierce fight
for dominion, during which no mercy had been manifest on either
side, but in which greater wisdom, with keenness and skill, also
fortune to some extent, were with Jinghis.

CHAPTER V

JINGHIS KHAN'S TRIUMPHANT ADVANCE BEYOND THE GREAT
WALL OF CHINA

MANY provinces of China had been subject to foreign rule
for three centuries. After the fall of the Tang dynasty,
which had ruled the whole country from 618 to 907, this immense
Empire fell to commanders of provinces and was cut up into ten
states co-existent and separate. Intestine wars, the result of this
parceling, favored the rise of a new power in Northern Asia.

The Kitans, who formed a part of the Manchu stock, held that
country from the Sungari southward as far as the present Shan
hai kuan, and from the Khingan range on the west to Corea.
These people had for a long time been vassals of Tartar Khans,
and next of Chinese Emperors. They were divided into eight
tribes, each with its own chief or manager. Abaki, the head of
the Sheliyu tribe, which owned the district known at the present
as Parin, gained supreme power in 907, and used the whole strength
of the Kitans to subdue Northern Asia. In 916, he proclaimed
himself sovereign, and when he died, ten years later, his dominion
extended eastward to the ocean, and westward to the Golden
Mountains or to the Altai.

Tekoan, the son of this first Kitan ruler, by giving the aid of his
arms to a rebel chieftain in China, secured victory, and a throne
for him. In return for such service the newly made Emperor,
who fixed his residence or capital at the present Kai fong fu on the
south bank of the Hoang Ho, or Yellow River, ceded sixteen districts to Tekoan in Pehche li, Shan si and Liao tung, engaging also
to furnish three hundred thousand pieces of silk as his annual
tribute.

The new Chinese Emperor took the position of vassal to the
Kitan, and termed himself his grandson and subject. The

successor to this Chinese ruler sought to modify these conditions. Tekoan made war on him; conquered all the provinces north of the Hoang Ho, seized Pien (Kai fong fu), captured the Emperor and sent him to regions north of China.

Following Chinese usage the Kitan took a new name for his dynasty, calling it Liao, that is Iron.

After the fall of the Tang dynasty five petty lines followed one another on the throne of Kai fong fu in the course of five decades. On the ruins of these dynasties in 960 the house of Sung united nearly all China. This house made war on the Kitans, but failed to win back the districts previously ceded to them, and in 1004, because of hostile action by the Kitans, the Sung Emperor, to gain peace, engaged to pay an annual tribute both in silk and silver.

The Kitan Empire lasted two centuries and assumed in its functions Chinese forms, at least externally, but Chinese methods made it feeble. After strong and warlike chiefs came weak and timid Emperors. At last a great man named Aguta rose among the Jutchis, a nomad people living in the lands between the Amoor, the Eastern Ocean and the Sungari River. These formed part of the same Tungus stock as did the Kitans, but they were untouched as yet by luxury.

In 1114 Aguta gained a victory over the Kitans, and the following year proclaimed himself Emperor of the Jutchis. The new State he called Aidjin Kurun (Kin kwe in Chinese), that is, Golden Kingdom. He would not act, he said, like the Kitans, who had taken the name of a metal that is eaten by rust very easily and ruined.

Aguta subdued the whole Kitan Empire, and died in 1123. Two years later his successor seized Yeliu yen hi, the ninth and last Emperor of the Kitan dynasty, which had endured nine years and two centuries.

The Sung Emperor had abetted Aguta, and even urged him towards victory, hoping thus to regain the lands lying between the Yellow Sea and the Yellow River. The Kitans were crushed in the conflict, but the new power (the Kin dynasty) was more dangerous for him than the old, as he learned to his cost very quickly. In 1125 the Kin Emperor invaded North China; the year following he reached the Hoang Ho, or Yellow River, and besieged Kai fong fu which lies south of it. The Sung Emperor, who visited the camp of the invader to find peace there if possible, was seized and sent to Manchuria with his family. One of his brothers, living then in the South, was made sovereign by the Chinese. The Kins advanced farther, reached the Yang tse and took Lin ngan in the Che kiang province. They forced the Emperor to acknowledge their conquest and promise a yearly payment of twenty-five thousand pieces of silk with two hundred and fifty thousand ounces of silver, and to avow himself a vassal in addition.

The rivers Hoaï and Han formed the boundary between the two Empires, and now the Kin Empire reached a line almost half way between the great rivers Hoang Ho and Yang tse. The Sung Emperor moved his capital to Lin ngan, known as Han chau somewhat later. The Kins took up arms to extend their new Empire still farther southward, but were confronted by failure. The war ended in 1165 by a treaty which retained former boundaries, but decreased the Sung tribute. The southern Emperor, moreover, instead of being a vassal to him of the north, acquired the relation of a nephew to an uncle. But in 1206 the Sung Emperor began a new war which brought defeat to him. To restore peace he was forced now to pay the original tribute.

About the middle of the 12th century the Kins had chosen the present Pekin as their residence; they called it Chong tu, or the middle capital. Lords over one third of China, they had adopted the customs and laws of that country. Their dominion extended on the north beyond China proper to Lake Baikal and the great Amoor River. The Kitans, once masters, had now become subjects to the Kin dynasty, but in 1162 they revolted; after that they were by force brought down to obedience.

Some years before, the Kins had had a struggle with the Mongols which for the Kins proved disastrous. They ended it by making concessions. The Mongol chieftain then took the title of Khan, which he kept ever after.

Jinghis, in beginning a war against China, was really attacking the Northern, or Kin dynasty, which had driven out that of the Kitans, hence, very naturally, he turned for co-operation to the Kitans. Madaku, the Kin Emperor, died in November 1209, and in 1210 an envoy informed Jinghis Khan that Chong hei, the eighth of the dynasty, had succeeded Madaku. The envoy demanded that the vassal, as he claimed to consider Jinghis, should receive the announcement while kneeling, in accordance with the etiquette of China.

"Who is this new Emperor?" asked Jinghis of the envoy.

"Prince Chong hei."

On hearing the name Jinghis spat toward the South, and then added: "I thought that the Son of Heaven must be lofty and uncommon, but how is this idiot Chong hei to sit on a throne, and why should I lower myself in his presence?" Then he mounted his steed and rode away without further word or explanation. He summoned his leaders at once, and said to them: "My forefathers suffered very greatly, as ye know, from Chinese monarchs; and still those same monarchs failed to conquer this land of ours after centuries of effort. Heaven has granted me victory over every opponent and permitted me to mount the highest round of fortune. If ye act with me faithfully, that same Heaven will grant a glorious triumph over China. Through this triumph the Mongols will win the greatest wealth and magnificence; their fame will never cease among nations."

All were delighted, all praised their conquering ruler. They agreed with him then to send an envoy to the Altyn Khan (Golden Khan)[1] with the following message: "Of course it has come to thy knowledge that we, by Heaven's favor, have been chosen from among all the Mongols to hold the reins of Empire and of guidance. The fame of our conquering host has gone forth, and is spreading. We are planting our banners over all the earth's surface, and soon every people and all nations will submit without delay or hesitation to our prosperous direction, and share in its many benefactions. But should any rise and resist, their houses, goods, property and dependents will be ruined without mercy. Praise and honor to High Heaven, our dominion is so well ordered that we can visit China. With us will go instruments of every sort, and crushing weapons. With us will march an army which is like a roaring ocean. We can meet enmity or friendship with the same tranquil feeling. If the Golden Khan in wisdom selects the way of friendship and concord, and meets us in congress, we will secure to him the management of China in proper form and strong possession. If he cannot come himself, let him send his honored sons to us as hostages with treasures. But should he resist, which

---

[1] Golden Khan, the title of the Kin Emperor in Mongol.

Heaven forbid, we must wait for warfare and for slaughter, which will last till Heaven puts the diadem of victory and power on the head of him whom it chooses, and puts the rags of misery and want on him whom it desires to wear them."

On receiving these words, such as no man had ever sent a sovereign in China, Chong hei burst into a blazing rage and dismissed the envoy with contempt and with injury. "If Jinghis has planned war and slaughter against us," replied he, "who can prevent him from tempting fortune?"

The last word had been uttered, and both sides made ready now for warfare.

Directing Tuguchar to guard home lands from every possible disorder, Jinghis moved from the Kerulon in March, 1211, to subdue the Chinese Empire. But before he left his native place he visited a lofty mountain. On the summit he loosed his kaftan, put his girdle round his neck and called High Heaven to help him : "Boundless Heaven," said he, "I am going to avenge the blood of Berkai and Ambagai, my uncles whom the Altyn Khans put to death with infamy and torture. If thou favor me send aid from out the lofty places, but on earth send men to help me; send also spirits good and evil."

His four sons, Juchi, Jagatai, Ogotai and Tului, accompanied the Mongol sovereign.

This army of invasion was held together by the sternest discipline and made up of mounted men only. The units of this force were ten, one hundred, one thousand and ten thousand warriors. The orders of the sovereign were given to the chiefs of ten thousand, and by them to subordinates. Each man had a strong rawhide armor and helmet; he carried a lance and a sabre with an ax, a bow, and a quiver; he was followed by a number of horses, which had no food save that which they found as they traveled. Immense herds of cattle were driven in the rear of the army. In time of forced marches each man carried with him some milk and a small portion of flesh food.

To reach the Great Wall the Mongols crossed a space of about twelve hundred miles consisting in part of the desert known as Sha mo in Chinese and as the Gobi in Mongol. The first success of the invaders was made easier by Ala Kush Tegin of the Onguts, whose duty it was to guard the Great Wall for the Emperor, but who favored the Mongols. In no long time Tai tong fu, called also Si king, an Imperial court northwest of Yen king or Chong tu, the Pekin of the present, was invested. The Chinese commander Kin kien sent Mingan, a trusted officer, to reconnoitre the Mongols. Mingan deserted and gave all needed information about places to the enemy, who attacked Kin kien and routed his forces; their mounted men trampled his infantry and cut it to pieces. The Mongols pressed on toward the chief Chinese army, which did not wait to engage them.

The success of the invasion was enormous. Expeditions were made to the walls of Chong tu the great northern capital. The terror stricken Emperor prepared to flee southward, but was stopped by his guards, who swore to fight to the death for their sovereign. During 1212 the Mongols succeeded at all points, and cut up the Kin armies wherever they met them. Still Jinghis could not capture Tai tong fu, though in August, 1212, he besieged it in person. He was wounded in front of the place by an arrow, and withdrew to the north for a period.

The Mongol invasion of China was aided now by an insurrection of Kitans. At the outbreak of hostilities Lyuko, a prince of the dispossessed Kitan dynasty, an officer serving in the Kin army, fled and levied men on his own account. He was ready to add his strength to Jinghis, when the latter sent Antchin Noyon to conclude an alliance against the common enemy. The two men ascended Mount Yen to finish the compact. On the summit they slew a white stallion and a black bull for their sacrifice. Turning then to the north they both held an arrow and broke it. Lyuko pledged his faith to Jinghis, and Antchin, in the name of his master, swore to uphold the Kitan prince against the Kin sovereign.

There was need of prompt help, since an army sixty thousand in number was marching to annihilate Lyuko. Gold and high dignities were promised to him who should bring the rebel's head to the Emperor. Jinghis sent three thousand warriors. With these, and his own troops, Lyuko defeated the Emperor's army, and took all its baggage, which he sent to Jinghis, and received then a new reinforcement. Chepé Noyon was despatched to give aid in winning the land of the Kitans, and he gave it successfully. Master now among the Kitans, who rushed in great crowds to him,

Lyuko, with the consent of Jinghis, proclaimed himself King of Liao.

In 1213 Jinghis resumed his activity in China, and again there was slaughter on all sides. The Mongol armies swept on till they almost touched the gates of Chong tu, where bloody scenes were enacted. The year before, Hushaku, the commander, had been stripped of his office and exiled. He was placed in command now in spite of protests from the governor, Tuktani, and others. Hushaku took command north of Chong tu, and, though the Mongols were near him, he passed his time mainly in hunting. Enraged because the Emperor cast blame on this conduct, he took a revenge which he had planned since his own reinstatement. He spread a report that Tuktani was rousing rebellion, and feigned that he, Hushaku, had been summoned to the city to repress it. Fearing military opposition he raised a false alarm to mask his real object. Horsemen rushed in hot haste to the city declaring that Mongols had come to the suburbs. Hushaku sent for Tuktani, the governor, as if to take counsel, and then with his own hand he slew him. Next he replaced the guard of the Emperor with his personal followers, and transferred to another edifice the Emperor, who was slain that same day by a eunuch.

Hushaku wished supreme power for himself, but saw soon that his plans were impossible. The throne fell to Utubu, the late monarch's brother.

Chepé Noyon had returned from the Kitans and was marching on the capital at that time. Hushaku had a wound in the foot, so he sent Kaoki to meet the Mongols, and threatened death should he come back defeated. Kaoki was forced to retreat on Chong tu, after desperate fighting. Fearing death from his chief he resolved to anticipate, and rushed to seize his superior and slay him. Hushaku tried to escape, but fell from his own garden wall while climbing it. Kaoki's people seized the man and then cut his head off. Kaoki grasped the head, bore it in hot haste to the palace, and asked for judgment immediately. The Emperor not only gave pardon, but made Kaoki chief commander.

While the Mongols were attacking the Kin Empire in the north, Tangut was attacking on the west, and in 1213 took King chiu, a border city.

Tangut and China had passed eighty years in mutual good feeling and friendship when the Tangut sovereign, attacked by Jinghis for the third time, asked aid from the Kin sovereign, but having failed to receive it, made an agreement (1210) with the Mongols, and severed relations with China. The Empire was weakened by defections so numerous that Jinghis Khan formed fifty-six brigades of men with officers and generals who had passed from the Chinese to his service. These were joined to his army, and now began an attack on all those lands bounded on the west and south by the Hoang Ho or Yellow River and on the east by the Hoang Hai or Yellow Sea, and forming the provinces of Shan si, Pe che li and Shan tung.

The Mongols sacked ninety flourishing cities, and in all that rich and great region there were only nine places which, through self-defence, escaped ruin. The booty was immense in gold and silk stuffs, in captives male and female, and in horses and cattle.

This great raid took place in the first months of 1214. All the Mongol armies were assembled with their booty in April of that year, at a place some leagues west of Chong tu. Jinghis would permit no attack on that capital. To the Emperor he sent two officers with the following message: " All places north of the Hoang Ho are mine, save Chong tu, which is all that remains in thy service. Heaven has brought thee down to this impotence; were I to harass thee still further I should dread Heaven's anger. Wilt thou treat my army well, and satisfy the generals? "

Kaoki wished to attack, but the counsels of other men triumphed. Envoys were sent to the invader, and peace was concluded. Jinghis received as wife the daughter of Chong hei, the late Emperor, with immense gifts in gold and precious objects. Five hundred youths, as many maidens, and three thousand horses went forth with his bride to the conqueror.

Peace now concluded with Jinghis, Utubu proclaimed complete amnesty to all, but not feeling safe, he left his heir in Chong tu, and set out for Pien king, the present Kai fong fu, better known as Nan king, on the southern bank of the Hoang Ho. On the way he attempted to deprive the Kara Kitans in his escort of the horses and arrows which had been given them. They revolted immediately, chose as leader one Choda and turned then toward Chong tu. Two leagues from the capital Choda met armed resistance, and though victorious, he sent envoys at once to Jinghis. These envoys tendered submission, and asked for aid straightway.

The Mongol Khan did not hesitate; he sent a division of Mongols under Samuka, and a division of Jutchis under Mingan, with orders to join the Kara Kitans and capture the capital. Mukuli, the best Mongol leader in China, was sent at the same time to strengthen Lyuko, from whom a Kin army had retaken the greater part of his kingdom.

When Utubu heard of this new Mongol inroad he summoned his son to Nan king immediately. Chong tu, the capital, was poorly provisioned, the Mongols were near it, their ferocity was famous; the besieged were in terror. Utubu hurried forward a great transport of food under Li ing, with a numerous army. The Mongols attacked this strong army. Li ing, who was drunk when they fell on him, was killed. The battle was lost, and the transport was seized and swept off by the victors. At news of this dreadful disaster the troops of two other Kin generals dispersed and the men went home to their families.

Connection with the city was broken. The investment was merciless; want came, and next famine, with hunger so cruel that the dead were devoured, and then living men killed to be eaten. Fu sing, the governor, proposed to Chin chong, the commandant, to attack the Mongols with every force in the city, and die arms in hand or else conquer. Chin chong had not this view of duty. Fu sing, unwilling to witness the loss of the city in which he was governor, made ready to die with propriety. He gave all he had to his servitors, took poison, and ended his earthly existence.

Chin chong hastened then to escape before the Mongols could enter. The Imperial princesses implored him to take them from the city, and save them, but, not wishing to hamper his flight, Chin chong asked some time to prepare for their journey. Once beyond the city, however, he fled and left those poor princesses to the Mongols. A great slaughter took place in the capital. The palace was fired, and burned, as is said, a whole month and even longer. Jinghis sent three officers to receive Imperial plunder, and give due praise to Mingan for his siege work.

Mingan had hardly captured Chong tu when Jinghis sent Samuka with ten thousand men to fall on Nan king and capture the Emperor. Samuka marched up so close to the city that he was only two leagues from it, but his troops being few, he was forced to retreat empty-handed. He made a second attempt the year following and was nearer success without reaching it.

Meanwhile the Kin dynasty was approaching its doom, and the day of extinction.

In the spring of 1216 Jinghis, from his home on the Kerulon, again sent Subotai against the brother and three sons of Tukta Bijhi, the last Khan of the Merkits. Tuguchar was to help should the need come. Subotai met the Merkits near the Jem River in the Altai and defeated them. Two sons of Tukta Bijhi and Kutu, his brother, were slain in the action; the third son, Kultuk Khan, a great archer, was captured and taken to Juchi, eldest son of Jinghis. When Juchi asked for a proof of his skill, the young man sent an arrow into a goal, and then split that first arrow with a second one. Juchi begged his father to spare this Kultuk,[1] but in vain. This great archer, the last son of Tukta Bijhi, had to die like the others.

While the Mongol Khan was in China, Baitulu, who was chief of the Tumats, withdrew from obedience. At command of Jinghis, Boroul marched in 1217 against the Tumats and crushed them, but lost his own life in the conflict, which was close and very bitter.

Jinghis had asked aid of the Kirghis. But they too rose against him, and Juchi was sent to reduce this recalcitrant people. He did the work thoroughly before leaving the upper waters of the Irtish and the Yenissei.

In 1214 Mukuli had been sent, as we remember, to the Kitans, whose country had been greatly overrun by Kin armies. During the two years which followed, this best of all Mongol leaders won back that whole region by excellent strategy, finesse, and grand fighting. This work was indispensable in the conquest of China. During 1217 this great general appeared before Jinghis encamped then on the Tula. Mukuli was rewarded beyond all other generals up to that day, and after it. Jinghis praised him in public, lauded his great mental gifts, and his services, called him Kwe Wang, or prince in the Empire, and made this title hereditary. He created him lieutenant commanding in China, and gave him a seal made of gold as a sign of authority. "I have conquered the North," said Jinghis, "subdue thou the South for me." And

[1] One of the faults with which Jinghis reproached Juchi was tenderness.

he dismissed him with an army of Mongols and Kitans, with the Jutchis, or Manchus, to help them.

In 1218 Jinghis marched on Tangut for the fourth time and brought it to obedience. During that year he received the submission of Corea. Next his activity was turned to a new side, and soon we shall see the opening scenes in that mighty movement begun by Jinghis and continued by his descendants, and still later resumed by his relative, the tremendous Timur, that World Shaking Limper and father of the Mongol rulers of India.

The first place which called the Grand Khan was Kara Kitai on the west, then conterminous with his own growing Empire. Kara Kitai had the following origin: When Kitan rule in North China was overthrown by the Kins, Yeliu Tashi, a relative of the last Kitan Emperor, and also his leading commander, took farewell of his sovereign in 1123, and with two hundred men journeyed westward. Governors and chiefs of tribes in those Chinese provinces through which he passed showed him homage as a descendant of Apaki, and gave armed warriors to strengthen him. At the head of these and his own men, he went farther. Bilik, prince of the Uigurs, from whom he asked a passage, went out to receive him at the boundary, with a large gift of sheep, horses, and camels. Bilik gave also as hostages a number of his sons and grandsons, and recognized the renowned man as overlord.

Yeliu conquered Kashgar, Yarkend, Khotan and Turkistan. Turkistan was at that time under Nahmud Khan, the twentieth prince of his dynasty, a ruler claiming descent from Afrasiab, so famous in Persian story. Nahmud was reduced to the possession of Transoxiana, and, as this region too was attacked somewhat later by Kara Kitans, he became Yeliu's vassal. Kwaresm met soon the same fate as Transoxiana; Yeliu's troops brought sword and flame to it, and Atsiz, the second prince of the dynasty of the Kwaresmian Shahs, obtained peace by paying thirty thousand gold coins for it yearly.

When Yeliu had brought under his dominion all regions between the Yaxartes and the Gobi desert, and between the headwaters of the Irtish and the Pamir highlands, he took the title of Gurkhan of Kara Kitai, and fixed his chief residence at Bela Sagun on the

next large stream east of the Yaxartes River. In 1136, while
preparing for war against the Kin sovereigns to win back the
Empire which they had snatched from his family, he died, leaving
only one son, then a minor. Till 1142 this son was under the
tutelage of his mother. Dying in 1155 he left a son, Chiluku, for
whom his aunt, Pussuen, was regent till 1167 when he came to
majority. When the son of the last Naiman ruler came in 1208
to seek an asylum in Kara Kitai, Chiluku was still ruling. He
showed the fleeing Khan a kind welcome, and gave him his daughter in marriage.

Chiluku was occupied mainly in hunting wild beasts, and in
seeking for pleasure. This weakness caused the defection of
great vassals: the Idikut of the Uigurs; the Khan of Transoxiana;
the Kwaresmian Shah, and now it led his perfidious new son-in-
law to dethrone him.

The Naiman Khan had attracted some of Chiluku's commanders, and on collecting the wreck of his late father's army he
saw himself at the head of considerable forces. To begin his
plot easily he begged leave of the Gurkhan to assemble the scattered remnants of the Naiman army, then wandering through
northeastern lands of the Kara Kitan Empire. These men
might be employed, he said, in Chiluku's service. The weak
and kindly old sovereign consented, gave his daughter's husband
rich presents, and confirmed his title Gutchluk, or the Strong
Man. The false son-in-law went on his mission. From Iwil,
Kayalik and Bishbalik, crowds rushed to his standard. He was
joined by the chief of the Merkits, who had fled before the Mongols.
These men began to win wealth by incursions in every direction.
Further hope of booty caused other bands to follow quickly. Still
Gutchluk could not seize the Empire without an ally, and the
Empire, or at least a large part of it, was his object.

He turned to Shah Mohammed who had withdrawn from subjection to Chiluku, and had received even the homage of Osman,
the Khan ruling then over Transoxiana and Samarkand. Gutchluk asked Shah Mohammed to fall on the Empire, and seize the
western part for this service. The Shah gave a favorable answer.
Meanwhile a Kara Kitan army was despatched to Samarkand by
Chiluku to bring Osman back to obedience. Shah Mohammed
hastened to render aid to his vassal, but before his arrival the

Kara Kitans were recalled to meet Gutchluk, who had now opened war on his father-in-law, the Gurkhan.

While Chiluku's army was absent in Samarkand, Gutchluk seized in Uzkend the state treasures, and hurried then by forced marches to surprise Bela Sagun. Chiluku, though old, took the field promptly in person, and defeated his son-in-law, who retired in despair after losing a large force of warriors who were killed or taken captive.

Meanwhile Shah Mohammed had crossed the western boundary accompanied by Osman, and met the Kara Kitan forces commanded by Tanigu. He attacked these and captured the commander. The defeated troops while marching home robbed their own fellow subjects and plundered without distinction; Bela Sagun, which preferred Mohammed, would not open its gates to them. Besieged by the troops of their own sovereign they fought for sixteen days, hoping daily to see the Shah's army. The city was taken by assault, and the people were slaughtered. Fifty-seven thousand persons perished under the sword edge.

As Kara Kitan treasures had vanished, the state treasury was empty. Mahmud Bai, an immensely rich general who feared for his own wealth and substance, advised the Gurkhan to force a restoration of all that had been seized by Gutchluk and his followers. The army chiefs, unwilling to yield up their plunder, were furious on hearing this proposal. Gutchluk appeared then on a sudden, and seized his father-in-law, the Gurkhan. Once master of the sovereign's person he used sovereign authority, so Chiluku, without power himself, retained a vain title till death took him off two years later.

In 1218 the Mongol Khan marched westward, but sent Chepé Noyon in advance, with an army twenty-five thousand strong, against the Kara Kitan usurper, his enemy. Gutchluk fled from Kashgar with a part of his forces. On entering the city Chepé proclaimed freedom of religion to all men. The inhabitants massacred Gutchluk's warriors, who had been quartered in their houses. Chepé hurried off in pursuit of the fugitive, and never drew bridle till he had hunted him over the Pamir, and caught him in the Badakshan mountains, where he cut his head off.

When Jinghis heard of this he commanded Chepé not to be proud of success, for pride had undone Wang Khan of the Keraits

and the Taiyang of the Naimans, as well as Gutchluk, and brought
ruin to every recent ruler.

This victorious Chepé some years later carried Mongol arms to
Armenia across Georgia and a large part of Russia. He was of
the Yissuts, a Mongol tribe which had fought against Jinghis,
known at that time as Temudjin. On a day Temudjin wrought
a crushing defeat on the Yissuts; Chepé fled with some others to
the mountains, and hid there from death, which he looked on as
certain in case he were captured. One day when Temudjin was out
hunting his beaters inclosed and caught Chepé. The Khan
wished to slay him, but Boörchu, his earliest comrade and one of
his four chosen leaders, begged for a combat with Chepé. Temudjin agreed, and gave him a white muzzled horse for the trial.
Boörchu shot an arrow which failed to reach Chepé. Chepé,
more adroit than his enemy, sent a shaft which brought down the
horse under him, and the next instant he rushed away with lightning speed. Reduced to want some time later Chepé offered his
service to Temudjin, the strong victor. Temudjin knew the man's
worth and accepted his offer. The Khan made Chepé a chief of
ten men to begin with, then of a hundred, later on of a thousand,
and at last of ten thousand warriors.

When Chepé brought back Gutchluk's head he wished to give
a recompense for the white muzzled horse which he killed when
Boörchu attacked him, so in Kashgar he collected a thousand
white muzzled horses and brought them to Jinghis as a present.

CHAPTER VI

THAT immense Kara Kitai, or Black Carthay, or Black China was added to the Mongol dominions which now were conterminous with the Kwaresmian Empire. This Empire, begun on Seljuk ruins, was increased soon by other lands, and in 1219 it extended from the Syr Darya or Yaxartes to the Indus, and from Kurdistan to the great roof of the world, those immense Pamir highlands. The sovereign at the opening of the thirteenth century was Alai ud din Mohammed, great-great-grandson of a Turk slave named Nush Tegin. The master of this slave was a freedman of Melik Shah the Seljuk Sultan, and this freedman transferred Nush Tegin to his sovereign. The slave became cupbearer to Melik Shah, and prefect of Khwaresm at the same time by virtue of his office. In Mohammedan history cases of Turkish slaves seizing sovereignty are frequent. Turkish captives in Persia were highly esteemed and appeared there in multitudes. Throughout the vast regions north and east of the Caspian various Turk tribes fought unceasingly; each seized the children of an enemy whenever the chance came, and sold them in the slave marts. These children, reared in the faith of Mohammed, were trained to arms for the greater part, and became trusted body-guards of princes. They served also as household officials, or managers. Those of them who earned favor gained freedom most frequently, and next the highest places at courts, and in armies. A lucky man might be made governor, and when fortune helped well enough he made himself sovereign.

Turkish slaves grew all-powerful in Moslem lands, till those lands were invaded at last by Turk warriors. Persia, lowered much by Arab conquest, recovered under Bagdad rule in some slight degree, till the eleventh century saw it conquered again by Turk nomads from those immense steppes north and east of the

Caspian. Under the descendants of Seljuk these fierce sons of wild herdsmen pushed their way on to the Propontis and to Palestine; camped in Persia, and in lands lying west of it. These self-seeking, merciless adventurers brought torture, oppression, and brigandage to all people equally, till at last intestine wars and social chaos put an end to Seljuk rule toward the close of the twelfth century.

Kutb ud din Mohammed, son of the manumitted slave, Nush Tejin, and also his successor, won the title of Kwaresmian Shah, a title used before the Arab conquest. Atsiz, son of Kutb ud din, raised arms repeatedly against Sindjar, the son of Melik Shah, and was forced to render tribute to the Gurkhan. When Sindjar died (1157) Il Arslan, son of Atsiz, seized West Khorassan; his son, Tukush, took Persian Irak from Togrul, who fell in battle. By the death of Togrul and Sindjar, both Persian Seljuk lines became extinct.

Tukush obtained investiture at Bagdad from the Kalif, and Persia passed from one line of Turkish tyrants to another. Mohammed, who succeeded his father Tukush, in 1200, seized the provinces of Balkh and Herat and made himself lord of Khorassan. Soon after this Mazanderan and Kerman passed under his power and direction. Mohammed now planned to shake off the authority of the Gurkhan of Kara Kitai, to whom he, and three of his predecessors, had paid yearly tribute. Besides he was urged to this step by Osman, Khan of Samarkand and Transoxiana, who, being also a vassal of the Gurkhan, endured with vexation the insolence of agents who took the tribute in his provinces. Osman promised to recognize Mohammed as his suzerain, and pay the same tribute that he had paid to the Gurkhan. The Shah accepted this offer with gladness; he merely waited for a pretext, which appeared very quickly: An official came to receive the yearly tribute, and seated himself at the Shah's side, the usual place in such cases, though it seemed now that he did so somewhat boldly. Mohammed's pride, increased much by recent victory over Kipchaks living north of the Caspian, would endure this no longer, so in rage he commanded to cut down the agent and hack him to pieces.

After this act Mohammed invaded the lands of the Gurkhan immediately (1208), but was defeated in the ensuing battle, and captured with one of his officers. The officer had the wit to declare that the Shah, whose person was unknown in those regions, was a slave of his. In a short time the amount of ransom for the officer was settled; he offered to send his slave to get the sum needed. This offer was taken and an escort sent with the slave to protect him. Thus did Mohammed return in servile guise to his dominions, where reports of his death had preceded him. In Taberistan his brother, Ali Shir, had proclaimed his own rule, and his uncle, the governor of Herat, was taking sovereign power in that region.

The following year Mohammed and Osman, the Samarkand ruler, made a second attack on the Gurkhan. Crossing the Syr Darya at Tenakit, they met their opponents, commanded by Tanigu, and won a victory.

They conquered a part of the country as far as Uzkend, and instated a governor. The news of this sudden success caused immense joy in the Kwaresmian Empire. Embassies were sent by neighboring princes to congratulate the victor. After his name on the shield was added " Shadow of God upon earth." People wished to add also " Second Alexander," but he preferred the name Sindjar, since the Seljuk prince Sindjar had reigned forty-one years successfully. After his return the Shah gave his daughter in marriage to Osman, and the Gurkhan's lieutenant in Samarkand was replaced by a Kwaresmian agent. Soon, however, Osman was so dissatisfied with this agent that he gave back his allegiance to the Gurkhan, and killed the Kwaresmians in his capital.

Mohammed, enraged at this slaughter, marched to Samarkand, stormed the city, and for three days and nights his troops did naught else but slay people and plunder; then he laid siege to the fortress and captured it. Osman came out dressed in a grave shroud; a naked sword hung from his neck down in front of him. He fell before Mohammed and begged for life abjectly. The Shah would have spared him, but Osman's wife, the Shah's daughter, rushed in and demanded the death of her husband. He had preferred an earlier wife, the daughter of the Gurkhan, and had forced her, the Shah's daughter, to serve at a feast that detested and inferior woman. Osman had to die, and with him died his whole family, including the daughter of the Gurkhan.

Mohammed joined all Osman's lands to the Empire, and made Samarkand a new capital. He further increased his Empire by a part of the kingdom of Gur, which extended from Herat to the sacred river of India, the Ganges.

After the death, in 1205, of Shihab ud din, fourth sovereign of the Gur line, his provinces passed under officers placed there as prefects. When Mohammed took Balkh and Herat, Mahmud, nephew of Shihab, kept merely Gur the special domain of the family, and even for this he was forced to give homage to the Kwaresmian monarch. Mahmud had reigned seven years in that reduced state when he was killed in his own palace. Public opinion in this case held the Shah to be a murderer, and beyond doubt with full justice.

Ali Shir, the Shah's brother, who had proclaimed himself sovereign so hurriedly when Mohammed was returning, disguised as a slave, from his war against the Gurkhan, was now at the Gur capital; he declared himself Mahmud's successor and begged the Shah to confirm him as vassal. Mohammed sent an officer, as it seemed, for this ceremony, but when Ali Shir was about to put on the robe of honor sent him the officer swept off his head with a sword stroke, and produced thereupon the command of his master to do so. After this revolting deed the Gur principality was joined to Mohammed's dominion (1213).

Three years later, 1216, Mohammed won Ghazni from a Turk general once a subject of Shihab ud din. This Turk had seized the province at the dissolution of Gur dominion. In the archives of Ghazni the Shah came on letters from the Kalif Nassir at Bagdad to the Gur Khans, in which he gave warning against the Kwaresmian Shahs, and incited to attack them, advising a junction with the Kara Kitans for that purpose.

These letters roused the Shah's wrath to the utmost. The Kalif, Nassir, who ascended the throne in 1180, had labored without success, though unceasingly, to stop Kwaresmian growth and aggression. He could not employ his own forces to this end, since he had none. The temporal power of the Prophet's successors had shrunk to the narrow limits of Kuzistan and Arabian Irak. The other parts of their once vast dominions had passed to various dynasties whose sovereigns were supposed to receive lands in fief from the Kalif. If these sovereigns asked for investiture it was simply for religious, or perhaps more correctly, for political reasons.

Outside the bounds of their own little state the Abbasid Kalifs had only two emblems of sovereignty : their names were mentioned in public prayer throughout Islam, and were stamped on the coins of all Moslem Commonwealths. They were not masters even in their own capital always.

When the Seljuk Empire, composed at that time of Persian Irak alone, was destroyed by disorder under Togrul its last Sultan, the Kalif, a man of quick mind and adventurous instincts, did much to bring on the dissolution of the tottering state, through his intrigues, and by calling in Tukush, the Kwaresmian monarch. He had hoped to win Persian Irak, but when Tukush had won that great province he would cede not a foot of it to any man. The Kalif saw himself forced to invest a new line with the sanction of sacredness, a line which threatened Bagdad far more than that which he had helped so industriously to ruin.

When Mohammed succeeded Tukush, Nassir roused Ghiath ud din of Gur to oppose him. This prince, lord already of Balkh and Herat, desired all Khorassan, and began war to win it. His death followed soon after. Shihab ud din, the next ruler, continued the struggle but lost his whole army, which was slaughtered and crushed in the very first battle. When at Ghazni, Mohammed found proof of the Kalif's intrigues, he despatched to Nassir an envoy; through this envoy he demanded the title of Sultan for himself; a representative in Bagdad as governor; and also that his name be mentioned in public prayers throughout Islam. Nassir refused these demands and expressed great surprise that Mohammed, not content with his own immense Empire, was coveting also the capital of the Kalif.

On receiving this answer Mohammed resolved to strip the Abbasids of the succession, or Kalifat. To do this he must obtain first a sanctioning fetva from Mohammedan theologians (the Ulema). So he proposed to that body the following questions : " May a monarch whose entire glory consists in exalting God's word and destroying the foes of true faith, depose a recalcitrant Kalif, and replace him by one who is deserving, if the Kalifat belongs by right to descendants of Ali, and if the Abbasids have usurped it, and if besides they have always omitted one among the first duties, the duty of protecting the boundaries of Islam, and waging sacred wars to bring unbelievers to the true faith, or, if they will not accept the true faith, to pay tribute ? ''

The Ulema declared that in such cases deposition was justified. Armed with this decision the Shah recognized Ali ul Muluk of Termed, a descendant of Ali, as Kalif, and ordered that in public prayers the name of Nassir be omitted. The Shah assembled an army to carry out the sentence against Nassir.

Ogulmush, a Turk general who had subdued Persian Irak and then rendered fealty to Mohammed, was murdered at direction of the Kalif, under whose control a number of Assassins had been placed by their chieftain at Alamut. In Persian Irak the name of the Shah was dropped from public prayers, after the slaying of Ogulmush. The princes of Fars and Azerbaidjan hastened promptly to seize upon Irak, at the instance of Nassir. Sád, prince of Fars, was taken captive, but secured freedom by ceding two strongholds, and promising the third of his annual income as tribute. Euzbek of Azerbaidjan fled after defeat, and the Shah would not pursue, as the capture of two rulers in the space of one year was unlucky. Euzbek, on reaching home, sent envoys with presents, and proclaimed himself a vassal. Mohammed annexed Irak to the Empire, and moved his troops on toward Bagdad.

Nassir sent words of peace to his enemy, but those words had no influence, and the march continued. Nassir strove to strengthen Bagdad and defend it, while Mohammed was writing diplomas, which turned Arabian Irak, that whole land of which Bagdad was the capital, into military fiefs and tax-paying districts.

The Shah's vanguard, fifteen thousand strong, advanced toward Heulvan by the way of the mountains, and was followed soon by a second division of the same strength. Though the time was early autumn, snow fell for twenty days in succession, the largest tents were buried under it; men and horses died in great numbers, both when they were marching through those mountains and when they halted. A retreat was commanded at last when advance was impossible. Turks and Kurds then attacked the retreating forces so savagely that the ruin of the army was well nigh total. This was attributed by Sunnite belief to Divine anger for that impious attack on the person of the Kalif.

The reports of Mongol movements alarmed the Shah greatly and he hastened homeward, first to Nishapur, and later on to

Bukhara, where he received the first envoys from Jinghis Khan, his new neighbor.

It is well to go back to the time when the Shah chose a new Kalif from among the descendants of Ali, the cousin and son-in-law of Mohammed. In the Moslem world there are seventy-three or more sects, varying in size and degree of importance, but the two great divisions of Islam are the Sunnite and Shiite, which differ mainly on the succession. Among Sunnites the succession was from Abbas, the uncle of Mohammed the Prophet of Islam; that is the succession which took place in history. Among Shiites the succession which, as they think, should have taken place, but which did not, was that through Ali, the husband of Fatima, the daughter of Mohammed.

The Shiites of Persia thought that the day of justice had come after six centuries of abasement and waiting, and that the headship of Islam would be theirs through the accession of Ali ul Muluk of Termid to the Kalifat. In their eyes the Kwaresmian Shah had become an agent of Allah, a sacred person. His act created an immense effect throughout Persia, and certainly no less in the capital of Islam at Bagdad, where the Kalif Nassir called a council at once to find means of defence against so dreadful an enemy as Shah Mohammed. After long discussion, one sage among those assembled declared that Jinghis Khan, whose fame was sounding then throughout Western Asia, was the man to bring the raging Shah to his senses.

The Kalif, greatly pleased with this statement, resolved to send an envoy, but the journey was perilous, since every road to the Mongols lay through Shah Mohammed's dominions. Should the envoy be taken and his message read, the Shah, roused by resentment and anger, would spare no man involved in the plot, least of all Kalif Nassir and his servants. To avoid this chance, they shaved the envoy's head and wrote out, or branded, his commission upon it. His skull was then covered with paint, or a mixture of some kind. The entire message to Jinghis was fixed well in the mind of the envoy, and he set out on his journey.

After four months of hard traveling he reached Mongol head-quarters, delivered his message in words, and was admitted soon after to the Khan of the Mongols in secret. The envoy's head was shorn a second time and the credentials traced with fire on his crown became visible. There was branded in also an invitation to invade the Kwaresmian Empire, and destroy the reigning dynasty.

Jinghis meditated over this invitation. The thought of conquering a new Empire did not leave him, but as he had spoken not long before with its ruler in friendship, he waited till a reason to justify attack should present itself.

In 1216–17 in Bukhara, as mentioned already, Shah Mohammed received three envoys from Jinghis; these men brought ingots of silver, musk, jade and costly white robes of camels' hair, all creations and products of Central Asia, sent as presents to the Kwaresmian sovereign. "The great Khan has charged us," said the envoys, " to give this message: ' I salute thee! I know thy power and the great extent of thy Empire. Thy reign is over a large part of the earth's surface. I have the greatest wish to live in peace with thee; I look on thee as my most cherished son. Thou art aware that I have subdued China, and brought all Turk nations north of it to obedience. Thou knowest that my country is swarming with warriors; that it is a mine of wealth, and that I have no need to covet lands of other sovereigns. I and thou have an equal interest in favoring commerce between our subjects.' "

This message was in fact a demand on Mohammed to declare himself a vassal, since various degrees of relationship were used among rulers in Asia to denote corresponding degrees of submission.

The Shah summoned one of the envoys in the night-time. " Has Jinghis Khan really conquered China? " asked he. "There is no doubt of that," said the envoy. " Who is this who calls me his son? How many troops has he? " The envoy, seeing Mohammed's excitement, replied that Mongol forces were not to be compared with his in any case. The Shah was calmed, and when the time came he dismissed the envoys with apparent good feeling and friendliness. When they reached the boundary of the Shah's land they were safe, for wherever Jinghis Khan became sovereign there was safety for travelers immediately, even in places where robbery had been the rule for many ages.

Since Kara Kitai had fallen, Mohammed's possessions reached the heart of Central Asia, and touched the land of the Uigurs, now tributary to Jinghis, hence commercial relations were direct and of very great value. Soon after the Khan's envoys had made their visit, a party of between four and five hundred merchants from Mongolian places arrived at Otrar on the Syr Daryá. Inaldjuk, the governor of the city, tempted by the rich stuffs and wares which those strangers had brought with them, imprisoned the whole party, and declared to the Shah that the men were spies of the Mongol sovereign. The Shah gave command to slay them in that case immediately, and Inaldjuk obeyed without waiting. When news of this terrible slaughter was borne to Jinghis he wept with indignation as he heard it, and went straightway to a mountain top where he bared his head, put his girdle about his neck, and fell prostrate. He lay there imploring Heaven for vengeance, and spent three days and nights, it is stated, imploring and prostrate. He rose and went down then to hurl Mongol strength at the Kwaresmian Empire.

The request of the Kalif of Islam ran parallel now with the wish of the Mongols. But before striking the Empire, Jinghis had resolved to extinguish Gutchluk, his old enemy, the son of Baibuga, late Taiyang of the Naimans. Meanwhile he sent three envoys to the Shah with this message: " Thou didst give me assurance that thou wouldst not maltreat any merchant from my land. Thou hast broken thy word! Word breaking in a sovereign is hideous. If I am to believe that the merchants were not slain at Otrar by thy order, send me thy governor for punishment; if thou wilt not send him, make ready for conflict."

Shah Mohammed, far from giving Jinghis Khan satisfaction, or offering it, slew Bajra, the first envoy, and singed off the beards of the other two. If Mohammed had wished to punish or yield up Inaldjuk he could not have done so, for the governor was a kinsman of Turkan Khatun, the Shah's mother, and also of many great chiefs in the Kwaresmian army.

And now it is important to explain the position of Turkan Khatun, the unbending, savage mother of Mohammed. This woman was a daughter of Jinkeshi, Khan of the Baijut tribe of Kankali Turks; she married Tukush, the Kwaresmian Shah, and became then the mother of Shah Mohammed. A large number of Kankali chiefs who were related to Turkan followed her with their tribesmen to serve in the Kwaresmian Empire.

The influence of this relentless, strong-willed woman, and the valor of Turkish warriors raised those chiefs to the highest rank among military leaders; their power was enormous, since commanders of troops governed with very wide latitude. Amid this aristocracy of fighters the power of the sovereign was uncertain; he was forced to satisfy the ambition of men who saw in all things their own profit only. The troops controlled by those governors were the scourge of peaceful people; they ruined every region which they lived in or visited.

Turkan Khatun, the head of this military faction, not only equalled her son in authority, but often surpassed him. When two orders of different origin appeared in any part of the Empire, the date decided which had authority; that order was always carried out on which the date was most recent, and the order of recent date was the order of that watchful woman. When Mohammed won a new province he always assigned a large part to the appanage of his mother. She employed seven secretaries at all times, men distinguished for ability. The inscription on her decrees was " Protectress of the world and the faith, Turkan, queen of women." Her device was: " God alone is my refuge." " Lord of the world " was her title. The following example shows clearly the character of the Shah's mother: She had obtained from Mohammed the elevation of Nassir ud din, a former slave of hers, to the position of vizir, or prime minister of the Empire; soon the Shah came to hate the man, for personal and also other reasons. His ability was small, and his greed without limit. At Nishapur the Shah appointed a new judge, one Sadr ud din, and forbade him to give the vizir any presents. Friends, however, warned the judge not to neglect this prime dignitary, so he sent Nassir ud din a sealed purse containing four thousand gold pieces. The Shah, who was watching both judge and vizir, caused the latter to send the purse to him. It was sent straightway, and the seal was intact on it. The judge was summoned, and when he appeared the Shah asked before witnesses what gift he had made the vizir; he denied having made any, persisted in denial, and swore by the head of his sovereign that he had not given one coin to the minister. The Shah had the purse brought; the judge was deprived of his dignity. The vizir was sent home without office to his patroness.

Nassir ud din went back to the Shah's mother. On the way he decided every case that men brought him. On the vizir's approach Turkan Khatun ordered people of all ranks and classes to go forth and meet him. The vizir grew more insolent now than he had been. The Shah sent an officer to bring the recalcitrant minister's head to him. When the officer came to her capital, Turkan Khatun sent him to the vizir, who was then in the divan and presiding. She had given the officer this order: " Salute the vizir in the Shah's name, and say to him: ' I have no vizir except thee, continue in thy functions. No man in my Empire may destroy thee, or fail in respect to thee.' "

The officer carried out the command of the woman. Nassir ud din exercised his authority in defiance of Mohammed; he could do so since Turkan Khatun upheld him, and she had behind her a legion of her murderous kinsmen. The sovereign, who had destroyed so many rulers unsparingly, had not the power or the means to manage one insolent upstart who defied him.

The murder of the merchants in Otrar was followed soon by such a tempest of ruin as had never been witnessed in Asia or elsewhere. Shah Mohammed had mustered at Samarkand a large army to move against Gutchluk, whom he wished to bring down to subjection or destroy altogether, but hearing that a body of Merkits was advancing through Kankali regions lying north of Lake Aral, he marched to Jend straightway against them, and learned upon reaching that city, that those Merkits, being allies of Gutchluk, were hunted by Jinghis, and that Gutchluk himself had been slain by the Mongols.

He returned swiftly to Samarkand for additional forces, and following the tracks of both armies, found a field strewn with corpses, among which he saw a Merkit badly wounded; from this man the Shah learned that the Jinghis had gained a great victory, and gone forward.

One day later Mohammed came up with them and formed his force straightway to attack them. The Mongol leader (perhaps Juchi) declared that the two states were at peace, and that he had commands to treat the Shah's troops with friendliness; he even offered a part of his booty and prisoners to Mohammed. The latter refused these and answered: " If Jinghis has ordered thee not to meet me in battle, God commands me to fall on thy forces. I wish to inflict sure destruction on infidels and thus earn Divine favor."

The Mongols, forced to give battle, came very near victory. They had put Mohammed's left wing to flight, pierced the center where the Shah was, and would have dispersed it, but for timely aid brought by Jelal ud din, the Shah's son, who rushed from the right and restored the battle, which lasted till evening and was left undecided.

The Mongols lighted vast numbers of camp fires, and retired in the dark with such swiftness that at daybreak they had made two days' journey.

After this encounter the Shah knew Mongol strength very clearly. He told intimates that he had never seen men fight as they had.

Jinghis, having ended Gutchluk and his kingdom (1218), summoned his own family and officers to a council where they discussed war with Mohammed, and settled everything touching this enterprise and its management. That same autumn the Mongol conqueror began his march westward, leaving the care of home regions to his youngest brother. He spent all the following summer near the Upper Irtish, arranging his immense herds of horses and cattle. The march was resumed in the autumn, when he was joined by the prince of Almalik, the Idikut of the Uigurs, and by Arslan, Khan of the Karluks.

Shah Mohammed was alarmed by the oncoming of this immense host of warriors, more correctly this great group of armies, though his own force was large, since it numbered four hundred thousand. His troops were in some ways superior to the Mongols, but they lacked iron discipline and blind confidence in leaders; they lacked also that experience of hardship, fatigue and privation, that skill in desperate fighting, which made the Mongols not merely a terror, but, at that time, invincible. The Kwaresmian armies were defending a population to which they were indifferent, and which they were protecting, hence victory gave scant rewards in the best case, while the Mongols, in attacking rich, flourishing countries, were excited by all that can rouse human greed, or tempt wild cupidity. The disparity in leaders was still more apparent. On the Mongol side was a chief of incomparable genius in all that he was doing; on the other side a vacillating sovereign with warring and wavering counsels. The Shah had been crushing and assassinating rulers all his reign, and now he feared to meet a man whom he had provoked by his outrages. Instead of concentrating forces and meeting the enemy, he scattered his men among all the cities of Transoxiana, and then withdrew and kept far from the fields of real struggle. Some ascribed this to the advice of his generals, others to his faith in astrologers, who declared that the stars were unfavorable, and that no battle should be risked till they changed their positions. It is also reported that Jinghis duped the Shah, and made him suspect his own leaders. The following is one of the stories:

A certain Bedr ud din of Otrar, whose father, uncle and other kinsmen had been slain by Mohammed, declared to Jinghis that he wished to take vengeance on the Shah, even should he lose his own soul in so doing, and advised the Grand Khan to make use of the quarrels kept up by Mohammed with his mother. In view of this Bedr ud din wrote a letter, as it were, from Mohammed's generals to Jinghis, and composed it in this style: " We came from Turkistan to Mohammed because of his mother. We have given him victory over many other rulers whose states have increased the Kwaresmian Empire. Now he pays his dear mother with ingratitude. This princess desires us to avenge her. When thou art here, we shall be at thy orders."

Jinghis so arranged that this letter was intercepted. The tale is, that the Shah was deceived by it and distrusted his generals, hence separated them each from the others, and disposed them in various strong cities. It is more likely by far, that he and they, after testing Mongol strength, thought it better to fight behind walls than in the open. They thought also, no doubt, that the Mongols, after pillaging the country and seizing many captives, would retire with their booty.

The Shah was light-minded and ignorant. He knew not with whom he was dealing. He had not studied the Mongols, and could not have done so; he had no idea whatever of Jinghis Khan and could not acquire it; he knew not the immense power of his system, and the far reaching nature of his wishes.

Jinghis arrived at the Syr Daryá with his army, and arranged all his troops in four great divisions. The first he fixed near Otrar and placed two of his sons, Ogotai and Jagatai, in command of it; the second, commanded by his eldest son, Juchi, was to act against the other cities, from Jend to Lake Aral; the third division he directed against Benakit on the river, south of Jend. While the three divisions were taking these cities on the Syr Daryá, Jinghis himself moved toward Bokhara to bar Shah Mohammed from the Transoxiana, and prevent him from reinforcing any garrison between the two rivers.

Otrar was invested late in November, 1218. The walls had been strengthened, and the city, with its fortress, provisioned very carefully. The strong garrison had been increased by ten thousand horsemen. After a siege of five months the troops and the citizens were discouraged, and the commander thought it best to surrender, but Inaldjuk, the governor, could not hope for his life, since he was the man who had slain the Mongol merchants; hence, he would not hear of surrender. He would fight, as he said, to the death, for his sovereign. The chief of the horsemen felt differently, and led out his best troops in the night to escape, but was captured. He and they offered then to serve the besiegers. The Mongols inquired about conditions in the city, and, when the chief had told what he knew, they informed him that he and his men, being unfaithful to their master, could not be true to another. They thereupon slew him, and all who were with him.

The city was taken that day, April, 1219, and its inhabitants driven to the country outside, so that the captors might pillage the place in absolute freedom. Inaldjuk, the governor, withdrew with twenty thousand men to the fortress, and fought for two months in that stronghold. When the Mongols burst in he had only two men left; with these he retired to a terrace. The two men at his side fell soon after. When his arrows were gone he hurled brickbats. The besiegers had orders to seize the man living. He struggled like a maniac, but they caught and bound him at last, and bore him to the camp before Samarkand. Jinghis had molten silver poured into his ears and eyes to avenge the slaughtered merchants. The surviving inhabitants of Otrar were spared but the fortress was levelled.

Juchi, before marching on Jend, went to Signak and asked that the gates be thrown open. Scarcely had the message been given when the furious inhabitants tore Hassan Hadji, Juchi's envoy, to pieces and called on God's name as they did so.

Juchi gave the order at once to attack, and forbade his men to cease fighting till the city was captured. Fresh troops relieved those who were wearied. After seven days of storming the Mongols burst in and slew every soul in that city.

Juchi made a son of Hassan Hadji commandant of the ruins; then he moved up the river and sacked every place that he visited.

As the Mongols drew near to Jend, Katluk Khan, the commandant, fled in the night time, crossed the Syr Daryá and took the desert road for Urgendj beyond the southern shore of the Oxus. Juchi demanded surrender through Chin Timur his envoy. Deserted by their chief, the people were in doubt what to do, and when Chin Timur came they wished to kill him, but he told them of Signak, and promised to turn aside Mongol vengeance in case they were prudent. The people then freed him, but very soon saw the enemy under the walls, which they thought proof against every besieger. The Mongols scaled those walls quickly, and rushed in from all sides. No hand was raised then against them. The inhabitants were driven to the open country and left nine days and nights there, while the pillage continued. Excepting those who had abused Chin Timur, the people were spared, since they had made no resistance.

Meanwhile a detachment of the army had seized Yengikend, the last town on the river, and Juchi's work was done on the right bank with thoroughness.

The third division of the army moved from Otrar to the left up the river, and attacked Benakit which was garrisoned by Kankalis. At the end of three days the officers wished to capitulate. Their lives were promised them, and they surrendered. The inhabitants were driven from the city. The Turks were taken out to one side, and cut down to the last man, with swords and other weapons. Being warriors whom the Mongols could not trust, they were slaughtered. The artisans were spared and divided among the Mongol army. Unskilled, young, and strong men were taken to assist in besieging; all other people were slain immediately.

The march was continued to Khodjend, and soon the invaders were in front of that city, and storming it. In Khodjend, Timur Melik, a man of great valor, commanded. He took one thousand chosen warriors to a fort on an island far enough from either bank to be safe from stones and arrows. The besiegers were reinforced by twenty thousand Mongols for conflict, and fifty thousand natives

of the country to carry on siege work.   These natives were employed first of all at bearing stones from a mountain three leagues
distant, and building a road from the shore to the fortress in the
river.   Timur Melik meanwhile built twelve covered barges,
protected from fire with glazed earth, which was first soaked in
vinegar.   Every day six of these boats went to each shore and
sent arrows, through openings, at the Mongols.   Night attacks
were made suddenly and wrought much harm on the invaders.

But despite every effort Timur saw that failure would come
if he stayed there.   He was met by preponderant and crushing
numbers at last.   So he put men and baggage in seventy strong
boats and his chosen warriors in the twelve covered barges;
and they sped down the swift river at night by the light of
many torches fixed on the boats of his flotilla.   The boats snapped
a chain stretched across from one bank to the other by Mongols
near Benakit, and passed along, hunted by the enemy on both
sides.

Timur learned now that Juchi had posted a large corps of men
on the two banks, close to Jend, captured recently; he learned
also that balistas were ready and that a bridge of boats had been
made near the same place.   He debarked higher up, therefore, and
took to horse to avoid capture.   Pursued by the enemy, he gave
battle till his baggage was brought near him.   He repeated this
day after day till forced at last to abandon the baggage.   Finally,
having lost all his men, he was alone and pursued by three Mongols.
He had only three arrows left, one of these had no metal point on
it; he shot that and put out an eye of the nearest pursuer.   Then
he cried to the other men: "There are two arrows still in my
quiver, ye would better go back with your eyesight."   They did
so.   Timur Melik made his way to Urgendj, and joined Jelal ud
din, whom he followed till the death of that sovereign.

Meanwhile Jinghis moved against Bokhara with his main
forces and arrived at that city during June of 1219.   On the way
he seized Nur and Charnuk, which he pillaged; then he took
from those places all stalwart men useful in siege work.   Bokhara,
the great city with a garrison of twenty thousand, was invested on
all sides, and attacked by relays of fresh warriors, who gave neither
respite nor rest to it.

After some days the defenders lost hope of success and resolved to burst through in the night time, trusting in that way to save themselves. They fell on the Mongols unexpectedly, and scattered them, but instead of pursuing this advantage and fighting, those escaping defenders hastened forward. The Mongol troops rallied, and hunted the fugitives to the river, where they cut down nearly all of them.

Next morning early, the Ulema and notables came out to give homage to the great Mongol Khan, and open the gates to him. Jinghis rode in, and going to the main mosque of the city entered it on horseback. Dismounting near the minbar, or pulpit, he ascended some steps of it and said to the people who assembled there quickly before him: "The fields now are stripped; feed our horses in this place!"

The boxes which had been used to hold copies of the Koran were taken to the courtyard to hold grain for Mongol horses; the sacred volumes were thrown under the hoofs of those animals and trampled. Skins of wine were brought into the mosque with provisions; jesters and singers of the city were summoned, and while wild warriors were revelling in excesses of all sorts, and shouting songs of their own land and people, the highest chiefs of religion and doctors of law served them as slaves, held their horses and fed them. While thus employed one great man whispered to his neighbor: "Why not implore the Almighty to save us?" "Be silent," said the other, "God's wrath is moving near us; this is no time for beseeching. I fear to pray to the Almighty lest it become worse with us thereby. If life is dear to thee hold their beasts now for the Mongols, and serve them."

From the mosque Jinghis went to the place of public prayer beyond the city, and summoned all people to meet there. He stood in the pulpit and inquired: "Who are the richest men in this multitude?" Two hundred and eighty persons were presented; ninety of these had come from other cities. The Khan commanded all those wealthy persons to draw near, and then he spoke to them. He described the Shah's cruelties and injustice, which had brought on the ruin of their city: "Know," continued he, "that ye have committed dreadful deeds, and the great people of this country are the worst of its criminals. Should ye ask why I speak thus, I answer; I am Heaven's scourge, sent to punish. Had ye not been desperate offenders I should not be standing here now against you." Then he said that he required no one to deliver wealth which was above ground, his men could discover that very easily, but he asked for hidden treasures. The wealthy men were then forced to name their agents, and those agents had to yield up the treasures, or be tortured. All strong men were set to filling the moats encircling the city; even copies of the Koran and furniture of mosques were hurled in to fill ditches. The fortress was stormed and not a man of its defenders found mercy.

When the fortress was taken, all its inhabitants were driven from the city with nothing but the clothes which they had on their bodies. Then began the great pillage. The victors slew all whom they found in any place of hiding. At last Mongol troops were sent out to surround the inhabitants on the plain, and divide them into parties. Deeds were done there which baffle description. Every possible outrage was enacted before those to whom it was most dreadful to be present, and have eyesight. Some had strength to choose death instead of looking at those horrors; among spectators of this kind were the chief judge of the city, and the first Imam, who seeing the dishonor of their women rushed to save them, and perished.

Finally the city was fired; everything wooden was consumed, nothing was left save the main mosque, and a few brick palaces.

Jinghis Khan left the smoking ruins of Bokhara the Noble, to march on Samarkand, which was only five days distant. He passed along the pleasant valley of Sogd, covered at that time with beautiful fields, orchards and gardens and with houses here and there in good number. All inhabitants of Bokhara taken to toil in the coming siege were driven on behind the army. Whoso grew weak on the way or too weary for marching was cut down at once without pity.

Samarkand was one of the great commercial cities of the world. It had a garrison which numbered forty thousand. Both the city and the citadel had been fortified with care, and all men considered that a siege of that place would continue for months, nay, for years perhaps.

The three other army corps appeared now, for every place on the lower river had been taken, and Northern Transoxiana was subjected. These divisions brought with them all captives who were young, firm and stalwart, men who might be of service in siege work; there was an immense host of those people arranged in groups of ten, and each ten had a banner. Jinghis, to impose on the doomed city, paraded his legions before it; cavalry, infantry, and at last those unfortunate captives who had the seeming of regular warriors.

Two days were spent in examining the city defenses and outworks; on the third morning early the Mongol conqueror sounded the onset. A host of brave citizens made a great sally, and at first swept all before them but not being sustained by their own troops, who feared the besiegers, they met a dreadful disaster. The Mongols retired before the onrushing people, who pressed forward with vigor till they fell into ambush; being on foot they were surrounded very quickly and slaughtered before the eyes of the many thousands looking from the walls, and the housetops. This great defeat crushed the hopes of the citizens.

The Kankali troops being Turks believed that the Mongols would treat them most surely as kinsmen. In fact Jinghis had promised, as they thought, to take them to his service. Hence this great multitude, the real strength of the city, issued forth that same day with their leaders, their families, and their baggage, in one word, with all that belonged to them. On the fourth day, just as the storm was to be sounded, the chief men of the city went to the Mongol camp, where they received satisfactory answers concerning themselves with their families and dependents; hence they opened the gates of Samarkand to the conqueror; but they were driven from the city save fifty thousand who had put themselves under the protection of the cadi and the mufti. These fifty thousand were safe-guarded, the others were all slaughtered.

The night following the surrender, Alb Khan, a Turk general, made a sortie from the citadel and had the fortune to break through the Mongols, thus saving himself and those under him. At daybreak the citadel was attacked simultaneously on all sides. That struggle lasted till the evening, when one storming party burst in, and the stronghold was taken. One thousand defenders took refuge in a mosque and fought with desperation. The mosque was fired then, and all were burned to death in it. The Kankalis who had yielded on the third day, that is the first day of fighting, were conducted to a place beyond the city and kept apart from others. Their horses, arms, and outfits were taken from them, and their hair was shaved in front, Mongol fashion, as if they were to form a part of the army. This was a trick to deceive them till the executioners were ready. In one night the Kankalis were murdered to the very last man.

When vast numbers of the citizens had been slaughtered a census was made of the remnant: Thirty thousand persons of various arts, occupations and crafts were given by Jinghis to his sons, his wives, and his officers; thirty thousand more were reserved for siege labor; fifty thousand, after they had paid two hundred thousand gold pieces, were permitted to return to the city, which received Mongol commandants. Requisitions of men were made at later periods repeatedly, and, since few of those persons returned to their homes, Samarkand stood ruined and unoccupied for a long time.

Jinghis Khan so disposed his forces from the first, that Shah Mohammed could not relieve any city between the two rivers; now all those cities were taken, and the forces defending them were slaughtered. The next great work was to seize Shah Mohammed himself, and then slay him, and with him his family.

Thirty thousand chosen men were employed now in chasing the Kwaresmian ruler. Never had a sovereign been hunted like this victim of the Mongols. He fled like a fox, or a hare; he was hunted as if he had been a dreadful wild beast, which had killed some high or holy person, or as if he were some outcast, who had committed a deed which might make a whole nation shudder. But here we must say a few words concerning the hunted man, and explain his position.

CHAPTER VII

FLIGHT AND DEATH OF MOHAMMED

WHILE the Mongols were ruining Northern Transoxiana Mohammed held aloof from every action, and was discouraged so deeply that his weakness affected all people of the Empire. While fortifying Samarkand he passed by the moat one day, and made this remark: "The Mongols are so many that they could fill this moat with their horsewhips." When Jinghis had captured the northern line beyond the Oxus, Mohammed moved southward by way of Naksheb, telling all people to care for themselves, since his troops could not protect them. The diversity of opinions among his commanders and ministers increased his hesitation. The best warriors declared that Transoxiana was lost, but that Khorassan and Irak must be guarded; that troops must be concentrated, a general levy enforced, and the Amu Darya be defended at all costs. Others advised to fall back upon Ghazni, and there meet the Mongols; if beaten the Shah might retire beyond the Indus. This being the most timid course Mohammed favored and chose it; but, joined at Balkh by Amad ul mulk, the vizir, he altered that plan at the instance of Amad, who was prime minister of Rokn ud din, the Shah's son who held Persian Irak as an appanage, and had sent Amad to his father hoping thus to be rid of him.

The position of Amad was of this sort: He wished to be near Shah Mohammed, his protector, and he was drawn toward his birthplace, the home of his family; so he persuaded the Shah to change plans and go to Persian Irak, where he would find men and means to force back the Mongols. Jelal ud din, the best son of Mohammed, in fact the only brave man in the family, was opposed to both projects; he would not talk of retreat, he would stop the invasion at the Oxus. " If thou retire to Irak," said he, " give

113

me thy forces. I will drive back the Mongols, and liberate the
Empire." Every discussion, however, was fruitless; the Shah
treated all his son's reasons as folly. " Success," said Mohammed,
" is fixed from eternity, defeat is averted by a change in the stars,
and not otherwise."

Before he left his position at Balkh Mohammed sent men to
Pendjde, a point north of Termed, to collect information of the
enemy's movements. Tidings came quickly that Bokhara had
been captured, that Samarkand had surrendered. Delaying his
journey no longer, the Shah started off in hot haste through
Khorassan. Most of the troops who went with him were Turks
whose chiefs were his mother's adherents and kinsmen; these
formed a plot very quickly to kill him. Forewarned of their
treachery, Mohammed left his tent during night hours; next morning it was seen to be riddled with arrows. His fears increased
greatly, and he hastened on till he reached Nishap, where he
halted, thinking that the Mongols would not cross the river Oxus
in any case.

From Samarkand Jinghis despatched Chepé with ten thousand,
Subotai with a second ten thousand, and Tuguchar with a third
corps of similar numbers. The order given these was to ride with
all speed to the camp of the Shah. If they found him at the head
of large forces to wait till reinforcements came up to them; if he
had few, to attack and secure him; if fleeing, to pursue, and with
Heaven's help take and keep him; to spare cities which yielded;
to ruin utterly those which resisted.

The pursuing Mongols swept through Khorassan untiringly.
This splendid province had four famous cities: Balkh, Herat,
Merv and Nishapur. Besides these there were others of considerable, though minor, importance. When the Mongols were
near Balkh that city sent forth a deputation with presents and
submission. A Mongol governor was placed in it. Zaveh closed
its gates and refused all supplies; unwilling to lose time there at
siege work the Mongols pressed forward, but since people mounted
the walls then, and stood beating drums and abusing them, they
turned and attacked that foolish city which reviled them. They
stormed the place, put to the sword every man in it, and burned
what they had not the power to take with them.

On and on rode the Mongols. People met on the way to

Nishapur were seized and put to torture till they told what they knew of the fleeing Mohammed. Cities were summoned to surrender; those that surrendered were spared and received new commandants. If cities which resisted were weak, they were stormed; if strong, they were left till a later occasion, since the work then on hand was to capture Mohammed.

When the Shah learned that the enemy had entered Khorassan he left Nishapur with a small escort under pretext of hunting. Consternation filled that place when the truth grew apparent. After the Shah deserted the city the vizir with the mufti and the cadi ruled, pending the arrival of a governor, who was on the way from Urgendj, the Kwaresmian capital. This man died when three days from the end of his journey; his household officials kept his death secret lest the escort might seize all his movable property. One of the regents went forth as if to meet him, and brought in his treasure. The escort, one thousand in number, would not stay in the city, but went in search of Mohammed. Next day those men, when nine miles from Nishapur, were met by a new host of Mongols who attacked very quickly and cut them to pieces.

The city was summoned to open its gates and the three regents gave answer as follows: "When Shah Mohammed is captured, Nishapur will surrender." The first Mongol party that demanded provisions received them and vanished. Day after day new bodies rushed up to the city, received what they asked for and rode away swiftly. At last Chepé came and commanded the vizir, the mufti and cadi to appear at headquarters. Three supposititious men were sent out to meet him with gifts and provisions. The general gave these men the Khan's proclamation in Uigur characters, and this was its import: "O commandants, officials and people! Know ye that Heaven has given me the Empire of the earth, both the east and the west of it. Those who submit will be spared; woe to those who resist, they will be slaughtered with their children, and wives and dependents. Give provisions to all troops that come, and think not to meet water with fire, or to trust in your walls, or the numbers of those who defend them. If ye try to escape utter ruin will seize you."

The three bodies of Mongols, ten thousand each which were speeding on now in pursuit of Mohammed were rushing toward

Irak. Subotai passed through Damegan and Simnan, and crossed the Kumus River. Chepé Noyon, who had gone by Mazanderan, rejoined Subotai at Rayi. This place they took by surprise, and then sacked it.

From Nishapur Mohammed hastened on to Kazvin, where his son Rokn un din had an army; there he took counsel with the leaders of that army which was thirty thousand in number, and sent for Hezerasp, prince of Lur, who advised a retreat across the mountain chain lying between Fars and Lur. The Shah wished to stay in Irak and increase his defense there; he had just stated that wish when news came that Rayi had been taken and plundered. Chiefs and princes fled straightway on hearing this. Each went his own road, and the whole army vanished immediately, so great was the terror inspired by the onrushing Mongols.

The Shah fled for safety to his sons in Karun. On the way Mongol forces were in sight and almost caught him, unwittingly. They sent arrows at the fleeing man though not knowing who he was and wounded the horse which he was riding, but the beast held out and bore him safely to the fortress. Next morning he fled farther along the road lying westward toward Bagdad. Barely had he ridden away when the Mongols, who knew now whose horse they had wounded, rushed in, thinking to seize the hunted man surely. They attacked the fort furiously at first, but learning soon that the Shah had escaped they hurried after him. On the way they met men who professed to be guides dismissed by Mohammed; from these men they heard that he was fleeing to Bagdad. They took the guides then and rushed forward, but the Shah was on a new road at that time. The Mongols soon saw that they had lost his trail, and were tricked, so they cut down the guides and returned to Karun.

Mohammed had fled to Serdjihan, a strong place northeast of Kazvin on a mountain. Seven days he remained there; he then fled to Gilan, and next to Mazanderan, where he appeared stripped of property and almost unattended. The Mongols had preceded him, having sacked two towns already, Amol the capital, and Astrabad a place of much commerce. "Where am I to find safety from Mongols? Is there no spot on earth where I can be free of them?" Such was the cry of Mohammed. "Go to some little

island in the Caspian, that will be the safest place!" said some
of his friends. This advice pleased Shah Mohammed, so he
stopped in a village on the seashore, intending to follow it. He
prayed five times each day in the mosque, had the Koran read
to him and promised God tearfully that justice would reign in
his Empire as never on earth up to that day, should power ever
come to him a second time.

While Mohammed was thus engaged in that village, Mongols
appeared on a sudden. They were guided by Rokn ud din, a
small prince of that region. This man's uncle and cousin had been
killed by Shah Mohammed, who seized their lands in the days of
his insolence and his greedy ambition. Rokn ud din's hatred had
sent him as a guide to the Mongols, and thus he recovered his family inheritance. The Shah had barely time to spring into a boat
and push out from shore when his enemies were upon him. Enraged at the loss of their victim, many horsemen sprang after the
boat, but they failed to reach it and were drowned in the Caspian.

Mohammed, who was suffering gravely from pleurisy and weakness, declared as he sailed from the shore, that after reigning over
many kingdoms and lands he lacked even a few ells of earth for
a resting place. The fallen man reached a small island and was
childishly joyous at finding a safe place of refuge. His house was
a tent with little in it, but the people of the coast brought him
food, and whatever else might be pleasing to the monarch, as they
thought. In return Mohammed gave them brevets of office, or
titles to land which they wrote themselves frequently, since he had
sent most of his small suite to bring his sons to him. Later on,
when Jelal ud din had regained some part of his possessions he
honored all gages of this kind.

The Shah's illness increased, and he lost hope of recovery. His
sons came and then he withdrew from Oslag the inheritance.
"Save Jelal ud din there is none of you who can recover the Empire," declared Mohammed. The failing monarch took his own
sabre which he girded on Jelal ud din, and commanded the younger
brothers to show him obedience. Mohammed breathed his last
some days later, January 10, 1221, and was buried on that island.
There was no cloth for a shroud, so he was buried in another man's
shirt. His funeral was small and the ceremony scant at his burial.
Such was the end which Jinghis gave a great sovereign who, till

his attack on the Kalif of Islam, ruled over a vast country and found success everywhere save in the struggles with his mother.

Before crossing the Oxus, Mohammed directed Turkan Khatun, who governed Urgendj, the modern Khiva, to retire to Mazanderan and live there in the mountains, taking with her his harem.   Jinghis, informed clearly of the quarrels between the Shah and his mother, sent Danishmend, his chancellor, to that relentless, harsh woman, and this was his message: " Thy son is ungrateful, I know that.   If thou agree with me I will not touch Kwaresm, which thou art ruling.   I will give thee, moreover, Khorassan when I win it.   Send a trusty man, he will hear this assurance from my own lips directly."

Turkan Khatun gave no answer, but left Kwaresm as soon as she heard that her son had fled westward.   Before going, however, she put to death all the princes whom the Shah had despoiled and imprisoned; among these were both sons of Togrul, the last Seljuk sultan of Irak; the Balkh prince and his son, the sovereign of Termed; the prince of Bamian; the Vakhsh prince, the two sons of the lord of Signak, and the two sons of Mahmud, last prince of Gur.   She had all these men thrown into the Oxus and drowned, sparing only Omar, Khan of Yazer, who could be of use on her journey, since he knew all the roads which led to his own land and birthplace.   In fact he served the woman well, till they were near Yazer, when his head was cut off at her order, as she had no further use for him.

When Mohammed had fled to Mazanderan he directed his mother, as we have seen, to live in Ilak, the best stronghold in all that great region of mountain.   Later on Subotai, who was hunting Mohammed, left a body of men to invest that strong fortress.   As Ilak was in a rainy, damp climate no reservoirs had been made for dry periods; while the place was invested that happened which came to pass rarely, a dry season.   After a blockade of some months drought forced a surrender.   But just after the Mongols had taken possession, the sky was covered densely with clouds which brought a great rainfall.

Turkan Khatun and the harem were taken to the camp of Jinghis, who was before Talekan at that time and besieging it. She was held captive there strictly.   All the sons of Mohammed found in the harem were put to death promptly.   Two of his daughters were given to Jagatai, who made one of them his concubine, and gave the other as a present to his manager; a third was given as wife to the chancellor, Danishmend. The widow of Osman, Khan of Samarkand, she who had insisted on the execution of her husband, and was the daughter of the Gurkhan, was given in marriage to a dyer, but by another account she was given to Juchi, who had by her afterward several children. Turkan Khatun, the strong, brutal woman, was taken to Kara Kurum, the Mongol capital, where she died eight years later. Just before she was captured a eunuch had urged her to find refuge with Jelal ud din, her own grandson, who was near by, he declared, with a numerous army. Turkan replied that captivity of any kind was sweeter to her than salvation at his hand. Such was the hate which she felt toward her grandson. Nassir ud din, the vizir who had defied Shah Mohammed, was put to death at Talekan with a number of others.

Mohammed's three elder sons made their way to Mangishlak by the Caspian and thence to Urgendj, the Kwaresmian capital. Since the flight of their grandmother the capital had been without rule; in her haste she had left no governor there. Seventy thousand men gathered round the three princes immediately. The commanders, being Kankali Turks, were dissatisfied that Jelal ud din had succeeded his father; they feared his strong will and plotted to kill him. The new Shah saw very clearly that his one chance of safety was flight, and he seized that chance quickly. With three hundred warriors under Timur Melik, that Khodjend commandant who had escaped through the Mongol investment, he fled across the desert to Nessa.

After the capture of Samarkand Jinghis stationed his troops between that place and Naksheb where they spent the spring of 1221 and also the summer. Toward autumn his forces were reorganized thoroughly. Having rested they were strong and now ready for action. The return of Mohammed's sons at Urgendj and the gathering of forces there roused the Khan's vigilance, so he despatched thither an army at once under his sons, Juchi, Jagatai and Ogotai. To cut off retreat toward the Indus he formed a cordon on the southern rim of the desert; a part of this cordon was already near Nessa when Jelal ud din and his party arrived there. He attacked this line of men valiantly, forced it to flight and pushed

on without stopping.   This was the first victory won over Mongols
in the Kwaresmian Empire.   The two younger brothers, hearing
of the advance on Urgendj, set out three days later, but failed of
such fortune as their brother, and perished near Nessa.   Their
heads fixed on lances were borne through Khorassan.

When the Mongol troops arrived before Urgendj, Juchi, who was
in command, sent to the capital a summons to surrender, informing
the people that his father had given him the city and that he did
not wish to injure it in any way.   As no attention was paid to this
summons the siege was begun at once.   The Mongols endeavored
to divert the waters of the Oxus above the town, but with no
success, for the workmen were killed by the garrison.   Quarrels
between Juchi and Jagatai impeded siege work very greatly.
Jinghis, angered by this delay, placed Ogotai in command.   Juchi
was enraged at being thus superseded by a younger brother, but
he could not withdraw.   The siege lasted seven months and gained
great renown through the desperate defense made by citizens.
After the general assault which decided the fate of the city the
people continued resistance with fury; driven from one street
they fought in the next.   Women and even children took part in
these struggles, which continued seven days and nights without
ceasing.   At last the inhabitants asked to capitulate.   " We have
felt thy wrath," declared they to the Mongol commander, " thy
time has come now to show favor."   " How ! " exclaimed Ogotai.
" They mention our wrath, they who have slain so many of our
army ?   We have felt their wrath very heavily and now we will
show them what ours is ! "

He ordered all the inhabitants to go forth from the city and wait
on the plain; the artisans were to group themselves separately.
These artisans were spared, but were sent to Mongolia.   Some of
them fearing such an exile, joined with the people and waited.
Except artisans no one was spared unless youthful women, and
also children; all were cut down by Ogotai, without mercy.

After this slaughter the Mongols plundered Urgendj of everything which had value.   Then they opened the sluices of the Oxus
and flooded the city; those who were hidden there perished.   In
other places some persons saved themselves always, but here,
those who escaped Mongol fury and hid themselves were drowned
by the water let in on them.

Jinghis camped that summer on the rich Naksheb steppes, where his vast herds of horses found rest and good pasture. In the autumn a new and great campaign was begun by the siege laid to Termed. This city, on the north or right bank of the Oxus, refused to surrender and was taken by storm on the tenth day of action. All the inhabitants were driven beyond the suburbs and massacred; a certain old woman stopped the sword above her head and promised a rare pearl if they spared her. When they asked for the treasure, she answered, "I have swallowed it." They ripped her body open and found the costly pearl in her stomach. Thinking that others might have swallowed jewels in like fashion, Jinghis commanded to rip bodies open thenceforward.

The Mongol Khan passed the next winter between Balkh and the Badakshan boundary, subduing, ravaging, destroying all cities of note, and every place of distinction or value. Before the winter had ended that whole region north of the Oxus was ruined, and was a horror to look upon. In spring he crossed the river at a ford and was met by a Balkh deputation with gifts and submission. Humility brought that rich famous place no salvation. Jinghis, who knew that Jelal ud din, the new sovereign, was at Ghazni with an army, would not leave a strong fortress behind him. Under pretext of making a census he directed the people in Balkh to assemble outside near the suburbs. They went forth and were slaughtered most brutally; the city was pillaged, then burned, and all its defenses demolished.

The time of terror came next to Nusrat i kuh in the Talekan district. This place, strong by position, by its works, and its garrison, defended itself for six months with immense strength, and successfully. Prisoners in large numbers were forced to fight in the front lines of investment. Those who turned back were cut down without mercy by the Mongols behind them. A huge earth mound was reared and catapults placed on it; with these the besiegers battered the interior of the fortress. At last the brave garrison made a great sally on foot and on horseback; the horsemen escaped to the mountains, but the foot forces were like wild beasts at bay; they fought till the enemy had slain every man of them. The Mongols then burst into the city; they spared no living soul in it and left not one stone on another.

While the Khan's army was destroying Nusrat i kuh, Tului

returned to his father after wasting Khorassan, the richest and most beautiful part of the Empire. When Tului had set out for this work of destruction Khorassan had been already ravaged by Subotai and by Chepé, who did the work only in part as they rushed along hunting Mohammed. These two chiefs left a commandant in each place which yielded. After they had passed, and when news came of victories won, as men said, by Mohammed, people hitherto terrified recovered their courage. For instance, the chief of militia in Tus killed the Mongol commandant and sent his head to Nishapur, the next city, as a trophy; but this chief suffered soon after for his levity and rashness. A strange captain came with a detachment to Tus, put nearly all native troops to the sword, and forced the Tus citizens to destroy their defenses.

When Tului received the command in 1220 to march on Khorassan he sent forward ten thousand men, under Togachar, as a vanguard. This body went on toward Nessa and when approaching that city a part of it met with resistance. Belgush, its commander, fell in the action which followed. Togachar, to avenge the death of Belgush, besieged Nessa. Shah Mohammed, when fleeing, had sent an official to advise Nessa people: " The Mongols," said he, " will abandon the Empire when they have plundered it, so flee to the desert, or to mountainous regions, unless ye wish to rebuild the old fortress, which was razed by my father " They rebuilt the old fortress.

Togachar attacked Nessa, using twenty catapults handled by captives, who, whenever they fell back, were massacred by Mongols behind them. On the sixteenth day at dawn a breach in the wall was effected; the Mongols burst through and drove out the inhabitants. On the plain near Nessa some were forced to bind others; when the hands of each man were bound behind his back the Mongols slaughtered all who were there, seventy thousand in number.

The ancient city of Meru, or Merv, renowned in Persian story, and still more in Sanscrit poems, was the first place attacked by Tului with the main army. It was one of the four ruling cities, and the one which Melik Shah and Sindjar, the Seljuk Sultans, had favored. It stood on a broad, fertile plain through which flowed the Murghab, or Bird, River. When Mohammed fled from Jinghis he directed Merv troops and officials to retire on Meraga, a neighboring fortress. " All people who remain must receive

Mongol troops with submission," this was his order.   Mohammed's fear, not his counsel, remained in that city.   His governor,
Behai ul Mulk, did not think Meraga strong and found elsewhere
a refuge; some chiefs returned to Merv, others fled to distant places.
The new governor, a man of no value, declared for submission,
and so did the mufti, but the judge and descendants of the Prophet
demanded resistance.   The governor lost his place soon and was
followed in office by a former incumbent named Mojir ul Mulk,
who managed Merv matters till Tului appeared with a force
seventy thousand in number, made up in some part of captives.
Next day he surrounded the outworks and within a week's time
his whole army had inclosed that doomed city, February, 1221.

The besieged made two sorties from different sides, but were
hurled back each time with great violence.   The assailants then
passed the whole night near the ramparts, so that no living soul
might escape them.   Mojir ul Mulk sent a venerable Imam next
morning to visit headquarters.   This holy man brought back such
mild words and fair speeches, that the governor himself went
to visit the camp, bearing with him rich presents.   Tului promised
him the office of governor, and the lives of all citizens.   He gave
him a rich robe of honor and spoke of the governor's friends and
adherents: "I desire to attach them to my person," said he,
"and confer on them fiefs and high office."   The governor sent
for his friends and adherents.   When Tului had all these men in
his power he bound them.   He bound Mojir ul Mulk also and
forced him to name the richest Merv citizens.   A list was drawn
up of two hundred great merchants and men of much property,
who were sent to the Mongols with four hundred artisans.   After
this the troops entered the city and drove out the people.   The
command had been given that each man must go forth with his
family and all he had of most value.   The multitude spent four
whole days marching out of the city.

Tului mounted a gilded throne on a plain near the suburbs and
had the war chiefs brought first to his presence.   That done he
commanded to hew off their heads in presence of the immense
wailing multitude of people, for whom no better lot was in
waiting.

Men, women, and children were torn from one another never
to meet in this life after that day.   The whole place was filled with

groans, shrieks and wild terror; the people were given in groups
to divisions of the army whose office it was to cut them down to
the last without pity or exception.   Only four hundred artisans
were set aside and some boys and girls intended for servitude.
Wealthy persons were tortured unsparingly till they told where their
treasures were hidden; when the treasures were found these
men were slaughtered as well as the others.   The city was plundered to the utmost; the tomb of the Sultan, Sindjar, was pillaged;
the walls of the ancient city and the fortress were made level with
the country about them.

Before he left that city of carnage and terror Tului appointed a
governor, one of the inhabitants whom he had spared for some
reason, and then he joined a Mongol commandant to that man.
When the army had marched away to destroy Nishapur, about
five hundred persons crept forth from underground places of hiding,
but short was the breathing space given them.   Mongol troops
following Tului wished also a share in the bloodshed.   Halting
outside the dark ruins, they asked that these ill-fated people bring
wheat to their camp ground.   The unfortunates were sent and
were slaughtered.

This corps cut down every man whom it met in the wake of
Tului.

Nishapur stood twelve days' journey distant from Merv and in
attacking it Tului was preparing to avenge Togachar, his sister's
husband, killed at Nessa.   The Nishapur people had done what
they could to the harm of the Mongols, and had prepared to
defend themselves with all the strength of their souls and their
bodies.   They had mounted three thousand ballistas on the walls,
and five hundred catapults.

The siege was begun by laying waste the whole province, of
which Nishapur was the capital.   Three thousand ballistas, three
hundred catapults, seven hundred machines to throw pots of burning naphtha, and four thousand ladders were among the siege
implements.   At sight of these, and of the vast multitude of savage
warriors surrounding their city, the leaders felt courage go from
them.

A deputation of notables, with the chief judge of Khorassan,
went to offer Tului submission, and an annual tribute.

Tului refused every offer and held the judge captive.   Next morning he rode round the walls and roused his troops to the greatest endeavor. They attacked all sides at once, fighting that day and the night following. In the morning the moats were full; in the walls were seventy breaches; ten thousand Mongols had entered. New assailants rushed in from every side, and there were desperate encounters at many points. Before that day had ended the city was occupied. The assailants took terrible vengeance. Togachar's widow, one of Jinghis Khan's daughters, rushed in herself with ten thousand warriors who cut down all before them. The slaughter continued four days without ceasing. The Mongols destroyed every living thing; even the cats and dogs in the city were killed by them (April, 1221).

Tului had heard that in the destruction of Merv many persons had saved their lives by lying down among corpses, so now he ordained that all heads be cut from the bodies; of these three pyramids were constructed, one of men's heads, a second from heads of women, and a third of children's heads. Fifteen days did destruction of the city continue; the place disappeared altogether, and the Mongols sowed barley on the site of it. Of the inhabitants only a few hundred men were left living; these were skilled artisans. Lest some should find refuge in underground places, troops were left near the ruins to slay all who might creep out later on into daylight.

The Mongol army marched now against Herat, the last city left in Khorassan. The governor, who had slain the envoy sent by Tului to summon the place to surrender, exhorted all men to fight desperately, to fight to the death. The struggle continued eight days, and Herat fought with immense resolution and fury; on that day the governor fell, and a small party sprang up which declared for submission. Tului knowing this state of mind in the city, promised to spare the people, if they would submit to him straightway. The offer was accepted. He spared all the citizens, excepting twelve thousand devoted to Jelal ud din, the new sovereign, and appointed a Mohammedan governor, with a Mongol commandant to help him.

Eight days later Tului received from Talekan a command to go to his father.

While Tului was ruining Khorassan, a small group of Turkmans, Khankalis, who were living near Merv, fearing the Mongols, moved westward, and after some wandering in Asia Minor, settled at last near Angora under Ertogrul their tribe chieftain. They numbered in those days four hundred and forty families. These Turkmans formed the nucleus of the Ottoman Empire, so famous in history until our day.

After he had destroyed Talekan, Jinghis held his summer camp for a time in the neighboring mountains. His sons, Jagatai and Ogotai, returned from Urgendj and other ruined places on the Oxus. Juchi went north of Lake Aral and in deep and unquenchable anger began to establish the monarchy of Kipchak, known later as the Golden Horde, and never again saw his father. Jinghis learning, toward the autumn of 1221, that Jelal ud din had large forces in Ghazni, directed his march toward that city to crush him.

The great Khan was detained a whole month at Kerduan, a firm fortress, but he destroyed it at last, with all its defenders. He crossed the Hindu Kush after that and besieged Bamian, where he lost one grandson stricken dead by an arrow; this was Moatagan, son of Jagatai. To avenge this death Bamian was stormed promptly, and taken. Jinghis would not have it in another way. The command was given to leave nothing alive, and take no booty of any kind. Every living creature had to die, and every thing of value was broken or burned. Bamian was renamed Mobalig (the city of woe), and the region about it was turned to a desert. A hundred years later it contained no inhabitants.

Just after this destruction came the news of Jelal ud din's victory over a Mongol division, commanded by Kutuku, who had been protecting the Khan's operations and those of Tului on the south side. This victory was gained at Peruan, not far from the Bamian boundary. It brought more harm to the victor, however, than profit, for it caused a sudden rupture between his commanders, some of whom deserted and led away many warriors. With reduced ranks he was forced to fall back upon Ghazni, and thence farther south when he heard that Jinghis was advancing rapidly to avenge the defeat of Kutuku, his general.

The Mongol army reached Ghazni fifteen days after its opponent had retreated. Jinghis left a governor in the city, and flew toward the Indus with all the speed possible to horses when men are sitting on them and urging them to the utmost. But this time the great

Mongol had to do with a man of more mettle than he had met in his warfaring thus far. Jelal ud din had gathered in forces from all sides; he sent urgent messages to the chiefs who had left him, but, though willing to return, they had no chance to do so at that day. Jinghis was between them and their leader.

The Mongols urged forward their horses with the energy of madmen. The great task was to stop the young Shah from crossing the Indus with his army and his harem — his wives and children were all with him. Time was in this case preëminent in value. The Mongols pressed Jelal ud din savagely, but he was, as ever, unterrified. Just before reaching the Indus he fell at night on the rear of his enemy's vanguard, and cut it down to a man very nearly.

On reaching the river there was no time to cross, so the Shah ranged his army for battle. The left wing was covered by a mountain, which ended sheer in the river. The mountain could not be turned, and could not be crossed, as the Shah thought; it protected the left from flank attack also; the Indus protected the right from flank movements, and Jelal ud din could be met straight in front only. His army was thirty thousand, while that of his enemy was many times larger.

And now began the unequal and desperate encounter. The Shah's right wing, to which he sent reinforcements repeatedly, repulsed the left wing of the Mongols, and he himself broke Jinghis Khan's center. For a time the Mongol conqueror was in personal peril, since a horse was killed under him in the struggle. Jelal ud din would have held his own, and perhaps won a victory, had not Bela Noyon been sent with ten thousand picked men to pass the mountain at all costs. Over cliffs and on the edge of abysses the Mongols crept carefully, pushing forward till at last they were in the rear of the weakened left wing and the center which, attacked from rear and front, were pierced through and forced out of contact with each other.

Rallying seven thousand men around him Jelal ud din made a desperate charge on the line of his enemy, which gave way for some distance, then he turned quickly, sprang on a fresh horse, threw off his armor and spurring to the Indus leaped from a bank given variously as from twenty to sixty feet higher than the plain of the water. His shield was at his shoulder, and his standard in his hand. Jinghis, who spurred to the river bank swiftly and gazed at his fleeing opponent, cried: "How could Shah Mohammed be the father of this man!"

The eldest son of Jelal ud din was a lad of eight years. He with his brothers were tossed into the Indus and drowned like superfluous puppies. Jinghis disposed of the harem and treasures as pleased him.

Jelal ud din vanished then for a time from the conflict to appear later on in various struggles till weakness, treachery and death put an end to him. Mongol generals crossed the river and pursued, but returned after fruitless endeavors.

Jinghis marched up the right bank of the Indus in the spring of 1222, and sent his son Ogotai to take Ghazni and destroy it. Here, as in most other places, the inhabitants were sent from the city, as it were to be counted, but were slaughtered most brutally; none were spared except artisans. An army corps was sent also to ruin Herat, the one city left in Khorassan. Herat had risen in revolt on hearing of the Peruan triumph over Mongols; the people had had such action in view since the time of surrender, and had stored away arms and supplies under pretext that they were for Mongol use should the need come.

Not far from Herat was the Kaliun fortress, known later on as Nerretu. To reach this strong place men had to pass single file on the high, narrow ridge of a mountain which resembled the back of a colossal hog of the razor-back species. The place was beyond reach of arrows, or of stones sent by catapults. Though they had attacked Kaliun twice, the Mongols had failed in their efforts to take it. The Kaliun men, fearing lest they might come a third time, and impress Herat people, had planned to involve that strong and wealthy city, which would then have one cause with them. They sent letters to the Mongol governors ruling in Herat stating: "We are ready to surrender, but fear Mongol rigor; we beg for a written safe-conduct."

The governors answered that they would give such a letter, and advised the petitioners to visit the city and come to them. This was all that the other men needed; so seventy strong warriors went down from Kaliun, disguised as simple huxters; they had arms covered up in the packs which they carried. They entered the city, each man by himself, combined later on and slew both

the governors.   Herat rose immediately, and killed every partisan
of the Mongols.

In addition to his own men the Mongol commander led now
fifty thousand impressed from conquered places.   A siege followed
soon and a desperate resistance.   Six months and seventeen days
did it last till the fall of the city.   The sword was turned then
on all save the choice youth of both sexes.   For one week the Mongols slew, pillaged, burned, ruined.   It was said that one million
six hundred thousand people perished in the conflict and subse-
quent slaughter.   Jinghis received the richest of the plunder, and
with it went several thousands of youthful captives.

When Herat was destroyed the commander went back to the
main army; somewhat later troops were sent to capture all who
might have escaped and appeared in the ruins; they found about
two thousand.   These they slew, and then returned to those who
had sent them.

Sixteen persons took refuge on a steep mountain peak, and
when they saw no Mongols coming back, they went down to Herat.
A few others came also and joined them.   There was then a new
population, forty persons in number.   Their only refuge was the
chief mosque of the city.

After its terrible ruin, Merv had been repeopled to some extent,
but later five thousand Mongols were sent to that city and they
slaughtered all whom they found in it.   When these five thousand
had done their work thoroughly a commandant, Ak Melik, was
left with the order to kill all who might reappear in the ruins.
This man did his best to find people and slay them.   He sent
muezzins to summon to prayer from the minarets.   Whenever a
Moslem crept out of his hiding place and entered the mosque he
was seized and his life taken.   Forty-one days did Ak Melik lurk
there and wait for more people.   The survivors were few when
he left the ruins.   Merv remained a sad desert till the days of
Shah Ruk, son of Tamerlane.

Jinghis cut down on the banks of the Indus all who had been
faithful to Jelal ud din, the new Shah, and now he destroyed all
who had deserted that sovereign and been foolishly treacherous.
On deserting Jelal ud din, Agrak had gone with Azam to Bekerhar.
After a visit there he set out for Peshawur, and from the first
halting place sent back this message: " Let not my mortal enemy

remain in thy country." This enemy was Nuh Jaudar, the chief of five or six thousand Kolluj families. Azam sent back this answer: " Never has there been among Moslems such need as there now is not to quarrel." And taking an escort of fifty, Azam followed to make peace between Agrak and Jaudar. He could not move Agrak or persuade him; they ate together and also drank wine; Agrak's brain grew excited, he mounted, took one hundred men and rode to the camp of the Kollujes. Jaudar thinking that Agrak wished peace rode forth with his son to greet him. On seeing his enemy Agrak drew his sabre as if to strike, and was cut down by Jaudar's men the next moment. When Agrak's adherents heard that their leader had been slain they thought that Jaudar and Azam had plotted his ruin, and right away they slew Azam. Then they attacked Jaudar's camp, where they massacred him and his children. Soon after this they encountered the Gur men and killed a great number. As a close to this tragic insanity of action a corps of mounted Mongols fell upon all and slew them indiscriminately; a small remnant fled in various directions.

CHAPTER VIII

JINGHIS had passed the winter of 1222-3 near the Indus, and in the spring of 1223 he resolved, rather suddenly as it seemed, to march up the Indus and return through Tibet to Tangut and China. The reasons given by historians for this move are various. There were troubles in Tangut and there was no imperative reason for remaining in Kwaresm, since that Empire was utterly helpless; it had been depopulated and ruined in most parts.

Some people thought that Jinghis, if not horrified, was at least set to thinking by the boundless slaughters committed at his direction. We have two accounts touching this matter which are of interest, though both bear the myth stamp, and are opinions of other men as to Jinghis, not the great Khan's own thoughts as expressed by his words or his actions. In the Chinese history "Tung Kian Kang Mu," the following cause is given for his sudden decision: When Jinghis was at the Iron Gate of North India his guards saw a creature which resembled a deer, but its head was like that of a horse with one horn on its forehead, and there was green hair on its body. This creature had power of speech, for it said to the guards: "It is time for your master to return to his own land." Jinghis, troubled by this message, consulted Ye liu chu tsai, who said: "That creature is Kotwan, it knows every language. It appears as a sign that bloodshed is needless at present. For four years the great army is warring in western regions. Heaven, which has a horror of bloodshed, gives warning through Kotwan. Spare the Empire for Heaven's sake. Moderation will give boundless pleasure."

The other account is quite different in character and import: "I was," says a Gurjistan cadi, "in Herat on a tower, which stood just in front of Tului's headquarters. Arrows came in such numbers that I went down and was lost in the dust, among Mongols. They seized and took me then to Tului. When he heard my adventure he wondered: ' An angel, or it may be a demon, is trifling with thee,' said he.   ' Neither,' replied I.   ' How then art thou here?' asked he.   'I looked at all things with the eye of a sovereign,' was my answer, ' hence no harm struck me.' This answer so pleased Tului that he showed me much favor. ' Take this gift,' added he, ' for thou art a man of rare wisdom. Be true to Jinghis the great Khan, for thou wilt now serve him.' He sent me then to his father, who received me in Talekan with high favor.   Jinghis spoke to me of Turkish sufferings repeatedly. ' Dost thou think,' asked he one day, ' that the blood which I have shed will be remembered against me by mankind?'   He held a dart in his hand while he looked in my face and put questions. ' I will answer,' replied I, ' if your majesty secures life to me.' ' Speak,' said the Khan, and I answered: ' If your majesty slays as many persons as you please, men will give you whatever fame pleases them.'   His face colored at these words, and he shouted in rage till the dart dropped from his fingers.   I felt death standing near me that moment, but he soon recovered and said: ' I have thought on the wisdom of sages, and see that I have plundered and slain without the right knowledge in that region where Mohammed's horse lost his way; but what care I for men?' and he went from the chamber.   I could remain in those places no longer, such was my fear in that horde, and I fled from it."

Before starting for home Jinghis gave command to kill all superfluous prisoners, that is, all who had done the work because of which they had been spared from death on the day when they were taken; only artisans were left, men needed for their skill in Mongolia.   This command was not carried out, however, till the captives had hulled an immense store of rice for the Mongols; that done they were slain in one night without any exception.

The Mongols took the road toward Tibet, but after some days they turned back from that difficult region and went to Peshawur, where were the roads along which they had come in the first place. As he passed Balkh on the Samarkand road Jinghis Khan issued orders to slay all who had made their way back to that city.

After the death of Shah Mohammed, Chepé Noyon and Subotai, two of the three who had hunted him down to extinction, plundered

Persian, that is Eastern, Irak and ruined it, and also the lands
between that vast province and the Caspian. On the west they
went great distances inland, including parts of Armenia, and also
Georgia as far as Tiflis. In 1222 those commanders received
from Jinghis reinforcements with a command to conquer the
Polovtsi, a people akin to the Mongols.

These Polovtsi led a nomad life in that region which stretches
westward from the Caspian to the Dnieper; they were neighbors
of the Russians whom they had harassed for centuries. The
Mongols had obtained from the Shirvan Shah ten guards to conduct them. The commanders began very strangely. They cut
off the head of one of these ten and declared that the other nine
would die by the same kind of death if they should deceive them
or use any treachery. Despite this cruel act the guides led the
army into ambush among northern foothills of the Caucasus, and
slipped away safely.

The Mongols, astray in mountains and woods, were attacked
upon all sides by various strong peoples; among these were the
Polovtsi, to whom they were bringing destruction. Pressed hard
at all points they sent to those Polovtsi this message: " Ye and
we are one people, why war with us ? Make peace. We will give
all the gold that ye need, and many rich garments. Ye and we
can work together with great profit."

Seduced by these words and by presents the Polovtsi gave
help and aid to the Mongols, gave them victory first, and then led
them out to the open country. When towns in the Caucasus
foothills and near them were ruined the Mongols turned on the
Polovtsi, slew their chief men and numbers of others, took back
the bribes to treachery, took every other thing of value and cut
down and slaughtered on all sides. The Polovtsi fled and spread
terror with their accounts of the Mongols. The whole people
left the best pastures and moved toward their northern and western
boundaries. Ten thousand families passed into Byzantine
regions. John Ducas, the Emperor, took those people then to
his service and gave them land in Macedonia and Thrace. Great
numbers fled into Russia, which for two centuries had been
scourged with their raids and their outrages. Among the fugitives was Kotyan, a Khan whose daughter had married the Galitch prince Mystislav the Gallant. Kotyan implored his son-in-

law to help him: "To-day," said he, "the Mongols have taken our land, they will take yours to-morrow. Assist us; if not we shall be beaten on one day and you the day following."

Mystislav called the Russian princes to a council, at which they resolved to give aid to the Polovtsi. "Unless we help them," said Mystislav, "they will go with the Mongols and strengthen them." A deputation went north to ask aid of the princes in Suzdal. Troops were collected and the Russian princes moved against the enemy in confidence. On the way they met Mongol envoys who delivered this message: "We have heard that, convinced by the Polovtsi, ye are marching against us, but we have not come to attack you. We have come against our own horse boys and slaves, the vile Polovtsi; we are not at war with you. If the Polovtsi flee to your country drive them out of it, and seize all their property. They have harmed you, as men tell us; they have harmed us also; that is why we attack them." The Russian princes gave answer by killing the envoys.

Some distance down that great river the Dnieper, a new Mongol embassy met the Russian princes with these words: "If through obedience to the Polovtsi ye have cut down our envoys, and are now bringing war on us, Heaven will judge your action; we have not harmed you." This time the princes spared the envoys.

When the Russians and Polovtsi had assembled at the Dnieper Mystislav crossed with one thousand men. He attacked the Mongol outposts and scattered them. After some hesitation the Mongols retired. Moving eastward, they lured on the Russians, who soon met a larger detachment of warriors. These they attacked and defeated, driving them far into the steppe land and seizing all their cattle. Encouraged by this success, the Russians moved forward eight days in succession till they neared the river Kalka. Then came an action with outposts and a third Russian victory. Mystislav ordered Daniel of Galitch, son of Roman, to cross the Kalka; after him went all the other princes and encamped on the steppe beyond the river. The Polovtsi were posted in advance, some of them serving as sentries. Mystislav rode forward to reconnoitre. Being satisfied with what was revealed to him he returned hastily, ordered out his own men and also Daniel, giving no command to other princes who were left in their camp awaiting orders; there was keen rivalry between

him and them. Mystislav thought, as it seems, to win victory
without them and believed that he had power thus to win it. He
knew not that he was to meet Chepé Noyon who had hunted to
death both Gutchluk and Mohammed, the sovereigns of two
Empires; he knew nothing of the Mongols, their numbers, their
power or their methods.

The battle was opened by Daniel who, in the forefront himself,
attacked with great valor and was wounded very early in the
action, which was obstinate. Observing the danger, Mystislav
supported him, and the Mongols were repulsed to some extent.
At this point, for some unknown cause, the whole force of the
Polovtsi stampeded, turned, rushed back in panic terror and filled
the Russian camp with disorder. The Mongols rallied quickly,
brought up fresh forces, and swept all before them. The Russians,
not engaged for the greater part, were waiting near the river. The
Polovtsi not only left the field, but in fact helped the enemy,
hence victory was perfect for the Mongols. " Never in Russia,"
states the chronicler, " was there a defeat so disastrous as this one
(1224)."

Three Russian princes, who had not taken part in the battle, held
their ground firmly near the river, on a hill which they fortified
with palisades. They fought there with two divisions of Mongols,
which remained at the Kalka — the others followed Mystislav
toward the Dnieper. Three days did those brave men fight at the
river, till assured that they would be freed on surrender, if ransomed. They trusted the plighted word of the Mongols and
yielded.

The Mongol chiefs bound those three princes hand and foot,
and laid them side by side on the ground at some distance one
from another. They then placed a heavy platform upon them,
sat on that platform and ate and drank while the princes were lying
beneath in desperate torture. Thus the three Russians died while
the Mongols were feasting above them.

Six princes and a great number of their men perished while
fleeing toward the Dnieper. Mystislav, and those in his company, including Daniel, reached the river and crossed it. The
prince burned his boats on the west bank, or had them cut
into pieces lest the enemy might follow him farther, but the
Mongols turned back before reaching the Dnieper. The north-

ern contingent, commanded by the Rostoff prince, Vassilko, heard at Chernigoff of the Kalka disaster and returned home, being too weak, as they thought, to face such an enemy.

On their way eastward the Mongols used fire and sword without mercy wherever they found men and property. They filled southern Russia with terror; they swept through the Crimea and ravaged it; they captured Bulgar on the Volga and ruined that opulent city. Sated with bloodshed and laden with booty they returned that same year to headquarters east of the Caspian. Thus one division of Jinghis Khan's great army overran an immense part of Europe without meeting effective resistance in any place.

On leaving Samarkand for Mongolia Jinghis gave command to the mother, the widows and the kinsfolk of Shah Mohammed to stand at the roadside and take a farewell look at their native land. They did this and wailed in loud voices as they saw it for the last time.

In February of 1225 the mighty manslayer had returned to his homeland between the rivers, where we may leave him for a time and turn to China:

After Jinghis left the Kin Empire in 1216 the Kins reoccupied the land seized from them excepting Chong tu and the northern rim of Pe che li and Shan si. Mukuli, the great Mongol general, reëntered China in 1217. During that year and the five years which followed he conquered all the lands of the Kin dynasty excepting one province, Honan, which lies south of the Hoang Ho and extends from the bend of that river at Tung kwan to its mouth at the Yellow Sea. Mukuli died in April, 1223, leaving his title and command to his only son, Boru.

After the death of this renowned warrior both Chinese dynasties became increasingly active and hostile. The king in Tangut followed also their counsel and influence. Beyond doubt, it was to meet this new growth of enmity that Jinghis had returned to Mongolia. The Kin Emperor had sent an embassy to Jinghis in the west with the offer to yield up all places north of the Hoang Ho, and to be a younger brother. This was refused. Jinghis answered that the Kin Emperor must be content with the title of Prince of Honan, and the position of a vassal. During the two years following there rose great and very active resistance.

Tangut favored the Kins, and its monarch prepared for armed action against the Mongols.

In view of this Jinghis toward the end of 1225 left his head-quarters to make war on Tangut. His formal complaint was that foes of the Mongol Khan had been favored and taken into service by the King who had refused also to send his son as a hostage.

Jinghis entered Tangut in 1226, during February. Between that time and the autumn following he passed from north to south, harassing the country most savagely. He laid siege to Ling chau, the capital. Li ti, the king, died in August, leaving the throne to Li hien, his son and successor. A new Tangut army was sent to strengthen Ling chau. Jinghis returned northward, put that new army to flight, stormed Ling chau, took the city, sacked it and slaughtered its inhabitants. Leaving a corps there he advanced to the south; seized Si ning with Lin tao and sacked both those cities. Establishing headquarters in Western Shen si he captured places all around in that region till the hot summer came when he retired to the Liu pan mountains and rested. The condition of the country at that time as described by Chinese annalists is as follows:

"Men strive in vain to hide in caverns and in mountains. As to the Mongol sword, hardly two in a hundred escape it. The fields are covered with the bones of slaughtered people."

In the month of July, 1227, Li hien sent an embassy with sub-mission. He asked merely one month in which to surrender his capital. The favor was granted, and Jinghis promised to regard him as his son in the future.

Soon after, the Mongol manslayer was taken ill and died eight days later. He had time, however, to instruct his sons how to live, and his generals how to capture Nan king, and destroy the Kin dynasty. He told them also how to deal with Tangut and its sovereign.

They were to hide the death of Jinghis very carefully, and when Li hien came out of his capital at the time fixed for surrender, they were to slay him and put all people of that city to the sword, without exception.

Jinghis died August 18, 1227, when sixty-six years of age. He had reigned twenty-two years.

The order to slay the Tangut sovereign and the people of the city was carried out strictly, and the kingdom of Tangut was added to the Mongol Empire.

"Since the beginning of time," writes the Chinese historian, "no barbarous people have ever been so mighty as the Mongols are at present. They destroy empires as a man plucks out herbs by the roots, such is the power in their possession. Why does Heaven let them have it?"

The remains of the great Khan were taken back to his birthplace. Lest his death might be known the troops who conducted them slew every person whom they met as they traveled. Only when they arrived at the home of Jinghis was his death published to all men.

As the life of Jinghis was unique and original, so were the circumstances of his death and the details of his funeral. A great number of causes were given for his death. It was ascribed to an arrow, to poison, to drowning, to lightning, to the witchery of Kurbeljin Goa the Tangut queen, who had the fame of great beauty, and whom Jinghis had taken as it seems from her husband and added to the number of his many wives. It is stated by some historians that he had more than 400 wives and concubines. But Bortai, the mother of Juchi, Jagatai, Ogotai and Tului always held the first place. Ssanang Setzen, the chronicler, a descendant himself of Jinghis, describes the last days, death and funeral of his ancestor. This account reads like one of those myth tales which I found in Siberia. First we have the life and death struggle between Jinghis and the King of Tangut whose name in the chronicle is Shidurgo. Shidurgo opens the struggle by becoming a serpent, Jinghis becomes king of all birds, and then Shidurgo turns into a tiger, Jinghis changes at once to a lion; at last Shidurgo is a boy and Jinghis appears as chief of the Tengeri or heavenly divinities, and Shidurgo is at his mercy. "If thou kill me," said Shidurgo, "the act will be fatal to thee; if thou spare me it will be fatal to thy children." Jinghis struck, but the blow did not harm his opponent. "There is only one weapon in the world that can kill me, a triple dagger made of magnet which is now between my first and second boot soles." With that the Tangut king drew forth the blade and gave it to his enemy. "Kill me; if milk comes from the wound it will foretoken ill to thee, if blood ill to thy posterity. Before taking Kurbeljin Goa, my wife, look to her previous life very carefully."

Jinghis stabbed Shidurgo in the neck, blood flowed and he died. Next the queen was brought in. All wondered when they saw her. "I had much greater beauty before," said she. "I am grimy from dust now, but when I bathe in the river my beauty will come to me." She went to the Kara Muren (the Hoang Ho) and plunged into it. When she returned she had all her former great beauty. The following night while Jinghis lay asleep she bewitched him; he grew feeble and ill and never gained strength again. She left him, went down to the Kara Muren and disappeared in that river.

Jinghis lay helpless in bed and at last death was near him. He spoke then to Kiluken, his old comrade, the gray hero: "Be thou a true friend to my widow Bortai Fudjin, and to my sons Ogotai and Tului, be thou true to them fearlessly. The precious jade has no crust, the polished dagger no dirt on it; man born to life is not deathless, he must go hence without home, without resting place. The glory of a deed is in being finished. Firm and unbending is he who keeps a plighted word faithfully. Follow not the will of another and thou wilt have the good-will of many. To me it is clear that I must leave all and go hence from you. The words of the boy Kubilai are very weighty; note what he says, note it all of you. He will sit on my throne some day and will, as I have done, secure high prosperity."

Kiluken and many princes went to bear the corpse of their mighty leader back to the Kentei Khan region, through the greater part of Tangut and across the broad Gobi. A long, an immense train of people followed it. As they marched they wailed and raised their voices together lamenting, Kiluken leading, as follows:

"In times which are gone thou didst swoop like a falcon before us. To-day a car bears thee on as it rumbles advancing.

O thou my Khan!

Hast thou left us indeed, hast thou left wife and children,

O thou my Khan?

Hast thou left us, hast thou left the Kurultai of thy nation,

O thou my Khan?

Sweeping forward in pride, as sweeps forward an eagle thou didst lead us aforetime,

O thou my Khan,

But now thou hast stumbled, and art down, like a colt still unbroken,

O thou my Khan.

Thou didst bring peace and joy to thy people for sixty and six years, but now thou art leaving them,

O thou my Khan."

When the procession had reached the Mona Khan mountains the funeral car stopped in blue miry clay and the best horses could not move it. All were discouraged and grief stricken, when a new chant rose, led by Kiluken the gray hero:

" O lion of the Tengeri, thou our lord, wilt thou leave us? Wilt thou desert wife and nation in this quagmire?' Thy firmly built state, with its laws and its much devoted people; thy golden palace, thy state raised on justice, the numerous clans of thy nation, all these are awaiting thee off there.

" Thy birth land, the rivers in which thou didst bathe, all these are awaiting thee off there.

" Thy subjects the Mongols devoted and fruitful are awaiting thee off there.

" Thy chiefs, thy commanders, thy great kinsfolk are awaiting thee off there.

" Thy birthplace, Deligun Bulak on the Onon, is awaiting thee off there.

" Thy standard of Yak tails, thy drums, fifes and trumpets, thy golden house and all that is in it, are awaiting thee off there.

" The fields of the Kerulon, where first thou didst sit on thy throne as Jinghis, are awaiting thee off there.

" Bortai Fudjin, the wife of thy youth, Boörchu and Mukuli thy faithful friends, thy fortunate land and thy great golden mansion, that wonderful building, are awaiting thee off there.

" Wilt thou leave us now here in this quagmire, because this land pleases thee? because so many Tanguts are vanquished? because Kurbeldjin Goa was beautiful?

" We could not save thy noble life in this kingdom, so let us bear thy remains to their last home and resting place. Let us bear thy remains which are as fair as the jade stone. Let us give consolation to thy people."

After this chant the car moved from the blue clay, went forward, passed over the mountain range easily and across the immense Gobi desert. It moved on amid wailing and chanting, and at last reached the home of the mighty and merciless manslayer.

The body was buried in a Kentei Khan forest near a majestic tree which had pleased Jinghis Khan very greatly in his lifetime. There were many smaller trees near this single large one, but soon after the burial all trees in the forest had grown equal in size and appearance, so that no man knew or could learn where the body of the conqueror was hidden.

Jinghis Khan is one of the great characters of history, perhaps the greatest that has appeared in the world to the present day. A man who, never hampered by conscience, advanced directly toward the one supreme object of his life, — power. His executive ability was wonderful, as was also his utter disregard for human life. Beginning with a few huts on the Kerulon he drew in tribe after tribe, country after country, till at his death he was master of more territory than had ever been ruled by one sovereign. He stands forth also as the greatest manslayer the world has ever known. From 1211 to 1223 in China and Tangut alone Jinghis and his assistants killed more than eighteen million five hundred thousand human beings. He demanded blind obedience from all men, the slightest infringement was punished with death; even his most distinguished generals submitted to the bastinado, or to execution.

In Jinghis Khan's Code of Laws the homicide, the adulterer, the cattle thief, and the person who for the third time lost a prisoner confided to his care was put to death. Torture was used to force confession. When an animal was to be slaughtered it must be thrown on its back, an incision made in its breast and the heart torn out. This custom prevails among the Mongols of the Baikal (the Buriats) to the present day when killing animals for sacrifice.

Jinghis Khan left great possessions to each of his sons and heirs. To Juchi, the eldest, he left that immense region north of Lake Aral and westward to the uttermost spot on which the hoof of a horse had been planted by Mongols at any time. The dominions of Jagatai extended from Kayalik in the Uigur land to the Syr Daryá, or Yaxartes.

Ogotai received the country watered by the Imil, while Tului, the youngest, inherited his father's home places between Kara Kurum and the Onon River region.

These dispositions, made somewhat earlier, agreed with Mongol custom and usage, by which elder sons received portions as they came to maturity; his father's house and all that belonged to it fell to the youngest son always.

When the last rites had been rendered, and the last honors paid to the great conqueror, each of the four sons returned to his possessions, and it was only after two years that the family held the Kurultai of election. In the spring of 1229 all assembled again on the Kerulon. They were met and received by Tului, acting as regent till they should choose a new sovereign.

From the regions north and west of Lake Aral came the descendants of Juchi, that eldest son who had dared to defy his own terrible father. Jagatai brought his sons and grandsons from the Ili; and Ogotai came from the Imil near which he had been living.

After three days of the Kurultai had been passed in feasting and pleasure, the assembly proceeded to choose a Grand Khan, or sovereign. Many were in favor of Tului, but Ye liu chu tsai, the great sage and minister, begged them to settle on Ogotai, the choice of Jinghis, and avoid all dissensions and discord. Tului did not hesitate in following this counsel and read immediately the ordinance of his father in which Ogotai was named as sovereign.

The princes turned then to Ogotai and declared him the ruler; Ogotai answered that his brothers and uncles were far better fitted than he for the sovereignty. He mentioned especially as the right man Tului who had remained with his father, or near him at all times, and was trained beyond any in the wisdom of the conqueror. "Jinghis himself has chosen thee!" cried the others to Ogotai, "how act against his command and his wishes?"

Ogotai still resisted, and forty days passed in feasting ere he yielded. On the forty-first day, which was pointed out by magicians as the time most propitious, he was conducted to the throne by Jagatai and by Utchuken his uncle, Jinghis Khan's youngest brother. Tului gave him the goblet used on occasions of that kind, and then all who were in the pavilion, and those outside, bared their heads, put their girdles on their shoulders and fell prostrate. Nine times did they fall before Ogotai, invoke on him prosperity, and salute him with his title Kha Khan, or Khaan, the White Khan of the Mongols.

The newly made monarch, followed by the assembly, went out then and bowed down three times to the sun in due homage. The immense throngs of people there present gave the like homage also. When Ogotai reëntered the tent a great feast was served straightway.

In choosing Ogotai the family swore to adhere to his descendants, and the following strange words were used by them: " We swear not to seat on the throne another branch of our family so long as there shall be of thy descendants a morsel of flesh which, cast upon grass, might stop a bullock from eating, or cast into fat might stop a dog from devouring."

Jinghis Khan's treasures were spoils from a great part of Asia, and Ogotai commanded to bring them before him; that done he distributed those precious objects to the princes, commanders, and warriors.

During three entire days they made offerings to the shade of Jinghis, their great ancestor. Ogotai chose from the families of princes and commanders forty most beautiful virgins; he had them attired in the richest of garments, and adorned with rare jewels. These forty virgins were slain, and thus sent to attend the mighty conqueror in that world which he occupied. With the virgins were slain and sent also the best and the costliest stallions of northern Asia.

The first work of Ogotai was to establish the code of Jinghis, and pardon offences committed since the death of the conqueror. Ye liu chu tsai, the sage who had exercised on Jinghis so much influence, and whose power still continued, prevailed then on Ogotai to fix the rank of each officer and official, and to define every difference between princes of Jinghis Khan's house and other subjects. He wished also to restrain the boundless power of Mongol chiefs in conquered places. Those men disposed of human life as each whim of theirs shaped itself; whenever they chose to condemn a man he died, as did also his family.

At Chu tsai's advice Ogotai refixed all forms of action in cases of this kind. The amount of yearly tribute was settled for the first time since the Mongol conquest. In the west it was a tax on every male person of legal age. In China the system of the country was chosen and the tribute was levied on houses. Lands taken from the Kin dynasty were divided into ten provinces in each of these was established a tribunal for assessment and collection of tribute. Chu tsai even proposed to the White Khan to use in governing his possessions the rules of Confucius. " The Empire has been conquered on horseback," said the sage, " but no man can rule it from the saddle."

The advice was listened to with benevolence, and scholars were placed by degrees in public office.

Now that the Mongols again had a sovereign they gave more force to their conquests along those vast lines of action which Jinghis had explained on his deathbed. Three great expeditions were arranged at the Kurultai of election: An army of thirty thousand was sent to destroy the rising power of Jelal ud din, who had returned from lands south of the Indus and regained some part of his father's dominions. A second army of similar numbers was sent under Kuyuk and Subotai to conquer the Kipchaks and other peoples. This Juchi would have done had he followed the advice of his father. On the third expedition Ogotai the Grand Khan set out with Tului and other princes to end the Kin Empire. These expeditions we will follow in the order mentioned.

CHAPTER IX

PERSIA AT THE TIME OF JINGHIS KHAN'S DEATH

WHEN Jinghis had returned to his birthplace Persia was left as a desert behind him. This was true of all Eastern parts of it, especially. "In those lands which Jinghis Khan ruined," exclaims the historian, "not one in a thousand is left of the people. Where a hundred thousand had lived before his invasion there are now scarce one hundred. Were nothing to stop the increase of population from this hour till the day of Judgment it would not reach one tenth of what it was before Jinghis Khan's coming."

The ruin inflicted by that dreadful invasion spread terror on all sides. People stunned by the awful atrocities committed in Persia, believed that the Mongols were dog-headed and devoured human flesh as their daily and usual nourishment.

Mohammed, the Shah of Persia, had three sons to whom portions had been given. Jelal ud din, the eldest of these sons, had sought a refuge at Delhi. At Sutun Avend Rokn ud din, the second son, had been slain by the Mongols, while Ghiath ud din, the third son, had retired to Karun, a Mazanderan stronghold, and saved himself.

When the Mongols had gone from the country Persian Irak was the cause of a conflict between the two Turk leaders Edek Khan and Togan Taissi the Atabeg. These rivals divided the province between them at last, and, since Ispahan fell to the former, Ghiath ud din wished to win him as a vassal. He therefore promised Edek his sister in marriage, but while settling the terms of agreement Edek was slain by his rival, the Atabeg, Togan.

Ghiath marched against Ispahan promptly, received Togan's homage, and gave him the sister just promised to Edek. In quick time he thus found himself master of Irak, Mazanderan and Khorassan.

Jelal ud din when defeated at the Indus, which he swam with
such daring, had been pursued fiercely in India by Jinghis Khan's
warriors until he was very near Delhi.

The sovereign at that capital was Shems ud din Iletmish, a
Turkman and once a slave of the Sultan of Gur, the last ruler of
his line in that country. When the Gur dynasty fell, Iletmish
seized a good part of north India and was ruling unchallenged.
He feared now the coming of so brave and incisive a man as
Jelal ud din, hence he sent him rich gifts and declared that the
climate of Delhi was unwholesome. Jelal would find, he felt
certain, a far better residence in Multan and a much more salu-
brious climate. Jelal withdrew, but he gathered much booty of
value as he traveled.

Meanwhile from Irak came many generals who were enraged
at Ghiath ud din, his brother. They brought with them warriors
who were ready for service since service meant plunder. Jelal
could meet now the Scinde prince, Karadja, whom he hated. He
entered Karadja's dominions, sacked many cities and routed his
army. Hearing that Iletmish was advancing to strengthen Karadja
he set out at once to encounter the Sultan of Delhi.

But Iletmish offered peace, and the hand of his daughter instead
of hostilities; Jelal took peace and the woman. Still Iletmish
made a league with Karadja and others to drive out the Kwaresmian if need be. Jelal, who could not make head against all,
took advice of his generals. Those who had quitted his brother
wished a return to home regions. It would be easy, they told him,
to snatch command from Ghiath his brother, a weakling, and
foolish. But Euzbeg, one of the generals, declared that Jelal
should remain where he was in full safety from Mongols who were
more to be feared than all the princes in India. Jelal ud din,
swept off by the hope of regaining his father's dominion, decided
on going to Persia. He left Euzbeg to watch over his fortunes
in India and to Vefa Melik he gave the whole government of Gur
and of Ghazni.

While crossing the desert lying north of the Indus Jelal lost
a part of his army by disease, exhaustion and hunger, and when he
reached Kerman, his whole force had shrunk to four thousand.
A Turk commander named Borak, with the surname Hadjib,
that is Chamberlain, had won that whole region. Borak had

served Shah Mohammed as chamberlain, hence the surname Hadjib from his service. Later on Ghiath ud din gave him office in Ispahan, making him governor, but, embroiled in the sequel with Ghiath's vizir, Borak got permission to go to Jelal then in India. While crossing Kerman the Kevashir governor attacked him, incited to do so by Ghiath, who wished at that juncture to seize all the baggage and women belonging to Borak's assistants.

The aggressor was beaten, put to flight and driven into a neighboring fortress, where Borak killed him. Borak not satisfied yet with this outcome had attacked Kevashir where the son of the recent, but then defunct, governor was commanding. While thus engaged he heard all at once that Jelal was in Kerman. Borak sent rich gifts to his visitor straightway and hurried off to receive him. He offered one of his daughters while greeting the Sultan, who took her in marriage without hesitation. When Jelal stood before Kevashir the place yielded and opened its gates to him.

The Sultan had passed a whole month in Kerman when he learned that his father-in-law was pondering treason. Orkhan, a general, advised the arrest of Borak and a seizure of all his possessions, but the vizir, Khodja Jihan, declared that if haste were exhibited in punishing the man who had been the first to acknowledge the Sultan many minds would be shaken, since there was no chance to prove clearly the existence of treason.

Jelal chose to feign ignorance, and continued his journey. Borak remained master of Kerman. After him nine of his family during eighty-six years succeeded in authority. These formed the Kara Kitan dynasty of Kerman, so called because of this Borak, the Hadjib, its founder.

Jelal advanced into Fars where for twenty-four years had been reigning the Atabeg, Sád, son of Zengwi, a prince who claimed his descent from a Turk chief named Salgar. Sankor, the grandson of Salgar, was established in Fars, and when the Seljuks had fallen he made himself master of that region, and princes descended from Salgar, that is the Salgarids, thus gained dominion.

On nearing Shirez, Jelal announced his arrival to the Atabeg, who sent his son with five hundred horsemen to welcome the Sultan, and excused himself saying that he had once made a vow not to meet any person whatever. Jelal accepted the statement. He knew that the Atabeg was hostile to Ghiath, who had invaded his country a short time before and had even retained certain parts of it. Jelal gave back those parts then to Sád and to gain the man thoroughly married his daughter.

The Sultan made a brief stay in Shiraz, being eager to win back Irak from his brother, for Ghiath could not restore peace to those countries given up to disorder and anarchy since the return of Jinghis to Mongolia. Each little district had its own cruel master and those petty tyrants completed in great part the ruin begun with such terror by the Mongols. Ghiath's name was repeated at prayer in the mosques, but no man gave him tribute. Having no money to pay his Turk troops he was forced to permit them to take what they could from the people and thus strip the country. When an officer of rank came for pay to the Sultan, the man had to take the next higher title, an emir was made melik, and a melik made khan. That was the reward for his service. He was forced next to subsist by real robbery in some shape.

After Jelal had reached Ispahan he set out very quickly with a picked band for Rayi near which his brother was recruiting an army. He had given all his horsemen white banners like those used by the Mongols. When Ghiath saw those white banners he thought that Mongols were advancing to attack him, and he took to flight straightway, but returned soon with a force thirty thousand in number. Jelal had recourse now to a stratagem. He sent to his brother, through an equerry, this message: " Having suffered cruel hardships I have come to find rest here, but since you meet me with swords, I withdraw to other places."

Ghiath believing this message, and thinking besides that his brother was powerless to harm him, came back to Rayi and dismissed his large forces.

Jelal sent out an agent who gave immense promises to the generals of his brother, and gave them rings also in proof of his favor. Many yielded while others went promptly to Ghiath and showed the rings given them. He had his brother's agent arrested. But Jelal, feeling that most of the warriors were with him, advanced with only three thousand picked horsemen. This advance was successful; Ghiath fled to a fortress but reassured by mild messages he left his asylum and went to his brother's headquarters.

The supremacy of Jelal was generally acknowledged; commanders came to him each with a shroud on his shoulders, and fell at his feet to win pardon. The Sultan treated these men with a kindness which scattered their fears and attached them to his fortunes. Soon he saw also at his court that entire horde of small tyrants who had sprung into power during anarchy in all parts of Persia. These men, in great dread lest they lose their sweet morsels, came of their own will to render him homage. Those who were best, or at least those whom he thought best for his own interests, got permission to return to their places.

Jelal's first campaign after securing power was against Nassir, the Kalif of Islam, and the enemy of his father. Marching to Kuzistan quickly he laid siege to Shuster, the chief place of that province. His army lacked all things and rushed through the country in various small parties to find what they needed. They drove back great numbers of horses and mules; they found what provisions were requisite, but at the end of two months the siege was abandoned, and the Sultan moved upon Bagdad directly. He halted at Yakuba, seven parasangs [1] distant from the capital.

Kalif Nassir strengthened Bagdad. He gave one million dinars [2] to his troops before sending them to battle; that done he waited.

Jelal begged by letter Moazzam, the Prince of Damascus and nephew of Saladin, to aid him in this struggle with Nassir who had brought, as he stated, savage people to Persia, and destroyed Shah Mohammed. Moazzam replied that he would make common cause with the Sultan in everything save only a struggle against the high chief of all Moslems.

Kush Timur led the forces of Bagdad which were twenty thousand in number. A pigeon was sent to Mozaffar who was prince then in Erbil with an order to attack the Sultan's rear guard and bar retreat to him. Since Jelal's forces were small he sent a message to Kush Timur saying that he had not come as an enemy; he desired the good-will of the Kalif whose aid was to him indispensable in that great struggle with the enemy who menaced all Islam. If the Kalif would act and agree with him he, the Sultan, could be the safe-guard of Persia.

Kush Timur's single answer was to range his men in order of

[1] About twenty-seven miles.   [2] A dinar is the fiftieth part of a cent.

battle. Jelal, forced to fight with an enemy greatly superior, put a part of his small army in ambush; he charged thrice after that with a troop of five hundred and fled, as it were, in disorder. The enemy followed, fell into the trap, and were attacked on both flanks with great fury. Kush Timur was cut down in the struggle; his army was broken and then pursued to the gates of the capital.

Jelal after winning this victory captured Dakuka (1225), and sacked it. Next he moved against Takrit, and learning that Mozaffar, the Prince of Erbil, was approaching with an army, and had gone ahead with a small force to surprise and take him, he set out with a handful of heroes and captured Mozaffar, whom he freed afterward on his promise to return to his own lands and stay in them.

Jelal dropped all his plans against Bagdad; Azerbaidjan was the place which now lured him. Marching first to Meraga he fell to clearing away the ruins, but left that task quickly on hearing that Togan Taissi, his uncle on the mother's side, and also his brother-in-law, was moving from Azerbaidjan to take Hamadan and the neighboring districts, the investiture of which had been given him by the Kalif. Togan had spent the whole winter in Arran and on his journey through Azerbaidjan he pillaged that country a second time.

Jelal arrived about midnight near the camp ground of Togan, around which were gathered vast numbers of sheep, mules, horses, asses, and cattle.

When this Turk general, who thought that the Sultan was then in Dakuka, saw his troops after daybreak, and knew by the regal umbrella that Jelal himself was there with them, he was so disconcerted that he forgot every idea save the single one of winning favor. He sent his wife, Jelal's sister, to make peace if possible. She made it and Togan thereupon ranged his troops with the Sultan's and under his banners; after that they returned to Meraga.

Euzbeg, who was ruler in Azerbaidjan, had gone from Tebriz to Gandja the capital of Arran. In spite of the dangers which threatened his country he passed his time drinking, leaving all cares of State to his consort, a daughter of Sultan Togrul, the last Seljuk ruler in Irak. She had remained in Tebriz, and Jelal, who was eager to win that famed city, laid siege to it. After five days of fighting and just as he was ready to storm it, the inhabitants asked to surrender. The Sultan reproached them with murdering, a year earlier, certain warriors of his father, and sending their heads to the Mongols. They assured him that not they but their ruler had to answer for that; they had been powerless to stop him.

The Sultan accepted this statement and spared them. They begged him to guarantee Euzbeg's wife the possession of Khoï, and a few other places. Jelal consented, and sent an escort to convey her to Khoï.

When Jelal had taken Tebriz he stayed for some days in that city. Meanwhile his men seized the neighboring districts. Then he set out on an expedition against Georgia (1226).

Since Euzbeg was neglectful and indolent the Georgians made raids into Arran and Azerbaidjan; they ravaged Erzerum also, and later on Shirvan. They had scourged the Moslems of these regions severely. Eager for vengeance Jelal had no sooner made himself master at the Caspian than he declared war on the Georgians, who sent back this answer: " We have measured our strength with the Mongol, who took all his lands from thy father and destroyed him. He was a man of more courage and power than art thou. Those Mongols who killed him met us, and ended by fleeing."

Jelal began by the capture of Tovin, which the Georgians had seized some years earlier; next he marched against the main Georgian army, seventy thousand in number, attacked it in the valley of Karni near Tovin, and put it to flight with a loss of twenty thousand. Many generals were captured, among others Shalové, the master of Tovin. The chief commander, Ivane, escaped to the fortress of Keghe, which the Sultan invested while the rest of his army spread out over Georgia, bringing fire and the sword to all places. He would have begun a real conquest had he not thought that he must go to Tebriz. When ready to march into Georgia the Sultan got news from his vizir that a plot had been formed in Tebriz to give back the country to Euzbeg. The Sultan kept this knowledge secret and only when Georgia was crushed did he tell the whole tale to his generals. He gave then command of his army to Ghiath his brother, hastened back to Tebriz, put its mayor to death, and arrested the ringleaders of the conspiracy. When he had strengthened thus his authority he married Euzbeg's wife, and while in Tebriz urged forward troops who took Gandja, the capital of Arran, whence Euzbeg made his way to Alandja.

Tebriz and Gandja being brought to obedience, Jelal returned quickly to Georgia, whose people meanwhile had raised a new army in which were found Alans, Lesgians, Kipchaks and others. This army struck now by Jelal lost heavily and was scattered. After the victory Jelal marched on Tiflis, which he captured through aid from Mohammedans who lived in that city. All Georgians were put to the sword except those who acknowledged the supremacy of the Sultan. Women and children fell to the conquerors, the city was yielded to pillage. Jelal took full vengeance on the Georgians for all that they had done to Mohammedans. His troops were enriched by the property of Christians, he slew a vast number of those " infidels," as he thought them, and drove their children and wives into slavery.

Leaving Georgia, a desert in great part he turned his face next to Khelat on the north of Lake Van in Armenia. This city belonged to Ashraf, an Eyubite prince, lord over Harran and Roha. His brother, Moazzam, the prince of Damascus, who defended himself against Ashraf, and Kamil, his eldest brother, who was Sultan of Egypt, had sent his chief confidant, an officer, to Jelal then in Tiflis, and begged him to make an attack upon Khelat, and give in this way assistance. Moazzam admired the Kwaresmian Sultan immensely, and held it an honor to wear a robe which had come from him, and ride on a steed which Jelal had thought proper to send him. During night banquets Moazzam never swore except by the head of the Sultan.

The Kwaresmian warriors laid siege to Khelat very willingly since the place promised booty in abundance. But they had barely arrived at the walls of the city when advice came to Jelal that Borak, the governor of Kerman, had withdrawn from allegiance, and even sent men to the Mongols to explain the increase and importance of Jelal's new army.

The Sultan abandoned the siege and set out for Kerman. Borak, who had learned that he was coming, withdrew to a stronghold and sent words of feigned loyalty and obedience. It would have been difficult to capture the stronghold, so Jelal thought it best to dissemble, to receive at their literal value the words brought to him; hence he sent a rich robe of honor from Ispahan to the faith-breaking Borak, and confirmed him in office.

Meanwhile news came from Sherif ul Mulk, the vizir, of hostile action by Ashraf against a corps of Kwaresmians which he had beaten.

The Sultan's troops left in Georgia lacked almost everything. They made an incursion toward Erzerum, drove away flocks and herds and took many women. While on the way back from this forage they passed near Khelat; the commandant rushed out from his fortress and seized all their booty. The vizir in alarm begged the Sultan to hasten with assistance.

Jelal moved to Tiflis by swift marches, and thence farther to Ani; he attacked this old city and Kars also with its very strong fortress. Returning soon to Tiflis he made a long march to Abhasia, October, 1226, as it were to subdue it. This was merely a feint to rouse false security in Khelat. Ten days only did he stay in Abhasia and turned then with great speed toward Khelat, which he would have captured had not the commandant been advised two days earlier by his confidants who were serving in the suite of the Sultan.

Jelal hurled his force on the city the day that he reached it; a second assault was made the day following. His troops took the outskirts which they pillaged, but were forced to withdraw from them. After some days of rest the assault was renewed, but resistance was so resolute that this plan was abandoned. The people knowing well the ferocity of Kwaresmians, and the deeds which they did in each captured city, resisted with desperate valor. Ashraf went to Damascus, moreover, and swore obedience to Moazzam, his brother, begging him meanwhile to stop Jelal from ruining Khelat, but Jelal remained till the cold and deep snow drove him from the place. Azerbaidjan also called him. A large horde of Turkmans were pillaging the people, and plundering caravans.

The Sultan made a swift march and came on them suddenly, shutting off their retreat to the mountains. Surrounding the robbers he cut them to pieces. Their families and all the rich booty which they had taken fell to the Sultan who retired to Tebriz with his captives. The Kwaresmians had abandoned Tiflis for the winter, so the Georgians at Ani, Kars and other places united.

They moved on Tiflis in a body and put to death all Mohammedans, and since they despaired of defending the city against
Jelal they fired it.

The Ismailians, that is, the Assassins of Persia, had just killed
a general to whom the Sultan had given Gandja and the lands
which went with it. To inflict vengeance for this act Jelal took
fire and sword to the land of those death dealing sectaries. A
division of Mongols meanwhile had moved westward toward
Damegan. Against this force the Sultan marched swiftly; he
repulsed and then hunted it for many days in succession.

While Jelal on the east was thus occupied Hussam ud din Ali,
Ashraf's commander at Khelat, appeared in the west unexpectedly,
invited to Azerbaidjan by those of the people who liked not the
Sultan's strange ways, and who were brought down to need by
the greed of his warriors. Euzbeg's former wife too was active.
She had had her own way with her first husband. Fixed now to
Jelal through marriage she could not endure the effacement that
came from this union. She remembered the past and joining the
people of Khoï took action. She invited Hussam to seize that
whole region. He consented and took many places; that done,
he marched back to Khelat, Jelal's new, but dissatisfied, consort
going with him.

But there was need soon to face a more serious opponent. The
Mongols were moving in force toward Irak and soon appeared at
its border. Jelal sent four thousand horsemen toward Rayi and
Damegan to watch them. Pressed by the Mongols these four
thousand fell back upon Ispahan, where the Sultan had fixed his
headquarters. The enemy following stopped one day's march
from the city, and east of it. The Mongol force, made up of five
divisions, was commanded by Tadji Baku, Anatogan, Taimaz and
Tainal. Astrologers counseled the Sultan to wait four days before
fighting; he complied and showed confidence of a kind to rouse
courage in all who came near him.

At the first news of that Mongol approach his generals were
alarmed and repaired to the palace in a body. He received them
in the courtyard, and talked long of things which concerned not
attack on the city, to show that he was in no way uneasy. Then
he seated them and discoursed on the order of battle. Before the
dismissal he made all take an oath not to turn from the enemy

or prefer life to the death of a hero.   He took the same oath himself, and appointed a day for the struggle.   Command was then given the chief judge and the Ispahan mayor to review the armed citizens.

Since Jelal did not move from the city the Mongols supposed that he had not strength or even courage to meet them, hence they prepared for a siege and sent two thousand horse into Lur to collect provisions.   The Sultan hurried three thousand men after them.   These took every defile in the rear of the foragers, and barred retreat; many Mongols were killed and four hundred were captured.   Jelal gave some of these men to the populace, by whom they were massacred in the streets of the city.   The Sultan cut off with his own hand the heads of others in the courtyard of his palace; and their bodies were hurled out to be eaten by vultures and dogs.

August 26, 1227, was the day fixed for battle — Jinghis had died in Tangut eight days earlier.   While the Sultan was ranging his men for the conflict Ghiath, his own brother, betrayed him, — deserted.   Jelal did not seem to take note of the defection.   Even when he saw the Mongols in order of battle he thought that his men were more than sufficient to conquer such an enemy, and ordered the Ispahan guards to reënter the city.   At the beginning of the conflict the two wings of the Sultan's forces were too far from each other for mutual assistance.   During a fierce onset his right wing pierced the left of the enemy, and pursued it to Kashin.   The left had not yet been in action.   The sun was declining and Jelal was resting at the edge of a defile.   Just then Ilan Buga, an officer, approached Jelal and said with animation: " We have long implored Heaven for a day such as this to take vengeance on those outcasts.   Success is now with us, and still we neglect it.   To-night this vile enemy will make a long two days' journey, and we shall repent when too late that we let them escape us.   Ought we not to make this day's victory perfect ? "

Struck by these words the Sultan remounted, but hardly had he crossed the ravine when a chosen corps of the enemy hidden by a height, rushed on the left wing, rolled it back on the center and broke it.   The generals of that wing now kept their oath faithfully and died weapons in hand, except three of them.

The Sultan remained in the center, which then was surrounded completely. He had only fourteen of the guards near his person, and he slew with his own hand his standard bearer who was fleeing; then he himself cut a way through the enemy. Fugitives from the center and left rushed in every direction. Some fled toward Fars, others toward Kerman, while Azerbaidjan was a refuge for a third group. Those who had lost their horses in the battle went back on foot to the city. At the end of two days the right wing came from Kashan, believing the rest of the army victorious. When they heard of its defeat they disbanded at once.

Though the Mongols won the battle, their sufferings and losses were greater than those of the Moslems. Advancing to the gates of the city they were repulsed and pursued with such speed that in three days of flight they reached Rayi whence by the Nishapur road they fled farther. On this retreat they lost many men both in killed and in prisoners.

No one knew whither the Sultan had vanished. Some sought for his corpse on the battle-field, others thought that the enemy had captured him. At Ispahan people talked of a new sovereign, while the mob wished to seize the women and goods of the Kwaresmians. But the cadi prevailed upon all to wait a few days till the Bairam feast opened. He agreed, however, with the principal citizens that should the Sultan not come to the prayer on that feast day they would choose as ruler Togan Taissi, who through his virtues deserved supreme power before others.

When the people had assembled on the feast day Jelal came to the prayer and caused great rejoicing. Fearing lest he might be besieged in the city he had not returned to it when the battle was over, but had waited on the Luristan side till the enemy had vanished. The Sultan now stayed some days waiting for fugitives and rewarding chiefs of the right wing by giving the title of khan to those who were meliks. He gave high rank also to simple warriors who had deserved fame for their action in the battle. Certain cowardly generals were led through the city with veils on their faces in the manner of women.

Ghiath ud din, Jelal's brother, had retired to the mountains and was striving to win back dominion through assistance from the Kalif. Hatred between the two brothers had been intensified by murder. Mohammed, son of Karmil, of a family illustrious in Gur, was in very high favor with Jelal who, charmed with his manners and speech, had admitted that youth to his intimate reunions. Some days before the late battle Mohammed had taken a few men to his service from the corps under Ghiath. These men had left Jelal's brother since no pay had been given them. One evening when Ghiath and Mohammed were at a feast given by Jelal, Ghiath asked Mohammed if he would send back his guardsmen. "They desire food," was the answer, "and serve him who will give it." Ghiath was roused by this statement, and the Sultan, who noted his anger, asked Mohammed to withdraw from the table. The young man obeyed, but a few moments later Ghiath went out also, entered the man's dwelling and stabbed him. Mohammed died some days later. The Sultan grieved greatly for his favorite, and sent this message to Ghiath: "Thou hast sworn to be a friend to every friend of mine, and an enemy of my enemies, but thou hast killed my best friend without reason. Thou hast broken thy oath and agreement. I am bound to thee no longer. I will let the law do its work, if the brother of thy victim comes to me begging for justice."

The Sultan commanded that the funeral procession move twice past the gate of the assassin. Tortured by this public punishment Ghiath took vengeance on the day of the battle by deserting. From his Kuzistan place of retirement he sent his vizir to Bagdad to declare that he had gone from his brother. He then proffered proofs that his reign had been friendly to the Kalif, while Jelal had acted with enmity, and had brought fire and sword to the suburbs of Bagdad. He begged aid of the Kalif in recovering his dominions, and promised true obedience to the heir of the Prophet.

The vizir was received with distinction, and a subsidy of thirty thousand dinars was then given him, but after the retreat of the Mongols Ghiath did not think himself safe from his brother. Jelal sent a corps of mounted warriors to follow the Mongols to the Oxus, and hurried himself to Tebriz for a season. He was playing ball with a mallet on the square of the city when he heard that his brother was returning to Ispahan. He set out at once for that city, but learning on the road that Ghiath was on his way to the land of the Assassins he changed his route quickly to follow, and ask the Alamut chief to surrender the fugitive. "Your brother," said the chief, "is here in asylum; he is a Sultan him-

self and his father was a Sultan, — we cannot surrender him, but
he will not take your dominions, we guarantee that. Should he
commit any act of hostility you are free to treat us as may please
you."

This statement seemed satisfactory to Jelal, and an oath added
strength to it. Jelal on his part swore to give the past to oblivion,
and the question was ended. But Ghiath himself went from
Alamut to seek refuge in Kerman. Some days after his arrival
Borak showed a wish to marry Ghiath's mother, Beglu Aï, who
had come with him. They were both in Borak's power and
resistance would have been futile. Still the princess yielded only
after much resistance. Conducted to Kevashir the capital of
Kerman, the mother and son had hardly arrived when two relatives
of Borak proposed to assassinate that governor and install Ghiath.
Ghiath rejected the offer, but Borak, hearing that his relatives
had made it, tortured the two men so cruelly that they confessed
to him. They were then cut to pieces in the presence of Ghiath
who, confined straightway in the citadel, was strangled with a
bowstring. His mother, who had rushed in at his cries, met her
death in the same way. The five hundred followers who had
come with him were cut down every man of them.

Borak sent the head of his victim to Ogotai Khan who received
it with gladness. This gift secured Mongol friendship and Borak
was confirmed in his Kerman possessions.

The Kankali Turks and the Kipchaks had been closely connected
with the reigning Kwaresmian family by marriages; because of
this fact, Jinghis Khan had attacked both those peoples inflexibly,
and Jelal now sought their friendship with growing endeavor.
After his Ispahan failure the Sultan sent to get men and aid from
the Kankalis. They agreed, as it seems, with much readiness
to give them. Kur Khan, one of their leaders, embarked with three
hundred men on the Caspian and passed the next winter with the
Sultan on the plain of Mughan, a rich pasture land in that season.
It was decided that Jelal was to gain the strong fort at Derbend
with its one narrow pass and retain it. By this pass alone could
large armies go south of the Caucasus from Kipchak. A force of
fifty thousand from the north was to aid in securing this road near
the sea, while Jelal was to give the prince ruling Derbend other
fiefs in payment for it. The plan failed, however. Jelal secured

now the district Gushtasfi between the rivers Kur (Cyrus) and
Araxes. This land was a part of the Shirvan Shah's kingdom,
and he had given it to his son Jelal ud din Sultan Shah and sent
him to Georgia to marry the daughter of Rusudan, the famous
and beautiful queen of that country. Detained there perforce he
was freed when Jelal took Tiflis and laid waste the country.

Jelal claimed tribute now from the Shirvan Shah for all his
possessions. This was done, since Jalal's house had succeeded
the Seljuks, to whom when in power those Shirvan Shahs had paid
tribute.

The unquiet ambition of Jelal had forced many people of the
Caucasus to a league with the Georgians against him. An army
made up from nine nations and forty thousand in number had
gathered north of Arran. The Sultan marched against this
army and pitched his camp at Mendur. Since his forces were
greatly inferior in number to those of the enemy, Sherif ul Mulk,
his vizir, advised at a council to limit all action to stopping provisions and meeting the enemy with advantage when want came.
This advice enraged Jelal so seriously that he struck his vizir on
the head with a writing case. "They are mere sheep; would a
lion be troubled by the number of such weak little animals?"
cried he, and he fined the vizir fifty thousand dinars for daring to
offer such counsel.

Next day the armies were facing each other. The Sultan, to
encourage his men, gave them presents, and shared with some his
best horses. From the top of a hill he saw two tumans of Kipchaks
who had come to give aid to the Georgians. By an officer he sent
bread and salt to those Kipchaks and told them that he had saved
the lives of many of their people taken captive by his father.
" Will you now raise the sword to repay me with bloodshed?"
asked he.

The Kipchaks withdrew on receiving this statement. The
Georgians advanced, but Jelal sent this message to their leader:
" Your men must be wearied by long marches; if they wish rest
for to-day the best warriors from both sides may amuse themselves
by trying their strength and address in the presence of the armies."
This proposition was accepted.

One of the bravest of Georgia's great veterans rode forth to the
space between the two forces. The Sultan rushed to meet this

strong champion, and pierced him through with one lance thrust.
Three sons of the man came forth then to avenge him and were
killed in succession by Jelal. Next came a fifth man, enormous
in stature. The Sultan's horse was wearied, there was no time for
a change, and had it not been for his marvelous skill in escaping
from blows and in parrying, Jelal would have seen his last hour in
that conflict. But when the Georgian was rushing lance in rest
at him, the Sultan sprang to the ground, disarmed the oncoming
giant, and killed him. He gave with his whip then a signal for
the onset, and, in spite of the truce, his whole army rushed at
the Georgians, surprised and defeated them.

Free of his enemies now Jelal marched in 1229 on Khelat to
besiege it a second time. He remained all the winter before it,
but was forced by keen cold and deep snow to lodge a great part
of his troops in the villages of that region. To his camp came the
Erzerum prince, Rokn ud din Jihan Shah, who belonged to a
branch of the Seljuks of Rūm. This prince, having had quarrels
before that with Jelal, wished now to arrange them, show homage,
and give presents ten thousand dinars in value.

The Sultan received him with every distinction, and in taking
farewell asked for siege engines. Rokn ud din sent a great catapult, shields and many engines of value. The princes of Amid
and Mardin sent their submission through envoys. Next came
an embassy from Bagdad. Nassir, the Kalif, had died during
1225 in the forty-sixth year of his rule, the longest rule of any man
in the whole line of Abbasids. Zahir, Nassir's son and successor,
had been only nine months in office when he died. Mostansir,
his son, then succeeded. Mostansir now sent an envoy to make
two demands upon Jelal; first that the Sultan would claim no
rights of a sovereign in Mosul, Erbil, Abuye and Jebal whose
princes were vassals of the Kalif; second that he would restore
the name of the Kalif in all public prayers throughout Persia.
Shah Mohammed, his father, had abolished this practice when he
was marching on Bagdad, and had not restored it. The Sultan
granted both requests straightway and commanded that in all
his states every Moslem should pray for Mostansir. When the
envoy returned a chamberlain of the Sultan went with him. This
chamberlain came back with two officials, who brought from the
Kalif a robe of investiture to Jelal, and splendid presents to him

and his highest officials. Jelal asked earnestly for the title of Sultan. Bagdad refused, having given thus far, as was stated, that title to no ruler, but while investing him the Kalif gave the title Shah in Shah (Shah of Shahs). In letters after that Jelal styled himself servant of the Kalif whom he called lord and master.

While besieging Khelat the Sultan commanded to adorn Ispahan with a college, and a domed mausoleum of rich structure. This building was to hold the sarcophagus of his father which meanwhile would rest on the Demavend mountain in Erdehan, a strong fortress three days' journey from Rayi toward the Caspian. He requested by letter his aunt, Shah Khatun, a widow of the Mazanderan prince named Ardshir, to attend the " great Sultan's " remains to the fortress. The chief men of her country and the Moslem Ulema were to go with her. Mohammed of Nessa, who indited the letter with this request, declares that he sent it unwillingly, since he knew well that Mohammed's remains were far safer on that island in the Caspian than they ever could be in the fortress; for the Mongols burned the corpses of all kings whose graves they found, believing them of the Kwaresmian dynasty. They dug up in Gur the remains of Mahmud, son of Sebak Tegin, though this prince had been dead two whole centuries. " The event failed not to justify my fears," adds Mohammed Nessavi.[1] " After Jelal had been slain the Mongols took the Erdehan stronghold and sent the body of Mohammed to Ogotai who burned it."

Before beginning the siege of Khelat, Jelal sent an envoy from Meraga to the Sultan of Rūm, Alai ed din Kei Kubad, with a letter expressing his wish for relations of friendship, and showing the need of close union, since they were one in the East and the other in the West, the two bulwarks of Islam against raging infidels. Kei Kubad read this letter with favor, and to strengthen an alliance proposed that Jelal give a daughter in marriage to his, Kei Kubad's, son, Kei Kosru. Two envoys from Kei Kubad came bringing friendly expressions to Jelal while he was in front of Khelat, and besieging it.

These envoys were forced to deliver their presents just as did subjects when bringing gifts to their sovereign. They asked a daughter of Jelal for Kei Kubad's son, and received a refusal.

---

[1] Mohammed of Nessa. Nessavi means of Nassa and applies specially to the historian.

They complained of hostility shown Kei Kubad by his cousin and vassal, the Erzerum prince, and asked that Jelal yield this prince up, and let Kei Kubad take his country. This request roused Jelal, who answered with spirit: "Though I have complaints against Jihan Shah, he has come to my court and now is a guest in it. It would not be proper for me to deliver him to an enemy." Discontent in the envoys was heightened immensely by insolence from Jelal's vizir.

One day when Nessavi was visiting this minister he heard rude speech and boasting: "If the Sultan permitted I would enter your country and subject it with the troops at my order," said Sherif. "When the envoy had gone I asked the vizir," says Nessavi, "for the cause of his rudeness, since Kei Kubad had testified friendship. 'The presents brought by those envoys,' replied the vizir, ' are not equal to two thousand dinars.' "

The envoys, accompanied by three others from Jelal, went home little pleased with their mission. When they arrived at the boundary of Rūm the two hurried on in advance to their sovereign. On hearing their narrative Kei Kubad despatched one of them straightway to make an alliance with Ashraf.

After six months of siege work Jelal stormed Khelat and took it April 2, 1230. He wished that his men should not pillage and ruin the city, but his generals declared that the siege had been long, that the warriors had lost many horses with cattle and property, that if he forbade pillage no new campaign would be possible at any time; all might desert in a body. The generals insisted so firmly that Jelal had to yield to them.

Khelat was given up for a time to the army; for three days and nights did wild, savage men work their will on it. A great many people expired under torture inflicted to force them to tell where their treasures were hidden. Women and children were saved for captivity. The Georgian wife of Prince Ashraf was taken by Jelal, who made her his concubine.

Two younger brothers, Yakub and Abbas, fell into the power of the conqueror also. The Sultan now had the walls of the city repaired, and gave land in that region to his generals. Jelal was preparing to strike Manazguerd when the Erzerum prince, who during the siege of Khelat had given him provisions, and thus earned the hatred of Ashraf, came to inform him that Ashraf and the Sultan of Rūm were concluding a treaty, hence he advised with all earnestness to forestall the two princes by attacking their forces before they could possibly unite them.

After the death of Moazzam of Damascus Ashraf had received from his brother Kamil, who was Sultan of Egypt, Damascus in barter for Surud, Harran, Roha and three other districts. When he heard of the fall of Khelat and the capture of his consort, Ashraf rushed away to his brother Kamil, who was at that time in Rakka. Ashraf met there that envoy from the Sultan of Rūm who was charged with concluding a treaty with him against Jelal. The Khelat Prince took advice from Kamil the Sultan of Egypt, who favored the alliance, but Kamil himself hurried back straightway to Cairo on learning that Salih, his son whom he had left there, was plotting to dethrone him.

Ashraf set out with seven hundred horsemen for Harran. There he demanded contingents from Aleppo, Mosul and the lands lying between the Euphrates and Tigris. When those troops had appeared he went at the head of them to join Kei Kubad at Sivas whence they would march with combined armies on Khelat.

Jelal had resolved to advance on Kharpert, hoping to attack the first of the armies which moved to join the other. He summoned his troops to Kharpert and went thither himself in advance of them, but falling ill at that place he was in such straits that the generals thought his life lost and were ready the moment breath left him to rush off and seize each man the province that pleased him. Jelal recovered, but meanwhile his enemies had united their forces. His army was small if compared with the troops ranged against it. He had not summoned in men from Arran, Azerbaidjan, Irak or Mazanderan who had gone on leave somewhat earlier. His vizir's corps was at Manazguerd, another corps also was attacking Berkeri, still he moved on and in Erzendjan met the enemy.

Kei Kubad's force was twenty thousand, Ashraf's only five, but all chosen warriors. Jelal was defeated most cruelly, and lost many warriors. Among prisoners was the Erzerum prince who had promised Jelal a good part of Kei Kubad's kingdom, but who was forced then to yield up strong places and treasures of his own to his cousin. The victors beheaded all the Kwaresmian officers whom they captured.

Jelal fled to Manazguerd, and taking the troops then besieging that fortress marched on Khelat which he stripped of all that had value and was movable; that done he burned the remainder. Then, taking with him the Georgian wife of Prince Ashraf and Ashraf's two brothers, Yakub and Abbas, he moved into Azerbaidjan. The vizir with his troops was posted in Sekman Abad to follow the movements of the enemy; he himself halted near Khoï. His generals had deserted.

Jelal's enemies did not pursue. On the contrary his vizir got a letter from Ashraf, who had parted with Kei Kubad after the victory, and gone to Khelat, which he found a sad ruin and deserted. "Your master," wrote he to Sherif, "is the Sultan of Moslems, the first rampart of Islam against Mongol enemies. We know that to weaken him signifies ruin to religion, that his losses will affect every Moslem. Why do you with your wonderful experience not give him peace-loving counsels? I guarantee to the Sultan true friendship with the strong aid of Kei Kubad, and my brother, the Sultan of Egypt."

These propositions were followed by discussion, and the two princes made peace. The Sultan agreed to cease all attacks upon Khelat, but despite every effort he would make no promise regarding Kei Kubad. He could not forgive him the alliance with Ashraf. He knew only later how his vizir had offended that prince's envoys. But when he learned that the Mongols were entering Irak he swore to respect all the lands of Kei Kubad.

This Mongol army, thirty thousand in number, was taken from all the troops under Ogotai. It was led by Chormagun, whom the Grand Khan had deputed to finish the conquest of Persia and establish himself there with his warriors. Chormagun, who wished first of all to hunt Jelal to death, as Jinghis the great Khan had hunted Jelal's father, moved through Khorassan very swiftly by the Esferain road, and past Rayi.

Jelal, who had gone from Khoï to Tebriz, hoped that these Mongols would winter in Irak; he needed delay of that length to gather in forces and concentrate. He despatched a Pehlevan straightway to Irak to watch all the movements of the Mongols. This man met a vanguard of the enemy between Zendjan and Ebher. He fled with fourteen men, all he had, and was the only survivor so fiercely did the Mongols rush after him. He came alone to Tebriz with his tidings to the Sultan.

Jelal did not delay; he left the place at once for the steppes of Mugan on the Caspian to gather in forces. Not having time to secure proper safety for his harem, it remained at Tebriz. He spent that winter in Mugan and in Shirvan. Two officers of distinction from Mazanderan and Khorassan were sent forward to have a keen eye on the enemy, report to Jelal, and keep relays of good horses at Firus Abad and at Ardebil.

While waiting for his warriors, summoned through heralds who presented red arrows, Jelal with a body-guard of only one thousand amused himself at hunts during daylight, and spent his evenings drinking with his intimates. One night two officers of the vanguard whom he had trusted to warn him let a Mongol division pass without challenge or notice. They surprised Jelal on a hill close to Shirkebut and he barely escaped from the peril by rushing on toward the river Araxes. The Mongols thought that he had crossed it and they hurried on farther toward Gandja, the capital of Arran, but Jelal had turned back toward Azerbaidjan and sent Prince Yakub his prisoner to explain to Ashraf, Yakub's brother, the great need of sending men promptly to drive back the Mongols, whose plan was to crush down and ruin the whole world of Islam.

Yakub was conducted to Sherif ul Mulk, Jelal's vizir, who had been directed to send with him an envoy having proper instructions. Sherif ul Mulk, who was now a full traitor, had a vizir of his own whom he sent, but with orders entirely opposed to those given by the Sultan. Jelal's harem left in Tebriz unprotected was sent now to Arran by Sherif and lodged in Sind Suruk, a strong fortress, while his treasures were hidden in various castles which belonged to the chief of the Turkmans of Arran. That done, Sherif went to Khizan and raised there the banner of rebellion. He was angry since the Sultan, because of Sherif's immense outlays, had taken from him command of the taxes, and income of all sorts. Thinking Jelal lost when he had fled in Mugan and had been almost captured, he wrote to Kei Kubad and Ashraf declaring that if they would leave Azerbaidjan to him coupled with Arran he would render homage for both and have the two princes' names mentioned at all public worship. " Fallen Tyrant " was the name given the Sultan in this letter. Many missives which were similar to this one in part went to governors to corrupt them. One of these was sent to the Sultan who knew now that Sherif stopped all Kwaresmian officers who came near his fort and wrung their possessions from them by torture. He learned also that Sherif had instructed the Turkman chief not to yield up the harem or treasures of the Sultan to any one, not even to Jelal himself should he come for them. In this letter also he styled him "Fallen Tyrant." The Sultan, knowing now the vizir and his treason, had orders sent to disregard his authority.

Jelal, who remained all the winter (1231) in Mugan, went to Arran in the spring upon hearing that the Mongols were moving from Odjan to find him. When near Sherif's castle he sent for the traitorous vizir and feigned to know nothing of his treason. Sherif came with a shroud on his neck. Jelal had wine brought to him, an act not agreeing with etiquette, since the Kwaresmian sultans never admitted vizirs to their banquets. Sherif thought himself then at the summit of favor, but soon he had reason to think otherwise, for though he followed the Sultan the latter assigned him no duties.

The bad condition of Jelal's affairs affected the people of the two Caspian provinces recently subjected. In Tebriz the population, roused to anger by the men who commanded in the name of the Sultan, were ready to massacre all the Kwaresmians and thus win good grace from the Mongols. Revolts broke out in many places of Azerbaidjan and of Arran. Men in the service of the Sultan were killed and their heads carried off as presents to the enemy.

Jelal wishing to assemble the troops of Arran, and unable to trust any Turkman in his service, prevailed on Mohammed of Nessa to accept this most delicate mission, which he carried out with such thoroughness and so deftly that Jelal soon had a strong force at his command. At report of this exploit the Mongol division which had marched into Arran withdrew to the main camp at Odjan. An envoy sent to the Bailecan governor to effect his surrender was brought before Jelal immediately. On being asked touching Chormagun's army, and promised his life if he told the truth sacredly (the man was a Moslem), he declared that the army roll counted twenty thousand on the day of review near

the Bokhará suburbs. Jelal, lest his troops lose their courage
and scatter, had the man killed at once.

Then, fearing that the vizir might rush away on a sudden and
rouse many men to rebellion, the Sultan set out for Jaraper followed still by the traitor. He ordered then the commandant of
the Jaraper fortress, a cruel old Turkman, to arrest the vizir and
put him in irons the moment that he, the Sultan, moved farther.
This was done, and soon after, the old Turkman sent six guards
to take life from Sherif. The moment he saw the men coming the
vizir knew that his last hour was present. He begged a short
respite during which to implore the Almighty. He made his
ablutions, then prayed, read some lines in the Koran, and said that
the guards might enter. On reappearing they asked him which
he preferred, the cord or the sabre. " The sabre," answered
Sherif. " It is not the usage that great people die by the sabre,"
said the guard, " and death by the cord is far easier." " The task
is yours," replied Sherif. " Do what seems best to you. I receive
that which comes to him always who trusts the ungrateful."
These were the last words of Sherif. He was strangled.

Jelal's next move was a quick march on Gandja, where the populace had slain all Kwaresmians in the city. He pitched his camp
at the wall and strove to persuade the seditious to obedience by
pleasant messages and mildness; but the crowd grew more insolent and rushed forth to fall on him. The Sultan charged fiercely.
The populace fled, and returned through the gate in disorder.
The victors were eager for plunder, but the Sultan restrained
them. He wished above all to discover the leaders of the outbreak.
Thirty were named and Jelal cut their heads off.

The Sultan remained fifteen days in the city, thinking on action.
At last he resolved to ask aid a second time of Ashraf. He hated
to do this, but yielded to counsel.

Ashraf, on hearing that envoys were coming from Jelal, took a
journey to Egypt. The envoys were made to delay at Damascus,
where the Syrian prince forced them to loiter and amused them by
letters declaring that he would return soon from Cairo with troops
for their master.

At last Jelal's envoys sent word to him that Ashraf would stay
in Egypt, as they thought, till the whole Mongol question was
settled without him. Jelal sent his chancellor then to Mozaffer,

who had received Khelat from Ashraf his brother. He invited this prince to come with his own troops and bring with him also the princes of Mardin and Amid, with their forces. He said that then he could win without Ashraf. His envoy was to explain to Mozaffer with all clearness possible that if they, with God's favor, should conquer the Mongols he would put Mozaffer in a country compared with which Khelat and its lands were as nothing. This was said by Jelal in the presence of his generals, but to Mohammed of Nessa when alone with him his speech was as follows: " I have no faith in the people to whom you are going, but these here," meaning his Turkman commanders, " are satisfied only with visions, and their highest desire is to escape serious fighting. Thus have they baffled every plan made by me. I send you now on this mission knowing well that you will bring back an answer taking from them all hope of aid."

The Sultan had fixed on Ispahan the capital as his stronghold. At his command six thousand men went to pillage in Rūm whence they drove back immense herds of cattle.

When Mohammed of Nessa gave Mozaffer the message, that prince replied in this fashion: " If I have given an oath to Jelal, I have given one also to Kei Kubad; I know too that your sovereign has ravaged Kei Kubad's country, and that is not what he promised on the day of the oath taking. Besides I am not my own master; I depend on my brothers, the Sultan of Egypt, and the ruler of Syria, I could not help any man unless those two permitted. Moreover what aid could my little army give Jelal, or others? As to the princes of Mardin and Amid, they are not my dependents. They are discussing with the Sultan touching aid. I know that, I know too that he is trying them. He will find soon that they are not truthful, while Ashraf is eager in the interest of the Sultan, and is faithful to promises. His only object in going to Egypt is to get troops and lead them back with him."

At the end of some days Mohammed took leave of Mozaffer while declaring that whatever the end was the latter would regret his decision. " If Jelal triumphs," said he, " you can never be reconciled; if he is conquered the Mongols will bring bitter grief on you if not destruction." The Khelat prince answered that he doubted not the words of the envoy, but added, " I am not my own master."

A letter borne by a pigeon from Perkri announced that the
Mongols were searching for the Sultan, and had passed by that
city. Jelal went to Hany, but finding there only the women and
baggage, he set out for Jebal Jor without waiting. A Mongol
escaping from punishment had come to the Kwaresmians and
declared that the Mongols were advancing. The man was a commander of one thousand who would not endure reprimands from
superiors, hence had fled from them. Following the advice of
this runaway Jelal left his baggage at the wayside, and settled in
ambush near by to fall on the Mongols while they were pillaging
it. Otuz Khan, one of his generals, with four thousand horsemen,
was to move on the enemy, engage and then flee after fighting, thus
luring them on into ambush. Otuz Khan being neither keen nor
courageous, came back and declared that the Mongols had gone
toward Manazguerd. On hearing this false statement the Sultan
came out of his ambush and went on to Hany where he was met
by Mohammed of Nessa whom he commanded to report in the
presence of all, on the outcome of his mission.

Convinced after listening to this report that no help would
come from any one, all resolved straightway to fall back on
Ispahan, taking only those of their children and wives who were
dearest to them.

Two days later, came an envoy from Prince Massud of Amid.
That prince wished the Sultan to make himself master in Rūm,
a conquest which he declared would be easy. Master of Rūm and
strong through the Kipchaks who were firmly attached to him,
Jelal could make himself terrible to the Mongols. Massud
promised to strengthen the Sultan with four thousand horsemen
and stay with him till Rūm should be conquered.

This entire plan of that Amid prince was caused by his rage at
Kei Kubad, who had snatched away some of his castles.

Jelal's ambition was roused to activity. He abandoned the
Ispahan journey and started off toward Amid without waiting.
Pitching his camp near that city he passed the whole evening in
drinking. At midnight a Turkman rushed in with tidings that he
had seen foreign troops at the place where the Sultan had passed
the night previous. Jelal declared this a lie, and a trick of the
Amid prince to force him from the country at the earliest. But at
daybreak the Mongols were present. They surrounded the

Sultan's pavilion while he was still sleeping off his carousal. One general, Orkhan, galloped up with his troops and drove the enemy away. The officers of Jelal's own household strove hard in this trial; they had barely time to give Jelal a light colored tunic, and put him on horseback. He thought at that moment of one of his wives who was with him, a daughter of the Fars prince, and commanded two of his principal officers to guard her while fleeing.

Seeing that the Mongols were terribly swift in pursuing, Jelal ordered Orkhan to rush in another direction with his forces, and draw off the enemy. He himself took the road to Amid with one hundred horsemen. The gates of that city were closed to him. Persuasion was powerless to open them, hence he fled on toward the Tigris, but soon turning aside he rushed back, and thus followed the counsel of Otuz Khan, who declared that the best way to flee from the Mongols was to double back and be behind them. He reached a small village in the region of Mayafarkin and stopped for the night at a granary. While he was sleeping Otuz Khan slipped away, and deserted. At daybreak the Mongols caught up with the Sultan, who had barely the time to mount and be off while his guards fought the enemy.

Most of Jelal's men were slain while defending their master that morning. Fifteen of the Mongols, on learning that he who had fled was the Sultan, rushed along after him madly. Two reached the swift rider, but he slew both of them. The others could not come up with the fugitive whose horse beyond doubt was superior.

Jelal hurried on alone now, and made his way into the mountains. There he was captured by Kurds, whose work was to strip every wayfarer and slay him. They stripped the Sultan at once and were going to kill him when he told their chief secretly who he was, asking the man to conduct him to the Erbil prince, Mozaffer, who would load him with benefits for doing so; if not to conduct him to some place in the Sultan's own kingdom. The Kurd chose the latter and taking with him to his own habitation the Sultan, whom he left in the care of his wife, he went out to find horses. Meanwhile another Kurd came in, and inquired of the woman who the Kwaresmian was, and why they had not killed him. She replied that he was under her husband's protection, and added, that he was the Kwaresmian Sultan. "How know that he is telling you the truth?" asked the Kurd. "But if he is the Sultan, he killed at the siege of Khelat my own brother, a far better man than he is." With that he sprang at Jelal ud din, pierced him with his javelin, and killed him. Aug. 15, 1231.

With Jelal ud din perished the Kwaresmian dynasty.

"Jelal ud din," says Mohammed of Nessa, "was of medium stature. He had a Turk face, his complexion was very dark, for his mother was from India. He was brave to excess, calm, grave and silent, never laughing except at the points of his lips. He spoke Turkish and Persian." Jelal ud din was no statesman, he had neither foresight nor wisdom; attached to his whims he reconciled no man. Music and wine gave him most of his pleasure. He always went to bed drunk, even at times when the Mongols were hunting him like bloodhounds. He did not retain the affection of his warriors, who receiving no pay had to live on the country and ruin it. Reckless conduct estranged from him those who might have upheld him. A wise and strong leader could have raised up and directed a resistance which would have stopped Hulagu in his conquests. What might have come afterwards is of course a new problem.

Soon after the death of this Sultan, Prince Mozaffer sent men to collect his effects. They found his horse, saddle and sabre. These, being shown to his generals, were recognized. Mozaffer then had his corpse brought and put in a mausoleum.

In after years report ran that Jelal had been seen in various places of Iran. A man at Ispidar gave himself out as the Sultan. The Mongol commanders called in men who had seen Jelal ud din. The imposter was discovered and put to death promptly. Twenty-two years after this death of the Sultan a poor man dressed as a fakir while crossing the Oxus spoke to the boatmen as follows: "I am Jelal ud din the Kwaresmian Shah reported as killed by the Kurds in the mountains of Amid. It was not I who was killed then, but my equerry. I have wandered about many years without letting men know me." Taken by the boatmen to an officer of the Mongols close to that river he was tortured, but insisted till death that he was Jelal ud din the Kwaresmian Sultan.

CHAPTER X

SAD was the fate of the people in Rūm through disunion, stupidity and thoughtlessness. After Jelal ud din lost his life in the mountains his warriors dispersed and were finished by land tillers, by Kurds, and by Beduins. The Mongols fell straightway to ravaging Amid, Erzerum and Mayafarkin. After a siege of five days they captured Sarad, two days' journey from Mardin, and east of it, and though the city had surrendered they slaughtered its inhabitants to the number of fifteen thousand, as is stated. Tanza met the same fate as also did Mardin, whose sovereign took refuge in the fortress. The district of Nisibin was changed to a desert, though the city itself was not taken by the Mongols who, entering the country of Sinjar sacked El Khabur and Araban. One division of them took the road to Mosul and hastened to pillage El Munassa, on the road between Mosul and Nisibin. The people of that place and the flat country around it took refuge in a building near the middle of the city where all save desirable women were massacred. A man of that region being hidden in a house looked out through a cranny and saw what was happening and afterward told Ibn al Athir, the historian. "Each time the Mongols slew some one they shouted ' La illahi.' This massacre finished, they pillaged the place and departed leading away the women selected. I saw them," said the hidden man, "rejoicing on horseback. They laughed, sang songs in their language and shouted while mocking the Moslems."

Another Mongol division marched on Bitlis. Some of the people fled to the mountains, others took refuge in the citadel. The Mongols set fire to the city and burned it. They stormed Balri, a fortified place in the region of Khelat, and slaughtered all the inhabitants. The large city of Andjish met a similar destruction.

A third Mongol force now laid siege to Meraga. This city surrendered on condition that the lives of all citizens be respected. The Mongols gave a promise to spare them, but notwithstanding this promise they slew a great number. They sacked Azerbaidjan, passed into Erbil, attacked Kurds and Turkmans, slaying every one whom they could reach with a weapon. They took fire and sword to all places, and committed atrocities without parallel.

Mozaffer, prince of Erbil, assembled his troops with great speed and got aid from Mosul. The Mongols withdrew then and marched on Dakuka. The prince thought it best not to pursue them.

During those two months which followed the death of Jelal ud din and the scattering of his army, the Mongols pillaged all lands between the Euphrates and Tigris; Diarbekr, Khelat and Erbil, without finding a single armed warrior to oppose them. The princes of those petty states hid away carefully, and the people were stupefied so great was the terror which had seized upon mankind. Deeds were done in that period which beggar belief. For example a lone Mongol horseman rode into a populous village and fell to cutting down people; no man had the courage to defend himself.

Another time a Mongol without weapons wished to hew off the head of a prisoner whom he had taken; he commanded the man to lie down and wait for him. The Mongol went off for a sabre, came back and killed the unfortunate, who was waiting obediently. Still a new tale from a third man: "I was on the road with seventeen comrades when a Mongol on horseback rode up to us, and commanded that each man tie the hands of another. My comrades thought it best to obey. 'This man,' said I to them, 'is alone, let us kill him.' 'We are too much afraid,' said they. 'But he will kill us. Let us kill him, God may then save us.' No man of them had the courage to do this. I killed him then with a knife thrust, and we fled and in that manner saved ourselves from other Mongols." These cases are but three out of thousands.

Three months after the death of Jelal ud din, people in general knew not whether he had been killed, or was hiding, or had gone to another country. Azerbaidjan was now seized by the Mongols. Their leader fixed his camp near Tebriz and summoned that city to surrender. It offered a large sum of money, many fabrics, wine and other products. The chief judge and the mayor with the principal people went to the Mongol commander, who ordered to send out to him weavers since he wished to have certain stuffs made for his sovereign. They obeyed and the citizens paid for those costly fabrics. He asked also a tent for his master. One was made for him of a kind that had never been equalled in that city. It was covered with silk embroidered in gold and ornamented with sable and beaver. Tebriz agreed to an annual tribute in stuffs and in silver.

The Mongols were sacking the lands of Erbil, a fief of the Kalif, Mostansir, who had summoned to assist him Mohammedan sovereigns as well as the Arabs. Kamil, Sultan of Egypt, whose dominions beyond the Euphrates were also threatened, had set out from Cairo at the head of an army and arrived at Damascus whence he moved eastward very promptly. His army being numerous, took various roads in crossing the desert. Since water was lacking, many horses died on that journey, and many men also. On learning at Harran that the Mongols had gone out of Khelat, Kamil besieged Amid. The capture of this place, which belonged to a grandson of Ortok, was the real cause of his coming from Egypt. With him was Ashraf, his brother, who had persuaded him to make the expedition. The Eyubite princes and the Sultan of Rūm marched also with Kamil.

The siege lasted five days altogether. Prince Massud, a weakling and a man enamoured of pleasure, surrendered his capital to Kamil, who gave it as an appanage (1232) to his faithless son Salih, who previously had wished to dethrone him. Massud received certain lands lying in Egypt; to those lands he went and settled down ignominiously as became him. Master of Amid Kamil attacked Hóssn-Keifa, which yielded also. He had now gained his object.

Mongol troops under Chormagun's orders, and after that general's death, under Baidju, continued during two entire decades to slaughter, rob, pillage and devastate lands west of Persia. They ruined whole regions, and cut down the people in wantonness and by thousands. In 1236-7 they made a second invasion of the districts near Erbil, and advanced to the Tigris. Next they took Erbil and found there rich booty. They burned a great number of houses, but could not take the fortress where the inhabitants had rallied, and though perishing from thirst fought with a marvelous valor. At the end of forty days the Mongols retired on receipt of large sums in gold from the people.

They ravaged after that the north edge of Arabian Irak as far as Zenk Abad and Sermenraï, which they pillaged. The Kalif made Bagdad defensible and in 1237 in his wish to rouse every Moslem, he asked the Ulema: "Which gives more merit, a pilgrimage to Mecca, or a war on the infidel?" "The holy war," answered all as one person. The war was proclaimed then. Great persons, men of law, common people, all went out daily to learn the art of wielding weapons. The Kalif himself wished to march with the forces, but prudent advisers dissuaded him. His troops met the enemy at Jebel Hamrin north of Tacrit, on the bank of the Tigris, put them to flight, cut down many, and freed all the captives seized at Dakuka and Erbil a short time before. In 1238 fifteen thousand Mongols invaded the territory of Bagdad, and advanced to Jaferiye, but retired at approach of the forces of the Kalif made up of Turks and Arabs.

That same year, Arabian Irak was reëntered by Mongols from ten to fifteen thousand in number. They advanced to Khanekin, a place some leagues south of Heulvan. The Kalif sent seven thousand horsemen against them under orders of Jemal ud din Beïlek. The Mongols, employing their old stratagem successfully, lured on the forces of Bagdad and attacked them from ambush. They put to the sword nearly all the detachment. Beïlek, their leader, disappeared without tidings.

In 1235 the Mongols took Gandja the capital of Arran, giving the city to flames and the people to slaughter. The year following, 1236, Chormagun left Mugan and swept through Armenia, Albania and Georgia, sacking all the best cities. Georgia had so recently been plundered by Jelal ud din that unable to defend themselves against the Mongol invaders, the princes and people sought refuge in the mountains. Queen Rusudan, a woman famous for her beauty and her lack of virtue, chose as asylum the impregnable fortress of Usaneth in Imeretia.

Chormagun seized the country between the Araxes and the Cyrus. One of his generals, Gadagan, took Kedâpagu and Varsanashod. Another one, Mular, seized Shamkar and every stronghold around it. Chormagun's brother Jola took the fortress of Katchen. Jelal, the master of the place, fled to Khok Castle near Kandzassar. When summoned to surrender he gave the Grand Khan allegiance with tribute and military service. Jagatai, another leader of Mongols, took Lori which belonged to Shah in Shah, prince of Ani, sacked the city and slaughtered the people. Next after this, and in 1239, the Mongols burst into Georgia and captured Tiflis with many other places. When Jagatai had made all his circuits through the country with terror in front of him and ruin behind, he swept again through Armenia, besieging now the old capital Ani. When the ancient city was summoned to yield, the authorities answered that without Shah in Shah they could not surrender, since he was prince of that region. The envoy was returning with this statement when the populace grew furious and killed him. Chormagun laid siege immediately to Ani. Not having supplies, the people learned soon the full meaning of famine. To escape from it many went out and surrendered. Chormagun met all those people with kindness, and gave them provisions; this enticed others till more than one half had gone out of Ani. After that those men, captured thus by their stomachs and Chormagun's cunning, were drawn up in companies and delivered to warriors, who cut them down to the very last person. Ani could not defend itself longer, so pillage and fire destroyed the old city.

On hearing of the dread destruction which had fallen upon Ani, and the slaughter of all who had lived in it, the inhabitants of Kars fearing the doom which, as they thought, would meet them unless they could avert it, carried the keys of their city to the Mongol commander. Notwithstanding this voluntary submission and surrender, a dreadful massacre followed, for Chormagun gave direction to put all to the sword except children, desirable women, and artisans of skill, who were needed by the Mongols.

When Kars had been ruined the invaders returned to the plains of Mugan, which abounded in rich winter pastures.

In 1240 Prince Avak of Tiflis and his sister Tamara went to give homage at Ogotai's court, and were met there with kindness. The Grand Khan gave them an order commanding Chormagun to reinstate them and other Georgian princes; a second command was sent also to take from them only the tribute agreed on already.

When people north of the Euphrates and Tigris had been thinned
out sufficiently and enlightened by slaughter, the Mongols turned
to take Rūm and subdue it.

Rūm had been ruled for a century and a half by a branch of the
Seljuks. Asia Minor was conquered about 1080 by Suleiman
Shah, whom his cousin Sultan Melik, Shah of Persia, had sent
toward the west with eighty thousand Turkman households to
bring down the infidel. Suleiman seized the central provinces of
that region from the Byzantine Empire, and made Konia the
capital of his newly won kingdom, which was called Rūm in the
Orient, but in the west with another vowel, Rome. From that
period on, the Turkman swarms which followed the banners of
the Seljuks spread over those conquered lands widely. Most
places were given them as fiefs, and the Christians of that entire
region passed under the yoke of unsparing and insolent nomads.

The Sultan Ghiath ud din Kei Kosru, eighth successor of Suleiman the first conqueror, had ruled over Rūm for five years when
in 1243 the Mongols set out to subject it. Chormagun was now
dead and Baidju, who succeeded him, had come with an army, in
which were Armenian and Georgian contingents, to invest Erzerum
where Sinan ud din Yakut was commandant. This Yakut was a
freedman of Sultan Kei Kubad, the father of Kei Kosru. At
the end of two months the walls were destroyed by twelve catapults;
the city was taken by storm, and one day later the citadel met with
a similar misfortune. The commandant and also his warriors
were put to the sword without exception. Artisans, workmen,
desirable women and children were spared to be driven into
slavery. When the city had been plundered and ruined the Mongols withdrew to their winter camp on the plain of Mugan.

Mongol warriors were sent in 1244 toward Syria. While they
were approaching Malattia, where news of the sack of Cesaraea
had spread dismay through every hamlet and corner, the prefect
and other officials of the Sultan took during night hours all the
silver and gold of the treasury, divided it among themselves and
set out to find refuge in Aleppo. At the same time the chief
citizens, both Moslem and Christian, tried to save themselves by
flight, but these, after journeying one day, were overtaken by
Mongols who slaughtered the old men and women; the young
of both sexes were spared and driven on into slavery.

The Mongols waited not to lay siege to Malattia, they sped forward at command of Noyon Yassaur to Aleppo, demanded a ransom, received it, and vanished. On his way back, Yassaur made a halt at Malattia and feigned an attack on it. The prefect collected much plate, also gold from church pictures, besides other treasures taken from the Nestorian cathedral; the value in all reached forty thousand gold pieces. After receiving this ransom Yassaur continued his march toward the boundary of Persia. Yassaur was the Mongol chief, probably, who in 1244, toward the end of the summer, summoned Bohemond V., Prince of Antioch, to level the walls of his cities, send in all the revenue of his princedom, and give besides three thousand maidens. The prince refused, the Mongol commander refrained from attacking, but later on the Antioch prince furnished tribute to the Mongols.

The Grand Khan's lieutenant had summoned all sovereigns in Western Asia to obedience. Shihab ud din in 1241 got a letter from an envoy of the Mongols. The letter sent to other princes as well as to him began in this way: " The lieutenant on earth, of the Master of Heaven, commands all the following princes to acknowledge his authority and level their defences; " the names then were given. The prince answered that he was a weak, petty ruler if compared with the sovereigns of Rūm, Syria and Egypt. " Go to them first," said he, " I will follow their example."

Hayton, the king of Cilicia, had promised to bring to the Sultan of Rūm a whole corps of Armenians; he delayed marching, however, and awaited developments. The kingdom of Rūm was now subject to Mongols, and Hayton thought it well to win Mongol favor if possible. On securing consent from the chief men of his kingdom he sent envoys in 1244, during spring, with rich presents to Baidju. The envoys turned to Jalal, an Armenian prince then in Katchen, who presented them to Baidju, to Chormagun's widow, and to Mongol commanders. Baidju asked first that Hayton deliver the wife, daughter and mother of Kei Kosru, who were then in Cilicia. That request made, he took leave of the envoys, and sent with them men of his own to their sovereign. The conditions were grievous to Hayton, but he yielded the women to Baidju's officials and sent on new envoys. The Mongol commander was satisfied, and concluding an alliance with Hayton, giving him a diploma which affirmed his position as vassal to the Grand Khan.

The Mongols during 1245 took regions north of Lake Van, among others Khelat, which through an order of Ogotai had been given to Tamara of Georgia. After this they marched into regions between the Euphrates and Tigris, taking Roha, Nisibin and other cities which the people abandoned at approach of the dread enemy. But great summer heat brought down most of their horses, hence the Mongols were forced to withdraw very speedily to save themselves.

Mongol dominion was extending continually. Bedr ud din Lulu the Prince of Mosul declared in a letter to the Prince of Damascus that he had in his own name concluded a treaty by which the inhabitants of Syria would give the Mongols a fixed tribute according to wealth and ability. The tax of the rich would amount to ten dirhems, medium men would pay five, and poor people one dirhem. This letter was published at Damascus, and officials began to collect the taxes decreed by it.

The same year, 1245, news came to Bagdad, by pigeons, that the Mongols had entered Sheherzur, eight days' travel northward from Bagdad, and sacked the whole city, whose prince, Melik ud din Mohammed, had fled to a stronghold.

The Mongols advancing in 1246 to Yakuba were attacked and driven off by Bagdad troops, and some of them were captured. Baidju did not feel himself master of Georgia while Queen Rusudan remained in Usaneth and refused all submission. In vain did he send her rich presents, and ask for an interview during which she and he might arrange, he declared, an alliance with friendship. The queen would not go from her stronghold, and gave no better answer to a message from Batu, who since Ogatai's death, in December,1241, was the first among Jinghis Khan's grandsons. She sent her son David, however, to Batu as hostage, and placed him under that strong Khan's protection. Baidju, wrathful at Rusudan's stubbornness, resolved to give Georgia a ruler subservient to Mongols. Rusudan's brother, Lasha, had a son born outside wedlock whom the queen had despatched into Rūm when her daughter went thither to marry Kei Kosru. This son of Lasha, named David, was detained for ten years in Cesaraea. Freed now for this special state trick, he was. brought to the camp of the Mongols where certain princes proclaimed him, and took the oath of allegiance. Georgian troops and Armenians went with David to Mtskhete the seat of the Patriarch, who anointed him.

David, the new king and tool of the Mongols, in 1246 attacked Rusudan in her fortress where, reduced to extremities, she took poison and in dying recommended her son to Batu the Khan of the Kipchaks and master at that time in Russia.

The young King of Georgia set out to be present at the installation of Kuyuk (1246). The names given of subject rulers present at this great Kurultai show how far-reaching was the power of the Mongols: the Prince of Fars; the ruler of Kerman; Bedr ud din Lulu, Prince of Mosul; Yaroslav, Grand Prince of Russia; Ambassadors from the Kalif of Bagdad; the Prince of the Assassin Kingdom; and many other noted rulers. There were present also two monks who came from the Pope — one of whom, Du Plano Carpino, has left us an account of the Kurultai— and Rusudan's son.

The rivalry of the King of Georgia and Rusudan's son brought about a division of their country. David got Georgia proper and Rusudan's son, Imeretia, Mingrelia and Abhasia. Both men were called kings, but David was the Suzerain. The Cilician King Hayton who sent Sempad, his brother, to be present at Kuyuk's enthronement, received from the Grand Khan more cities seized from Cilicia by the Sultans of Rūm.

In 1249 fresh alarm rose in Bagdad, for the Mongols advanced to Dakuka and killed Bilban the prefect. In 1250–1 Nassir the Prince of Damascus got a letter of safe-conduct from the Grand Khan and bore it in his girdle. Splendid gifts were a proof of his gratitude and pleasure. Lands between the Euphrates and Tigris were again visited by the Mongols. The districts of Diarbekr and Mayafarkin with Reesain and Sarudj were given over to pillage. The invaders cut down in this raid more than ten thousand people. A caravan which had set out from Harran for Bagdad was attacked by those Mongols, who massacred every man in it. They took a large booty; among other objects they got six hundred camel loads of sugar and cloth stuffs from Egypt, besides six hundred thousand dinars in money. After such splendid robbery they went back to Khelat for enjoyment.

A corps under Yassaur, who eight years before that had struck at Malattia, attacked now this city's environs and slew all the

people whom it could reach with a weapon. Kei Kosru had died
in 1245. Yzz ud din Kei Kavus with his two brothers, Rokn
ud din Kelidj Arslan, and Alai ud din Kei Kubad, had succeeded
their father. The names of all three appeared on the coinage,
and were mentioned in mosques at public service. Some great
lords of Rūm wished Rokn ud din as chief sovereign. Shems ud
din of Ispahan, the grand vizir, put many of those partisans to
death. He married Yzz ud din's mother and, wishing to eliminate
Rokn ud din, had him sent to the court of Kuyuk with the tribute
and presents agreed on in the treaty of submission made recently.

When Rokn ud din had appeared at the court of the Grand Khan
he and an officer of his suite, Behaï ud din Terjuman, accused the
vizir of doing to death powerful people who favored Rokn ud din,
of marrying the late Sultan's widow, and of raising a sovereign to
the throne without consent or command of the Grand Khan. On
hearing this statement, Kuyuk commanded that Rokn ud din
take Yzz ud din's place, and that Terjuman take Shems ud din's
office. When the latter heard of this change he despatched to
Kuyuk, Rashid ud din, the prefect of Malattia, with much gold
and many jewels. The new order destroyed him and he hoped
now that the Grand Khan would revoke it. But when his envoy
was nearing Erzerum the newly made Sultan with his vizir were
approaching that city. Overcome by the greatness of his task
the weak envoy placed his treasures in the stronghold of Kemash
and fled with all speed to Aleppo. Terjuman appeared at Malattia
very promptly with two thousand Mongols, and proclaimed the
new Sultan.

Shems ud din wished to take Yzz ud din to the seacoast from
Konia, but he was seized and held captive before he could do so.
Terjuman then sent Mongols to Konia to torture that active
vizir and thus learn where his treasures were hidden; by these
men he was finally killed.

Meanwhile it was settled that Rūm must go to both brothers.
All that lay west of the Sivas was given to Yzz ud din, and everything east of that river fell to Rokn ud din, but the officials of
the latter wished him to have all that Kuyuk had first given him.
Yzz ud din's partisans declared that their sovereign was resigned
to the will of the Grand Khan, and would take whatever appanage
his brother might give him. Rokn ud din credited this statement

and went to a meeting place. He was seized with his vizir and taken to Konia. No harm was done him, however. Yzz ud din joined in the sovereignty Alai ud din his third brother.

Kuyuk died in 1248; Mangu his successor was inaugurated July, 1251. In 1254, three years after Mangu's elevation, Yzz ud din was called to Mongolia, but he feared to absent himself, knowing that Rokn ud din had many partisans, hence he decided to send Alai ud din the third brother, who set out, with many presents, traveling along the Black Sea and the borders of Kipchak. Yzz ud din craved forgiveness from Mangu for sending his own younger brother instead of appearing in person. This, he said, he regretted most keenly, but he was forced to remain and defend his possessions from Greeks and Armenians, his most implacable enemies; he hoped soon, however, to offer homage in person.

Rokn ud din's partisans now sought means to uphold the claims of their master in the presence of the Grand Khan. They forged a letter from Yzz ud din to Tarantai and his colleague, in which the Sultan commanded to confide Alai ud din and the presents to the chancellor Shems ud din and the Emir Seif ud din Jalish, the bearers of the letters, who would go with the prince to Mongolia. Tarantai and his colleague were summoned to Konia.

The Emir and the chancellor set out with this letter and overtook Alai ud din at Sarai, Batu's capital. Batu gave them an audience and to him they explained how Yzz ud din had discovered Tarantai's evil plotting and also that of his colleague. On a time, as they said, Tarantai had been stricken by lightning, hence should not stand in the presence of Mangu. Shuja ed din, his associate, was a leech greatly skilled in all magic, and had with him poison to use for the Grand Khan's undoing; hence the Sultan had sent them to replace those two envoys, who must go back immediately to Konia.

Batu commanded to search the effects of the envoys; certain roots were found in them, among other things scammony. They directed Shuja to swallow the drugs in his baggage. He swallowed parts of each except scammony. Batu thought this last to be poison, but his doctor declared it a plant used in medicine. After that the Khan decided that Alai ud din must go with the new envoys, while the two others must take with them the presents.

Each party went its own way. Alai ud din died on the journey.

When they arrived at the court of Mangu, the opposing officials defended each two of them their own cause. The Grand Khan decided that Rūm must be given to both brothers, Yzz ud din getting everything west of the Sivas, and Rokn ud din all that lay east of that river, as far as the Erzerum border. The tribute was fixed, which each Sultan must send in annually.

After Alai ud din had set out for Mongolia, Rokn ud din's partisans, thinking that Yzz ud din wished to be rid of this brother, had him slip away from the capital where agents were watching him. He went to Cesaraea, gathered troops there and led them to Konia where, defeated in battle, he was captured and imprisoned.

In 1255, one year later, Baidju being impatient at Yzz ud din's loitering with the tribute, entered Rūm, marched against Konia, and met the Sultan's forces between Ak Serai and the capital where he scattered them. Yzz ud din fled and found refuge in the stronghold Anthalia.

Baidju then took Rokn ud din out of prison and installed him as Sultan in all the Rūm provinces. Yzz ud din fled now a second time and found refuge with the Byzantine Emperor who was visiting Sardis. This emperor, Theodore Lascaris, fearing Rokn ud din's partisans, as well as the Mongols, advised the fleeing Sultan to return to his kingdom. Yzz ud din took the advice, and offered submission to Hulagu, who upheld the division of Rūm between the two brothers.

When Mangu became Grand Khan in 1251 the Cilician king, Hayton, begged Batu to recommend him to the new Mongol sovereign. Batu counseled him thus wise: " Go to Mangu and stop on the way to confer with me." The Armenian, alarmed by the length of the journey, and knowing that evils might happen to the country in his absence, was fearful to leave it. Meanwhile Argun, the collector, with a great horde of Moslem assistants, appeared in Armenia. These men caused immense hardship to Christians. " Whoso could not pay," declares an Armenian historian, " suffered torture. Owners of land were driven from their places, their children and women were sold into slavery. Any man trying to emigrate and caught in the act was stripped, beaten and torn to pieces by raging dogs kept for that purpose."

The King, learning of these savage deeds in Armenia, decided to go to the Grand Khan and intercede for the people of his nation, but the death of his queen, Isabella, detained him. He set out at last in 1254 and, traveling in disguise, crossed Asia Minor. He passed through Derbend to the court of Batu, and to that of Sartak, Batu's son, said then to be a Christian. From Batu's Horde he spent five months in reaching Mangu, who received him with distinction. Letters patent were given the King. These were to serve as a safeguard to him and his country, and as a charter of freedom to the church in Armenia. He remained fifty days at the court, and returned in 1255 to Cilicia through Transoxiana and Persia. Hulagu had at this time arrived with his army.

Great was the ruin effected by Mongols in Asia Minor between Jelal ud din's death and the coming of Hulagu. Great too were the ravages wrought by Jelal through his various adventures. Though Chormagun's army and that under Baidju were vastly inferior to those of the princes in Western Asia, the dissensions of those princes were so hopeless and their wretched self-seeking so pitiful and paltry that the enemy brought most of them down to death or submission, and thousands upon thousands of people to destruction or torture.

After Jinghis Khan had returned from the west to Mongolia his eldest son, Juchi, left Chin Timur in Kwaresm as its governor. When Chormagun was sent out by Ogotai against Jelal ud din, Chin Timur was commanded to march with the troops of Kwaresm, and keep guard in Khorassan while Chormagun was destroying the Sultan. Chin Timur remained in Khorassan as governor, having as colleagues four officers appointed by the heads of the four groups in Jinghis Khan's family, namely: Kelilat by the Grand Khan; Nussal by Batu; Kul Toga by Jagatai, and Tunga by the widow and sons of Tului. Those countries west of the Transoxiana, and south of it, were the undivided inheritance of Jinghis Khan's family. Despite all the horrors committed in Khorassan there was something still left there to pillage. Many districts had escaped through ready submission, and at their first coming the Mongols knew not precisely the value of treasures, but Chin Timur knew the value of jewels and gold, and was eager to get them. People were tortured by him to disclose hidden wealth, and on learning where it was he killed them very promptly. The few who were spared had to buy back their homes. Besides there was still another misery. Kwaresmian bands ravaged

actively in Khorassan. They killed all the prefects whom Chormagun the Mongol general sent to various places, and searched
out and slew Kwaresmians who were faithful to Mongols. These
bands were parts of a corps of Kankalis, ten thousand in number,
or thereabouts, who occupied chiefly the Tus and the Nishapur
mountains. Togan Sangur and Karadja, two of Jelal ud din's lieutenants, commanded them.

Chin Timur attacked thrice these Kankalis, but did not master
or crush them. At last, Kelilat, his lieutenant, succeeded at Sebzevar, after three days of desperate fighting. In this struggle he
lost two thousand warriors. Karadja fled to the Sidjistan country
to save himself, while Sangur sought refuge in the Kuhistan
mountains. Three thousand Kankalis went to find safety in
Herat. Kelilat sent four thousand horsemen to end them. After
three days of hard struggle those four thousand forced the grand
mosque where the three thousand had hoped to find safety, and
there every man died at the sword edge. Of course the attackers
lost heavily.

Sair Bahadur who commanded at Badghis had been commissioned by the Grand Khan to march against Karadja and take
fire and sword to all rebels. He was on the road when he heard
that Karadja, defeated by Kelilat, had shut himself up in Arak
Seistan. Sair invested the place, but only after two years of hard
toil did he take it.

This general now informed Chin Timur, that the Grand Khan
had given him Khorassan to govern, and that he, Chin Timur,
had no further power in that country.

Chin Timur reproached Kelilat with seeking those districts of
Khorassan which had been recovering from ruin, and whose people
were innocent of Karadja's excesses, and forewarned Sair that
he was sending a report to the Grand Khan through an officer,
and would wait for his orders. Meanwhile Chin Timur and the
others received from Chormagun a command to march with their
forces and join him, leaving Mazanderan and Khorassan to Sair
Bahadur. Chin Timur thereupon counseled with his officers.
It was settled at last that Kelilat should go to Ogotai, and get
Mazanderan and Khorassan for Chin Timur. As this officer
served the Grand Khan directly, he was chosen as the best man
for the mission. To secure a good hearing he took from those two

great regions various small princes who had given their submission.

Kara Kurum now beheld for the first time princes of Iran. When Ogotai heard of their coming he was gratified greatly. He compared Chin Timur's methods with Chormagun's action. Chormagun, master in rich and broad countries, had never sent to his sovereign even one from among vassal rulers. Chin Timur was made governor, and with him was associated Kelilat; both were free of Chormagun and every other commander. Ogotai gave feasts to honor the Persian princes, his vassals. He showed them many marks of high favor, and when they were going he confirmed each one of them in his own region.

Chin Timur made Sherif ud din of Kwaresm his sealkeeper, and Behai ud din Juveini the minister of Finance. Commanders of troops belonging to the three other branches of Jinghis Khan's family had each one an agent in the ministry of Finance.

Chin Timur dying in 1235 was succeeded by Nussal, a Mongol commander who was nearly one hundred years old when he took up his office, and soon he gave way to Kurguz, Chin Timur's chancellor and favorite. It is said that Kurguz had organized honestly and well the affairs of Khorassan and had repressed a whole legion of fiscal extortioners. This of course made him enemies among whom were Sherif ud din, the vizir, and Kelilat, the commander, who were working at Ogotai's court to destroy him.

Kurguz was an Uigur and a Buddhist and had risen mainly through merit. Born in a village not far from Bishbalik, the Uigur capital, he had striven in early life to master Uigur letters and penmanship. That done, he began service with an officer attached to Prince Juchi. One day while the prince was out hunting a letter was brought him from his father. None of his secretaries were present, so search was made for a man to read Uigur. Kurguz was brought in and he read Jinghis Khan's letter to Juchi; he was the only man in that party who could read it. Juchi took him then to his service. Since his penmanship was beautiful, Kurguz was sent to teach letters and writing to the children of Juchi which he did till Chin Timur was made governor of Khorassan. Kurguz was then attached to him as secretary; he soon won his confidence and was made minister. He kept his office under Nussal, but was summoned to Mongolia to explain the affairs of Khorassan. Danishmend Hadjih, an enemy of Chinkai, Ogotai's minister and the special friend of Kurguz, was toiling at that time to put Ongu Timur, Chin Timur's son, in the place held before by his father, while Chinkai was using every effort to make Kurguz master, hence, choosing a moment when he was alone with the Grand Khan, Chinkai explained that the chief men of Khorassan were anxious that Kurguz should manage their country, and he obtained an ordinance from Ogotai, by which Kurguz was sent to collect for a time all the taxes and make a census of Mazanderan and Khorassan. While this task was in progress no man was to trouble him for any cause. If Kurguz did his work well he would be rewarded.

Kurguz came back to Khorassan with this patent and commenced work with vigor. Nussal, set aside by this document, was old and quite powerless, but Kelilat, his aid, being a man of capacity and keenly ambitious, raised his voice in opposition. Kurguz showed his patent: " Here is the order that no man may trouble me in my labor." Kelilat found no answer on that day. Kurguz reorganized Mazanderan and Khorassan, putting down as he did so a whole army of extortioners and tyrants.

Meanwhile Sherif ud din, the vizir, and Kelilat, who were powerless against Ogotai's patent and Kurguz, with his strong will and purpose, urged Ongu to ask with insistence for the place of his father. The vizir, while feigning to be the fast friend of Kurguz, was rousing up every power possible against him. Swept away by these efforts, Ongu sent a nephew to Ogotai with false accusations, incriminating Kurguz. These accusations were upheld with activity by all who were hostile to Chinkai. Ogotai now sent Argun with two others to investigate and report to him. Kurguz, on learning that Ongu had sent an agent to Ogotai, set out himself to explain the position, leaving Behai ud din to manage in his absence. At Tenakit he came on the members of Argun's commission, who declared that he must go back to Tus with them. He refused. Thereupon there was violence and he lost one tooth in a personal encounter. He returned, but before starting he sent a trusty friend in the night time to Ogotai, bearing one of his garments which was blood stained.

When the commission arrived at Khorassan the commanders

of troops with Kelilat, Ongu and Nussal, expelled from the residence of Kurguz his secretaries and other assistants. Kurguz himself wanted simply to hold the position till his messenger returned from Mongolia. This man came at last with an order to the civil and military chiefs to state each man his case before Ogotai, who had been incensed by the bloody garment.

Kurguz communicated this order to his enemies, and set out at once without waiting for their answers. Many persons of distinction went with him. Kelilat, Ongu and others followed quickly and both parties reached Bukhara simultaneously. In the time of a feast which was given them by the governor, Kelilat was assassinated.

When the opponents reached Ogotai's capital the Grand Khan wished to dine in a beautiful tent which Ongu had just given him. After the meal he went out for some minutes, intending to reënter, but as soon as he had left the pavilion a blast of wind overturned it. The Grand Khan, through annoyance and superstition, commanded to rend the tent in pieces immediately.

Some days later a tent was erected which with its contents Kurguz had given Ogotai. Inside were displayed curious things of many kinds and much value; all these were gifts to the Grand Khan. Among other objects was a girdle set with stones known as yarkan. When Ogotai put on this girdle he was freed from a pain in the loins which had troubled him somewhat. He drank that day freely and was in excellent humor. Kurguz might consider his cause as triumphant. Chinkai, his protector, had been appointed with other Uigurs to examine all statements of the rivals. On one side was Kurguz, helped by persons of value, position and substance; he himself had much keenness. On the other, since Kelilat's death, there were only that general's sons, who were still little children, and Ongu, a young man devoid of experience. But at the end of some months the affair was still pending. Ogotai, wishing peace between the two rivals, commanded Ongu and Kurguz to live in one tent and drink from the same goblet. Care had been taken to remove every weapon. This plan proved resultless, and Chinkai and his aids gave in their report to the sovereign.

Ogotai summoned the two sides before him. When he had questioned each one he condemned both Ongu and his partisans.

" But," said he to Ongu, " since thou art under Batu I will refer the whole matter to him; he it is who will punish thee."

Chinkai, taking pity on Ongu, approached him, whispered, and then spoke aloud to the Grand Khan: " Ongu Timur has said this to me. ' The Grand Khan is higher than Batu. Should a dog, such as I am, cause these two sovereign to deliberate? Let the Grand Khan fix my fate; he can fix it in one moment.' "

" Thy words are wise," replied Ogotai, " Batu would not pardon his own son had he acted as thou hast."

Ongu's adherents were punished. Some were bastinadoed immediately while others were given to Kurguz with the wish that he put the kang on each man of them, and all had to go back with the victor. " Let them learn," said the Grand Khan, " that according to Jinghis Khan's Yassa and justice, calumny brings with it death for the sake of example, but since their children and wives are awaiting them I bestow life on those people, if they offend not a second time. But tell Kurguz too that he, like those who are punished, is also my servitor, and should he cherish hatred toward any he himself will be subject to punishment." After that he gave Kurguz rule over all the lands south and west of the Oxus.

Persian lords also begged patents, but Kurguz convinced Chinkai that if others got patents of any kind they would assume independence of the governor. It was settled then that no patent should be issued save the one given Kurguz.

Sherif ud din continued double dealing; he feigned friendship for Kurguz while working as an enemy in secret. On noting Ogotai's action, an adherent of Ongu gave Kurguz certain papers in Sherif's own hand, which proved the entire recent trouble to be the sole work of that trickster. When he learned this, Ogotai did not wish the vizir to go back to Persia lest he suffer from Kurguz. Sherif was rejoiced to escape, but some friend warned Kurguz not to lose sight of an enemy who would take the first chance to destroy him Kurguz got permission to take with him Sherif, whose presence, as he said, was important. The taxes had not yet been brought to Khorassan and collectors might charge some of these to Sherif in his absence.

Kurguz went back to Tus and there fixed his residence. He summoned promptly the chief men in Khorassan and Irak, as well as the Mongol commanders, and marked his accession to power by a festival which lasted some days, during which the new ordinances were issued.

He sent his son with officials of finance to take from Chormagun's officers control over districts in Azerbaidjan and in Irak which they were ruining by exactions. Every noyon, every officer acted with absolute power in the region or city where he functioned, and seized for himself the main income of the treasury. These petty despots lost their places and were forced to restore even large sums of money.

Kurguz protected the lives and the property of Persians against Mongol officers, who now could not bend people's heads when they met them. The warrior lost power to vex peaceful people along roads over which he was marching. Kurguz was both feared and respected. He raised Tus again from its ruins. On the eve of his coming there were only fifty inhabited houses within its limits. When he had chosen it as a residence Persian lords came to live in that capital and within a week land rose a hundredfold as to value.

Herat too reappeared out of ashes and fragments. After the ruin and sack of that city in 1222 its site had been occupied by very few persons, but in 1236, when Ogotai commanded to raise up Khorassan, it was planned to repeople Herat, once so prosperous. An Emir, Yzz ud din, whom with one thousand families Tului had transported to Bishbalik from Herat, received now command to come back with one tenth of his following. These people at first had much difficulty in finding subsistence, through lack of draught cattle. Men of all ranks had to draw ploughs in the manner of oxen. Earth tillers were forced to irrigate land out of water pots, all canals being choked up and ruined. When the first harvest was gathered, twenty strong men were chosen to bear each twenty menns of cotton to the country of the Afghans, and sell it. They did so and brought back implements for tillage.

In 1241 the chiefs of this settlement sent to the Grand Khan for more people. At the end of five months two hundred new families were added to Herat. A census taken the year following showed the city as having six thousand nine hundred inhabitants. In following years the increase became rapid.

On arriving at Tus Kurguz put a kang on his enemy Sherif. He drew from him afterward confessions which were sent to the

court in Mongolia. His messenger learned on the road that the
Grand Khan was dead. Kurguz himself had set out to explain
the whole system introduced by him recently in Persia. While
passing through Transoxiana he had a quarrel with an officer
of Jagatai's household. Threatened with complaint before that
prince's widow he replied that he cared not. This answer when
taken to the widow roused wrath and keen hatred. Alarmed by
the quarrel and hearing of Ogotai's death with the loss of protection,
he judged best to turn back and he did so.

Meanwhile the wife of Sherif had sent people promptly to the
Jinghis Khan princes imploring protection for her husband. Those
messengers had been seized on the way save one among all of them.
This man escaped and reached Ulug Iff, the chief residence of
Jagatai, whose wives and sons sent Argun out with orders to bring
them Kurguz of his own will or, if need be, in spite of him. On
hearing this order Kurguz, who had given Sherif to the prefect of
Sebzevar who was to kill him, sent command straightway to stay
the execution. When Argun was approaching, Kurguz found
retreat in a storehouse. Since the governor would not yield himself
willingly, Argun required aid of the district commanders and got
it. These men were all foes of Kurguz since he had fought their
abuses. When they were ready to burst in and take him, he threw
the gates open declaring that he was no enemy.

Kurguz was taken to Jagatai's sons and examined. After that
he was sent to the court of Turakina, Ogotai's widow, who was
regent in Mongolia. Chinkai, his protector, was gone. He had
fled from the hatred of the regent which intrigue had roused
wrongfully against him. To crown his misfortune, the governor
of Persia was penniless, hence had no power to establish his
innocence. He was sent back at command of the regent to Jagatai's sons to be judged by them. He answered straightforwardly
all questions which they put to him, nevertheless, Kara Hulagu
adjudged death to the governor. His mouth was crammed then
with earth and in that way they strangled and killed him.

Kurguz being dead, Sherif had a chance now to prove himself,
and he did so; he engaged to collect four thousand balishes due,
as he stated, from Mazanderan and Khorassan. This Sherif,
destined to death by Kurguz very recently, was the son of a porter
of Kwaresm. He became page to the governor of the country,

who chose him because of his personal beauty. When Chin
Timur was commanded to enter Khorassan and assist Chormagun
in that country he wanted a secretary. No man wished that office
because the incumbent must act against Moslems, and the issue
of the enterprise seemed doubtful. The governor of Kwaresm,
whose feelings had cooled toward Sherif, who by that time had lost
youthful freshness and was acting only as secretary, gave him to
Chin Timur. Sherif had learned the Mongol language already
and, being the only man able to interpret, all business passed
through his hands and he became greatly important.

When Argun went as governor to Khorassan many agents of
Turakina, the regent, went with him. These he left in the province
to gather the imposts and taxes, going himself into Azerbaidjan
and to Irak to rescue those countries from Mongol commanders,
who acted as if the whole conquest had been made by them only,
and for their sole personal profit. At Tebriz he received envoys
from Rūm and from Syria, who implored his protection. He sent
men to those countries to gather tribute.

All this time Sherif, who had received from Argun perfect
liberty of action, wrested taxes from people with unparalleled
audacity and harshness. Each collector was bound and instructed
to spare no man. To extort from the victims all that was
humanly possible, armed warriors of the garrison were quartered
in houses; people were seized and imprisoned, kept without food
or even water, nay more, they were tortured. Moslem ulemas,
exempt from all tribute to Mongols and hitherto treated respect-
fully, came to ask mercy for themselves and for others. Widows
and orphans, exempt by the laws of Jinghis and Mohammed,
came to implore simple justice. These people were treated with
the utmost contempt, and were flouted by Sherif's assistants. Men
pledged at Tebriz their own children, and sometimes they sold
them to find means to pay taxes. One collector on entering a
house where a dead man was laid out for burial, and finding no
other property to seize, had the shroud stripped from the body, and
took it.

Sherif's agents assembled at Rayi after passing through Irak on
their great round of robbery. They brought the fruits of their
merciless activity and extortion to the chief mosque, and placed
them in piles there. Beasts of burden were driven into that edifice,

which was sacred for most of the people. Then the carpets of the
mosque were taken and cut into sizes that suited the robbers. In
those pieces they wrapped all the wealth which they had gathered
and took it away on the backs of pack animals. Happily for
Persia, and for most people in it, Sherif ud din met his death
some months later (1244).

Argun did what he could, as it seems, to correct those abuses.
He remitted taxes not paid before Sherif's death, and freed all
who were in prison for non-payment. Argun had been summoned to the Kurultai which elected Kuyuk and there an important
abuse became prominent. Since Ogotai's death the various princes
of Jinghis Khan's family had given to some orders on the revenue
of districts in Persia, and given also orders of exemption to others.
Argun collected these orders and delivered them to the Grand
Khan in person. Of all presents brought to Kuyuk this was the
one which gave him most pleasure. The orders were delivered
in the presence of the princes who had issued them. Kuyuk
continued Argun as the governor of Persia, and those whom Argun
favored obtained whatever offices he asked for them.

On returning to Persia, Argun was received in Merv splendidly.
But he saw very soon that powerful opponents at court were in-
triguing against him, hence he set out again for Mongolia. While
on the road he learned of Kuyuk's death and turned back to make
barracks for troops sent by that Grand Khan to reduce populations not subject as yet to the Mongols. Now arrived also agents
of various princes with orders on the revenues for years in advance
of collection. This abuse, which was ruinous, endured till the
interregnum was ended.

Argun reached the court only after the election of Mangu in
July, 1251. He complained of those orders on the income and he
condemned the great hordes of officials who went to collect them.
These people lived on the country, he said, and they ruined it. It
was decided at last that each man in Persia should pay in proportion to his property. This tax was varied from one to ten dinars,
and was to maintain the militia and post routes; also envoys of
the Grand Khan. Nothing more would be asked of the people.

Argun retained his high office of governor. Persia was divided
into four parts; in each was a lieutenant under Argun. Evil
doers were punished, at least for a season, and here is a striking

example of this justice: Hindudjak, a general and chief of ten thousand, who had taken life from a melik of Rūm without reason, was put to death, though a Mongol, outside the Tus gate by direction of Mangu. His property, family and slaves were divided among the four parts of the Jinghis Khan family.

When he had fixed administration in Persia, Argun at command of the Grand Khan went back to Mongolia to explain the position.

East Persia had been given by Mangu as a fief to Melik Shems ud din Mohammed Kurt, lord of the castle of Khissar in Khorassan. Osman Mergani, his grandfather, had been made governor of this stronghold by his brother, Omar Mergani, the all-powerful vizir of Ghiath ud din of the Gur line of princes. When Osman died Abu Bekr succeeded him. Abu Bekr married a daughter of Ghiath ud din; from this union came Melik Shems ud din Mohammed, who in 1245 lost his father and inherited the Gur kingdom. He went to the Kurultai and arrived on the day of election. He was presented by Mangu's officials, who informed the Grand Khan of the merits of the father and grandfather of the man then before him, not forgetting, of course, Shems ud din's own high qualities.

Mangu received Shems ud din with distinction and invested him with Herat and its dependencies which extended from the Oxus to the Indus, including Merv, Gur, Seistan, Kabul, and Afganistan. Mangu commanded besides, that Argun deliver to his agents fifty tumans as a present.

Next day at an intimate audience the Grand Khan gave the favorite a robe from his own shoulders, three tablets, and objects of the value of ten thousand dinars; a sabre from India, a club with the head of a bull on it, a battle axe, a lance and a dagger. Shems ud din then set out for Herat attended by one of the Grand Khan's own officers. He turned aside on arriving in Persia to go with a salutation to Argun, to whom the commands of Mangu were exhibited. The governor treated him with great respect, and had fifty tumans delivered to his agents.

Shems ud din reigned in Herat as a sovereign and took many strongholds in Afganistan, Guermsir, and other places.

Kerman was held at that time by the son of Borak Hadjib. After slaying Ghiath ud din, the brother of Jelal ud din, the last Shah of Persia, Borak asked the title of Sultan from the Kalif, and received it. Kutlug Sultan was the name which he gave himself. When Sair Bahadur laid siege to Seistan at the head of a Mongol division, he summoned Borak to show the Grand Khan obedience and furnish troops also. Borak declared that he could take the place with his own men, the Mongols might spare themselves trouble. His great age, he added, hindered him from going to the Grand Khan, but his son would go thither instead of him.

In fact he sent Rokn ud din Khodja. While on the road to Mongolia this young prince heard of the death of his father, and the usurpation of power by Kutb ud din his own cousin. He continued the journey, however, and was received well by Ogotai, who, to reward him for coming so far to look on the face of the Grand Khan, gave him Kerman which he was to hold in his character of vassal with the title and name of his father, Kutlug Sultan.

Kutb ud din now received a summons to appear at the court in Mongolia. Shortly after his arrival he was sent to China under command of Yelvadji. After Ogotai's death Kutb ud din went to that Kurultai at which Kuyuk was elected, and strove then to get Kerman, but met only failure. Chinkai, the minister, was the firm friend of his rival, and he himself was commanded to go back to Yelvadji. Soon after, he went with this governor from China to the new Kurultai, which chose Mangu from whom, and with the aid of Yelvadji, he obtained the throne of Kerman. When Kutb ud din was approaching Kerman, Rokn ud din was departing with treasures to Lur where he asked an asylum from the Kalif. The Kalif, not wishing to anger the Mongols, refused it, and now Rokn ud din resolved to repair to the court of Mangu to find justice.

The two rivals were summoned to the Grand Khan's tribunal. Rokn ud din lost his case and was given to his cousin, who struck him down with his own hand, and killed him. Kutb ud din ruled in Kerman till his death in 1258. He was son of that Tanigu the treacherous prefect of Taraz under the last sovereign of Kara Kitai. Tanigu was Borak Hadjib's own brother.

When Hulagu came with his army to Persia, Kutb ud din met him at Jend to show homage and honor.

This was the position in Persia in 1254 when Hulagu went to that country to conquer, to slaughter, and to regulate. His very first task was to root out and destroy the Ismailians who had formed

the famed mountain Commonwealth of Assassins, and then he
was to bring to obedience or ruin the successor of Mohammed
the Abbasid Kalif at Bagdad.

That the importance of this expedition may be understood
a brief sketch of the origin and history of the Assassins must be
given.

CHAPTER XI

THE Ismailians, known later by their enemies as Molahids (lost ones), and by all Europe in the sequel as Assassins, were an offshoot from one of the two great divisions into which Islam ranged itself after the death of the Prophet in 632. These divisions were caused by the problem of finding a successor to Mohammed — a Kalif.

The founder of Islam had died without saying whom he wished to succeed him. The first of the Kalifs, Abu Bekr, father-in-law of Mohammed, was elected by Medina, only one voice opposing. Abu Bekr on his death bed named Omar, who was confirmed by the people of Medina in 634. The second Kalif, when mortally wounded by a murderer, named electors to choose the third Kalif. Those electors chose Othman and when he was slain by insurgents, Aly, the son-in-law and cousin of Mohammed, was elected by Medina directly. A. D. 656.

Various and intricate causes brought about civil war, and deep hatred followed quickly; after that came the election in Damascus of Muavia, the governor of Syria, as a Kalif to overthrow Aly, whom many Mohammedans would not acknowledge. The father of Muavia had been one of the most bitter enemies of the Prophet. This hatred was shared fully by the son, who left nothing undone to rouse Syria to the utmost against Aly; he even had the blood-stained clothes of Othman exhibited in the principal mosque of Damascus. A fierce but drawn battle at Siffin between these two Kalifs was fruitless; an arbitration as to who should be Kalif settled nothing and pacified no man.

Next came the winning of Egypt by Muavia as the first Ommayad Kalif. There were two Kalifs now ruling de facto in Islam,

Muavia at Damascus, and Aly at Kufa.   In 661 Aly fell by the
hand of an assassin. Aly's son, Hassan, succeeded him, but resigned after six months of rule, and retired to Medina where one
of his many wives poisoned him, incited, as partisans of Aly
insisted, by Muavia. Muavia was now the sole Kalif of Islam.

Election had been attended with peril; there was danger of
outbreaks and slaughter. In three cases the chance had been
narrow, and the fourth choice had brought bitter warfare. Three
elections had been held at Medina, and made by the men of that
city; the fifth, that of Hassan, at Kufa. Muavia had been chosen
at Damascus. Since Medina was no longer the capital really, it
could not choose a Kalif or confirm him. Election must be at the
chief place of government, if anywhere.

Troubles such as those which had followed the election of Aly
might recur in the future and threaten, or even cut short the
existence of Islam. The system of election was unsafe in that
turbulent society. To avoid these great perils Muavia planned
to choose a successor while he himself was still ruling. His own
son Yezid was the candidate. If he could win for Yezid an oath
of allegiance from most of the Moslems he would secure power for
his family and prevent a contested election. After working a time
with great industry and keenness Muavia succeeded. Deputations
from all the chief cities, also from each province, appeared at
Damascus to do the hidden will of Muavia.

These deputations all named Yezid as heir of the Kalif and
chose him. They gave then an oath of allegiance and homage.
Arabian Irak and Syria also joined in this oath.

Muavia went next to the two holy cities as it were on a pilgrimage, but his great ruling purpose was to win or to force the
consent of Medina and Mecca to the recent election. The chief
dissentients in Medina were Hussein, son of Aly, Abd al Rahman,
son of Abu Bekr and both Abdallahs, sons of Omar and Zobeir.
Muavia treated them so rudely that to avoid offense they departed
immediately for Mecca. The rest of the people accepted Yezid
and gave him the oath without waiting. Muavia went on then to
Mecca, where he bore himself mildly toward all men, but near the
end of his visit he spoke to the city concerning an heir to the Kalifat.
It was answered that the election of an heir was opposed to prece-
dent but Mecca men offered to accept any one of three methods:

first, that of the Prophet who left the election to Medina, or that of Abu Bekr who chose a Kalif from the Koreish, or of Omar who appointed electors to choose from among themselves a candidate; the Kalif omitting, like Omar, his sons and the sons of his father.

" As for the earliest method," said Muavia, " there is no man among us who is like Abu Bekr to be chosen by the people. As to the other two methods I fear the bloodshed and struggles which will follow if the succession be not settled while a Kalif is living."

Since all his reasons proved powerless, Muavia summoned his attendants and forced Mecca men at the sword point to give the oath of allegiance to Yezid.

The example of Syria, Irak and the two holy cities was followed throughout the whole Empire, and this new method conquered in large measure afterward.

The theory of a right of election residing in the people existed in form, but the right was not real. In practice the oath of allegiance was obtained by the sword against every refusal.

After the days of Muavia, the Kalif in power proclaimed as his heir or successor the fittest among all his sons — that one of course who most pleased him. To him as the heir an oath of allegiance was given. To increase the assurance of safety two heirs were sometimes created, one of whom was elected to follow the other. This method begun by the Ommayed line was continued by the Abbasids.

Muavia died in 680. Yezid, who succeeded, made those first of all take the oath to him who had refused it at Medina. The sons of Omar and Abbas gave this oath straightway, but Hussein, son of Aly, and the son of Zobeir went to Mecca asking time to consider. No one had dared to attack that holy city since its capture by Mohammed, and there in full safety every plotter could work out his plan against the Kalif or others.

Ibn Zobeir, as Muavia had noted, was eager for dominion, but while Hussein was living he feigned to work only for that grandson of the Prophet. Offers of support went from Kufa to Hussein with advice to appear there immediately. True friends of Hussein at Mecca distrusted these offers and strove to dissuade him from going, but Ibn Zobeir, who in secret burned to be rid of this rival, urged him on always. Hussein yielded at last and set out for Kufa. Muslim, his cousin, had been sent ahead to prepare for his coming. This move became known at Damascus, so Yezid summoned hastily to Kufa Obeidallah, then governing in Bussorah with unpitying severity. On arriving he sought and found Muslim, who was lodging with Hani, an adherent of the Alyite family.

At first a majority of the people sided with Hussein and rose promptly against Obeidallah. They attacked him in his castle and came very near killing him, but their ardor cooled quickly. Obeidallah was triumphant, Muslim was taken and killed with his co-worker Hani.

Toward the end of 680 Hussein rode out of Mecca with his family and a small band of followers, all kinsmen. When the desert was crossed, and he was advancing on Kufa, news came to him that Muslim's life had been taken. He might have turned back then to Mecca, but Muslim's kinsmen were clamorous for vengeance. Besides there remained the wild hope that those who had invited him might rally at last; but each man whom he met gave darker tidings.

Farazdak the poet, who had left Kufa recently, had only these words to offer: "The heart of the city is on thy side, but its sword is against thee."

The Beduins, ever ready for warfare, had been coming to Hussein, but when they saw his cause weakening they fell away quickly, and no one was left except the original party. A chance chieftain passing southward advised him to turn to the Selma hills and to Aja. "In ten days," said the man, "the Beni Tay and twenty thousand lances above them will be with thee."

"How could I take these children and women to the desert?" asked Hussein, "I must move forward."

And he rode northward till a large troop of horsemen from Kufa, under an Arab named Horr, stood before him.

"Command has been given me," said Horr, "to bring thee to the governor. If thou come not, then go to the left, or the right, but return not to Mecca."

Leaving Kufa on his right, Hussein turned to the left and moved westward. Obeidallah soon sent a second man, Amr, son of Sad, with four thousand horse, and a summons. Hussein now fixed his camp on the plain of Kerbala near the river, five and twenty miles above Kufa. There he denied every thought of hostility

and was ready to yield if he might take one of three courses:
" Let me go to the place whence I came, or attend me to the Kalif
of Damascus. Place my hand in the hand of Yezid, let me speak
face to face with him. If not, let me go far away to the wars and
fight against enemies of Islam."

Obeidallah insisted on absolute surrender, and directed that
Amr stop every approach to the river, thus taking water from the
party. Hussein, fearing death less than the governor of Kufa,
adhered to his conditions. He even brought Amr to urge Obeidallah to lead him to the Kalif. Instead of agreeing, Obeidallah sent
a certain Shamir to urge action. " Hussein," said he, " we must
have dead or living in Kufa immediately; if Amr loiters, Shamir
must depose him."

Amr then encircled the camp very closely. Hussein was ready
to fight to the death, and the scenes represented as following
swiftly are retained in the minds of believers to this day with
incredible vividness.

Hussein received a day's respite to send off his family and
kinsmen, but not one person left him.

On October 10th of 680 the two sides faced each other, and
opened a parley. Hussein's offer was repeated, Obeidallah rejected
it. Hussein slipped down from his camel, his kinsmen gathered
round him, and the whole party waited. From the Kufa attackers
at last came an arrow which opened that struggle of tens against
thousands. One after another Hussein's brothers, sons, nephews,
and cousins fell near him. No enemy struck Hussein till tortured
by thirst he turned toward the river, and Shamir cut him off from
his people; then, stricken down by an arrow, he was trampled by
horses. Hussein's attendants were slain every man of them. Two
sons of his perished and when the action was over, six sons of Aly
were corpses, also two sons of Hassan and six descendants of Abu
Talib, Aly's father. The camp was plundered, but no harm
inflicted on the living, mainly women and children, who with
seventy heads of the slain were taken to Obeidallah. A shudder
ran through the multitude of people as the bloody head of the
Prophet's grandson was dropped at the feet of the governor.
When he turned the head over roughly with his staff an aged man
cried to him: " Gently, that is the grandson of the Prophet.
By the Lord I have seen those lips kissed by the blessed mouth of

Mohammed." Hussein's sister, his two little sons, Aly Ashgar and Amr, with two daughters, sole descendants of Hussein, were treated with seeming respect by the governor, and sent with the head of their father to the Kalif. Yezid disowned every share in the tragedy. Hussein's family were lodged in the Kalif's own residence at Damascus for a time, and then sent with honor to Medina, where their coming caused a great outburst of grief and lamentation. Many objects in that city made the day of Kerbala seem dreadful. The deserted houses in which had dwelt those kinsmen of Mohammed who had fallen; the orphaned little children, and the widows, gave great reality to every word uttered. The story was told to weeping pilgrims in that city of the Prophet by women and by children who with their own eyes had looked at the dead and the dying and had lived through the day of Kerbala. The tale, repeated in many places, was heightened by new horrors; retold by pilgrims in their homes and on their journeys from Medina, it spread at last to every village of Islam.

The right of Aly's line to dominion had been little thought of till that massacre, but compassion for Aly's descendants, who were also the great grandsons of Mohammed, sank into men's minds very deeply after that dreadful slaughter on the field of Kerbala. The woeful death of the grandsons of the Prophet seized hold of the Arab mind mightily, and fascinated millions of people. This tragic tale helped greatly to ruin the Ommayed dynasty and when, through it and other causes, the Abbasids rose to dominion and hunted to death or to exile the descendants and kinsmen of Muavia, that same tale affected the Abbasids and made it possible to raise up against them a nation in Persia and a dynasty in Egypt. So strong were men's feelings on this point in Islam and so many the people who favored the descendants of Aly that Mamun, the son of Harun al Rashid, made an effort to consolidate the Alyite and Abbasid families. Moreover the teaching of Persian adherents of Aly had such influence that they captured this Kalif intellectually.

In Mamun's day the Moslem world became greatly imbued with ideas from Persia and India, and with Greek theories and learning. The Koran was treated as never before till that period. Opinions and systems of all sorts were brought into Islam. A time of tremendous disturbance succeeded as the fruit, or result, of these teachings and these were all connected, both in life and in politics with views touching Aly.

One Babek, a man of great energy, appeared in 816 of our era as a leader in religion, in practical life, and in management of people, preaching indifference of action and community of property. Through various mystic doctrines most cunningly compounded with incitements to robbery and lust and dishonor, he rallied multitudes to his standard, and during twenty whole years he visited many parts of the Empire with ruin and slaughter. He had fixed himself firmly in those strong mountain places west and south of the Caspian, and thence scattered terror in various directions through sudden attacks which were ever attended by terrible bloodshed, till at last his forces were defeated in great part and driven westward.

In 835 Motassim, the Kalif, sent Afshin, one of the best among all his Turk generals, to seize this arch enemy and destroyer at all costs. Only after two years of most desperate fighting and many deceitful devices, were Babek's strong places all taken and his own person captured. Thousands of women and children were taken with him, and restored to their families; and all the treasures which during two decades had been gathered by this murderous deceiver fell now to the Turk general, Afshin.

Babek had defeated six famous generals of Islam and slain, as some state, a million of people during twenty years of rebellion. One of his ten executioners declared that he alone had taken the lives of twenty thousand men; so merciless was the struggle between the partisans of the Kalifat and the advocates of freedom and equality.

The prisoner was brought by his captor to Samira in chains and confined there. Motassim went in disguise to the prison to look at this demon of Khorassan, this " Shaitan " (Satan), as they called him. When the Kalif had gazed at Babek sufficiently the captive was exhibited through the city as a spectacle, and brought at last to the palace where Motassim, surrounded by his warriors, commanded Babek's own executioner to cut off the arms and legs of his master, and then plunge a knife into his body. The executioner obeyed, Babek meanwhile smiling as if to prove his own character, and the correctness of his surname, " Khurremi " (The Joyous). The severed head was exhibited in the cities of Khorassan, and the body impaled near the palace of the Kalif.

In the ninth century, and contemporaneous with these horrors, there lived in Southern Persia, at Ahwas, a certain Abdallah, whose father, Maimun Kaddah, and grandfather, Daisan the Dualist, had taught him Persian politics and religion. This Abdallah conceived a broad system, and planned a great project to overturn Arab rule in his country and reëstablish the ancient faith and Empire of Persia. This involved complete change in the structure of Islam, and all its present ideals. He could not declare open war against the accepted religion and dynasty, since all the military power was at their command; hence he decided to undermine them in secret.

From Ahwas he went to Bussorah and later to Syria where he settled at Salemiya, whence his teachings were spread by Ahmed, his son, by two sons of that Ahmed, and also by his Dayis, men who performed each of them all the various duties of spy, secret agent, and apostle. The most active of those Dayis was Hussein of Ahwas, who, in the province of which Kufa was the capital, instructed many agents in the secrets of revolt and in perversion of the teachings of Islam. Among these agents the most noted was one famous later as Karmath. This man delayed not in showing his character and principles "through torrents of blood, and destruction of cities." Crowds of men rallied to his war cry.

The Karmathites declared that nothing was forbidden, everything was a matter of indifference, justified by the fact of its existence, hence should receive neither punishment nor reward. The commands of Mohammed were pronounced parables disguising political maxims and injunctions. They differed from Abdallah's disciples in that they began action immediately, and, in most cases, openly, while the others were preparing for a new throne in Islam to be occupied by a man of their own, a true and zealous co-believer.

The Karmathite outbreak was more terrible, continuous, and enduring than that begun twenty years earlier by Babek, and far more dangerous. The Karmathites fought savage battles in the East and the West, in Irak and Syria. They plundered caravans and destroyed what they found with tiger-like fury unless it was valuable and they could bear it away with them. They attacked the holy city of Mecca and captured it through desperate fighting. More than thirty thousand true Moslems were slain while defending the temple. The sacred well, Zemzem, was polluted by corpses hurled into it by people to whom nothing whatever was sacred. The temple was fired, and the black, holy stone of the Kaaba, which in Abraham's day had come down from heaven into Mecca, was borne off to be ransomed for fifty thousand gold coins two and twenty years later.

This Karmathite madness, after raging at intervals for a century and torturing most parts of Islam, was extinguished in bloodshed. The career of the Karmathites proved the wickedness and folly of their method. Its turn came now to the system of Abdallah.

Ismailian teaching had spread through the Empire of Mohammed and reached even Southern Arabia. About 892 a certain Mohammed Alhabib, who claimed his descent from Ismail, son of Jaffar es Sadik, sent one Abu Abdallah to the north coast of Africa. Abu Abdallah impressed the Berber tribes greatly, and his success was so enormous that they drove out the Aglabid dynasty then ruling them. He roused expectations to the highest degree by announcing a Mahdi, or infallible guide for believers. He then summoned in Obeidallah, a son of that Mohammed Alhabib, who had sent him to Africa.

Obeidallah, after many strange deeds and adventures, and finally an imprisonment from which Abu Abdallah released him, was put on a throne in 909 and made the first Fatimid [1] Kalif at Mahdiya, his new capital near Tunis. Abu Abdallah, the successful assistant and forerunner, was assassinated soon after at command of Obeidallah, who owed him dominion, but who now had no wish for his presence. The new Kalif, since this man knew, of course, many secrets, might well think him safer in paradise. Obeidallah now proclaimed himself the only true Kalif, a descendant of the Prophet through Fatima his daughter, and became a dangerous rival of the Abbasids. By 967 his descendants had won Egypt and Southern Syria. A fortified palace was built near the Nile, and called Kahira. [2] Around this palace rose the city known later as Cairo.

---

[1] Called Fatimides because they professed to trace their descent to Fatima the daughter of the Prophet (Mohammed).
[2] The Victorious.

In 991 Aleppo was added to the Fatimid Empire which, beginning at the river Orontes and the desert of Syria, extended to Morocco. In view of this great success and its danger to the Abbasids the world was informed now from Bagdad that the Fatimid dynasty was spurious; that the first Kalif installed at Mahdiya was no descendant of the Prophet, he was merely the son of that Ahmed who was a son of Abdallah, son of Maimun Kaddah, son of Daisan the Dualist, his mother being a Jewess. Hence he was son of that Ahmed whose emissary, Hussein of Ahwas, had raised up and trained the detestable Karmath, whose crimes, and the crimes of whose followers, had tortured all Islam for a century.

That society, or order, which met at the famed House of Science in Cairo, was dreaming of power night and day and struggling always to win it. Power it could reach by supplanting the Abbasids, but not in another way, hence this order aimed at the overthrow of the Abbasids. It also spread secret doctrines by its Dayis (political and religious missionaries) continually. Through this activity the Fatimids were rising. Meanwhile the Abbasids were failing till Emir Bessassiri, a partisan of the Fatimids, seized and held for one year the two highest marks of dominion in Islam, the mint and the pulpit at Bagdad in the name of Mostansir the Kalif at Cairo, and would have held them much longer had not his career been cut short in 1058 by Togrul the first Seljuk Sultan, who hastened to the rescue of the Abbasids. Meanwhile the Dayis from Cairo and their aids filled a great part of Asia with their labors.

One of these Dayis, Hassan Ben Sabah, founded a sect, the Eastern Ismailites, renowned later as the Assassins. This Hassan was son of Ali, a Shiite of the old city Rayi, who claimed that his father, Sabah Homairi, had gone from Kufa to Kum and later to Rayi. People from Tus in Khorassan, and others insisted that his ancestors had passed all their lives in Khorassan. Ali, suspected of heresy, made lying oaths and confessions to clear himself; since his success was but partial he strove to increase it by sending Hassan, his son, to the Nishapur school of Movaffik, a sage of eighty years at that period, and the first scholar among Sunnite believers.

This sage, it was said, brought happiness and good fortune to all whom he instructed. His school was frequented by multitudes, and the success of his pupils was proverbial. Among his last students were three classmates, later on very famous: Omar Khayyam, the astronomer and poet; Nizam ul Mulk, the first statesman of the period, and Hassan Ben Sabah, who founded a sect upon sophisms, and a State upon murder.

Hassan's ambition was active from the earliest; while in that Nishapur school he bound both his classmates by a promise. Nizam ul Mulk himself tells the story: " ' Men believe,' remarked Hassan one day to us, ' that the pupils of our master are sure to be fortunate; let us promise that should success visit one of us only, that favored one will share with the other two.' We promised." Years later when Nizam ul Mulk was grand vizir to Alp Arslan, Sultan of the Seljuks, he showed Omar Khayyam sincere honor and friendship, and offered him the dignity of second vizir, which the poet rejected, but at his request the vizir gave him one thousand gold pieces each year instead of the office. Thenceforward Omar Khayyam was enabled to follow his bent and do great work, as astronomer and poet.

Hassan Ben Sabah lived on in obscurity till the death of Alp Arslan in 1072.

Nizam ul Mulk retained his high office with Melik Shah the new Sultan. Hassan Sabah went now to his friend and quoting bitter words from the Koran reproached him with forgetting sacred promises, and mentioned their agreement of school days. The vizir, who was kind, took his classmate to the sovereign and gained for him favor.

Hassan Sabah, who had reproached his old friend out of perfidy, soon won great influence through cunning, feigned frankness and hypocrisy. In no long time Melik Shah called him frequently to his presence, advised with him, and followed his counsels. Soon Nizam ul Mulk was in danger of losing his office. Hassan had resolved to ruin his benefactor and classmate; in one word to supplant him. Each apparent omission of the great man was reported by tortuous ways to the sovereign, whose mind was brought to doubt the vizir, and to test him The most painful blow of all, according to Nizam ul Mulk's own statement, was given when Hassan promised to finish in forty days the whole budget of the Empire. Nizam ul Mulk needed ten times that period for the labor.

Melik Shah gave all the men called for by Hassan, and with their aid the work was accomplished. But to defeat the vizir was not easy; Nizam ul Mulk had abstracted certain pages, hence Hassan's budget was imperfect. He could not explain why the pages were lacking, and he could not restore them, so he went on a sudden to Rayi and to Ispahan somewhat later. In the latter city he lived in concealment at the house of Abu Fazl, the mayor, whom he converted, and who became his most intimate adherent.

One day in 1078, when complaining of Nizam ul Mulk and the Sultan, Hassan added: "Had I but two friends of unbending fidelity I would soon end this rule of the Turk and the peasant (Sultan and vizir)." These words describe Hassan's forecast completely, and show the germ of the Assassin creation, which was cold-blooded murder, carefully pondered, thought out with slowness, but executed on a sudden. Abu Fazl could not credit that statement, and thought Hassan demented. To restore his mental balance he placed on the table before him meat and drink mixed with saffron which was believed at that time in Persia to be a mind strengthening herb. Hassan noted his meaning immediately, was angry, and would not remain longer. Abu Fazl did what was possible to detain the apostle of murder, but every effort on his part was fruitless; Hassan left Ispahan quickly for Egypt.

The Ismailite mysteries of atheism and immorality had been taught to Hassan Ben Sabah by a Fatimid apostle in Persia. He had also conversed long and intimately with others. He knew all the secrets of Cairo, and had been tried and found worthy to spread the beliefs of the great House of Science. The fame of his learning and gifts, and the high position which he had held at the court of Melik Shah, went before him. Mostansir desired to show honor to a servant who might help him to wider dominion. The chief of the new House of Science was therefore sent to the boundary with greetings; a residence was assigned to the visitor, while through ministers and dignitaries he was loaded with favors until a great quarrel broke out on a sudden in Egypt.

Mostansir had declared his son, Nesar, as his successor, and heir to the Kalifat; thereupon rose a faction. The commander-in-chief of the war forces was at the head of it. He insisted that Mosteali, another son of Mostansir, was the only one fitted for the dignity. Hassan was in favor of Nesar, and this enraged the commander, who had Hassan imprisoned in Damietta. The apostle was barely in prison when a great tower fell in the city without evident reason. The amazed and terrified people saw in this accident a miracle performed by Hassan, so his enemies and admirers joined straightway in bearing him off to a vessel just ready to sail for West Africa. Soon after starting a storm rose and terrified every man on the ship except Hassan. When asked why he was not alarmed he answered: "Our Lord has promised that no harm shall meet me." The sea became calm soon after. All on board turned then to Hassan, accepted his teaching and became devoted and faithful disciples. As the voyage continued a contrary wind drove the vessel to Syria where the apostle debarked and went to Aleppo. Thence he traveled farther, to Bagdad, Isaphan, Yezd, Kerman and many other places, publishing his doctrines with the greatest industry.

In Damegan Hassan spent three years, and made numerous converts. Rayi he could not visit since Nizam ul Mulk had instructed the governor to seize him. Dayis converted by Hassan and attached to him personally had gone to Kirdkuh and many other fortresses and cities in that marvelous region. He passed now through Sari, Demavend, Kazvin and Dilem and halted at last at Alamut.

Hussein Kaini, one of Hassan's devoted and skilful Dayis, had been sent some time before to Alamut to secure an oath of allegiance and fidelity to Kalif Mostansir. Most of the inhabitants had already given the usual oath, but the commandant, Ali Mehdi, who held the fortress in the name of Melik Shah, refused, declaring that he would acknowledge the spiritual dominion of no one save the Kalif of Bagdad of the family of Abbas, and submit to no sovereign but Melik Shah of the family of the Seljuks. Hassan then offered to pay him three thousand ducats for the fortress, but Mehdi refused this bribe. Finding all persuasion useless Hassan took possession by force and Mehdi was driven out. As if to show his great influence and authority Hassan then gave Mehdi a letter to Reis Mosaffer, commander of the fortress of Kirdkuh, instructing him to pay Mehdi three thousand ducats. Mehdi, knowing well the confidence placed in Mosaffer by the Seljuk Sultan, was amazed when the three thousand ducats were paid to him. He learned then that Mosaffer was a devoted follower of Hassan Ben Sabah, and one of his earliest adherents.

Alamut[1] was the largest and strongest of fifty castles in that country. It was built in 860 by Hassan Ben Seid Bakeri, and now in 1090 Hassan Sabah, who had hitherto sought in vain for a stronghold, was in possession of it. He at once began to build walls and ramparts around his fortress and had a canal dug which would ensure a water supply. Gardens and orchards were planted in the surrounding country and the inhabitants were soon engaged in agricultural pursuits. Men of power in the Seljuk country Hassan won by secretly placing Assassins at their service; whoso wished in those days to ruin any man had but to accuse him of connivance with Hassan Ben Sabah. Informers increased, suspicion was general. Melik Shah distrusted his most intimate associates and servants whom ill-will or envy strove to ruin. But now an Emir to whom Melik Shah had given Rudbar in fief, that is the whole region in which Alamut was the main stronghold, stopped every road to the fortress and cut off all supplies. The inhabitants were ready to abandon the place, but Hassan assured them that fortune would soon show them favor, as in fact it did, and the name "Abode of Good Fortune" was bestowed on the castle. Melik Shah, who hitherto had treated Ismailians with contempt, resolved now to crush them. He commanded Arslan Tash, his Emir, to destroy Hassan Sabah with all his followers.

Though Hassan had only seventy men, and not much food to give them, he defended the fortress with great courage till Abu Ali, his Dayi, hastened up in the night time with three hundred men. These, with the seventy of the garrison, attacked the besiegers and dispersed them.

Melik Shah who was greatly alarmed by this defeat sent troops from Khorassan against Hussein Kaini, Hassan Sabah's main agent, who was spreading heresy in the Kuhistan province. Hussein retreated to a castle in Mumin where soon he was besieged and in no less danger than Hassan had been very recently in Alamut.

Up to this time Hassan had acted as a political agent and religious nuncio in the name of Mostansir, but now he saw an opportunity for securing power for himself and he did not hesitate.

---

[1] Eagle's nest.

Knowing well that lawlessness of the people brought destruction to the throne, he established a system of religion and politics based upon atheism and absolute freedom of action which became the tenet of the Assassins, known, however, to but few and concealed under the veil of religion.

Hassan determined to deliver his first great blow at this juncture and begin his career of surprises. He had resolved to rid himself of opponents unsparingly, and to terrify those of his enemies whom he left living. His first victim was Nizam ul Mulk, his classmate, friend and benefactor, a statesman renowned throughout one half of Asia as chief vizir under three Seljuk Sultans, the first of their dynasty, a man of profound wisdom and keen foresight, whose *Treatise on the Principles of Government* was written for Melik Shah and adopted as his code. In this code the wise vizir explains in the clearest terms the duties of a sovereign. Melik Shah, the most famous and best of the Seljuk Sultans, died three weeks later (1092). The sudden deaths of these two great men filled Western Asia with terror. The vizir was cut down by Hassan Sabah's Fedavi, or devoted assistants. Melik Shah died of poison. His loss was greatly lamented for he had ruled with justice and made his country prosperous. He was both a statesman and a warrior. To extend commerce he had built bridges and canals; to ensure the safety of merchants and all who traveled he had made each village and hamlet responsible for the crimes committed within its precincts. In this way the entire population assisted in the suppression of robbery, one of the great evils of that time. Hassan had made a notable beginning — he had alarmed all Asia.

What were the doctrines of the Ismailians, used by Hassan Ben Sabah?

The Ismailian apostles trained in the House of Science in Cairo, which had been founded and developed in the Fatimid interest, taught their secret doctrines to a few chosen followers. These doctrines were communicated slowly and with many precautions. The chiefs or apostles at Cairo, the prime masters of all sacred wisdom, initiated disciples. There were nine degrees through which those of the faithful had to pass to receive the great mystery. But before giving the first degree to any novice whatever the Master took from him an oath devoting the applicant to the greatest calamities of this life, and the keenest sufferings of the next, if he

kept not strict silence touching that which was revealed to him,
or if he ceased to be the friend of all friends of the Ismailians,
and the enemy of all their enemies.   When the oath was accepted
the Master took a fee for that which he was going to communicate,
and he never advanced any novice from degree to degree, till he
saw that the man had assimilated to the utmost everything taught
him.

The first step in instruction was that God has at all times given
the task of establishing His worship, and preserving it, to Imams,
his chosen ones, who are the sole guides of the faithful.   As God
has created the most beautiful of all things and the noblest, by
sevens, such as the heavens and the planets, he has fixed the
number of Imams at seven, namely: Aly, Hassan, Hussein, Ali
Zayn al Abidin, Mohammed Bakir, Jaffar es Sadik, and Ismail,
or Mohammed, the son of Ismail, who surpasses all other Imams
in occult wisdom and in knowledge of the mystic sense of things
visible.   He explains these mysteries to those of the initiated who
inquire, for he has been instructed by God himself, and he com-
municates his marvelous gifts to the Dayis, or Ismailian apostles,
to the exclusion of all other sectaries of Ali.

Like the Imams, the word-endowed prophets sent to establish
new religions were seven in number.   Each prophet had one vicar
(siwes) as aid who upheld true religion after the death of his
principal, and six other vicars, who appeared after him among
men.   In distinction to the word-endowed prophets the vicars were
called "the dumb," because they merely walked in the way
which had been traced for them previously.   When these seven
vicars pass from the earth, a new prophet comes who sets aside the
preceding religion and is followed by seven mute vicars.   These
changes follow one another till the coming of the seventh word-
endowed prophet, who is the lord of the present, that is, lord of
the age in which he is manifest.

The first prophet was Adam, for whom his son Seth served as
vicar; after Adam his religion had seven successive vicars.   Noah
was the second prophet, and his vicar was Sem; Abraham was
the third prophet, his son, Ismail, was his vicar; Moses, the fourth,
had Aaron his brother first as vicar, after Aaron's death Joshua,
son of Nun, was his vicar.   The last of his vicars was John, son
of Zachary; Jesus, son of Mary, the fifth prophet, had Simeon as

vicar. With the sixth prophet, Mohammed, was associated Aly. After Aly were six mute chiefs of Islam. These are the Imams whom we have named from Hassan to Ismail. Ismail is the seventh and most recent prophet. When he appeared preceding religions were abolished. Endowed with an all-knowing wisdom he alone can explain sacred teaching. All people owe him obedience, and it is only through his guidance that man can advance in salvation.

These were the doctrines taught in the first four degrees. In the fifth degree the disciple learned that the Imam, as supreme priest, should have apostles to visit all places. The number of these was fixed by Divine wisdom at twelve like the months of the year, the tribes of Israel, the companions of Mohammed, for God in all he does has views of deep wisdom.

In the sixth degree the Master commenced by explaining the mystic significance of the precepts of Islam touching prayer, alms, pilgrimages, and all other practices which were, as he showed, to turn men from vice to perfection. He recommended the study of Aristotle, Pythagoras, and Plato; he warned against blind belief in tradition, against yielding credit to simple allegations, and against taking accepted proof unless it be rational.

In the seventh and the eighth degree the Master taught that the founder of every religion requires an associate, a vicar to hand down his precepts; the latter is the image of the world here below enveloped by that which is above it; one precedes the other as cause does effect. The first principle has neither attribute nor name; one may not say that it exists, or does not exist, that it is ignorant, or knowing. And thus farther on with all its attributes, for every affirmation regarding it implies a comparison with things that are created, every negation tends to deprive it of an attribute; it is neither eternal nor temporal, but its commandment, its word is that which exists from eternity. The disciple — that is, he who follows — aspires to the height of the one who precedes him, and he who is endowed with the word on earth aspires to be one with him who is master of the word in heaven.

In the ninth degree, which is the last, the teacher restates all that he has taught up to that time, and on seeing that the disciple understands he removes the last veil, and says to him in substance.

All that is said of creation and of a beginning, describes in a simile the origin and changes of matter. An apostle delivers to mankind that which heaven has revealed to him. For the sake of justice and order, he adapts his religion to the needs of the race. When this religion is needed for the general welfare it is binding, but the philosopher is not bound to put it into practice. The philosopher is free, is bound to nothing; knowledge for him is sufficient, since it contains the truth, that towards which he is striving. He should know its whole meaning, all that it binds men to execute, but he need not be subject to vexations, which are not intended for sages. Finally it is explained to the disciple that if word endowed apostles have the mission to uphold order among mankind in general, sages are charged to teach wisdom to individuals.

From all that has been preserved by the chroniclers of those days regarding the Assassin kingdom, it is clear that in great part these teachings were borrowed from Greece, Palestine, and Persia.

The Fatimid Kalifs of Egypt had many secret agents in Persia and Syria. The Assassins went to Syria about the same time as the Crusaders. In the first year of the XIIth century Jenah-ed-devlet, then Prince of Emesa, died by their daggers while he was hastening to the castle of the Kurds, Hosn Ak Kurd, which the Count of St. Gilles was besieging. He had been attacked four years earlier in his palace by three Persian Assassins, but had succeeded in saving his life. Risvan, the Prince of Aleppo, was suspected of causing this attack. There was reason to suspect him, since he was a bitter enemy of Jenah-ed-devlet, and a friend of the Assassins.

Risvan had been won to the Order by one of its agents who was very persuasive; an astrologer and a physician, who had the power to attract by methods of his own, which were separate from those of the Order. Four and twenty days after this unsuccessful attempt, the astrologer died, but his place was soon filled by a goldsmith from Persia named Abu Tahir Essaigh, who roused Risvan to still greater activity. This Prince of Aleppo was hostile to every Crusader, and to his own brother, Dokah, the Prince of Damascus. He was anxious for a new influx of Assassins, since their acts favored his policy.

Abul Fettah, the nephew of Hassan Sabah, was at that time

Grand Prior in Syria; his chief residence was Sarmin, a fortified place one day's journey from Aleppo.

Some years later, when the people of Apaméa implored aid of Abu Tahir Essaigh, the goldsmith, now the commandant in Sarmin, against Khalaf, their governor from Egypt, he had Khalaf slain by Assassins under Abul Fettah, and took Apaméa for Risvan, but he could not hold it against Tancred, who seized the place and took Abu Tahir to Antioch where he kept him till ransomed. Abul Fettah expired under torture. Other captives were given to Khalaf's sons. Tancred took from the Assassins the strong castle of Kefrlana.

Abu Tahir on returning to the Prince of Aleppo used all his influence to kill Abu Harb Issa, a great Khojend merchant, who had come to Aleppo with five hundred camels bearing much merchandise. This man had done what he could to cause harm to the Order. A man named Ahmed, who was secretly an Assassin, had been present in the caravan from the boundary of Khorassan, and was watching to avenge his brother slain by the people of that merchant. On reaching Aleppo he went to Abu Tahir and Risvan, whom he won through accounts of Abu Harb's immense wealth, and his hatred of the Assassins. On a day, while the merchant was counting his camels, the murderers fell upon him, but his slaves, who were near, showed their courage and slew the attackers before they could injure Abu Harb. The merchant complained to Syrian princes and they reproached Risvan bitterly, but he denied every share in that action. No one believed him, however. Abu Tahir, to save himself from punishment, fled to North Persia and remained there for a season.

Hassan's policy swept through the country, selecting its victims from the powerful and the rich. In 1113 Mevdud, then Prince of Mosul, fell, stabbed to death while walking with Togteghin of Damascus through the forecourt of the great mosque in that prince's capital. The Assassin who killed him was decapitated straightway. That same year died Risvan, Prince of Aleppo, who had long protected the murderous Order most carefully, and had used it effectually in extending his own dominions.

Risvan's son, Akhras, succeeded him. This youth of sixteen was assisted in governing by Lulu, a eunuch. He began rule by condemning to death all people belonging to the Assassin Order. By this sentence more than three hundred men, women and children were slain, and two hundred were thrown into prison. Abul Fettah, a son of Abu Tahir the goldsmith, and his successor as head of the Assassin Order in Syria, met with a death no less terrible than that of his namesake, the nephew of Hassan Ben Sabah. The trunk of his body was hacked into pieces at the gate looking eastward toward Irak, his legs and arms were burned, and his head was borne through Syria as a spectacle. Ismail, a brother of that astrologer who had brought the Order into friendship with Risvan, died with the others. Many Assassins were hurled into the moat from the top of the fortress. Hossam ed din, son of Dimlatsh, a Dayi who had just come from Persia, fled from the rage of the people to Rakka where death found him promptly. Many saved themselves by flight, and were scattered in towns throughout Syria; others, to avoid all suspicion of belonging to the Order, denounced their own brothers, and killed them. The treasures of the Order were searched out and taken. Thus did Akhras, Prince of Aleppo, take vengeance on the Assassins for their evil influence over his father.

Later on the Order avenged this " persecution " in various ways, and most cruelly. In an audience given by the Kalif of Bagdad to Togteghin, the Atabeg of Damascus, three murderers attacked and killed the Emir, Ahmed Bal, then governor of Khorassan, whom they mistook, as it seems, for the Atabeg. The Emir was their enemy, but not the enemy whom they had come to destroy with their daggers, — though of this they were ignorant.

In 1120 Ilghazi received a command from Abu Mohammed, the chief of the Assassins in Aleppo, to surrender the castle of Sherif. Ilghazi, who feared the Order, feigned to yield up the castle, but ere the envoy could return with this answer the people had pulled down the walls, filled the moats, and joined the castle to Aleppo. Khashab, who had thought out this exploit and saved a fortress from the Assassins, paid with his life for the service. Bedü the governor of Aleppo became their victim, as did also one of his sons. His other sons cut down the murderers, but a third slayer sprang forward and gave one of them, wounded already, his death blow. When seized and taken to Togteghin the surviving

Assassin was punished with simple imprisonment, for Togteghin did not dare to mete out justice.

A few years later Nur ed din, the famous Prince of Damascus, received from the Assassins a command to surrender the castle of Beitlala. He yielded apparently and then roused up the people in secret to prevent the Order from gaining the fortress. They did this by destroying it hastily. So greatly did the princes fear the Assassins that they dared not refuse to obey their commands; they would promise obedience, and then rouse the people to pull down their own strongholds.

Governors of provinces both in Persia and Syria were the chief agents in keeping peace and good order, hence were opposed to the Assassins, and were exposed to their daggers more than all other men.

In Persia as in Syria the Assassins murdered many of the most distinguished men, men whom the Order feared or whom they removed to win favor or money. Sindjar, Sultan of the Seljuks, sent troops to retake Kuhistan castles which the Ismailians had seized. Hassan Sabah sought peace more than once with this Sultan through envoys. When all efforts proved futile, he won over officers of Sindjar's own household who spoke in his favor, and even prevailed on a servant of that prince to thrust a dagger into the floor before his bedside while he was sleeping. When Sindjar woke and saw the dire weapon he resolved to say nothing, but soon he received from Hassan Sabah a note with the following contents: "Were I not well inclined toward Sindjar, the man who planted that dagger in the floor would have fixed it in the Sultan's bosom. Let him know that I, from this rock, guide the hands of the men who surround him."

This letter made such an impression on Sindjar that he ceased to disturb Ismailians. His reign thereafter was the period of their greatest prosperity.

Hassan Ben Sabah died thirty-four years after his entrance into Alamut, and during that time he never came down from the castle, nay more, he never left, except twice, his own dwelling. He passed his life studying and writing on the dogmas of his system, and in governing that murderous Commonwealth which began in his brain, and was of his own invention.

He showed the truth of his doctrine by concise, captious arguments. " As to the knowledge of God," said he, " one of two courses must be followed : Claim to know God by the sole light of reason, or admit that one cannot know him by reason, but that men need instructors. Now he who rejects the first statement may not reject another man's reason without admitting thereby the necessity of guidance." Hassan combated in this way the claims of Greek sages. " The need of a guide being admitted we must know if every teacher is good, or if we must have infallible instruction. Now he who maintains that every teacher is good may not reject his opponent's instructor without acknowledging the need of a teacher deserving the obedience and confidence of all men. It is shown," added he, " that mankind has need of a true and infallible teacher. This teacher must be known so that men may accept his instruction with safety. He must have been designated and chosen; he must be installed; his truth must be proven. It would be folly to go on a journey without a skilled guide and director. This guide must be found before starting on the journey.

" Variety of opinion is a real proof of error, accord in opinion shows truth, and unity is the sign of it. Diversity is a clear sign of error; unity comes from teaching obedience, diversity from freedom of thought; unity indicates submission to an Imam, freedom of thought goes with schism, and many leaders."

Apparently austere in his morals and respecting the Koran, Hassan Sabah forced all his subjects to live just as he did. The sternness of his methods may be known from these examples. He had one son clubbed to death for mere suspicion of being connected with the slaying of the Kuhistan governor without orders; the other for wine drinking and dissolute conduct. In the execution of his elder son he gave to his subjects an example of the penalty paid for interfering with the prerogative of the Grand Prior. The execution of the younger showed them the result of disobedience to principles — the principles ruling at Alamut.

Just before his death in 1124 Hassan Sabah made his old comrade Kia Busurgomid his successor. Under this second chief murder increased very greatly; not merely enemies of the sect fell now by the dagger, but any prince or man who had an enemy could hire one of the Order to murder him. Rather than expose themselves to death, sovereigns and men of authority lived in apparent accord with the Assassins and obtained from the chief as a price of good-will a number of his devotees as aids in carrying out their own evil schemes for aggrandizement. Those men slew all pointed out to them, frequently, however, whole populations were punished for these crimes of their co-religionists. Kia Busurgomid was a man of great activity who followed the methods of Hassan, destroying the most illustrious leaders of the enemy.

Mahmud, the successor of Sindjar, at first met the Assassins with their own tactics of murder and deceit; but, for an unknown reason, after being in open war with Kia Busurgomid for some time, he asked that an envoy be sent to discuss terms of peace. The envoy from the Assassins was received courteously by the Sultan, but upon leaving the presence of Mahmud he was seized and murdered by the enraged populace. The Sultan sent an envoy to Alamut immediately to assure Kia Busurgomid that this unfortunate incident was due wholly to the hostility of the citizens, and that he himself was in no way to blame.

Kia Busurgomid replied that he had believed in the assurances of safety which the Sultan had given. If the Sultan would deliver the murderers of the man to the Assassins there would be no difficulty, otherwise he would take revenge for the death of his envoy. Mahmud fearing the rage of the people gave no reply, and was shortly after attacked by a large number of Assassins who killed four hundred men and carried off many horses and camels.

In 1129 the Sultan got possession of the Alamut fortress, but was soon forced to relinquish it. Not long after Mahmud died, probably by poison administered by a member of the Order.

In Risvan's time, as already stated, the Assassins enjoyed immense influence at Aleppo, but under his son they were hunted down and slaughtered. A somewhat similar fate struck them in Damascus where during Busi's time, Behram, an Assassin from Astrabad, won over to his side the vizir who gave him in 1128 the castle of Banias, which immediately became the center of influence in Syria, and so remained until twelve years later when the Assassins made Massiat their capital. On gaining a firm foothold in Syria by possession of Banias, the Assassins flocked to their new capital from all sides. No prince now had courage to give any man protection against them. But the career of Behram the shrewd Assassin was of short duration.

Dohak, the chief man in Taim, a part of the district of Baalbek, determined to avenge the death of his brother who had been murdered at command of Behram, hence he summoned the warriors of Taim with assistance from Damascus and places around it. Behram planned to surprise Dohak and his army and crush them, but he fell into their power unwarily, and they killed him. His head and hands were taken to Egypt, where the Kalif had them borne in triumph to Cairo, and gave a rich gold embroidered robe to the man who brought them. Those Assassins who escaped fled from Taim to Banias, where before the expedition Behram had given chief command to Ismail, an Assassin from Persia.

Tahir, the vizir, was as ready to negotiate with Ismail as he had been with Behram. Ismail had as aid Abul Wefa, a man without faith or principle, but adroit and successful. The Crusaders, whose power was then rising in Syria, seemed to Abul Wefa the best allies possible for Assassins. Enemies of Mohammedanism, they were friends to its opponents. Attacked from without by Crusaders and corrupted from within by Ismailian teachings, Abbasid Mohammedanism seemed nearing its downfall. Abul Wefa now made a treaty with the King of Jerusalem, through which he engaged to give him Damascus on a certain Friday. While Busi, the Emir, and his great men, were assembled in the mosque at devotion all approaches were to be opened to the king and his forces. In return for this service the king was to give Abul Wefa the city of Tyre on the seacoast. The Templars' earliest Grand Master, Hugo De Payens, appears as main agent, it is stated, in urging the king to this arrangement.

During a decade of years after its organization, the Order of Templars remained in obscurity, observing vows of poverty, chastity, and obedience, and performing the labor of protecting all pilgrims. It was, however, merely a private society at that time without distinguishing habit or statutes. Rules given by St. Bernard and confirmed by the Pope raised it to be a great Order created to defend the Holy Sepulchre and pilgrims.

During this year, 1129, Hugo arrived in Jerusalem with a numerous escort of pilgrims and knights, who through his influence had taken the cross and raised arms in defence of Christ's sepulchre.

The winning of Damascus was now decided upon, but mar-

velous events happened meanwhile to prevent the carrying out
of this plan.   Tahir Ben Saad, the vizir, who, as we have seen,
exercised supreme power at direction of Tajul Muluk Busi, Prince
of Damascus had arranged with Abul Wefa, the surrender of
Damascus in secret.   Tajul Muluk Busi, discovering the treachery of his vizir and the plot of the Assassins to get possession of
Damascus, had Tahir Ben Saad put to death immediately, and
then commanded a slaughter of all the Assassins in the city.   It
is stated that " six thousand fell by the sword which thus avenged
many victims of the dagger."

While this was taking place a strong Christian army was rapidly
approaching Damascus to take possession of the city.   Of this
army a large number, while marching, went with knights to
plunder villages and obtain provisions, permitting, as was cus-
tomary, a considerable force of pilgrims to accompany them.
They advanced without order and were in great part cut down
by a picked corps of warriors from Damascus.   On hearing of
this disaster the rest of the Christian army hurried forward to attack those men of Damascus.   While they were thus hastening
dreadful darkness appeared on a sudden, darkness broken only
by flashes of lightning; then came a tempest with the roaring of thunder and a downrush of rain which overspread
everything.   When the roads were all flooded and the whole
country covered with water, a great cold set in quickly; frost of
amazing severity turned flood and rain into ice and snowflakes.
When light came again it disclosed winter scenery.   The disaster,
storm, change and frost were considered by the Christians as
manifestations of Heaven's terrible anger because of their great
sin in making a compact with murderers

The only advantage obtained from this league with criminals
was the restoration of the castle of Banias.   Ismail remembering
the fate of Damascus Assassins restored Banias, but three years
later, in 1132, he retook it, and the Christians in the end gained
nothing whatever.

CHAPTER XII

THE valiant and powerful Prince of Mosul, Aksonkor Burshi, was one of the first victims of the second Grand Prior. He was just and daring, a man greatly feared not only by the Assassins but also by the Crusaders with whom he had recently fought a battle. Shortly after his return from this encounter he was attacked by eight Assassins who, disguised as dervishes, fell upon him in the chief mosque of Mosul while he was taking his place on the throne. Protected by armor he defended himself with immense courage. Three of the Assassins he killed, but before his assistants could come to his aid he received a wound which soon proved fatal. All the other Assassins were slain save one who fled and escaped from the wrath of the people. When the mother of this man learned of Aksonkor's death she adorned herself immediately through pride in the success of the onset for which, as she supposed, her son had given his life. But when he came home uninjured she cut off her hair and blackened her face in deep sorrow, since he had not died with his comrades in honor — such was her view of honor.

Busi the Prince of Damascus was marked for destruction. Tahir the friend of the Assassins had been executed and six thousand of the Order had been massacred in 1129 at that prince's command; therefore there was no escape for Busi. Within two years of that massacre he was attacked by a band of Assassins and escaped with difficulty; the year following, however, brought death to him from the effects of wounds received in that encounter.

The vengeance of the Assassins continued for years; it waited for time, opportunity, and place, nay more, it passed from one generation to another. They never forgot and never forgave. Shems ul Muluk, son of Busi, as well as many other people of renown fell under the daggers of the Order. The mufti of Kasvin and the mayors of Ispahan and Tebriz were among those who perished. Besides rulers and great men a multitude of merchants and ordinary men were murdered by the tools of Hassan Ben Sabah and his successors the so-called apostles of Islam.

But in spite of the bitter enmity between the Abbasids and the Fatimids and the fact that the Assassins, an offshoot of the Fatimids, had worked long and industriously to overthrow their opponents, the throne of the Kalif of Bagdad had not been stained with the blood of its occupants thus far. But the time had now come when the Order dared to murder even the successor of the Prophet. Through a strange retribution, however, Kalif Abu Ali Mansur the tenth of the Fatimid dynasty was the first to die by the hand of an Assassin, but whether this death was effected by the policy of the Order or by private revenge is unknown. It was thought by many that the murderer was employed by the family of Efdhal, the grand vizir.

Efdhal had been as dangerous for the Kalif at Cairo through the immense power which he wielded in Egypt as for the Crusaders because of his hatred for them and the great energy with which he warred against them. He was cut down by two men who belonged to the Order. No one knew who had employed those two persons, whether the murderers were the tools of the Crusaders, or of the Kalif. At first suspicion fell on the Kalif. The son of Efdhal, Abu Ali, who was imprisoned immediately upon the death of his father, was set free after the assassination of the Kalif and given the office and titles of the vizir. But Assassins soon attacked and killed Abu Ali. It may be that all three murders were caused by the machinations of unknown enemies.

Egypt from this time on presents scenes of turmoil and disorder produced by great struggles between partisans of the Kalifs of Bagdad and Cairo, or in other words between the Abbasids and the Fatimids.

Mostershed the twenty-ninth Abbasid Kalif held power from 1118 to 1135, but his power was limited and his throne most insecure. When they made themselves guardians of the Kalifs at Bagdad the Seljuk Sultans took from them all marks of temporal power except the Friday prayers from the pulpit, and the coinage of money. When Massud became Sultan he immediately took this last evidence of authority from the Kalif and appointed Friday prayers in his own name. This encroachment was tolerated by Mostershed but he did not accept it. Some time later a number of officers with the men under them left Massud and joined the Kalif's army. These officers assured the Kalif that it would not be difficult to conquer Massud. Deceived by their statements Mostershed marched against the Sultan, but, deserted by his warriors in the first onset, he was captured by Massud and taken to Meragha. He was freed however on his promise to remain thereafter in Bagdad and pay a yearly tribute to the Sultan.

The Ismailians had hoped that this war would end the Abbasids; hence they were bitterly disappointed, and determined to take the work into their own hands at once and at all costs. When Massud left Mostershed in his camp near Meragha, the Assassins cut down the Kalif and his attendants. Then not satisfied with the murder, they mutilated the corpses by cutting off their ears and noses.

People had scarcely recovered from the terror caused by this slaughter of Mostershed when they learned that his successor Rashid had been killed. The Assassins had thought that by the murder of Mostershed they would bring about the ruin of the Kalifat. But hope deceived them. Rashid on taking the throne planned his own policy and determined to begin his rule by avenging the death of his father. He went first, however, on a journey to Ispahan, intending when he returned to deal with the Assassins. The Order ever alert and watchful discovered his purpose. Four active adherents followed Rashid, and at last when the chance came they stole into his tent and stabbed him. He was buried in Ispahan, and the warriors whom he had assembled to march against the Order scattered at once.

When news of the Kalif's death came to the Grand Prior there was great joy in Alamut. For seven days and nights kettledrums sounded to announce the happy event to that whole mountain region. This murder brought alarm and terror to the Abbasid world. It is said that after the death of Rashid Abbasid Kalifs very rarely, if ever, showed themselves in public. Agents of the Order now went in crowds through Asia. Fortresses already held by them were strengthened while new ones were built or else purchased. In Syria they obtained Kadmos in 1134, Kahaf four

years later, and Massiat in 1140. The first and the second they
bought, the third they took by the strong hand, with violence,
and made it the center of their activity in Syria.

Kei Busurgomid had ruled the Assassin kingdom for fourteen
years when, realizing that his last hour was near, he made his
eldest son, Kia Mohammed, Grand Prior. The ruler at Alamut
while increasing the power of the Order and extending its influence
in every direction did not call himself sovereign or claim sovereign
power. He ruled in the name of an invisible Imam of whom he
called himself an apostle, an Imam who was to appear in the
future and establish his rule over mankind. The real tenets of the
Order were known only to the Grand Prior and to his chosen and
tested associates who were bound to secrecy by the most dreadful
oaths. The vast majority of people who were under the control
of the chief of Alamut thought themselves devout followers of
Mohammed the Prophet whose teachings they observed with the
utmost fidelity. They looked upon the Grand Prior as an apostle
whose wisdom was beyond question and obeyed his commands
with willingness and the most implicit confidence. Those of his
his disciples whom he employed as tools to carry out political
schemes or private revenge requiring the removal of men by the
use of the dagger thought they were working for a holy cause and
removing enemies of their faith and their country. As the
books and manuscripts of Hassan Ben Sabah and of those
Alamut chiefs who succeeded him were destroyed at the coming of
the Mongols it is difficult to obtain at this time much information
regarding the internal government of the Assassin kingdom.
Their real doctrine was carefully concealed and its supporters
appeared only as upholders of Islam. This is shown by answers
given the Sultan Sindjar who sent an envoy to Alamut to gain
information concerning the doctrine of the Order.

"The Ismailian doctrine is as follows," replied the Prior.
" We believe in one God and recognize that alone as true wisdom
which accords with His holy word and the commands of His
Prophet, Mohammed. We obey these as given in the sacred
Koran; we believe in all that the Prophet taught touching creation
and the last day, rewards, punishments, the judgment and the
resurrection. To believe thus is needful for salvation, and no man
may give an opinion on God's commands, or alter one letter in

them. These are the rules on which rests our religion, and if they please not the Sultan let him send a theologian to talk with us."

In 1138 began the rule of Kia Mohammed, a man not only lacking in wit and ability but wholly untrained in the art of governing. The power of the Order had now reached its height. Its authority and influence were apparent in many countries of Asia. There was need of a strong man at Alamut. Nearly fifty years had passed since Hassan Ben Sabah began his career of murder; years during which all the teachings of Islam were observed with the greatest strictness by the common people who believed in their rulers and yielded ready obedience. But Kai Mohammed did not win the confidence of his subjects; they greatly disliked him. Hassan, his son, was a man of unlimited ambition, and early in life gained the love of the people and the reputation of having keen insight and much learning, a reputation which he used for the attainment of his own objects and not for the advancement of the Order. He knew and did not contradict the report which his partisans spread very carefully that he was the Imam whom Hassan Ben Sabah had promised. But the Prior of Alamut heard of his son's action; of the opinions of the people and the report that Hassan was the long looked for Imam, and he declared his displeasure at once. "Hassan is my son," said he. "I am not the Imam but one of his precursors; whoever thinks differently is an infidel!" and he ordered the immediate execution of two hundred and fifty of Hassan's associates and partisans; others were banished. Hassan through fear for his own safety wrote against his adherents and supported his father. He avoided punishment thus by removing suspicion. Since he drank wine in secret, however, and practised many things which were forbidden, his adherents thought him surely the promised Imam whose coming was to end prohibition of all kinds.

But now appear the men destined to destroy the Fatimid dynasty of Egypt, — Nur ed din Mahmud Ben Amed Es Zenky, son of Zenky, son of Ak Sunkur, and Saladin, son of Eyub the friend of Zenky. Ak Sunkur, a slave whom Melik Shah made his court chamberlain and later the governor of the Province of Aleppo, died in 1094 leaving a son, Zenky, ten years of age. Not long after his father's death Zenky was summoned to the court of Kur Buga then Prince of Mosul. He soon became a favorite and companion of the prince and accompanied him on his campaigns. In 1122 the prince gave him Wasit and Basra in fief. When in March of the following year the Arabs, led by Dubeg a renowned Emir of the Asad tribe, marched against Bagdad, Mostershed the Kalif crossed the river with his army and was received on the bank by his vassals the Prince of Mosul, Zenky of Basra, and others. The combined armies then attacked Hilla the enemy's stronghold, and though Dubeg's army was much larger than that of the Kalif's the Arabs were defeated owing chiefly to the skilful movements of Zenky. Somewhat later Zenky went to Hamadan to the court of the Seljuk Sultan, Mahmud, and soon married the widow of Kundughly, the richest noble of the court. In 1124 he returned to Basra and Wasit where he ruled with great severity. In a battle between the Sultan and the Kalif, Zenky took the part of the Sultan and sent him reinforcements, thus obliging the Kalif to make peace. When after this victory the Sultan took up his abode in Bagdad Zenky received a high office. In 1127 he was made governor of Mosul and Jezira and took upon himself the task of defending the country against the Crusaders. Not long after this he became master of Aleppo. In 1131 the Seljuk Sultan died and there was a bitter conflict over the succession. Zenky now determined to get possession of Damascus but his attempt, made four years after the death of the Sultan, brought him no success. In 1144 he besieged and captured Edessa held at that time by the Crusaders. Two years after this great victory he died by the hand of one of his own attendants, leaving a son, Nur ed din, to finish his work by becoming master of Damascus.

In 1132 when fleeing from Karaja by whom he had been defeated in battle, Zenky was saved by Eyub commandant of the castle of Tenkrit on the bank of the Tigris. This service was never forgotten. In 1138 on a night when Eyub, who had been driven from the castle of Tenkrit, was seeking an asylum with Zenky at Mosul a son was born to him. This son he named Yessuf Salal ed din (Saladin). A year later Zenky took possession of Baalbek and Eyub was made governor there. Saladin was nine years old when Zenky was murdered. Zenky's possessions were shared by his two sons, Seif ud din who received Mosul, and Nur ed din who ruled the Syrian province.

Nur ed din was a wise and just ruler, as well as a brave and fearless warrior, and a resolute defender of Islam. Being master of Mosul and Aleppo he was also master of North Syria, but in the south he lacked power through not having Damascus. Mejr ed din Abak the last of the Seljuks of Damascus ruled there, or more correctly, his vizir ruled at his commission. After Zenky's death Damascus sent troops to retake Baalbek. Eyub made terms and surrendered the city receiving in return ten villages in that region. A few years later he became commander-in-chief of the Damascus army, a position which he held when Nur ed din marched against Damascus in 1154. Shirkuh, brother of Eyub, had meanwhile taken service with Nur ed din. When the Syrian army appeared before the city Shirkuh opened negotiations with his brother and Eyub surrendered the place to the son of his old friend. Thus Damascus abandoned its hereditary sovereign and Mejr ed din withdrew from the city. He received in exchange Emesa, then Balis, and went finally to Bagdad.

An earthquake had nearly ruined Damascus, but Nur ed din restored the city and made it his capital. During his reign of twenty-eight years he captured fifty castles or more and established mosques and schools in every city of his dominion. Policy as well as religion caused Nur ed din to favor the Abbasid line instead of the Fatimids of Cairo. The time seemed to him ripe then to end Cairo helplessness, a genuine helplessness since civil war raged there between Dargham a commander and Shawer the vizir who under the Kalif were struggling for mastery.

Early in 1163, the year following that in which Nur ed din had conquered Haram and taken possession of many Syrian fortresses, Shawer who had been driven from Cairo came to Damascus and promised not only to pay the cost of an invasion but afterward to yield up one third of the income of Egypt if Nur ed din would give him certain aid against Dargham. Nur ed din was not opposed to obtaining a foothold in the country, still he withheld assistance till April of the following year, when he sent his able and ambitious governor of Emesa, Essed ed din Shirkuh, with an army into Egypt. Dargham was slain and Shawer was restored to his former position. Freed from his enemy and safe, as he thought, he refused to fulfil the conditions he had made. Shirkuh enraged by his treachery seized the eastern province, Sherkiya, and the chief town, Belbeis.

Shawer, who was an artful unprincipled man, false to his friends, to his warriors and to his own interests, then called in Amalric, Count of Askalon and king of Jerusalem, to act with the Crusaders against Shirkuh. The friend of the Egyptian vizir was now his foe, and the Crusaders had become the ally of their erstwhile enemy. Between Amalric and Nur ed din there was keen rivalry, for neither man would permit the other to become master in Egypt.

Shirkuh fortified Belbeis and for three months resisted all attacks from his opponent. Nur ed din now made an expedition to Palestine and Amalric had need to hasten home to protect his own kingdom. An armistice was arranged and both armies left Egypt.

But in 1167 Amalric again advanced at the head of a large army. Rumors of this advance having reached Nur ed din he at once sent Shirkuh to Egypt with a force of two thousand horsemen. He had barely crossed the Nile when Amalric appeared on the opposite bank. Shirkuh halted at Giza, and Amalric took up his position at Fustat. Shawer allied himself with Amalric, who dictated his own terms and insisted that the Kalif should ratify the treaty.

Shirkuh, alarmed by the strength of the combined armies, retreated to Upper Egypt. Pursued by his opponent, he turned and gave battle, April 18, 1167, at a place a few miles south of Minya. The Egyptians were defeated, but Shirkuh, not having troops sufficient for a march on Cairo, withdrew to Alexandria, where he left Saladin in command with one-half of the army, and moved toward the South to collect contributions. Alexandria was soon besieged and blockaded. Provisions were lacking in the city and there was talk of surrender when news came that Shirkuh was advancing rapidly to their relief. He halted before Cairo and invested that city. Amalric then raised the siege of Alexandria and a peace was made by which Shirkuh and the king promised to withdraw their troops from Egypt. It is stated that Shirkuh received fifty thousand ducats, and the king twice that amount from the revenues of Egypt. There remained at Cairo, moreover, a general of Crusaders with a large number of men as a guard against Nur ed din.

But peace was of short duration; the advantage which came to the King of Jerusalem by the terms of the treaty induced him to violate his promise in the hope of eventually getting control of the country. Incited by the Hospitalers, whose chief wished to keep his Order in Belbeis which he had charged with a debt of more than one hundred thousand ducats, Amalric advanced early in the winter of 1168 but this time he entered Egypt as an enemy.

He arrived at Belbeis in November, captured that city and slaughtered its inhabitants. He then besieged Cairo. A wall at which women and children were toiling both by day and by night had been raised around the city. November 12th Fustat the most ancient part, called usually Old Cairo, was by command of Shawer set on fire to hamper the enemy, and it continued to burn for fifty-four days and nights. Adhad, the Kalif, despatched courier after courier with letters to Syria imploring Nur ed din to help him, and to picture the greatness of his need he inclosed locks of hair from the heads of his wives, as if saying: " The enemy are dragging our women by the hair. Come and rescue! "

Nur ed din was in Aleppo and Shirkuh at Emesa. Nur ed din, however, at no time indifferent to the importance of gaining influence and power, gave two hundred thousand gold ducats to Shirkuh and sent him to Egypt immediately (December, 1168). Six thousand chosen Syrians marched with him and two thousand picked Turkman warriors from Damascus. Saladin, urged by his uncle, accompanied the expedition.

Meanwhile Shawer and Amalric were negotiating — the former to liberate, the latter to win Cairo. Shawer promised a million of ducats in the name of the Kalif, and the King of Jerusalem was glad to receive fifty thousand in ready money. The Crusaders withdrew when the Syrians under Shirkuh appeared before Cairo in January, 1169. The Kalif went to the camp on a visit immediately, and complained very bitterly of Shawer who had brought the Crusaders into Egypt, burned Fustat, and ruined the country. He begged Shirkuh to obtain for him the head of the vizir, he himself being unable to get it.

Shawer felt now his own danger, and, while feigning friendship for the Syrians, resolved to destroy, under cover of a banquet, both Shirkuh, and Saladin, his nephew, with the princes of their suite. The plot became known in good season, however, and when Shawer was approaching on a visit to Shirkuh, he was seized and killed, and his head was sent to the Kalif.

Shirkuh took Shawer's place as vizir and the Kalif gave him the title of Al Melik Al Mansur (The Victorious King).

Shirkuh died two months later, March 26, and his nephew Yussuf Salah ed din, now thirty-one years of age, was invested with the same dignities of office and received the same title.

Saladin was now the vizir of the Kalif, and Nur ed din's commander, thus his position was peculiar; he was the vizir of a Shiite Kalif and the commander of a Sunnite king. He therefore caused the name of Nur ed din to be mentioned in public prayers every Friday after that of the Kalif.

Nur ed din thought that the time had come to abolish the Fatimid Kalifat, but Saladin delayed since the people clung to Adhad, the last representative of the dynasty. Adhad fell ill, however, and died opportunely. Saladin transferred the prerogative of prayer then from the Fatimid line to that of the Abbasid September 10, 1171. In this way Saladin delivered the blow which destroyed the main branch of the Western Ismailites. The Abbasid Kalifat now prevailed over that of the family of Ali for which the Ismailites had taught and conspired and in whose name they had deceived the people for nearly three centuries.

This was an event of vast importance in the history of the East, as well as in that of the Assassin Order before whom Saladin, now a famous warrior and an ardent champion of the Abbasids, stood forth as a powerful and dangerous enemy.

Eight years before the fall of the Fatimid dynasty Mohammed the Grand Prior of the Assassins died, and Hassan II assumed power. As we have seen, Hassan began his career during his father's life, by winning partisans and spreading the belief that he was the promised Imam. In his youth he had spent many years in acquiring a thorough knowledge of philosophy and history, and in receiving instruction regarding the mysteries of the Order. Unprincipled and profligate he now determined not only to indulge without limit in every vice but to favor a like indulgence in others. To cast aside all concealment and give the secrets of the Ismailians to the world. To announce the same license to the leaders of the Order and favor impunity of vice not merely by example but by preaching from the pulpit that crime is permissible and innocent. In Ramadan of the 559th year of the Hegira — 1163 — the inhabitants of Rudbar were assembled at Alamut by his command. A pulpit was placed at the foot of the castle and looking toward Mecca to which all professors of Islam turn when praying.

Hassan ascended the pulpit and made known to his hearers the maxims of a renewed and strengthened religion. He announced to them that they were freed from all obligations of the law, for they had come to an era in which they were to know God by intuition; they were released from the burden of every command and brought to the day of Resurrection, that is to the manifestation of the Imam before whom they were now standing. They were no longer to pray five times each day, or observe other rites of religion. Then, after he had explained that an allegorical sense should be given to the dogmas of Resurrection, Hell, and Paradise, he descended from the pulpit and the people held a great banquet, yielding themselves to pleasures of all kinds, to dancing, to music, to wine and to sport in celebration of the day of Resurrection, the day when the Imam was made manifest.

From that hour when all things were lawful according to Hassan the name Molahids, or the Lost Ones, which previously had been given to the Karmathites and other great criminal disturbers, was given not only to the disciples of Hassan but to all the Ismailians. Through their Grand Prior the Order after concealing its true doctrine from mankind for years had revealed it on a sudden and exposed to the world a society founded on atheism, assassination and immorality. Thenceforth the Order was doomed to rapid internal destruction.

The Ismailians had adopted the view that the universe had never begun and would never end. The end in their eyes meant merely a phase, the close of an epoch in existence which would be followed by another whose length would depend upon the movements and position of the heavenly bodies. By Resurrection was meant the presence of men before God at the close of an epoch, and when that term came every practice of religion was included, since man's one concern is the estimate of his actions.

The 17th Ramadan was celebrated with banquets and games, not only as the feast of the manifestation, but as the true date of publishing their doctrine. As the followers of Islam reckon their time from the flight of the Prophet, so did the Molahids from the manifestation of the Imam, the 17th of Ramadan in the 559th year of Hegira. As Mohammed's name was never mentioned without adding " The Blessed," so after that day the words " Blessed be his memory " were added to Hassan's name. The Grand Priors had called themselves simply missionaries or precursors of the Imam, but Hassan insisted that he was the Imam; in him lay all power to remove the restrictions of the law. By this claim he appeared before the people as a lawgiver. In this spirit he wrote to the different princes. His letter concerning Reis Mossafer, the Grand Prior of Kuhistan, a namesake of whom had been Grand Prior in Irak under Hassan Ben Sabah, was as follows:

" I, Hassan, declare to you that on earth I am God's vice-gerent. Reis Mossafer is my vice-gerent in Kuhistan. The men of that province will obey him; they must listen to his words as to mine."

Reis had a pulpit erected in the Mumin Abad castle, his residence. From the pulpit he read this epistle to the people, most of whom listened to it with pleasure. There was a great festival with music and sports; they fell to dancing, they drank wine at the foot of the pulpit, and in every way possible made known their joy at liberation from the bonds of the law. A few who remained faithful to Islam withdrew from the Order; others who did not believe but could not decide to take this step remained and shared the reputation of the " Lost Ones."

Profligacy, atheism, infidelity and freedom from all restraint now ruled supreme, and Hassan's name was heard from every pulpit of the Order as that of the real successor of the Prophet, the long waited for Imam.

But it was much easier for Hassan to make himself a teacher of atheism and immorality than to assume the character of Imam.

To convince the people that he was the Imam Hassan was driven to prove himself descended from the Fatimid Kalifs. He was declared to be a son of Nesar and a grandson of the Kalif Mostansir during whose reign Hassan Ben Sabah had been in Cairo, and in the political disputes of the day had taken the side of Mostansir's elder son Nesar. For this he had been ordered by Bedr Jimali, the commander-in-chief, to leave Egypt. A certain Abul Hassan Seid, a favorite of the Kalif, had come to Alamut a year after the death of Mostansir, and had brought with him a son of Nesar whom he confided to Hassan Ben Sabah. Hassan treated the envoy with great respect and gave the young man, also called Nesar, a village near the castle as a residence. Nesar married and had a son to whom the name " Blessed be his Memory " was given. When Nesar's wife was delivered of her child the wife of Mohammed, the Grand Prior of Alamut, also had a child. A nurse carried " Blessed be his Memory " into the castle and substituted him for the son of Mohammed.

This tale instead of satisfying the people was received with ridicule and declared to be untrue. Then as, according to new Ismailite teaching, all was indifferent and nothing forbidden, the builders of Hassan's genealogy found it best to maintain that Nesar had met Mohammed's wife in secret, the result being Hassan, the Grand Prior, Imam, and Kalif, " Blessed be his Memory."

Ismailites who in this way tried to prove that Hassan was a descendant of Nesar were called by their opponents " the Nesari," a title which involved extreme obloquy.

Crime and immorality now reigned wherever the Order had power or influence. Men who had hitherto been Assassins through obedience to those in power and in the belief that they were fulfilling a religious duty by removing persons who were harmful to Islam, now murdered people wantonly.

Hassan II died in the fourth year of his reign by the dagger of his brother-in-law at the castle of Lamsir.

Disorders caused through the revelation by Hassan were not stopped by his murder. Crimes of every kind increased greatly during the reign of his son and successor, Mohammed II, whose first act was to avenge the murder of his father. Nanver, the late Prior's brother-in-law and assassin, died by the axe of the executioner, and with him died all his kindred, male and female.

Mohammed II preached and taught with even more insistence than had Hassan, his father, the doctrine of license, crime, and vice, and like him claimed to be the Imam. Deeply read in philosophy he thought himself unequalled in this and other forms of knowledge. He was a man devoted to evil, and though he reigned for forty-six years there is but little information to be obtained regarding the Order during that period.

In the eyes of the Orthodox the Assassins were a band of vile heretics, an assemblage of outcasts; but that Order was still defiant and mighty. Fakhr ul Islam of Ruyan was the first doctor of the law to pronounce it impious. This he did in Kazvin by a fetva. On his return from Kazvin to Ruyan he fell by an Assassin. A doctor of greater reputation was treated more tenderly: Fakhr ud din Rasi, a professor of theology at Rayi, never failed in his lectures to refute all their doctrines, adding as he did so: " May God curse and destroy them." The Ismailian Prior sent an agent to Rayi. This man appeared as a student, heard lectures and bided his time. At last, finding that Fakhr ud din was alone in his cabinet, he walked in, shut the door, placed the point of a dagger at the breast of his master and waited. " What is this ? " cried the latter in terror. " Why do you curse the Ismailians and their doctrines unceasingly ? " asked the Assassin. " I will speak of them no more," said the teacher, " I swear this to you most solemnly." " Will you keep this oath ? " After strong assurance the agent was satisfied, drew back his dagger, and continued: " I had no command to kill you; if I had nothing could have turned me from duty. My master salutes you and says that he cares not for common men's words, but he regards your discourses, since they will live in the memory of people. He invites you to visit him at Alamut, for he wishes to prove his high esteem to you in person."

Fakhr ud din would not go, but promised silence. The agent then put down a purse of three hundred miskals, and said: " You will receive every year a purse such as this. I have brought you two tunics of Yeman besides; they are now in my lodgings." That said the man disappeared. Some time after this a disciple of the teacher asked why he did not curse the Ismailians. " How can I curse them ? " replied Fakhr ud din, " their arguments are so trenchant."

In Arslan Kushad, the Ismailians surprised in the night a castle two leagues from Kazvin on the top of a high mountain. The people of that place were in despair at having such neighbors, and implored various princes to free them but in vain, till a certain Sheikh, Ali, persuaded the Kwaresmian Sultan, Tagash, to assist him. The Sultan laid siege to the castle, took it, allowed the Ismailians to withdraw, and placed a small garrison on the moun-

tain. Barely had the investing troops gone when the Ismailians
reëntered the stronghold at night through an underground passage
known to them only and slew the whole garrison. The Sheikh
Ali implored Tagash again and he came now in person. The people
of Kazvin joined his forces and after a siege of two months the
Ismailians yielded the castle on condition that they should be
allowed to retire unmolested. They promised to leave in two
divisions. If the first passed in safety the second would follow,
if not it would keep up the struggle. The first party descended,
rendered homage to the Sultan and vanished. The besiegers
waited for the second division, waited long and discovered at
last that the garrison had gone in one party. The castle was then
razed at command of the Sultan. But the Ismailians took vengeance on Sheikh Ali. While returning from a pilgrimage to
Mecca he was slain by one of their Assassins in a mosque at
Damascus.

Syria and Egypt at this time demand attention since it was there
that the enemies of Saladin were acting.

In Cairo was the Sultan's great palace where for two hundred
years the Fatimids had been collecting the wealth not only of
Egypt, but of Syria and Arabia. When after the death of the
Sultan, Saladin took possession of this palace, he found there
jewels of a value beyond estimate. There were magnificent pearls;
an emerald " a span long and as thick as a finger," there was furniture of ebony and ivory, there were coffers inlaid with gold and
ornamented with precious stones. There was wealth of every kind.
There was also a splendid library containing, as some historians
state, 2,600,000 volumes, others mention a much smaller number
but it was, in any case, at that time the largest library in Europe.

Some of those treasures Saladin gave to the officers of his army,
some he sent to Nur ed din and others were disposed of to obtain
sums needed for campaigns against the Crusaders and for erecting
fortifications, mosques and schools.

Though there was a strong party in Cairo hostile to Saladin, a
party composed of officers in the Egyptian army, palace dependents
and even some of the Syrian officers who were embittered by the
rapid advance of so young a man, still his adherents were increasing. Nur ed din saw with alarm the influence and power of
his lieutenant but he knew well that embroiled with the Crusaders

and the Sultan of Rūm he could not recall the master of Cairo. Hence though alert and watchful he remained in apparent friendship, and Saladin was prudent enough to render him homage as ruler of Syria and Egypt. Meanwhile to secure his own position he gathered his family around him, made his brothers, his nephews, and his relatives commanders in the army; and strengthened the fortifications of Cairo.

In June, 1173, by the Atabeg's command he laid siege to Karak, but scarcely were his troops in position when news came that Nur ed din was approaching with his Syrian army. Saladin withdrew hastily and returned to Cairo, giving his father's illness as a reason for the withdrawal. In 1174 he sent his elder brother, Turan Shah, with an army against Yemen, a place which he thought would be convenient for defence in case he were attacked by the Atabeg of Syria.

Abdennebi, a follower of the impious Karmath, was master of that region and had done much to oppress and demoralize his people. Turan Shah soon conquered the Yemens and for more than fifty years the province remained in the possession of the Abbasids.

Nur ed din died May 6, 1174, and was succeeded by his son Salih, a boy eleven years of age. The young prince, incapable of governing, was under control of guardians among whom was the eunuch Gumushtegin, a man greatly disliked by the Syrians of Aleppo. Master of Egypt and with a large army at his command Saladin could have seized power had he so wished, but he remained true to the interests of Salih and at once ordered that the name " es Salih, son of Nur ed din " should be mentioned in the Friday prayers and engraved on the money.

But trouble began immediately. The Prince of Mosul seizing the opportunity threw off allegiance, and annexed Edessa. The Crusaders ever anxious to get possession of Damascus threatened the city and withdrew only when the governor, Ibn al Mokadden, gave them a large sum of money. In August Gumushtegin took Salih to Aleppo where the commander of the army assumed the guardianship of the young prince. The people of Damascus alarmed by the proximity of the Crusaders, and in dread of an attack from Aleppo, now begged aid of the Prince of Mosul. When he refused they turned to Saladin, who moved by quick marches

across the desert and entered the city on the 27th of November.
Making his brother Governor of Damascus he set out for Aleppo.

Upon his arrival at that place he sent to assure the prince that
he was in Syria to defend cities threatened by Crusaders and by
Seif ed din of Mosul. When the governor and Gumushtegin
closed the gates and refused him entrance Saladin laid siege to
the city, declaring that he did so to rescue his sovereign.

The eunuch now had recourse to the Assassins. Rashid ed din
Sinan, the Grand Prior in Syria lived in those days at Massiat,
the strongest of the fortresses belonging to the Ismailians of that
country.

He was the most politic and learned as well as one of the worst
of the rulers of the Assassin Kingdom and was at this moment
all-powerful in the mountains of North Syria. Saladin as a strong
champion of the Abbasid Kalifs and a man who seemed likely to
become sovereign was the natural enemy of the Order, hence
Sinan was willing to assist Gumushtegin especially as his request
that Saladin should die at the earliest was accompanied by a large
sum of money. Three Assassins were sent at once who although
they reached Saladin's tent and even his presence failed of their
purpose and were cut down by his attendants.

At this critical moment the Christians made an attack upon
Emesa where a part of the Egyptian troops were stationed. Saladin
was obliged to raise the siege of Aleppo and march to Emesa
where he soon had possession both of the town and the citadel. A
few days later he occupied Baalbek.

The Prince of Mosul and his brother alarmed by the success of
Saladin now joined their forces to those of Aleppo and advanced
against him. The armies met April 13, 1175, near Hamath. The
troops of Aleppo and Monsul were routed most thoroughly and
pursued even to the gates of Aleppo.

Saladin, now the greatest power in Egypt and Syria, waited no
longer; he at once proclaimed himself King and named the
dynasty which he founded "The Eyubite dynasty" in honor of
his father. Twelve months later the Prince of Mosul, who had
brought together a numerous army, met Saladin near Aleppo
where a fierce battle was fought April 22, 1176. Seif ed din was
defeated and lost his camp and his army.

Very soon after this victory Saladin took three important fortresses: Bosaa, Manbidj, and Azaz, the latter only after a siege lasting nearly a month. During this siege the king was again attacked by Assassins; the first struck at his head with a knife but Saladin seized the man's hand and an attendant rushed forward and killed him. A second and even a third murderer sprang forth but met with no better success.

Saladin, greatly alarmed by these repeated attacks, determined to destroy the Assassins, or at least drive them out of Syria. In 1177, after peace was established with Mosul and Aleppo, he advanced with a large force and blockaded Massiat which was built on an almost inaccessible peak commanding a deep ravine. Moslem historians assure us that he would have captured this all-important fortress and thus ended the Order in Syria had not his uncle, Shihab ed din, Lord of Hamath, begged him to make peace on the assurance of Sinan that the king would thereafter be protected from Assassins. Other historians assert that he was terrified by the threats of Sinan and relate how on a night Saladin awoke and found by his bed some hot scones of a size and shape peculiar to the Assassins. Near them, pinned down by a dagger, was a paper containing a threat and a warning. Whatever the cause may have been Saladin withdrew to Damascus without capturing the Assassin stronghold. Then leaving Turan Shah in command of Syria he returned to Cairo after an absence of two years.

Thereafter Saladin campaigned both in Egypt and Syria, took possession of the principal cities held by the Crusaders, and won the Holy Land for Mohammedans, but was never again attacked by Assassins.

Mohammed II died at Alamut in 1213 from poison, as is stated, leaving a son, Jelal ud din Hassan, who was twenty-five years of age at that time. From boyhood he had been opposed to the practices of the Assassins. As years passed this opposition became so intense that father and son feared each other and when Mohammed died suddenly suspicion rested on Jelal. As soon as the new Grand Prior assumed command he announced his return to the true tenets of Islam, and gave notice to the Kalif at Bagdad, the Kwaresmian Shah and the Governor of Irak of this change in the teachings at Alamut, undertaking at the same time to bring all

Ismailians to follow his example. Belief seems to have been given
to these assurances, for when his wife and mother went on a pilgrimage to Mecca they were received with distinction at Bagdad
and the party of pilgrims who marched under the banner of the
Alamut ruler preceded all others. He lived only twelve years after
coming to the throne but during those years he built mosques,
established schools and called in learned men to teach his people the
true faith. Some historians consider Jelal ud din a shrewd politician
rather than a reformer and assert that he remained an apostle of
atheism. Be this as it may he did for a short time suppress assassination but it reinstated itself quickly when poison removed
him and his son, Alai ed din Mohammed, a boy nine years of age,
reached the throne. During Alai ed din's reign women of the
harem ruled at Alamut. Every law established by Jelal ud din, his
father, was abolished and atheism and the dagger held sway as in the
days of Hassan Ben Sabah. When nearing manhood Alai ed din
showed symptoms of mental disorder but no man had the courage
to say that the chief was in need of assistance. Had a physician
dared to tell the truth on that subject he would have been torn
limb from limb by the rabble at Alamut. As his illness increased
his conduct became almost beyond sufferance, though his associates
declared that what he said and did was divine in its origin. When
Alai ed din was eighteen years of age a son was born to him.
This son he named Rokn ud din Kurshah and made him his
successor.

From childhood the Ismailians looked upon Rokn ud din as
their future Grand Prior and showed him honor equal to that
given his father. This roused anger in Alai ed din and he resolved to depose his son and appoint another successor. When
his advisors declared that the nomination was final he was enraged
and from that time on annoyed and tormented his son, till at
last Rokn ud din disclosed his whole mind to those courtiers who
were as much dissatisfied with his father as he was. He declared
that Alai ed din was ruining the Commonwealth, and that Mongol
arms would destroy it because of his conduct. " I will withdraw
from my father," said he, " send envoys to the Grand Khan and
make terms with him."

The greater number of the chief men agreed with Rokn ud din
and promised to defend him to the utmost, but in case of attack

by his father the person of the chief, as they said, must be sacred.
A short time after this pact and agreement Alai ed din when drunk
fell asleep in a thatched wooden building near one of his sheep
pens, a place which he visited whenever he indulged in his favorite
amusement of acting as shepherd. He was found dead in that
house about midnight, his head cut from the body. A Turkman
and a native of India were found wounded near him.

At the end of eight days, after many had been tortured on suspicion they discovered the murderer. He was a certain Hassan of
Masanderan, the late chief's nearest intimate, his inseparable
companion, a man whom he loved till his death though tormenting
him in every way possible.

Rokn ud din instead of bringing this Hassan to trial had him
slain quickly, an act which confirmed the suspicions which rested
on the youthful chief, who gave an additional example of savagery
by burning with the body of Hassan two sons and one daughter
of the Assassin. Of course they were innocent, though not only is it
possible but probable, that they possessed knowledge which Rokn
ud din would suppress at all hazards. Thus Alai ed din was murdered by an Assassin hired by his own son.

The first act of this new ruler was to order his subjects to observe
every practice of Islam, and next he took measures to suppress
robbery and murder. But only one year had passed when the
Mongol tempest came. Though Rokn ud din and the Ismailians
could not foresee it the doom of Alamut and all who belonged
to it had been settled. The Grand Khan had instructed Hulagu
to destroy them, and the master of Persia was advancing to the
execution.

Rokn ud din sent an officer to Yassaur, at Hamadan to
assure him of his submission to the Mongol Empire. This general
advised him to visit Prince Hulagu, who had just come to Persia.
Rokn ud din, alarmed for his own safety, answered that he would
send his brother, Shahinshah, in advance. Yassaur consented to
this and charged his own son to go with Shahinshah. But meanwhile he entered the Alamut region with an army corps of Persians
and Turks, and attacked that great fortress June, 1256. After a
sharp struggle his men were forced back, and out of revenge he
destroyed all the harvest, and ravaged the country.

Hulagu had commissioned Guga Ilga and Kita Buga to finish

the conquest of Kuhistan which the latter had begun two years earlier. He had made rather slow progress alone, but aided by Guga Ilga he captured Tun and slew all the people, excepting young women and children. This done both commanders joined Hulagu.

After Hulagu had received Shahinshah at headquarters he sent Rokn ud din this message: "Since thou hast sent thy brother with expressions of submission we will forgive the crimes committed by thy father. Raze thy castles and come to our camp. No harm will be done to the country."

When Rokn ud din had demolished several castles and dismounted the Alamut gates with those of Meimundiz and Lemsher, Yassaur left Ismailian territory. But Rokn ud din, while giving assurances of obedience, and receiving a Mongol governor, asked the term of one year in which to do homage to Hulagu.

Hulagu sent envoys a second time to induce the Alamut ruler, through promises and threats, to visit him. When these envoys were returning Rokn ud din sent with them a cousin of his father, and his own vizir Shems ud din Kileki, who were to present his excuses and obtain the delay which he asked for. He begged also to retain the three castles, Alamut, Lemsher and Lal, engaging in this case to surrender all others. He hoped by this yielding to win the delay which he needed. He was merely waiting for winter, which would stop every action in that entire mountain region.

The only answer given by Hulagu, who had just captured the castle of Shahdiz, was a summons to his camp pitched at that time near Demavend. He added that if Rokn ud din needed a few days to bring his affairs into order he might have them, but he must send his son straightway.

Rokn ud din, in great dread on receiving this message, replied that he was sending his son, and also a contingent of three hundred warriors. He declared that he would demolish castles if the land were not invaded. But instead of his son he sent his half brother, a boy of seven years, the son of his father and a Kurdistan woman. Hulagu saw the trick, but dissembled, was kind to the boy and sent him back saying that the child was too young. He required of Rokn ud din now his second brother, Shahinshah. The Alamut chief sent this brother, hoping that his own presence would not be demanded. Later on winter would come, as he thought, and confine him to his castle; it would also ward off every enemy.

At this juncture Hulagu sent Shaninshah to Rokn ud din with the following message: "Thou must destroy Meimundiz, and come quickly. If thou come thou wilt find here good treatm...t, if not God knows and He alone what will happen."

Rokn ud din repeated his worn out excuses. Hulagu would not receive them, and commanded his troops to march into Rudbar from various points simultaneously. The right wing moved from Mazanderan, the left by the Khar route and over Lemnan, while the center went by the Talekan highway. By order of Hulagu, who advanced with the center, the three hundred men sent by Rokn ud din were cut down near Kazvin, slain in secret. Reaching Meimundiz he made a tour of the fortress and summoned a council. Five days were given Rokn ud din for surrender. If he yielded in that time no harm would be done him or his subjects, but after that term an assault would be ordered.

It was answered that Rokn ud din was then absent, that without his command no man could surrender. The Mongols prepared for immediate action. Trees were cut down and shaped into beams of right size, borne by men to the neighboring summits and made into catapults. Hulagu fixed his tent on the highest position. On the morrow the conflict had already begun when Rokn ud din sent a message declaring that since he knew now where the prince was he asked that all action be suspended, and on that day, or the morrow, he would visit headquarters. Next day he desired to surrender in writing. The vizir Ata ul Mulk Juveini was deputed to frame the surrender. The paper was sent to Rokn ud din and he promised to yield up the stronghold, but when his brother was leaving the fortress such a tumult arose that he was stopped, and every man threatened with death who declared for surrender.

Rokn ud din informed Hulagu of this trouble, and the peril in which he then found himself. In answer Hulagu begged him not to expose his life needlessly. Meanwhile the catapults were mounted and the following morning an attack was begun from all points. The combat lasted till evening and was strenuous on both sides. At a season when tempests and snow had till that year made all mountain places impassable the weather was favorable for siege work and a new attack. The fourth day was opening when Rokn ud din thought it best to abandon the fortress. He sent his chief men with his son to the camp of the Mongols, and went himself the next morning to fall prostrate in presence of Hulagu. With him went his minister, the famous astronomer, Nassir ud din, and two great physicians, who had always advised a surrender.

Next day the Mongols marched into Meimundiz. Hulagu treated Rokn ud din kindly, but Mongol officers watched him and he was forced to direct Ismailian commandants to surrender their fortresses. He himself had to go with Hulagu's agents to effect every transfer. More than forty strong castles surrendered; all were destroyed when their garrisons had withdrawn. Alamut and Lemsher were the last strongholds left standing and their commandants declared that they would yield only when Hulagu came in person, and Rokn ud din ordered the transfer.

Hulagu set out for Alamut and halted nine days at Sheherek, the ancient residence of the Dilem rulers, where he celebrated the happy end of his enterprise. After that he appeared before Alamut and sent Rokn ud din to summon his people to surrender. The commandant refused. Hulagu sent now a large corps of men to lay siege to the fortress. At this the garrison offered to yield, and sent deputations repeatedly to Rokn ud din to intercede in their favor, and save them.

Three days were given to remove what belonged to the garrison personally. On the fourth day the Mongols and Persians marched in, seized what was left and set fire to the buildings. Hulagu, it is said, himself visited the fortress and was amazed at the height of the mountains around it.

The library of Alamut was renowned in those regions, but the vizir and historian, Ata ul Melik Juveini, who asked and obtained Hulagu's permission destroyed every manuscript which related to Ismailian opinions and teaching.

The foundations of this famed fortress were laid in 860, and the castle, enormously strong through its works and position, was richly provisioned. This was the true head and capital of that kingdom of murder. Connected with the castle were great apartments cut into the rock, for storage of provisions both solid and liquid; of the latter there was wine, honey and vinegar. It was said that those stores had been put there one hundred and seventy years earlier, in the days of Hassan Ben Sabah, and were preserved perfectly owing to the cleanliness of the place, and the pure mountain air of that region. The waters of the river Bahir, conducted to the foot of the fortress, filled a moat which inclosed half the stronghold.

A Mongol officer of Persian and Mongol militia now received the command to raze Alamut. Much time and great labor were needed to do this.

Hulagu then went to Lemsher, but as that fortress would not yield he left Tair Buga with a strong corps to take it, and returned to headquarters where he gave a great feast, eight days in duration.

Rokn ud din followed Hulagu to Hamadan whence he sent officers with those of Hulagu to Syria to order the commandants of Ismailian castles in that country to surrender to the Mongols. While in Hamadan the late master of Alamut became enamored of a Mongol maiden of low origin. Hulagu gave the girl to him and he married her. Thus far the fallen chief had been useful to the Mongol who had treated him with kindness while commanding him to deliver up strongholds which might have stood the siege for years had the Ismailians resisted. When he had no further use for the man he wished to be rid of him, but he had given such a promise of safety that he did not like to break his word openly. Rokn ud din saved him from embarrassment by expressing a wish to visit the court of Mangu, the Grand Khan. Hulagu beyond doubt suggested this idea very deftly through others. He sent the fallen chief with nine attendants of his own people under an escort of Mongols (1257).

When Rokn ud din reached the Mongol court Mangu would not see him, and said that the authorities in Persia should not have permitted the journey, which wearied post horses for nothing. Rokn ud din turned homeward, but when near the mountain Tungat, the escort cut him down with his attendants. According to Rashid, Mangu had him killed on the way to Mongolia, not while returning.

Since the Grand Khan had given orders to exterminate the Ismailians, Rokn ud din's subjects had been distributed among Mongol legions. When the Assassin chief had set out on this journey, which was ignominious and doleful, command was given Mongol officers to slay the Assassins, and spare no man, woman or child; hence all were massacred. Infants at the breast were not spared any more than their mothers. Not a child or a relative of Rokn ud din was left living.

This last ruler of the Assassins was among the most loathsome of characters in history — a pitiless coward who had caused the death of his own father, killed the murderer of that father without trial lest he tell what he knew of his master's evil doing, and burned the children of the murderer with the corpse of their father lest they too might expose him. He gave away power without an effort to save it, and lost his own life with indignity.

CHAPTER XIII

DESTRUCTION OF THE KALIFAT

HULAGU had destroyed the Assassins: he was now to extinguish the line of the Abbasids. In August, 1257, this Mongol master of Persia sent his envoys to Bagdad, with a letter to Mostassim, the Kalif then in office, who was a grandson of Nassir, that successor of the Prophet who had invited Jinghis Khan to destroy Shah Mohammed.

After certain introductions and complaints in the letter, Hulagu warned against resistance substantially as follows: "Strike not the point of an awl with thy fist, mistake not the sun for the glowing wick of a flameless taper. Level the walls of Bagdad at once, fill its moats; leave government to thy son, for a season, and come to us or, if thou come not, send thy vizir with Suleiman Shah and the chancellor. They will take to thee our counsels with precision; thus wilt thou use them correctly and we shall not be forced then to anger. If we march against Bagdad thou wilt not escape us, even shouldst thou hide in the deepest earth, or rise to highest heaven.

"If thou love thy own life and the safety of thy house give ear to these counsels; if not the world will behold Heaven's anger without waiting."

The answer to this letter showed no sign of fear or humility. "Young man," replied the Kalif, "seduced by ten days of favoring fortune thou art in thy own eyes High Lord of the universe, and thinkest thy commands the decisions of destiny. Thou requirest of me that which will never be given.

"Knowest not that from the West to the East all who worship God and hold the true faith are my servitors? Had I the wish I could make myself master of Iran. With what is left of its people I could go beyond Iran and put every man in his real position. But

247

I have no wish to rouse war, that scourge of all nations. I desire
not that troops should at my command wring curses from my
subjects, especially as I am a friend to the Grand Khan, as well as
to Hulagu. If thou sow seeds of friendship how canst thou be
concerned with the moats and ramparts of Bagdad? Walk in
the ways of peace and return to Khorassan."

Three officers carried this answer; they went with Hulagu's
envoys, who were met outside Bagdad by an immense mass of
people who covered them with insults, tore their clothes, spat in
their faces, and would have slain them all had not guards rushed
out and saved the men promptly.

"The Kalif is as crooked as a bow," said Hulagu on receiving
Mostassim's sharp answer, "but I will make him as straight as an
arrow. Heaven has given the Empire of the earth to Jinghis Khan
and his descendants. Since your master refuses submission to
this power," added he to the envoys at parting, "war is all that
remains to him."

Mostassim in doubt what to do turned to his vizir who advised
him to send precious gifts to the Mongols. "There is no better
use for wealth," said he, "than to spend it in defending the
Kalifat."

The chancellor accused the vizir of high treason, and added:
"We hold every road touching Bagdad; if gifts are sent out to
the enemy we will seize them." The Kalif told the vizir that his
fears were unfounded, that the Mongols would merely threaten;
that should they make bold to move on the Abbasids they would
rush to their own certain ruin.

Suleiman Shah, the chief general, and others hastened to the
vizir and stormed against the Kalif, saying: "Given over to
buffoons and to dancers he has no mind left for warriors or
seriousness. If measures be not taken immediately we shall see
the foe at our gates, and Bagdad will suffer the fate of all cities
taken by Mongols; neither high nor low, rich nor poor will escape
death by massacre. We are able to collect a large army; we hold
all approaches; we may fall on the enemy and triumph, or if
fortune should fail us we can at least die with honor."

These words were brought to the Kalif and roused him. He
charged the vizir to make levies, strengthen Suleiman, and guard
with all power the safety of Bagdad. The vizir made the levies,

but made them very slowly. The troops were ready only at the end of five months. Even then the neglectful Mostassim would not give the coin needed. Mongol spies knew what was happening at all points. There was no chance at that day to stop Hulagu's armies, or surprise them.

The Kalif sent envoys a second time to warn Hulagu against war on the Abbasids whose house would endure, as he said, till the end of all ages. Cases were cited of those who had touched that sacred house to their own ghastly ruin, the last being Shah Mohammed, who died in dire misery on an island of the Caspian. " Keep their fate in mind if thou hast their plans in thy counsel." This was the Kalif's sharp warning.

Hulagu paid small attention to warnings of that kind. He was preparing troops to besiege a great city which might have many defenders. His chief camp was at Hamadan, and Bagdad must be taken, hence his first point was to seize all the roads between those two cities. One road, that over which the left wing of his army must travel, lay among mountains and over high passes, snow-covered almost at all times. In these difficult districts was the fortress Daritang which commanded a defile and guarded Arabian Irak at its boundary. In Daritang the commandant Aké was a man who had griefs of his own brought about by the Kalif. Hulagu sent for this person, seduced him with favors, engaged him to yield his own fortress, and win over other commandants if possible.

Once at home Aké felt his heart change; he repented. Through a friend he made known at Bagdad the plans of the enemy, and declared that if the Kalif would send him one corps of trained horsemen he would furnish a hundred thousand good warriors, Turkmans and Kurds; with these he would stop every Mongol advance against Bagdad. This offer was laid before the vizir, but the Kalif refused it. Hulagu knew all these details soon after and sent a strong mounted force to settle with the Daritang commandant. The Mongol on nearing the fortress called out the commandant to consult with him, as he said. Aké appeared and was seized that same moment. "If thou wish to save life for thyself, and save also thy office, call out all thy people; we are taking a census." Aké was submissive and called out the people. "If faithful, thou wilt tear down the fortress." The commandant saw that he had been discovered, still he obeyed calmly and had the fortress demolished. Then he was slain with all the men under him, and also his household. Emir Säid, Aké's son, fled quickly and wandered about in the mountains, but he sought safety in Bagdad at last where they killed him.

The Daritang road once secured, Hulagu called in the astrologer whom the Grand Khan, his brother, had given him, to choose days propitious for action of all sorts. This man, a religious adherent of the Kalif, and bribed perhaps also, predicted six great calamities should Mongols lay siege to the capital of Islam. Nassir ud din, the astrologer of Alamut, a Shiite, was summoned. Hulagu asked him: " Will these six things predicted come true ? " " Surely not one of them." " What then will happen ? " " The city of the Kalif will be taken by Hulagu," replied the adherent of Ali. Nassir then met the other astrologer and overcame him by naming the Kalifs who had been killed without causing calamity to mankind.

Command was now given the Mongols to converge upon Bagdad. Those in Rūm and the West were to march through Mosul, halt somewhat west of the capital and encamp there. These men would form the right wing of Hulagu's army. The left wing would march on the road by Daritang to camp northeast of the capital. Hulagu himself was to be in the center, hence he took the road through Heulvan by which Mohammed Shah had advanced when he met his disaster. From Essed Abad new envoys were sent to the Kalif inviting him to visit headquarters. Mostassim refused this, but promised an annual tribute if Hulagu would lead away all his warriors. The prince answered that being so near he could not go back without seeing the Kalif. But before going farther Hulagu despatched a third embassy asking to send the vizir, with the chancellor.

Meanwhile Luristan in greater part had been taken by the Mongols. When the right wing was drawing near on the southern bank of the Tigris a real panic seized all people who were living in that region and immense crowds sought refuge in Bagdad. Such was the panic that men and women rushed into the water in their great anxiety to cross the river. Rich bracelets, or all the gold coins which a hand could grasp, were given gladly to boatmen for a passage to the city.

Now the chancellor who with the general, Feth ud din, had an army disposed on the Heulvan roadway, moved to meet this strong Mongol division. He attacked the vanguard which was beaten, and then pursued till it reached the main army. There the Mongols faced the pursuers and a second battle began which continued till nightfall. The two armies camped face to face until daybreak. During the night the Mongols opened canals from the Tigris and submerged a great plain in the rear of their opponents, thus making retreat very difficult, and in places impossible. At daybreak a fresh battle followed in which most of the Bagdad men perished. The chancellor fled to the city with a very small party. Only then did the Kalif's advisers set about strengthening the walls and defending the capital. Some days later the right Mongol wing touched the suburbs along the west bank of the Tigris. Hulagu himself attacked the eastern side of the city. Just after the chancellor had fled from the field to the city defences the Kalif sent his vizir to headquarters; with him went the Nestorian patriarch. The vizir took this message: " I have yielded to Hulagu's wishes, and hope that the prince will remember his promise." Hulagu gave this answer: " I made my demand when in Hamadan. I desired then to see the vizir and the chancellor. I am now at the gates of the capital, and my wish may be different."

Next day the vizir, the home minister, and many among the chief citizens went in a body to Hulagu. He would not receive them. The attack was renewed then and lasted six days in succession. At the end of that period the whole eastern wall had been seized by the Mongols. The investment was absolute, escape by the river was impossible either down with the current, or upward against it. The chancellor tried to escape but was met by a tempest of stones, burning naphtha and arrows. He was driven back after three of his boats had been captured and the men in them slaughtered.

The Kalif saw now that he must bend to the Mongols, and he bent in his own foolish fashion: He sent two officials with presents, not too rich or too many lest the Mongols might think him over timid, and become too exacting. Hulagu refused these envoys an audience. Next the youngest son of the Kalif and the Sahib Divan went to the camp of the enemy bearing this time rich presents, but they gained no sight of the great Mongol. The eldest son of the Kalif took the vizir and with him made a new trial,

but these two had no more success than the others. On the following day Hulagu sent two messengers into the city with this order.
" Bring to me Suleiman Shah with the Chancellor. The Kalif may
come, or not come, as he chooses." These two men were brought,
and then sent back to the city to say to all people with whom they
had contact that they would be taken to Syria, and were to issue
forth through the gates without hindrance. In the hope of finding
safety in some place many persons left Bagdad. These people
were all parceled out among Mongol divisions, and died by the
sword every man of them. The Chancellor was put to death
first, then Suleiman was led with bound hands into Hulagu's
presence. " Since thou hast knowledge of the stars, why not
see the fatal day coming, and give to thy sovereign due notice ? "
asked the Mongol. " The Kalif was bound by his destiny, and
would not hear faithful servants," replied the commander.
Suleiman was put to death, and his whole household died with
him, seven hundred persons all counted. The son of the Chancellor
died with the others.

It was the Kalif's turn then; he went forth with his three sons
from Bagdad, three thousand persons went with him, high dignitaries and officials. When he appeared before Hulagu the prince
asked about his health very affably, and then said that he must
proclaim to the city that all men were to lay down their arms, and
come out to be counted. Mostassim returned and proclaimed to
the people of Bagdad that whoso wished for his life had to lay down
his arms and repair to the camp of the Mongols. Then all people,
both warriors and civilians, pressed in crowds toward the gates of
the city. When outside they were slaughtered, slain every one of
them, save the Kalif and his sons who were taken to the army
on the left wing, and guarded there strictly. From that
moment the high priest of Islam could see his own fate very
plainly.

Three days later on began the sack and the pillage of Bagdad.
The Mongols rushed in from all sides simultaneously; they spared
only houses of Christians and those of a few foreigners. On the
second day of the city's undoing Hulagu went to the palace in
Bagdad and gave a great feast to his commanders; toward the
end of that feast the Kalif was brought in to stand before Hulagu.
" Thou art master of this house," said the conqueror, " I am the

guest in it. Let us see what thou hast which might be a good and proper gift to me."

The Kalif had two thousand rich robes and ten thousand gold dinars brought and many rich jewels also. Hulagu would not look at them. " Our men," remarked he, " will find all wealth of that kind, which is for my servitors. Show hidden treasures." The Kalif described then a place in the courtyard. Men went to work straightway and dug till they came to two cisterns filled with gold pieces, each piece a hundred miskals. In various parts of the palace the Mongols found gold and silver vessels; of these they made no more account than if they had been tin or copper.

Hulagu desired then that all persons in the harem be counted. Seven hundred women and slave girls were found there, and one thousand eunuchs. The Kalif begged to have those women given him who had never been under sunlight or moonlight directly. The conqueror gave him one hundred. Mostassim chose relatives and they were led forth from the palace. All the Kalif's best treasures were taken to Hulagu's camp ground. Around the immense tent of Jinghis Khan's grandson were piled up great masses of wealth, being a portion of that which the Abbasids had taken from men during half a millennium.

The sack of the city continued seven days and nights in succession; most of the mosques were burned during that time. A deputation came then to beg pity of the conqueror. Seeing that the place if he spared it might yield him some profit he relented after eight hundred thousand human beings had been slaughtered. Those who had hidden from death came forth now into daylight with safety; few were they in number and pitiful to look at. Many Christians had assembled in a church strongly guarded and were saved from death and every evil by the Mongols. The Nestorian Patriarch had power to effect this. A few wealthy Moslems had entrusted the best of their treasures to the Patriarch to keep for them; they had hoped to survive, but all perished.

Hulagu withdrew to the village of Vakaf, some distance from Bagdad, because the air of the city had grown pestilential and loathsome. He summoned Mostassim. The trembling Kalif asked Ibn Alkamiya if there was no way of salvation. " My beard is long," replied the vizir, referring to a taunt of the chancellor.[1]

[1] " Long beard, short wit," an Arabic proverb.

The Kalif and his eldest son were placed each in a felt sack, and trampled to death under horse hoofs. Mostassim's attendants were cut down, and slaughtered by various methods. Next day the youngest son of the Kalif died, and all of the Abbasids whose names were on the list of that ruling family were then put to death.

The Kalif, whose mother was an Ethiopian slave, was the thirty-seventh of his line. He was forty-six years of age when he died, February 21, 1258, after a reign of fifteen years. Hulagu appointed new dignitaries for Bagdad. The old vizir, Ibn Alkamiya, was continued in office. Among new men was one quite deserving of notice; this was Ben Amran, prefect of a place east of Bagdad and touching it. This man had been a servant to the governor of Yakuba. One day when stroking the soles of that governor's feet to bring sleep to him Ben Amran himself began to slumber. Roused by his master he said that he had just had a marvelous vision. "What was it like?" asked the governor. "I thought that Mostassim and the Kalifat were gone, and that I was the governor of Bagdad." His master gave him in answer a kick of such force that he fell over backward. Being in Bagdad during the siege days Ben Amran heard that provisions were scarce in the camp of the Mongols. He tied a letter to an arrow and shot it over the wall with this message: "If Hulagu would learn something of value let him send for Ben Amran." The letter was taken to the Mongol, and he sent for Ben Amran. The Kalif, who was foolish in all things, permitted the man to go from the city. When brought to the chief of the Mongols he declared that he could obtain a great stock of provisions. Hulagu, though not greatly believing his phrases, sent him off with an officer; Ben Amran took the man to large underground granaries near Yakuba where there was wheat enough to supply all the Mongols for a fortnight, and thus he enabled Hulagu to continue the siege without trouble. Ben Amran received the reward of his treachery, and now was made prefect.

Ibn Alkamiya, the vizir, was accused of treason both before the fall of the city, and afterward. For a long time the books used in schools bore this sentence: "Cursed of God be he who curses not Ibn Alkamiya." On the Friday next after the death of the Kalif these words were pronounced in place of the usual invocation: " Praise to God who has destroyed high existences, and condemned to nonentity dwellers in this abode (of humanity). O God, assist us in woes such as Islam has never experienced: but we belong to God and return to Him."

Hulagu was now master of Bagdad, and he proposed to the Ulema this question: " Which man is better as sovereign, an unbeliever who is just, or a Moslem unjust in his dealings ? " The assembled Ulema gave no answer till Razi ud din Ali, a sage esteemed greatly, wrote as follows: " The unbeliever who is just should be preferred to the unjust believer." All the Ulema subscribed to this answer.

Every place from the Persian Gulf to Bagdad was subjected. And it is of great interest to note the conduct of some and the fate that befell them. The story of Ben Amran, the prefect, is in strong contrast with that of Teghele, son of Hezerasp, who had given good advice in his day to Shah Mohammed. Teghele had joined the Mongol forces, but expressed regret at the ruin of Bagdad, and the death of the Kalif. Hulagu heard of this and grew angry. Teghele, informed of his peril, left the camp without permission and withdrew to his mountains. A force was despatched to Luristan to bring back the fugitive, whose brother, Shems ud din Alb Argun, set out to appease Hulagu and gain pardon. Argun was met on the Luristan border by Mongols who put him in chains, and slew his whole escort. The Mongols went on then and summoned Teghele to yield himself. At first he refused through distrust of their promises, but he made no active resistance. When at last they gave him Hulagu's ring as a token of favor he believed, and they took him to Tebriz where Hulagu had him tried, and put to death on the market place.

The throne of Luristan was then given to Alb Argun the brother of the dead man. About this time appeared at headquarters the rival Sultans of Rūm, Rokn ud din Kelidj Arslan, and Yzz ud din Kei Kavus; the latter had come with some fear since he had roused Hulagu by resistance. When admitted to audience he offered the Mongol a pair of splendid boots with his own portrait painted inside on the soles of them. " I hope," added he, " that the monarch will deign to show honor with his august foot to the head of his servitor." These words, and the intercession of Dokuz Khatun, Hulagu's wife, obtained the grace which he needed and was seeking. The brothers were reconciled and Rūm was divided between them.

Hulagu now summoned Bedr ud din Lulu of Mosul to his presence. This prince was then more than eighty years old and very crafty. He had been a slave of Nur ud din Arslam, Shah of Diarbekr, who at death left him as guardian to his son Massud. Lulu governed Mosul for this Massud who died in 1218 leaving two sons of tender years. These boys followed their father to that other existence before two years had passed, and the former slave became sovereign. He had reigned in Mosul forty years lacking one, before coming to Hulagu's presence with splendid gifts and apparently unlimited obedience. When leaving Mosul, Lulu's friends were in dread for his safety, but he calmed them, and gave this assurance: "I will make the Khan mild, and even pull his ears while I speak to him."

Lulu was received by Hulagu very graciously and when the official gifts had all been delivered he added: "I have something for the Khan's person specially," and he drew forth a pair of gold earrings in which were set two pearls of rare beauty. When Hulagu had admired them Lulu continued: "If the Khan would but grant me the honor to put these two jewels in their places I should be exalted immediately in the eyes of all rulers, and in those of my subjects." Permission was granted, so he took the Khan's ears and put the two rings in them very deliberately. Then he glanced at his own suite, thus telling them that he had kept his strange promise.

The fate of both Christians and Jews had been painful and bitter under Abbasid dominion. Favor and solace now came from the Mongols. The invaders cared no more at that time for Christians than for the followers of Mohammed, but when attacking new lands it was to their interest to win populations which were hostile to the dominant nation. The protection of the conquerors, and the shattered condition of Islam, weakened by such dire devastation, had roused hopes among Christians to dominate those who had trampled them for centuries. Upon the choice which the conqueror would make between the religions their fate was depending, and the issue of that struggle to win the Mongols was for some time uncertain, but surely momentous. Christians of the Orient, as well as Crusaders, were rejoiced to see Hulagu

making ready to march upon Syria, and to them it seemed sure
that they saw in advance the destruction of Islam in regions where
Christian blood had been shed so abundantly.

On the eve of this Mongol invasion Syria was ruled by Salih,
a descendant of Saladin, but Saladin's grand-nephews had lost
Egypt a little before that. While the army of Saint Louis was in
Damietta the Sultan, Salih, died (1249). His death was kept
secret till his son Moazzam Turan Shah should arrive from his
appanage between the two rivers, that is the Euphrates and Tigris.
The French army was ruined, and Saint Louis was captured.
Three weeks later on Turan Shah fell by the daggers of men who
had been Mameluk chiefs in the reign of his father. He had wished
to replace these by friends of his own, so they slew him. After
this deed the chiefs gave allegiance to Shejer ud dur, the late
Sultan's slave girl and concubine. She had enjoyed his full confidence, and was governing till Turan Shah might reach Cairo.

Eibeg, a Mameluk chief, was elected commander. Shejer ud dur
now married Eibeg and when three months had passed she resigned in his favor. In mounting the throne the new Sultan took
the title Moizz, and chose as associate El Ashraf, an Eyubite
prince six years old, the great-grandson of Kamil the Sultan.
This revolution, which placed a Mameluk chief on the throne of
the Eyubites, shows how powerful these warriors had become then
in Egypt. Saladin, on gaining power in 1169, had disbanded the
troops of the Fatimid Kalifs. Those troops were negro slaves,
Egyptians, and Arabs, and he put Kurds and Turks in their
places. This new force was formed of twelve thousand horsemen.
Saladin, and the Sultans who followed him, were fond of buying
young Turks, whom they reared very carefully to military service,
but Salih, ruling sixth after Saladin, preferred Mameluks to others.
Before coming to power this prince had tested the Mameluks and
esteemed them; when Sultan he increased the number of them
greatly, by purchase. These new men were brought from regions
north of the Caucasus and the Caspian, from those tribes known
in the Orient as Kipchak, and as Polovtsi by the Russians. At
first it was difficult to obtain them, but after the Mongol invasion
of Russia young prisoners were sold in large numbers into Egypt
and Syria. Salih had a thousand, whom he lodged in the fortress
of Randhat, on an island in front of Cairo; he called them the

Bahriye, or men of the river. These young slaves were brought
up in the practice of arms, and in the religion of Islam. The
guard of the Sultan was composed wholly of Mameluks. Salih
chose from their chiefs the great officers of his household, and his
most trusted advisers. They attained the highest military offices,
enjoyed the richest fiefs, and received the best revenues; they
saved Egypt at Mansura, and did most to destroy the French army;
their power lay in *esprit de corps* and ambition. Their chiefs
rose to dominion in Egypt, and then put a check on the Mongols.

Syria belonged now to Nassir Salah ud din Yusseif, who from
his father, Aziz, a grandson of Saladin, inherited the principality
of Aleppo in 1236, and took in 1250, after the slaying of Turan
Shah, the principality of Damascus, which belonged to the Sultan
of Egypt. Master now of the best part of Syria, Nassir Salih
undertook to drive from the throne of Egypt the Turkish freedman, who had recently usurped it, but he was beaten by Eibeg,
and an envoy of the Kalif proposed mediation; peace was made,
and Nassir 1251 ceded to the Sultan Jerusalem, Gaza and the coast
up to Nablus. Faris ud din Aktai, a great chief among Mameluks,
was assassinated at command of Eibeg, whom he had offended.
Seven hundred troopers of this chief and some Bahriye officers
fled, among others Beibars and Kelavun, both of whom occupied
the Egyptian throne later on. They left Cairo in the night,
went to Syria, and obtained of Prince Nassir permission to appear
at his court. They received money, robes of honor, and then
they advised him to march on Cairo. Nassir was distrustful of
these men, against whom Eibeg had roused his suspicions by letter,
but he made use of the incident to demand back the lands which
he had ceded to Egypt, because the Mameluks who had received
them as fiefs were now in his service.

Eibeg gave back the lands, and Nassir confirmed the Mameluks
in the use of them. But those river Mameluks did not remain
faithful to Nassir, since they thought him too feeble for their
projects. They went to another Eyubite, Mogith Omar, Prince
of Karak, and asked him to aid in the attack upon Eibeg, alleging
falsely that they had been called to that action by generals in
Cairo.

Mogith, a son of the Sultan Adil, had been confined by
Turan Shah in the castle of Shubek, when Turan had been

slain Mogith was set free by the castle commandant. In 1251 this same Mogith became sovereign of Karak and also of Shubek. Circumstances seemed to favor a descent upon Egypt. The Prince of Karak marched against Egypt, but was beaten by Kutuz, Eibeg's general, who seized many Bahriye chiefs captive and cut their heads off immediately.

Some years before his defeat by Eibeg Prince Nassir had sent to Hulagu his vizir, Zein ud din el Hafizzi, who brought back with him letters of safety to his master. The immense progress of Hulagu's arms and his menacing plans disturbed Nassir, who grieved now that he had not sent homage earlier to the conquering Mongol. In 1258 he despatched his son, Aziz, still a boy, with his vizir, a general, and some officers, giving also a letter to Bedr ud din Lulu, the aged and crafty Mosul prince, whom we know as having pulled Hulagu's ears at an audience.

When Nassir's envoys were received by Hulagu, he inquired why their master had not come with them. "The Prince of Syria fears," said they, "that should he absent himself his neighbors, the Franks, who are also his enemies, would invade his possessions, hence he has sent his own son to represent him." Hulagu feigned to accept this false answer. The envoys, it is said, requested Mongol aid to save Egypt from the Mameluks. Hulagu detained Aziz some months, and when at last he permitted the boy to take leave and return to his father, the vizir received a message for Nassir, which was in substance as follows: "Know thou, Prince Nassir, and know all commanders and warriors in Syria, that we are God's army on earth. He has taken from our hearts every pity. Woe to those who oppose us, they must flee, we must hunt them. By what road can they save themselves, what land will protect them? Our steeds rush like lightning, our swords cut like thunderbolts, our warriors in number are like sands on the seashore. Whoso resists us meets terror; he who implores us finds safety. Receive our law, yours and ours will then be in common. If ye resist, blame yourselves for the things which will follow. Choose the safe way. Answer quickly, or your country will be changed to a desert. Ye yourselves will find no refuge. The angel of death may then say of you: 'Is there one among them who shows the least sign of life, or whose

voice gives out the slightest of murmurs ? ' We are honest, hence
give you this warning."

Since Nassir had no hope of aid to fight Hulagu he chose to
make common cause with every Mohammedan, and sent back a
brave answer. These are some words of it: " Ye say that God has
removed from your hearts every pity. That is the condition of
devils, not sovereigns. But is it not strange to threaten lions with
bruises, tigers with hyenas, and heroes with clodhoppers? Resistance to you is obedience to the Highest. If we slay you our
prayers have been answered; if ye slay us we go into paradise.
We will not flee from death to exist in opprobrium. If we survive we are happy; if we die we are martyrs. Ye demand that
obedience which we render the vicar of the Prophet, ye shall not
have it; we would rather go to the place in which he is. Tell
the man [1] who indited your message that we care no more for his
words than for the buzz of a fly or the squeak of a Persian fiddle."

Hulagu gave command to his army to march into Syria. He
summoned Bedr ud din Lulu, who, excused because of great age,
had to send his son, Melik Salih Ismail, with the troops of Mosul.
When this young man arrived at the camp of the Mongols Hulagu
made him marry a daughter of Jelal ud din, the last Shah of
Kwaresm. Kita Buga went with the vanguard, Sinkur, a descendant of Kassar, and Baidju led the right wing, the left was commanded by Sunjak. Hulagu set out with the center, September
12, 1259. He passed Hakkar, where all Kurds whom they met
were cut down by the sword, not one man being spared. On
entering Diarbekr Hulagu took Jeziret on the Tigris, and sent
his son Yshmut with Montai Noyon to take Mayafarkin, an old
and famous town northeast of Diarbekr, whose Eyubite prince,
Kamil Nasir ud din Mohammed, he wished to punish for hostility
to the Mongols. He was all the more angry since this man
had been received well years before that by Mangu the Grand
Khan, and given letters which put his lands under that sovereign's
protection. Hulagu accused Kamil now of crucifying a Syrian
priest, who had come to his court with the Grand Khan's safe-
conduct; with having expelled Mongol prefects, and with having
sent a corps of troops to help Bagdad at demand of the Kalif —

---

[1] This man was Nassir ud din the astronomer who had been at Alamut, and
had confounded the astrologer favorable to the Kalif.

these troops when they had gone half the distance turned back on learning that the capital had fallen. To finish all, Kamil had been in Damascus asking Prince Nassir to march on the Mongols. It was at this time that Hulagu sent his son to punish Prince Kamil, who had barely returned with vain promises when he found himself sealed in at Mayafarkin securely.

Hulagu summoned next to obedience Saïd Nedjmud din el Gazi, Prince of Mardin. That prince sent his son, Mozaffer Kar Arslan, his chief judge, and an emir with presents, and a letter in which he alleged severe illness as his excuse for not giving personal homage. Hulagu sent the following answer, making the judge go alone with it to his master: " The prince says that he is ill, he says this because he fears Nassir of Syria, and thinks that if I should triumph he must be friendly with me hence he feigns this illness, and if I fail he will be on good terms with Nassir."

The son of Bedr ud din Lulu was sent against Amid. Hulagu himself took Nisibin. He had encamped close to Harran, and received the submission of its people, who were spared, as were also the inhabitants of Koha, who followed the example of Harran; but the people of Sarudj, who sent no deputation to beg for their lives, were cut down with the sword every man of them.

Hulagu's march spread dismay throughout Syria. Prince Nassir had spent his time thus far in discussing with Mogith. The year before a corps of three thousand horsemen came to Syria; these were deserters from Hulagu's army, so called Sheherzurians, doubtless Kurds of Sheherzur. Nassir took these men to his service, and gave them good treatment; on hearing that they wished to desert him for Mogith he doubled his bounty, but still they passed over to Mogith. With these men and the Mameluks Prince Mogith considered that he could master Damascus. Nassir went out to meet him and camped near Lake Ziza. He staid there six months discussing conditions with Mogith, through envoys. It was agreed at last that the latter would yield up his Mameluks to Nassir, and discharge the Bahriyes.

This treaty concluded, Nassir went back to Damascus. On learning that Hulagu was at Harran, he consulted his generals and resolved on resistance. Nassir fixed his camp at Berze, a short distance north of Damascus, but he could not confide in his army; volunteers, Turks and Arabs, he knew that his generals and soldiers greatly feared Hulagu's victors. He himself was a man of weak character who roused no respect in his army.

Seeing Nassir's alarm, Zein ud din el Hafizzi, the vizir, extolled Hulagu's greatness and counseled submission. Indignant at this an emir, Beibars Bundukdar, sprang up one day, rushed at the vizir, struck the man, cursed him, and said that he was a traitor seeking the destruction of Islam. Zein ud din complained to Nassir of these insults. Nassir himself was assailed that same night in a garden, by Mameluks, who had determined to cut him down immediately, and choose a new Sultan; he barely succeeded in fleeing to the citadel, but returned later on to the camp at the prayer of his officers. Beibars left for Gaza whence he sent an officer named Taibars to Mansur the new sovereign of Egypt with his oath of fidelity.

At a council, held to discuss coming perils, it was settled without any dissent, that the prince, his officers, and his warriors should send their families to Egypt. Nassir sent thither his wife, a daughter of Kei Kobad, the Seljuk Sultan, he sent also his son, and his treasures. Next followed the wives, sons and daughters of officers, and a great throng of people. The fears of individuals were communicated to the army, officers went, as if to take farewell of their families, but many of those officers never returned to their places. Thus Nassir's army was disbanded.

Nassir now asked assistance of Mogith, and besides sent Sahib Kemal ud din Omar to Cairo to obtain aid from the Sultan. Eibeg had just been slain by the hands of Shejer ud dur, his wife, who, convinced that he was ready to slay her, had been too quick for him. Prompt punishment was inflicted: Shejer was given to the widow of Sultan Aziz, who, assisted by eunuchs and females, beat her to death, stripped her body and hurled it over the wall to the moat of the fortress, where it lay several days without clothing or burial.

Eibeg's son, Mansur, a boy fifteen years of age, was raised to the throne, with Aktai, a former comrade of his father, as guardian, or Atabeg, to be followed soon by Kutuz, who had once been a slave of his. When Nassir's envoy arrived the Egyptian general held council in presence of the Sultan. At the council this question was put to the chief judge and the elders: " Is it possible to levy a legal war tax on the nation? " The answer was that after needless

objects of value had been taken from people, and sold, a tax might
be levied. This was accepted by the council. The Sultan was a
boy who had been spoiled by his mother, hence was unfitted for
rule at that terrible period. Kutuz desired supreme power and
was ready to seize it as soon as the generals would start for Upper
Egypt. When they had gone he imprisoned the Sultan with his
brother and mother, and was then proclaimed sovereign.

Captured by Mongols in boyhood, Kutuz had been sold in
Damascus, and later in Cairo. He declared himself a nephew of
the Kwaresmian ruler, Shah Mohammed. Manumitted by
Moizz ud din Eibeg he added El Moizzi to his name, thus following the Mameluk custom.

When generals condemned Kutuz for taking the dignity from
Mansur he referred to Hulagu, and the fear caused by Prince
Nassir of Syria. " All I wish is to drive out the Mongols. Can we
do that without a leader ? When we have driven out this enemy,
choose whom you please as the Sultan." Thus he pacified his
rivals and, feeling sure in his power, removed Mansur with his
mother and brother to Damietta. In the following reign they
were sent to Stambul, the Turkish capital, and remained there.

The new Sultan imprisoned eight generals, then, receiving the
oath of the army, he prepared his campaign against the Mongols.
First he sent an assuring epistle to Nassir, swearing that he would
lay no claim to that prince's possessions; that he looked on himself as Nassir's lieutenant in Egypt, that he would put him on the
throne if he would come at that juncture to Cairo. If the prince
wished his services he would march to his rescue, but if his presence
was disquieting the army would go with the chief whom Prince
Nassir might indicate.

This letter, borne to the prince by an officer from Egypt, who
went with the envoy whom the prince had sent to Egypt asking for
aid, allayed the suspicions of Nassir. Danger was imminent,
Hulagu had just marched into Syria. Master of all lands between the Euphrates and Tigris, Hulagu laid siege to El Biret on
the first of these rivers, and took it. In that citadel Said, the
Eyubite prince, who had been nine years in prison, was freed by
Hulagu and put in possession of Sebaibet and Banias. The Mongol
then crossed the Euphrates by bridges of boats at Malattia, Kelat
ur Rūm, El Biret, and Kirkissia; he sacked the city Mahuj, and

left garrisons in El Biret, Nedjram, Joaber, Kallomkos, and Lash, having put to the sword their inhabitants. After that he marched with all his armed strength on Aleppo.

The terror which preceded the Mongols drove multitudes of people from the city to seek shelter in Damascus, while still greater numbers were fleeing from Damascus to Egypt. The season was winter, many perished from cold on the journey, the majority had been robbed of their property, and to complete their distress and great wretchedness the plague was then raging throughout Syria and worst of all in Damascus.

One Mongol division came now and camped near Aleppo, a part of it marched on the city from which the garrison sallied forth followed by volunteers from among the lowest people. These, finding the enemy superior in numbers, and resolute, returned through the gates very quickly. Next day the bulk of the Mongol division approached the walls closely. The chiefs of the garrison went out to the square where they counseled. Though Prince Moazzam Turan Shah, the governor, had forbidden attacks on an enemy so evidently superior, a part of the troops, and with them a crowd of common people, marched out to the mountain Bankussa which they occupied. Seeing Mongols advancing, some of those on the mountain hurried down to attack them. The Mongols turned to flee, the others pursued for the space of an hour and fell into an ambush. Those who escaped from the trap fled back toward Aleppo, pursued by the enemy. When abreast of Bankussa the people who had remained on the mountain rushed down toward the gates of the city, and a great number perished. That same day the Mongols appeared at Azay, a town somewhat north of Aleppo, and took it.

In a few days Hulagu came and summoned Prince Moazzam, its governor, to surrender: "Thou canst not resist us," said Hulagu. "Receive a commandant from us in the city, and one in the citadel. We are marching now to meet Nassir; should he be defeated the country will be ours, and Moslem blood will be spared by thee. If we are beaten thou canst expel our commandants, or kill them." The Prince of Erzen ur Rūm bore this summons to which Moazzam answered: "There is nothing between thee and me but the sabre."

The walls of Aleppo were strong, and inside was a good stock of weapons. The besiegers made in one night a firm counter wall;

twenty catapults were trained on the city, which was taken by
assault on the seventh day of investment January 25, 1260. When
Aleppo had been sacked during five days and nights, and most of
the inhabitants had been cut down, Hulagu proclaimed an end to
the massacre. The streets were blocked up with corpses. Only
those men escaped who found refuge in four houses of dignitaries,
in a Mohammedan school, and a synagogue, all these were safe-
guarded. One hundred thousand women and children were sold
into slavery. The walls of Aleppo were leveled, its mosques were
demolished, its gardens uprooted and ruined. One month later
on the citadel yielded. The victors found immense booty in the
stronghold and also many artisans whom they spared for captivity.

Prince Nassir was in his camp at Berze near Damascus, when he
received news of the sack of Aleppo. His general advised to
retreat upon Gaza and implore the Sultan Kutuz for assistance.
Nassir left Damascus defenseless and set out for Gaza with the
Hamat Prince, Mansur, and a few others who had clung to him.
By Nassir's command all who could go to Egypt were to start
immediately. Terror reigned in Damascus; property was sold
for a song, while the value of camels was fabulous.

Nassir halted a short time at Nablus, and when on the way
from that city to Gaza two officers whom he had left there with
troops were captured by Mongols and slaughtered. This swift
approach of the enemy made him retire to El Arish, whence he
sent an envoy to Sultan Kutuz, imploring him to send succor
quickly.

After Nassir had gone Zein ud din el Hafizzi, the vizir, closed the
gates of Damascus, and decided with the notables to surrender to
the envoys who had been sent by Hulagu to see Nassir at Berze.
Hence a deputation of the most distinguished men went with rich
presents and the keys of the city to Hulagu's camp near Aleppo.
Hulagu put a mantle of honor on the chief of these men, and
made him grand judge in Syria. This cadi returned to Damascus
immediately and called an assembly. Appearing in the mantle,
he read his diploma, and an edict which guaranteed safety to all
men. But in spite of grand words of this kind consternation and
dread were universal.

Two commandants came now, one a Mongol, the other a Persian, who gave orders to follow the wishes of Zein ud din el Hafizzi,

and treat the inhabitants with justice. Soon after this Kita Buga arrived with a body of Mongols, safety was proclaimed at his coming, and respect for life and property. The citadel refused to surrender but was taken after sixteen days of siege labor. The commandant and his aid were beheaded at Hulagu's direction. Ashraf, the Eyubite prince and grandson of Shirkuh, who after the departure of Nassir for Egypt went to give homage to Hulagu near Aleppo, had been reinstated in the sovereignty of Hims, which Nassir had taken from him twelve years before, giving Telbashir in exchange for it. Hulagu now made Ashraf his chief lieutenant in Syria. Ashraf arrived at Merj-Bargut and Kita Buga commanded Zein ud din el Hafizzi and the other authorities of Damascus to yield up their power to him.

After reducing Aleppo Hulagu moved against Harem, a fortress two days' journey toward Antioch. The garrison was summoned to surrender with a promise under oath that no man would be injured. The defenders replied, that the religion which Hulagu held was unknown to them, hence they knew not how to consider his promise, but if a Moslem would swear on the Koran that their lives would be spared, they would surrender the castle. Hulagu asked whom they wished as the man to give oath to them; they replied Fakhr ud din Saki, last commandant in the citadel of Aleppo. Hulagu sent this man with directions to swear to everything asked of him. On the faith of his oath the place was delivered. All then were ordered to go forth from Harem. Hulagu, angry that his word had been questioned, put Fakhr ud din to death straightway, and slaughtered the whole population, not pitying even infants. He spared one person only, an Armenian, a jeweller of skill, whom he needed.

CHAPTER XIV

HULAGU received news now of the death of Mangu, the Grand Khan, and deciding at once to return to Mongolia, he made Kita Buga commander of the armies in Syria, and when departing ordered him to level the walls of Aleppo and its citadel. A deputation of Crusaders came at this time to Kita Buga.

It is said by historians, that Hulagu had resolved to take Palestine from the Moslems, and give it to Christians, and that he was about to do this when news came of Mangu's demise in Mongolia. He turned homeward immediately, intending to strive for his own elevation, but he learned in Tebriz that his brother, Kubilai, was elected, and this stopped his journey.

From El Arish Nassir had hastened on toward Kathia, but Kutuz, now in Salahiyet, not desiring an Eyubite prince as a ruler for Egypt, wished to render him harmless. He wrote to the chiefs under Nassir's command, among others the false Sheherzurians, and requested them to enter his service, offering high places, and money as he did so. Seduced by these offers the Turks and Kurds deserted Nassir. There remained with the prince, but his brother and a very few other men. On reaching Kathia he dared not go farther toward Egypt, so changing his road he went on by the desert toward Shubek; when he arrived there, he and the men with him had naught but their horses and two or three servants. He held on farther toward Karak; the sovereign of that place sent horses, tents, and all needed articles to Nassir with the statement that he might stay with him or go to Shubek. Nassir would do neither; he continued his journey to Balka, but, betrayed by two Kurd attendants who informed Kita Buga of his whereabouts, he was seized near Lake Ziza by Mongols and taken to their general, who was laying siege then to Ajalon. The general forced Nassir to order the commandant to surrender that fortress to the Mongols. The commandant obeyed after certain resistance and Ajalon, that stronghold built by Iziz ud din, one of Saladin's emirs, was leveled to the ground. The Mongols had a short time before taken possession of Baalbek and ruined that city and its citadel. Kita Buga now sent Nassir to Tebriz with his brother and Salih, son of the Hims prince. Mogith, Prince of Karak, sent his son Aziz, a boy six years of age, with him. When they passed through Damascus Nassir was greatly affected and when he saw the ruins of Aleppo he wept, unable to restrain his grief.

Hulagu received Nassir well and promised to reinstate him in Syria when he should subdue Egypt.

Egypt, up to that time a refuge for those who were fleeing from Mongols, now felt the terror of a threatened invasion. The Mongols had conquered all lands invaded by them thus far, hence most men felt certain that they would take Egypt. The Africans living in Cairo returned to their distant homes because of this conviction. Soon after Hulagu's departure for Persia envoys announced themselves in Cairo, and summoned the Sultan to obedience; war was threatened in case of refusal. Kutuz called a great council immediately to decide upon final action. Nassir ud din Kaimeri, a Kwaresmian general who had just left the service of Nassir, favored war and declared for it. "No one," he said, " could believe Hulagu who has broken faith with the Alamut chief, with the Kalif, with Aké, commandant of Daritang, and with the Prince of Erbil." Beibars, the emir from Damascus, called for war also. After some debate every chief present agreed with the Sultan. " It is well," said Kutuz. " We take the field. Victors or vanquished we shall do our whole duty, and Moslems hereafter will never make mention of us as of cowards."

It was then decided that Hulagu's envoys must die, hence they were thrown into prison to await execution. The Sultan made immense efforts; he levied tribute, illegal in Islam; he taxed revenues, he taxed heads, but that was still insufficient; then he seized the goods of all who had deserted Nassir for his sake. Nassir's wife had to yield up a part of her jewels; other women were forced to make similar sacrifices. Those who did not part with their jewels willingly were ill-treated. When ready for marching Kutuz took an oath of fidelity from his generals, and set out from his castle called the Castle of the Mountain July 26, 1260. His forces of a hundred and twenty thousand strong were composed of the army of Egypt, of Syrians who had passed to his service, of Arabs, and also of Turkmans. On the day of departure he had the chief Mongol envoy and the three next in dignity beheaded, one in each quarter of Cairo. The four heads were exposed at the gate of Zavila; of the twenty-six envoys remaining he spared only one, a young man whom he placed in a company of Mameluks. A summons was issued throughout Egypt for every warrior to march in that struggle for Islam. All had to go, if any man tried to hide himself the bastinado was used on him without mercy.

Kutuz sent an envoy to demand aid of Ashraf of Hims, the chief governor of Syria under Hulagu's orders, and Säid, who had been liberated from prison in El Biret and had received Sebaibet and Banias as his portion. Said abused the envoy, but Ashraf received him, and in private prostrated himself in his presence through respect for Kutuz, who had sent him, and added in answer to the message: "I kiss the earth before the Sultan, and say to him, that I am his servant, and subject to his orders. I am thankful that God has raised up Kutuz, for the succor of Islam. If he combats the Mongols our triumph is certain."

At Salahiyet Kutuz held a council; the greater part of the leaders refused to go farther; they wished to wait at Salahiyet. "O chiefs of Islam," said the Sultan "I march to this holy war, the man who is willing to fight in it will follow me; he who is unwilling may return, but God will not take his eye off that recreant. On his head will be counted the dishonor of our women and the ruin of our country." From every leader who liked him he took an oath then to follow and next morning he sounded the signal to march against the Mongols. The chiefs who had wished not to go were borne away now by the example of others; the whole army moved forward and entered the desert. Beibars, who commanded the vanguard, had, with other Bahriyan chiefs, quitted Nassir and joined Kutuz, who gave him the district of Kaliub as an income. Beibars found the Mongols at Gaza, but they left the place straightway, and he entered it unopposed. The Sultan made only a brief halt at Gaza, and moved along near the coast line. Kita Buga, who heard at Baalbek of this hostile advance, sent his family and baggage to Damascus, collected his troops, and set out to encounter the forces of Egypt.

The two armies saw each other first on the plain of Ain Jalut (Fountain of Goliah), between Baissan and Nablus. Before the battle Kutuz spoke with great feeling to his generals, and strengthened them for the conflict. He mentioned the peoples whom the Mongols had ruined, and he threatened his hearers with the same lot unless they won victory. He roused them to liberate Syria, and vindicate Islam; if not they would earn Heaven's wrath and dire punishment. Moved by his words they shed tears, and swore to do all that was in them to hurl back the enemy.

The two armies met September 3, 1260. The Egyptians entered the battle without confidence. At first they were timid and confusion appeared in the left wing which turned to flee; at that moment the Sultan cried out: " O God, give Thou victory to thy servant Kutuz." He charged then in person, cut into the thick of the enemy, and performed miracles of valor. He charged again and again, encouraging others to meet death, and fear nothing.

Meanwhile the left wing had rallied, re-formed, and reappeared on the battlefield. These warriors fought now with invincible fury, and stopped not till they had broken the ranks of the Mongols, who fled after having lost most of their officers. Kita Buga was killed in the action. A Mongol division entrenched on a neighboring height was attacked, and cut to pieces. The emir, Beibars, surrounded the fugitives, of whom only a very small number escaped. Some hid among reeds near the battle-ground; Kutuz set fire to the reeds and all those men perished. When the great battle was over the Sultan came down from his horse, and returned thanks to God in a prayer of two verses. Prince Said, who had fought on the side of the Mongols, came now to surrender. On dismounting he went to the Sultan to kiss his hand, but Kutuz kicked his mouth, and commanded an equerry to cut his head off immediately.

In the rage of that terrible battle the young Mongol placed by Kutuz among Mameluks found a chance, as he thought, to avenge his father; but one of those near him seized his hand in time to turn aside the missile which, missing Kutuz, killed the horse on which he was riding.

The camp of the Mongols, their women, and children, and

baggage fell into the hands of the conquerers. Hulagu's commandants were slaughtered wherever the Moslems could seize them. Those in Damascus were able to save themselves. News of the Mongol defeat arrived there September 8 in the night between Saturday and Sunday. The commandants rushed off immediately. Seven months and ten days had they occupied Damascus. September 9 the Sultan sent from Tiberias a rescript to Damascus, announcing the victory which God had given Islam. This news caused a joy all the greater since Moslems had despaired of deliverance from the Mongols, deemed until that day invincible. Their delight was unbounded, hence they rushed straightway to the houses of Christians where they pillaged and slew all unhindered. The churches of Saint James and Saint Mary were burned. Jew shops were plundered most thoroughly, and the houses of that people with their synagogues were saved only by armed forces. Next the turn came to Moslems who had been partisans and agents of the Mongols; these too were massacred without pity.

Kutuz arrived at Damascus with his army, and entered the city two days later. He hanged a number of Moslems, who had favored the Mongols, among others the Kurd who had betrayed Nassir; he hanged also thirty Christians and forced the remainder to contribute one hundred and fifty thousand drachmas.

Beibars, who was sent to pursue the fleeing Mongols, hurried forward to Hamath. The fugitives, when almost overtaken, abandoned their baggage, let their prisoners go free, and rushed toward the seacoast, where they were captured, or slain by the Moslem inhabitants. Noyon, who was powerless to resist the Egyptians, withdrew to Rūm with the remnant of his warriors.

Kutuz, who had saved Egypt and become master of Syria as far as the Euphrates, was the only man of that period who could have turned back the tide of Mongol conquest. He now gave fiefs and rewards to whomever his good-will selected. He gave the government of Damascus to Sindjar; and of Aleppo to Mozaffer, a son of Bedr ud din Lulu; Prince Mansur was confirmed in possession of Hamat; Ashraf, Prince of Hims, Hulagu's chief lieutenant in Syria, asked grace of the Sultan and got it. When he had named all his lieutenants in Syria Kutuz left Damascus for Egypt Oct. 5th. Beibars, who had shown immense valor in battle, asked for the government of Aleppo, and failing to get it, conceived such resentment that with six other malcontents he formed a plot to assassinate the Sultan.

Between Koissem and Salahiyet the Sultan left his road for a short hunting trip; the conspirators followed till they found him unattended. Beibars then approached Kutuz and begged for a favor which was granted; he took the Sultan's hand to kiss it; that moment one of the six struck Kutuz on the back of the neck with a sabre, a second man pushed him down from the horse, a third pierced his body with an arrow, and Beibars with a last blow took life from the Sultan, October 25, 1260. The assassins left the body of Kutuz where he died and hastened on to his camp at Salahiyet. They entered the Sultan's pavilion and immediately set about enthroning Bilban, an emir, the most considerable person among them. Fari ud din Aktai, the Atabeg, ran in and asked what they were doing. " Taking this man for Sultan," said they as they pointed at Bilban. " What is the Turk usage in cases of this kind ? " inquired Aktai. " The slayer succeeds," was the answer. " Who slew the Sultan ? " " That man," said they pointing to Beibars. The Atabeg took Beibars by the hand and led him to the throne of the Sultan. " I seat myself here in the name of the Highest," said Beibars, " now give your oath to me." " It is for thee to swear first," said the Atabeg, " to treat them with loyalty and give them advancement." The new Sultan made promises in that sense and swore to them, the others then gave their oath of allegiance.

After this unexpected enthronement Beibars started for Cairo where he arrived just at midnight. The city had been adorned at all points for Kutuz, the deliverer of Islam. The people were waiting and expecting to see their famed ruler, and rejoice at the victory of the faithful. What was their wonder and amazement when heralds at daybreak passed through all Cairo and shouted: " O people, implore divine favor for the soul of El Mozaffer Kutuz, and pray for Ez Zahir Beibars your new Sultan."

All were in great consternation for they feared the Bahriyans and their tyranny. Beibars, a man of the Kipchak, or Polovtsi Turks, had been sold at Damascus for eight hundred drachmas, but the purchaser found a white spot on his eye and broke the bargain. He was bought then by Emir Eidikin Bundukdar;

following Mameluk usage he called himself Beibars el Bunduk-dari. In 1246 the Eyubite Sultan, Salih, disgraced Eidikin, took his Mameluk, and advanced Beibars until he became one among the highest Bahriyans.

Beibars now made his old owner a general, and gave him the government of Damascus. Hulagu had given Damascus and its province to Prince Nassir, and had sent him from Hamadan, with an escort of three hundred Syrians, on the eve of the day when news came that the Mongols were crushed at Ain Jalut. It was suggested to Hulagu then by a Syrian that Nassir on getting Damascus would join Kutuz surely. Thereupon Halagu sent three hundred Mongols on horseback to follow Nassir. They came up with the prince in the mountains of Salmas where they killed him, and spared no man of his suite except the astrologer, who gave the historian Bar Hebraeus the details of this slaughter. Hulagu was impatient to avenge the defeat of Ain Jalut, but, occupied greatly by the death of Mangu, he could not begin an expedition at that time.

As we have stated, Mayafarkin had been summoned to surrender and then besieged by Yshmut while his father, Hulagu, was advancing on Aleppo. Prince Kamil of Mayafarkin gave this answer to the summons: " I have learned from the fate of other sovereigns to put no trust whatever in Mongols and will fight to the utmost." Inflaming the courage of his people, he opened all his supplies and every treasure, not wishing, as he said, to act like the Kalif of Bagdad who lost life and an Empire through avarice. He began by a sortie, in which he slew many besiegers. He had in his service a man of rare skill in hurling great stones with catapults. This man did immense harm to the assailants; they too had a man of much art in this matter whom they got from Bedr ud din Lulu, late prince of Mosul. It is said that once the two men discharged their engines at the very same instant and the two stones from their catapults met in the air and shivered each other to fragments. Two champions of wonderful strength came out of Mayafarkin each time with a sortie, and never retired till they had left on the plain many Mongols. The siege turned in time to a blockade, and with the blockade appeared famine. The besieged were forced to eat dogs, cats, shoes, and at last they ate people. After the blockade had continued a full year and resistance was exhausted, the inhabitants sent to Yshmut declaring that there were no more defenders in Mayafarkin. He sent Oroktu Noyon, who found only seventy half famished people. The Mongols rushed in to pillage. The two champions went to a house top whence they killed men as they passed them; surrounded at last they refused to surrender and died fighting desperately. In the spring of 1260 the famous old town of Mayafarkin was in the possession of Mongols. Prince Kamil and nine Mameluks were captured, taken to Telbashir, and led into the presence of Hulagu, who put Kamil to death in a horrible manner: bits of flesh were torn from his body and thrust down his throat until life left him. His head, cut off and fixed on a lance, was borne from Aleppo to Hamath, and taken finally to Damascus. There it was carried through the streets and tambourines and singers moved before it. At last it was tied to the wall next the gate El Feradis (Paradise) where it hung till Kutuz made his entry after the victory of Ain Jalut. The Sultan had this head placed in the mausoleum of Hussein, son of Ali.

Of the nine Mameluks in Mayafarkin eight were put to death. The last man was spared because he had been chief hunter for the Prince of Mayafarkin, and Hulagu took him into his service.

Yshmut now attacked Mardin at command of his father. Hulagu had invited Säid of Mardin to come to him, but Säid was distrustful, and sent his son Mozaffer, to render homage at Aleppo; Hulagu sent him back to Mardin and said: " Tell thy father to come; prevent his revolt and thus save him." The father would not listen and imprisoned Mozaffer; then Hulagu sent troops against Mardin. The place was on a height beyond reach of projectiles, and the attackers were forced to blockade it. At the end of eight months an epidemic and famine had produced fearful ravages; Prince Säid died of the malady or, as some historians state, of poison administered by his son. Mozaffer was set free then and surrendered; Hulagu gave him Mardin which he kept till his death in 1296.

After the capture of Bagdad and the destruction of the Kalifat Abul Kassin Ahmed, an uncle of the Kalif Mostassim, had succeeded in escaping and had found a refuge among Beduins in Irak till 1261, when he went to Damascus attended by Arabs. Beibars sent orders at once to treat this descendant of Abbas with distinction, and conduct him to Egypt. When Kassin Ahmed approached Cairo, June 19, 1261, the Sultan went out to meet him with a great suite of military leaders, also cadis, ulema and an immense throng of people, followed by Jewish Rabbis bearing their Scriptures, and Christian priests bearing with them the Gospels.

Four days later the chief functionaries and the ulema assembled in the palace, and Ahmed's genealogy was established. Taj ud din the chief justice gave him the oath of allegiance, next the Sultan pledged his homage and faith in case the new Kalif acted always according to the Divine law of Islam, and all traditions of the Prophet, commanded what the law commands, forbade what the law forbids, and walked in the ways of the Almighty. Also that he received legally in the name of God the contributions of the faithful and gave them to those who had the right to receive them. The Kalif then invested Beibars with the sovereignty of countries submitted to Islam, and those which God might permit him to free from unbelievers. This act of investiture was fixed in a diploma, which was given to the Sultan. Then every man present pledged faith to the Kalif, now called Al Mostansir Billahi, and gave him homage. The Sultan sent an order to every prefect in the provinces to have the new Kalif recognized, his name mentioned in public prayers and stamped on new coinage. The Kalif gave the Sultan a mantle of the House of Abbas. Some days later this successor of Mohammed rode forth in public on a white steed with black trappings. He wore a black turban, a violet mantle, a collar of gold, and the sabre of a Beduin. On the day of installation the Kalif invested the Sultan with robes of office, and put a gold chain on his neck. After that the vizir read the diploma conferring sovereign power upon Beibars. The Sultan now mounted and rode through the city with great pomp and the utmost solemnity, preceded by the vizir and the grand marshal, who carried alternately above their heads the diploma given by the Kalif. All houses were decorated, and the Sultan's horse walked on the richest of stuffs which had been spread on the streets of his passage.

The following Friday the Kalif preached in the mosque of the citadel; the Sultan, uncertain of the effect which he might produce, and to be sure of results in every case, so arranged as to shower gold and silver coins from above on his person, and thus interrupt the discourse which he was giving.

Beibars now formed for the Kalif a household with all the officers, horsemen and servants which were requisite. He added one hundred Mameluks, each having three dromedaries and three horses; he gave also two thousand mounted warriors, and a body of Beduins.

The Sultan and the Kalif left Cairo for Damascus September 4th, 1262. On the 10th of October the Kalif took the road for Bagdad, attended by the generals Seïf ud din Bilban and Sonkor of Rūm who had been deputed to go with him to the Euphrates, and to hold themselves ready to follow into Irak at the first signal from the Kalif.

The three sons of Bedr ud din Lulu, then princes of Mosul, Jeziret and Sindjar, set out with the Kalif, but halted at Rahbah despite his entreaties, leaving with him, however, sixty Mamluks. Mostansir was joined at that place by Yezid, an emir who was chief of the Al Fazl, and had with him four hundred Beduins, and by Eidikin, an emir who brought with him thirty horsemen from Hamath.

Advancing by the western bank of the Euphrates they met at Ana the Abbasid Iman, Al Hakim, attended by seven hundred Turkmen; Al Burunli, the Marmaluk chief who had seized command of Aleppo in spite of the Sultan, had made Al Hakim set out with these horsemen. The Kalif overtook Hakim and his party at the river where the seven hundred Turkmen deserted.

Thereupon Hakim adhered to Mostansir, and was ready to assist in installing him at Bagdad. The people of Ana had refused to receive Hakim. The Sultan of Egypt, they said, had recognized a Kalif who was coming; to him alone would they open the gates of their city.

When Mostansir appeared he was met with due homage. Haditse acted like Ana, but Hitt refused sternly to open its gates and was taken by violence. The Kalif entered the city November 24 with his warriors, who plundered both Christians and Jews without mercy.

Kara Buga, the commander of those Mongols who guarded Arabian Irak, hearing of Mostansir's approach marched against Anbar with five thousand cavalry. Anbar was friendly to the

Kalif and might give him aid. Kara Buga entered the city on a sudden and cut down the people on all sides. Bahadur Ali, governor of Bagdad, went hither also with the troops in his garrison. These two commanders after joining their forces near Anbar encountered the new Kalif who, ranging the Turkmans on his right, the Arabs on his left, charged himself in the center. Bahadur's troops took to flight and the greater part threw themselves into the river. Kara Buga put some of his forces in ambush and waited. When the Turkmen and Arabs met the Mongols they fought very little, and rushed off in panic. The center, now left unsupported, was surrounded and overpowered, crushed into disorder and cut to pieces. The Kalif was lost in that chaos, and was never seen again. According to some he was killed, others said that he escaped to Arabs and died of his wounds while among them.

Mostansir was, as is said, a man of great strength and good courage, with a loftiness of bearing very different indeed from Mostassim, the last Kalif of the Kalifat, who was trampled to death under horsehoofs at Hulagu's camp ground. But whatever his merits this adventure reached the acme of folly. It is difficult to explain how the Sultan of Egypt with all his shrewd management could have spent so much treasure on a journey foredoomed beyond doubt to disaster, unless he had a sinister motive in the enterprise, and wished it to end in the destruction of that Kalif whom he had perhaps inaugurated through diplomacy and for his own aggrandizement. One historian declares that Beibars was sending ten thousand warriors to set up the Kalif in Bagdad, and giving him as aids the Prince of Mosul and his brothers, when one of these warned the Sultan that the Kalif if settled in Bagdad might take Egypt from him. We may well suppose that Beibars wished simply to establish his own power with firmness, and give himself freedom in Islam, and that he wished to be rid of the new Kalif so as to put in his place a man who could not be strong, and who would be obedient. Hakim, who met the late Kalif at Anbar, claimed to be fourth in descent from Mostershed who was slain in 1135 by the Assassins. This Hakim now fled to Egypt, where Beibars received him with distinction and gave him a residence in the palace called Munasir al Kebesh. His duties were simply to legitimize with the holiness of Islam the Sultan of Egypt, and ward off all Fatimid pretensions. His power beyond that was as nothing. He was styled " Shadow of God upon Earth, Ruler by command of God." He lived this life for forty years and was first in that line of Egyptian Kalifs who were puppets of the Mameluke sovereigns. An end was put to that line only when Egypt was conquered by Selim I. and the Turkish Sultans took to themselves the Kalifai, and became the successors of Mohammed.

Salih, the eldest son of Bedr ud din of Mosul, met a worse fate by far than the Kalif. Soon after the accession of Beibars Salih's brother Säid, who had been driven from Aleppo by the Mamelukes, went to Egypt, whence he wrote to his brother advising a visit to Beibars, who when he had conquered the Mongols could make Salih ruler not of some petty place in the West but of great Eastern regions. This letter was kept very carefully by Salih, who took it to bed with him. Ibn Yunus, an official who had been a great personage in Bedr ud din's day, stole it from under the coverlet while Salih was sleeping. He set out immediately for Baashika his birthplace in the province of Nineveh.

On missing the letter Salih sent two slaves to Baashika. Ibn Yunus, fearing dire punishment if caught, turned toward Erbil and at Bakteli, on the way, he advised one Abad Ullah to flee with all his people without waiting, for Salih would destroy every Christian and escape straightway to Egypt. He fled then to Erbil.

Meanwhile Salih, fearing lest Ibn Yunus might give the letter to the Mongols, withdrew with his son, Alai ul Mulk, toward Syria. Turkan Khatun, his wife, would not go with him. She remained in Mosul with Yasan, the Mongol prefect. She and Yasan shut the gates and prepared a defence for the city. One of Salih's officers, Alam ud din Sanjar, left him while journeying and returned to occupy Mosul. He found the gates closed and began to attack them. This attack lasted several days unsuccessfully. At last a number of citizens threw the gates open and he entered. The prefect and Salih's wife fled to the citadel.

Sanjar killed all the Christians who would not accept Islam, hence many renounced their religion to save themselves.

Meanwhile the Kurds attacked places in the surrounding country, and slew a great number of Christians. They took the Kudida convent by storm and put to death many of its inmates.

The monastery of Mar Matthew they besieged during four months
with warriors on foot and one thousand on horseback. They
attempted to storm it, but the monks repelled every effort, and
burned all scaling ladders with naphtha. The Kurds now let down
two immense rocks from a neighboring mountain top. One of
these remained fast in the wall and was fixed there like a stone in
its setting; the other passed through and left a wide breach behind it. When the Kurds tried to rush through the opening the
monks met them with a desperate valor, using stones, darts, and
every weapon in the monastery. They kept the Kurds out and
filled up the great breach. The Abbot, Abunser, fought with the
foremost and lost one eye in that venomous struggle. But in time
the defenders were failing and would have been forced to surrender had the attacks been continued. But the Kurds too had
their weakness. They greatly feared an attack from the Mongols,
though this they concealed very cleverly, and even extorted a
ransom. The monks gave the silver and gold of the churches,
and all the treasure which they could get from the people, after
which the Kurds left them.

At Erbil the Mongol emir, Kutleg Beg, cut down men and
women without mercy. Salih's officer, Sanjar, having heard that
the Mongols were moving on Mosul, marched out and engaged
them; he was killed and his forces defeated. Salih, the Melik of
Mosul, and his son had gone meanwhile to Beibars who was then
at Damascus with the new Kalif. He was received with great
pomp by the Sultan, as were also his brothers. Horses and banners and robes of honor were presented to them, also diplomas
confirming their titles. These diplomas were strengthened further
by the Kalif. The three brothers then escorted the Kalif to
Rahbah, as has been already stated, where they left him, each
going back to his own place.

Salih returned to Mosul which was at that time invested by
Mongols. Samdagu, the commander, having learned from a spy
that Salih was coming, withdrew to a point not remote from the
city where he waited. When Salih had passed the gate, Samdagu
reinvested it with two tumans of warriors and twenty-five catapults. He then began siege work which lasted from December
till summer.

Salih gave good gifts to his garrison, and promised that the Sul-

tan would send reinforcements. The defence was a brave one and
effective. One day eighty Mongols succeeded in scaling the bulwarks, but were killed every man of them and their heads shot out
from catapults to their comrades.

Samdagu felt need of reinforcements which came to him promptly
from Hulagu. At last the Sultan commanded Akkush, who was
governing Aleppo, to march on Mosul and relieve it. He set out,
and sent a pigeon with news of his coming. This bird settled
down, by a wonderful chance, on a catapult in Samdagu's army,
was caught, and through the letter attached to it gave notice not
to the Prince of Mosul but to Samdagu.

Samdagu sent straightway a strong corps of warriors to beat
Akkush back and destroy him if possible. The Mongols were
placed in three ambushes where they waited. The Egyptians
suffered partly from these ambushes and partly from a fierce wind
which blew in their faces, and hurled clouds of sand at them.
The Sultan's army was slaughtered except a mere remnant. The
Mongols attacked then the people of Sinjar, killed nearly all the
men and seized captive the women and children. Next they put
on the clothing of Akkush's dead warriors and moved toward
Mosul. When nearing that city they were seen from the watch-
towers by the people, who mistook them for forces sent by the
Sultan, and went out in large numbers to meet them. These
citizens were surrounded immediately by the Mongols and slain to
the very last person.

When the siege had continued six months the fierce heat of
summer was raging and each side ceased its action. The Mongol
commander made a promise to spare all and send Salih to Hulagu
with a request for full pardon. Thereupon Salih yielded and sent
to Samdagu a letter containing the terms of surrender.

He went to the Mongol camp from the city June 25, 1262, with
presents and dainties, preceded by dancers, musicians and har-
lequins. The Mongol commander, forgetting all promises, would
not receive Salih, or look at him, nay more, he put the prince under
a strong guard immediately.

But Samdagu reassured the people; they were to be of good
cheer he declared and fear nothing. Meanwhile they must tear
down the walls and remove them. They did this work straightway, and when all was cleared, and the whole place was laid open,

a massacre began in that woebegone city. Nine days did that terrible slaughter continue, till the sword had finished every one. Mosul was deserted, not a soul now remained there. It was only when the Mongols had moved far away that eight or ten hundred people who had hidden in the hills and in caverns crept out and came back to inhabit the city.

The first governor of this spectral and death-stricken Mosul was that Ibn Yunus who had stolen the letter from Salih and betrayed him.

Salih was sent to Hulagu for a judgment. The sentence was revolting and hideous. The late Prince of Mosul was deprived of his clothing and wrapped in a sheepskin just stripped from the animal. This skin was fastened firmly round Salih who, exposed to the sun of July in that climate, suffered terribly. The skin was soon covered with a life most repulsive and the all conquering worm now lived with Salih. The Prince had passed a whole month in that horrible sheepskin when death came to him.

His son, Alai ud din, a boy of three years, was sent back to Mosul and put to death there. They made the child drunk, tied cords around his middle very tightly in such fashion as to force upward his entrails; they then cut his body across into two pieces and hung one on each bank of the Tigris, on a gibbet. Mohai, son of Zeblak, who with others had opened the gates to Salih, was beheaded.

Samdagu after his triumph at Mosul marched on to Jeziret to which he laid siege all the following winter and spring and a part of the summer of 1263. This place was saved from destruction by the bishop, Hanan Yeshua (Grace of Jesus), a Nestorian, who through his knowledge of alchemy was a favorite of Hulagu, to whom he went straightway and obtained a yarlyk, or decree securing their lives to the people. The gates were thrown open to Samdagu, who had the walls leveled at once. Gulbeg, an officer of the Jeziret prince, was made governor, but Samdagu on learning soon after that Gulbeg had given the late prince's messenger gold which that prince himself had secreted, put Gulbeg to death promptly.

About this time Salar of Bagdad, a deserting emir, went from Irak to Egypt. This man was a native of Kipchak and had once been a Mameluk of Dhahir, the Kalif, and from him received rule

over Vassit, Kufat and Hillet; this he retained under Mostassim
and Mostansir. After the ruin of Bagdad by Hulagu, Salar
joined his forces with others in resisting the Mongols, but finding
that they had not strength to do anything effective he went to the
desert of Hidjaz and was six months in it when a message from
Hulagu bestowed former rule on him. He went and took it.
When Beibars became Sultan he wrote to Salar repeatedly inviting
him to Cairo. Salar was inclined to the visit but deferred it; he
wished to secure all his treasures.

Meanwhile the Sultan said one day to Kilidj of Bagdad: "Salar
thy friend is coming to see me." "I do not think he will come,"
said the other, "he is ruling in Irak, why leave what he has which
is certain for something in Egypt?" "Very well," said the Sultan,
"unless he comes of himself I will force him." Beibars then sent
a messenger to Salar with letters, as it were in reply to some others;
he sent a second man also to kill the first as soon as he crossed
Salar's boundary, and leave the man where he fell with the letters
upon him. All this was done as Beibars had commanded. Mongol outposts discovered the body and searched it. The letters were
sent to the court for perusal. In Hulagu's service there were sons
of former Mameluks of the Kalif. These men told Salar directly
what had happened and he knew straightway that Beibars
had tricked him. He received soon an order to appear at
the Mongol court, but fearing death there from Hulagu he
fled to the Sultan of Egypt, leaving behind both his family and
property.

Beibars received him with distinction and bestowed on the
fugitive a military command with a fief of good value.

Hulagu was stopped now very seriously in his plans against
Syria and Egypt by the Golden Horde Khan, Berkai, his cousin,
son of Juchi. The death of Batu, 1255, was followed quickly
by that of Sartak his son and successor. Next after Sartak came
Sartak's infant son, Ulakchi, under the care of his mother. The
child died some months later and Berkai, the third son of Juchi,
was put on the throne in 1256. Berkai had been converted to
Islam and was spreading its doctrines effectively. Strong through
support of Mangu, the Grand Khan, whom he had helped to
the Empire, Berkai now reproached Hulagu with needless cruelties, with slaughter of both friends and enemies; with the

ruin of many cities; with the death of the Kalif, brought about
without sanction of the Jinghis Khan family.   There were
still other causes of complaint.   Three descendants of Juchi
had marched into Persia with Hulagu: Balakan and Tumar,
a grandson and great grandson of Juchi.   These two at the
head of Batu's contingent, and Kuli, also a grandson of Juchi.
Kuli led the contingent of Urda's, his father.   Tumar was accused before Hulagu of attempting to harm him, through witch-
craft.   He confessed guilt when examined while in torture.
Hulagu out of respect for Berkai sent Tumar to him attended
by Sugundjak, a commander.   Berkai, thinking that Tumar's
offence had been proven, sent him back to Hulagu, who had
the prince put to death without waiting.   Balakan died soon
after as did also Kuli.   Berkai supposed these deaths caused by
poison and was enraged.   The families of those princes escaped
then from Persia.   Policy may have played a large part in these
murders, for Berkai and the descendants of Juchi desired the
election of Arik Buga, while Hulagu favored Kubilai in the contest
for Grand Khanship.   Hulagu, tired of excessive reproaches from
Berkai, was ready for warfare.   On hearing this, Berkai declared
his intention of avenging the blood of his relatives and many
thousands of others.   He sent southward an army of thirty thousand commanded by Nogai, a cousin of Tumar, who marched
on and camped near Shirvan beyond the Caucasus.   When the
troops of the princes descended from Juchi saw war breaking out
between their own sovereign and Hulagu they left Persia quickly.
One part went home through Derbend, another, pursued by
Halagu's warriors, passed through Khorassan to seize upon Gazni
and lands touching India.

Hulagu left Alatag, his summer camp ground, and marched at
the head of an army gathered in from all Persia.   On November
11, 1262, his vanguard commanded by Shiramun was thoroughly
defeated near Shemaki, but some days later Abatai repaired this
reverse by a victory near Shirvan.

Hulagu advanced to continue this victory and met the enemy
north of Derbend near the Caspian.   Nogai was put to flight and
pursued by a large force of warriors who seized a camp left by
him north of the Terek in which were vast numbers of cattle and
of women and children.   Hulagu's army remained at that camp

and for three days continued to drink, and to yield themselves up
to every indulgence accessible.

All on a sudden Nogai reappeared with his army. Hulagu's
men were surprised near the river and thoroughly defeated (January 13, 1263). The only escape for survivors was to cross the
frozen river. They tried this, the ice broke and immense numbers
sank in the Terek. Hulagu returned to Tebriz greatly grieved and
cast down by the overthrow, but he summoned at once a new army
and avenged his wrath on those merchants of Kipchak whom he
found in Tebriz at his coming. He put them to death, and then
seized their property. Berkai answered straightway by killing all
traders within his reach who were subjects of Hulagu, and living
in Kipchak. Hulagu next killed Bokhara people. Population
had grown in that city, though not greatly, since its ruin. It reached
seventeen thousand according to a census. Of these five thousand
were subjects of Kipchak, three thousand belonged to Siurkukteni,
the mother of Hulagu, and the rest to the Grand Khan. Hulagu
commanded that those five thousand subjects of Berkai be driven
to the plains near the city; there the men were slaughtered with
swords; the women and children were reduced to captivity.

In 1264, the year following, report ran that Nogai was to lead
an attack on lands south of the Caucasus. While Hulagu was
preparing to meet this, Jelal ud din, son of the second chancellor
to the late Kalif, told Hulagu that there were thousands of
Kipchaks then living in Persia who would serve in the vanguard
with readiness. They knew northern methods of warfare, and
would be, as he said, of use beyond others in the campaign against
Berkai. Hulagu sent this man to summon those warriors, and
commanded that supplies, arms, and money be given him in
sufficiency, and that no one should thwart him.

When Jelal had assembled those people of Kipchak he declared
that Hulagu would put them in the vanguard to be slain there.
" I do not wish this," said he. " Follow me and we will free ourselves from Mongols." He gave the men money and arms from
the treasury and arsenals of Bagdad; then, he told the commandant
of the city that to gather provisions he was making a raid against
Kafadje Arabs, at war with Hulagu; that done, he would
march toward Shirvan. He crossed the Euphrates, all his men
following, taking with them their families and baggage. Then he

declared to them that he was going to Syria and Egypt. Hulagu was beside himself with anger when he learned of Jelal's treachery.

Beibars, the shrewd Sultan of Egypt, noting Hulagu's alertness, and the movements of Berkai, which might mean, as he thought, an invasion of Syria, sent mounted men toward the boundary of Persia to reconnoitre. Later on he commanded the people of Damascus to move to Egypt with their families for safety, and thus leave more food for his warriors. He instructed the governor of Aleppo to burn all the grass in the regions toward Amid. This was done to the width of ten days' journey. Information came next to the Sultan that a Kipchak detachment had appeared in his territory. These men, people told him, were subjects of Berkai and were from the contingent given Hulagu on his coming to Persia. Berkai had recalled them, if stopped they were to take refuge in Egypt.

The Sultan commanded his officials to treat these men well, to give them provisions and clothing. They came to Cairo about two hundred strong and under four captains. Each captain received the land given to commanders of a hundred. Beibars gave also clothing, horses and money. All became Moslems. This generous treatment induced others to seek an asylum in Egypt.

When he had talked with these strangers concerning their sovereign and country the Sultan resolved to send envoys to Berkai. He chose for this office Seïf ud din Keshrik, a man who had once served Jelal ud din the Kwaresmian Sultan; he knew the country to which he was sent and its language. Madjd ud din, a juris-consult, went with him. Two men of the Kipchaks who had received hospitality from Beibars were attached to the party. The envoys bore a letter from Beibars assuring Berkai of the Sultan's good feeling and urging him to act against Hulagu.

The Sultan's troops made up of many nations were lauded; his vassals, Mohammedan and Christian, were mentioned; the letter ended by stating that a body of warriors had visited Cairo and declaring themselves subjects of Berkai, had been received gladly because of him. To this letter the pedigree of the new Kalif, Hakim, was added.

The envoy and his associates set out for the Volga, but were stopped in Greek regions by the Emperor Michael[1] who had com-

[1] Michael Palæologus.

plaints against Berkai whose troops had been raiding his possessions. Michael had sent some time before a Greek document in
which he had sworn peace and amity to the Sultan.

Beibars summoned straightway the Patriarch and bishop to get
their decision on oath breaking. They declared that by breaking
an oath a sovereign abjures his religion. Beibars sent to the Emperor this document signed by the Patriarch and bishops; he sent
also a letter to Berkai, in which he implored him to stop all attacks
on the Empire.

Michael now freed the envoys, who sailed over the Black Sea
and landed at Sudak whence they crossed the Crimea and went to
Sarai situated somewhat east of the Volga. They were twenty days
making that journey. Berkai's vizir, Al Furussi, went out to meet
them. When instructed in Sarai ceremonial they were taken to
Berkai, who was in a tent large enough for five hundred persons.
They left behind every weapon and were careful not to touch the
threshold while entering. Presented on the left of the throne they
were taken with the suite to the right of it, after the letter from
Beibars had been read before Berkai. At the right of the Khan
sat his principal wife. Fifty or sixty high officers occupied stools
near him.

The Khan addressed several questions to the envoys. He did
not detain them at Sarai without need and sent with them envoys
to the Sultan at Cairo where Seïf ud din arrived after an absence of
two years.

About six months after the Sultan's men had started from
Cairo two envoys from Berkai arrived in that city; both men were
Mussulmans and had passed through the Byzantine capital. One
was an officer, Jelal ud din el Kadi, the other a Sheik, Nur ud din
Ali. Beibars, who had just come from Syria after the taking of
Karak, gave them an audience in the Castle of the Mountain in
presence of his commanders and a numerous assembly.

Berkai announced in a letter that he with his four brothers had
received Islam. He proposed an alliance against Hulagu, asking
to send a corps of Egyptians toward the Euphrates. He expressed
also interest in one of the Rūm Sultans, Yzz ud din, and asked
Beibars to aid him.

The Sultan gave these envoys from Berkai many proofs of
munificence, and when they were going he added his envoys to the

company. These envoys took with them an answer on seventy pages half margin. Rich presents went also to Berkai, a copy of the Koran, made, as was stated, by Osman the Kalif, with Osman's pulpit and prayer carpet; tunics, candelabras and torches from Barbary; all kinds of linen from Egypt; cotton stuffs, morocco, tapestry, sabres, bows, arms, helmets, breast pieces, saddles, bridles, boxes filled with arrow heads, vases of dried grapes, gilded lamps, black eunuchs, women who could prepare delicate dishes, Arab horses, dromedaries, white camels, wild asses, a giraffe, and some balsam. A turban which had been in Mecca was added also, for Beibars had sent an officer in Berkai's name on a pilgrimage to the holy city, and messengers to Medina and Mecca to put the Khan's name next his own in the public prayer of each Friday; this was done also in Jerusalem and Cairo. He sent to Berkai the first Friday sermon of the new Kalif.

Beibars sent back with the Berkai envoys the two hundred warriors from Kipchak.

Three months after the envoys had gone thirteen hundred Kipchaks set out for Cairo. Beibars commanded to treat them well on the way, and he went out to meet them. They dismounted and bowed to the earth when they saw him. Soon after a second and a third party came. Among these were ten officers of distinction with the title of Aga. All were treated most liberally. Beibars asked them to accept Islam. This they did, accepting the faith in his presence.

The Sultan received also in Cairo a number of high officers from Fars, chiefs of the Arab tribe, Kafadje, and the emir of Arabian Irak. These came to seek an asylum in Egypt, and he gave them fiefs. The next year he sent Shuja ud din, one of his chamberlains, to Berkai, begging him to stop his people from raiding the lands of the Byzantine Emperor, who had asked his good offices. He sent at the same time three turbans to Berkai which he had worn while making the pilgrimage to Mecca, two marble vases and other presents.

While Hulagu was defending his northern frontier against Berkai's armies Hayton, the King of Cilicia, attacked Egyptian regions. Hayton when returning from Hulagu's court saw at Heraclea Rokn ud din, the Rūm Sultan, with whom he formed a close friendship. On reaching home he summoned troops and marched against Aintab.

Beibars, informed always with accuracy of what was happening near his borders, had already commanded troops in Hamat and Hims to march on Aleppo. Egyptian troops followed quickly. The Armenians were surprised, and put to flight with some loss. Hayton summoned in seven hundred Mongols, who were in Rūm at that juncture, and advancing, was joined by one hundred and fifty from Antioch. This little army encamped on the steppes of Harem where it suffered from rain, snow and scant food and was at last forced to retreat, losing meanwhile many warriors.

Hayton had a thousand Mongol coats and caps which he put on his men to make it seem that Mongol troops had come to him. This trick merely brought more Egyptians against him. They attacked Hayton in force and dispersed his small army; after that the Sultan's men rushed into Antioch lands, and committed great havoc.

Beibars was informed now by secret servants in Irak that Hulagu had sent two agents to corrupt leading officers of Egypt, and that these men would visit Siss as they traveled. This news was confirmed by his agents in that capital of Armenia. The Sultan learned afterward from Acre that those two agents had gone to Damascus; he commanded to arrest them directly. Brought to Cairo they could not deny the accusation, so Beibars hanged them promptly.

The Egyptians intercepted this same year a letter from Hulagu to Mogith, Prince of Karak; this seemed an answer to some communication, from which it might be inferred that the prince had been asking the Mongols to take Egypt, and also Syria to Gaza. Beibars set out straightway for Gaza, and feigning great friendship for Mogith invited him to Gaza. Mogith made the visit, but the moment he entered the camp he was seized.

Beibars next summoned the chief judge of Damascus, the princes, feudatories, commanders and notable persons, also European ambassadors, and had Hulagu's letters to Mogith read in their presence. He declared thereupon that this letter was the cause of the prince's detention. After that he seized Karak and returned to Cairo where he took Mogith's life without waiting.

Hulagu was interested greatly during the last year of his rule in building a palace at Alatag, and in finishing the observatory at Meraga. Though not a scholar himself he liked to converse with learned men, especially astronomers and alchemists, but beyond all the latter, who had known how to captivate his fancy, and on whom he expended large sums of money.

Administration had now, (1264), become greatly important. Hulagu's rule extended from the Oxus to Syria and the Byzantine Empire. He gave his eldest son, Abaka, Mazanderan, Irak and Khorassan; to Yshmut his third son, Azerbaidjan and Arran; to Tudan, one of his commanders, Diarbekr and Diarrabiat up to the Euphrates; Rūm he gave to Moyin ud din Pervane; to the Melik Sadr ud din, the province of Tebriz, and Fars to an emir, Ikiatu. According to Rashid he gave Kerman to Turkan Khatun, but this is questioned by some historians. In 1263 he had put to death his vizir Seïf ud din Bitikdji while on the march from Shemaki to Derbend, and put in his place Shems ud din Juveïni, whose brother, Alaï ud din, Ata ul Mulk, was made governor of Bagdad. This same year Hulagu condemned to death Zein ud din Muyyed Suleiman, son of the emir El Akarbani, better known as El Hafizzi, a name which he had taken from his former master, Prince Hafizzi. He was accused of having turned to his own profit a part of the income from the province of Damascus. Hulagu reproached him for his perfidy. "Thou hast betrayed me," said he, "thou didst betray also Prince Nassir, and before him Prince Hafizzi, and earlier than all the Baalbek prince."

The death sentence which struck down El Hafizzi included his family, his brothers, his relatives and clients, fifty persons in all. Only two escaped, one was his son, and the other his nephew.

The troubles in Fars at this time roused Hulagu's attention very keenly. The princes of that region were subject to Mongol dominion from the first. After the death, in 1231, of the Atabeg of Fars, Säid Abu Bekr, his son and successor, sent his brother Tehemten with his homage to Ogotai and also rich presents. The Grand Khan gave a patent of investiture with the title Kutlug Khan. Fars had been saved by prompt submission from every Mongol hostility. Its sovereign paid the Grand Khan each year thirty thousand gold dinars, a small sum if the wealth of that region be considered; presents also were given.

When Hulagu came to the Transoxiana Abu Bekr's nephew, Seljuk Shah, came with rich presents to greet him. Seljuk Shah was befittingly received at the Oxus by Hulagu; but was afterward imprisoned.

Abu Bekr died in 1260, after a reign of thirty years. His son Säid succeeded him but died twelve days after reaching the throne, leaving a son of tender years in the care of his mother, Turkan Khatun. This child, named Mohammed, died in 1262, and the Fars throne fell to Mohammed Shah, one of his uncles, a son of Salgar Shah and grandson of Säid, son of Zengwi. This prince had commanded the contingent of Fars in Hulagu's great campaign against Bagdad. Brave, but unsparing and dissolute, his tyranny had roused great complaints upon all sides. Called to the camp by Hulagu, who feigned a desire to consult him concerning Fars matters, the prince delayed him under various excuses till Turkan Khatun, now his wife, who was displeased with his conduct, but especially with his treatment of herself, had the man seized as he was passing the harem and taken to Hulagu, whom she informed that Mohammed Shah was unfitted to govern. This decision of the princess found favor with Hulagu, so she had her husband's brother, Seljuk Shah, freed from prison, and though his temper was untamed and fiery, she married him soon after.

One night when flushed with wine at a banquet Seljuk Shah was taunted with having risen through the favor of his wife, and not through any other cause, and when besides her conduct was described, a fit of fury seized the man. He commanded a eunuch to cut her head off immediately and bring it to him. When the black man brought the head of the princess, Seljuk Shah tore two splendid pearls from the ears, and threw them to musicians who were playing at the banquet.

When this raging man heard that Hulagu's prefects in Shiraz, Ogul Beg and Kutluk Bitikdji, disapproved of this horrible action, instead of trying to appease them he killed one with his own hand, and cut down the other through his servants; he murdered also the people attached to them. At news of these horrors Hulagu commanded to execute Mohammed Shah, to whom he had just given permission to return to his country, and ordered his generals, Altadju and Timur, to march against Seljuk Shah. Their two divisions were to be strengthened by troops from Ispahan, Yezd, Itch and Kerman.

Altadju sent Seljuk a message from Ispahan, stating that if

he repented he might yet obtain pardon, and that he would act in his favor. The raging prince maltreated the messenger cruelly. Altadju marched after that into Fars with the forces of the sovereign of Kerman, the Atabeg of Yezd, Seljuk's brother-in-law, and other forces. Seljuk Shah retired to the Persian Gulf border. The magistrates and notables bearing flags, food and copies of the Koran went forth to meet Altadju. He reassured them, and commanded his troops, who were eager for pillage, not to harm them in any way. He marched with speed after Seljuk, who met him at Kazerun and displayed wondrous valor, but yielded to necessity at last and fled to the tomb of the holy Sheik Morshed, which the Mongols surrounded.

At bay and in his last refuge Seljuk rushed to the sepulchre of the saint and broke with one blow of his club the flat covering of stone which was over the body. " O Sheik, give thy aid! " cried the fugitive. It was known in that region that the saint had declared, " When peril threatens, give notice on my tomb and I will save you."

The Mongols burst in the door and killed many of Seljuk's people who had sought refuge there also. They then seized the fleeing Seljuk whom they killed at the tomb. No Salgarid was left save two daughters of the Atabeg Säid, son of Abu Bekr. One of these, Uns Khatun, whose mother Seljuk Shah had beheaded, was placed on the Fars throne by Hulagu (1264).

When Seljuk Shah's life was ended Timur wished to put all Shiraz men to death, and thus give a warning to people such as Seljuk and his partisans, but Altadju insisted that the citizens were innocent, and that punishment like that might be given only at Hulagu's order. The army was dismissed, and Altadju taking the most notable people of Fars went to Hulagu's court with them.

In 1265 another storm made its appearance in Fars: Sherif ud din, the Grand Kadi, a chief man among the descendants of the Prophet, who had lived many years in Khorassan and won signal fame by his piety, tried now to use this reputation to further his ambition. He had the people show him homage, and many joined him in each town and village which he visited. Multitudes believed him to be that Madhi expected in the fulness of time by the Shiites, and thought that he had the power to work wonders. Assuming the insignia of royalty he advanced from Shebankiare towards Shiraz with his followers who already formed a small army.

The Mongol commander at Shiraz and Uns Kahtun's chief minister took proper measures and marched against this descendant of Mohammed. They met near Guvar. Many thought that the " Madhi " was assisted by spirits, and that whoso attacked him would be paralyzed. For some time no man in the army of Shiraz would raise a hand against Sherif. At last two warriors ventured to discharge arrows at him, others followed this example. The Mongols then charged the insurgents, who fled; Sherif was killed in the mêlée with most of his followers.

At the first news of this uprising Hulagu commanded to bastinado Altadju for sparing the people of Shiraz, and he ordered a tuman of warriors to punish them. When he learned, however, that Sherif ud din had been slain, and that the people of Shiraz were innocent, for the greater part, he recalled his first order.

When Uns Khatun had ruled for one year she was sent to the Ordu to marry Mangu Timur, son of Hulagu, to whom she brought a rich dowry. Fars was managed thenceforth by the Divan, though in the name of Uns, who died during 1287 in Tebriz. With her died the Salgarid dynasty.

At the end of 1264 the Mongols laid siege to El Biret. This place was considered the master stronghold of Syria. Akkush commanded for the Sultan of Egypt. The Mongols filled up the fosse of the fortress with wood. The besieged made a tunnel to that fosse and burned all the wood which then filled it. The Mongols worked with seventeen catapults, but they met firm and active resistance, women showing more courage than men in that struggle.

News had reached Beibars earlier that Franks were advising the Mongols, by letter, to march into Syria during spring when the troops were at home, and their horses were out grazing. As soon as he heard that the Mongols were attacking El Biret, the Sultan sent a corps of four thousand to oppose them. He sent four days later another four thousand, who were to reach El Biret by forced marches. The Sultan himself set out January 27, 1265, and by February 3 was at Gaza, where he learned that the enemy had raised the siege and retreated.

The Mongols at approach of their opponents had removed all

their catapults, sunk their boats, and fled quickly. Beibars gave command to bring in arms and supplies for a siege that might last a whole decade. Three hundred robes of honor and a hundred thousand drachmas in money were sent out by him to reward those who had fought in El Biret.

Hulagu died suddenly February 8, 1265, at the age of forty-eight. He was buried on the summit of that mountainous island called Tala in the lake of Urumia where a fortress had been built to contain his chief treasures. According to the custom of Mongols much gold and many gems were placed in the grave with him. Youthful maidens of rare beauty, richly dressed and adorned to the utmost, were buried alive to go with him. Four months and eleven days later died Dokuz Khatun, his chief wife, who was a Christian. She was the grand-daughter of Wang Khan and so wise a woman that Mangu had in 1253 enjoined on Hulagu to take no step without consulting her. Rashid ud din states that through her influence Hulagu had favored the Christians and permitted them to build churches in many parts of the Empire.

The death of Hulagu and his consort was deplored by the Christians, to whom both had shown great respect. Near the entrance of Dokuz Khatun's palace was a church with its bell which tolled at all seasons. Hulagu had five wives; from these, not counting other women, he had thirteen sons and seven daughters.

Accounts have come down to us of interesting judgments connected with Hulagu. On a time certain people came to him for justice; a file-maker had killed a near relative of theirs, and they asked that the criminal be given them for punishment. " Are file-makers numerous in the country? " asked Hulagu. " They are few," was the answer. Hulagu thought a moment and answered: " I will give you a maker of pack saddles; since there are many of these we can spare one more easily than a file-maker." The friends of the dead man declared that they wanted the murderer. Hulagu would not yield, and gave them a cow as an equivalent.

A man lost his eye in a quarrel with a weaver, and came to get justice: The prince put out the eye of a maker of arrows in satisfaction. Some one asked why he did this. " A weaver," said he, " needs both his eyes, while one is enough for the arrowsmith;

he always closes the other when he tests the straightness of an arrow."

A letter without signature or date was sent to Hulagu from a Pope, supposed to be Alexander IV, though assigned to 1261. In this letter the Pope declared his delight on hearing that Hulagu wished to be a Catholic. "Think," continued he, "how your power to subjugate Saracens will be increased if Christian warriors assist you openly and with force, as with God's grace they would, sustained by Divine power under the shield of Christianity. In shaping your actions by Catholic teaching you will heighten your power and acquire endless glory." Hulagu is credited not only with favoring Christians, but learned men of all creeds.

In the spring of 1266 Berkai began a second campaign in lands south of the Caucasus. Abaka, who was Hulagu's eldest son and successor, held the right bank of the Kur with his forces. Abaka sent forward Yshmut, his brother, who met Berkai's first army commanded by Nogai. A stubborn engagement took place near the Aksu. Nogai's army was forced to retreat on Shirvan in disorder, Nogai himself being wounded. Abaka now crossed the Kur, but hearing of Berkai's advance with a numerous army, he recrossed and destroyed all the bridges.

Berkai came up with his forces and the two armies camped on opposite sides of the river. They remained fifteen days in their places discharging arrows at each other, and sending words of defiance and ridicule. Neither could cross, hence no battle was possible. At last Berkai marched up the river intending to cross at some point east of Tiflis, but he died on the road, and that ended hostilities. His body was taken to Sarai, and there it was buried, 1266. His army disbanded.

We must now return to the Kin Empire.

CHAPTER XV

NIN KIA SU, the Kin Emperor (his Chinese name was Shu siu), had sent to Ogatai in 1229 his ambassador Ajuta with offerings to Jinghis Khan's spirit, but the new sovereign would accept naught from a ruler who had refused to acknowledge Jinghis as his overlord.

The Mongols, not regarding the death of Jinghis, had continued their warfare in China and pushed on through Shen si to the edge of the Sung Empire. At the end of 1227 they besieged Si ho chin, a city southeast of Kong chang and thirty leagues distant. The commandant defended the place with great valor, but, seeing that the Mongols would conquer at last, and then seize him, he invited Li shi, his wife, to think on her destiny. "We have enjoyed the good will of our sovereign," said the woman, "we should die for the dynasty;" thereupon she took poison. Two of his sons and their wives followed her example. When he had burned the five bodies the commandant stabbed himself. Twenty-eight of his dependents died with him.

In 1228 the Mongols pushed still farther south and Wanien Khada, the Kin general, sent to oppose them a mounted force under Cheng ho shang, who crushed a detachment eight thousand in number. This was the first triumph won by the Chinese in three decades, and roused the desire of resistance very greatly.

In 1228 the Mongol general Tukulku invested King yang fu, when a second Kin envoy was sent to Mongolia with presents, which were not accepted. Ogotai now gave command over all Chinese troops in his service to three generals of that race, and made two of them governors.

In 1230 the Mongols were beaten a second time by Yra buka, a Kin general, who stopped the siege of King yang by a victory.

Elated by success, Yra buka freed from confinement an envoy whom during his regency Tului had sent with peace messages. While dismissing him the Kin general boasted unwisely in the following phrases: " We have had time to make ready. If ye wish battle now ye have only to come to us." This challenge was taken to Ogotai who acted at once and set out with his brother Tului for China. They crossed the Hoang Ho and pushed on toward the southern part of Shen si, where they took sixty forts and laid siege to Fong tsiang, a large city.

The Kin government now saw the error in their treatment of the envoy, and sent new terms of peace to the Mongols. The Grand Khan tried to persuade this envoy to visit Fong tsiang and obtain its surrender, but though threatened with death the man was immovable. Ogatai had the beard of the envoy cut off and then he imprisoned him. The siege of Fong tsiang was continued with vigor.

The Kin emperor, seeing that his generals were slow in sending aid, hurried off Bai kua, his assistant, to urge them. They replied that their troops were too few to challenge the great Mongol army. The Emperor commanded to take men from Tung kwan, the strong fortress, give battle at once to the enemy, and force the relief of Fong tsiang which was sorely beleaguered.

An attack was made soon, but the battle was indecisive. The Kin forces fell back the night following, however, and left the place to its own strength and fortune. Antchar, who commanded the Mongols, blockaded that city, captured places around it, kept out all provisions, and when food and supplies were exhausted Fong tsiang had no choice save surrender.

Master of Shen si, Ogotai was eager now for Honan, the last land of the Kin Emperor, but this region was difficult to capture. On the north it was bounded by the Hoang Ho, on the west it was guarded by high rugged mountains, and the strong Tung kwan fortress. The Mongol officers were seeking for means to overcome or elude these great obstacles when Li chang go, a Kin officer, who had joined Ogotai's service only after Fong tsiang had surrendered, proposed to enter Honan from the south, and traced out a route for the conquest. Tului saw that the plan was the same as that traced by Jinghis on his death bed, and commended it to Ogotai, his brother, immediately. Ogotai consulted his generals, accepted the plan, and commissioned Tului to follow it.

It was agreed that the armies of the north and the south should meet at Nan king in the following February. Ogotai sent Chubugan to the Sung Emperor for permission to pass through a part of his country, but the envoy was killed after crossing the boundary. The deed astounded the Mongols, since the Sung court had requested their alliance somewhat earlier. This killing gave a good pretext later on, however, for attacking the Empire.

Tului marched straightway on Pao ki where he assembled thirty thousand mounted warriors. First he captured the fortress Ta san kuan, destroyed the city Fong chin and opened a way through the Hwa mountains, though with immense labor. This mountain chain divides the Hoai water system from the Han and formed for some distance the boundary between the two Empires in China. Tului crossed this chain and thus entered Kin regions. When he had taken one hundred and forty towns and strong places, slain people in vast numbers, and driven others to barren regions where they perished, he fixed his camp near the Han and there he rested.

On seeing the enemy at the southern border the Kin Empire was terrified. At the council called by the Emperor to find means of defence the majority were in favor of placing the army in towns near Nan king, where great stores must be gathered in quickly. The Mongols, worn out by long marching, could not attack in the open and would be forced back by sure famine. This plan did not please the Kin Emperor. He declared that his subjects had made every sacrifice for the army, he would not leave them then in that peril. He must defend Honan on the north and the south at its boundaries; that was his final decision.

In view of the Emperor's wishes an army corps was formed north of the Hoang Ho, and another at Teng chu on the southern border. This second army was composed of the forces of Wanien Khada and Yra buka who arrived at Teng chu in 1232 during January, and were joined by Yang wu yan, Cheng ho shang, and Wu shan, three Kin generals. While these generals were discussing whether they were to fall on Tului at the crossing of the Han, or after he had crossed it, they learned that he was on their side already. They marched immediately and discovered the enemy at the foot of Mount Yui in a chosen position. The Kin forces attacked and a sharp struggle followed. The Mongols were inferior in numbers and withdrew, but withdrew unmolested.

After some days the Kin generals were informed that the enemy had retired to a forest. They resolved to return to Teng chu, subsist on the provisions of the city, and spare their own rations. They passed by mere chance near the forest; the Mongols sallied forth and attacked, but only feigned serious fighting. Meanwhile the Kin cavalry seized the Mongol baggage.

On reaching Teng chu the Kin generals reported that they had won a great victory. Rejoicings at the court were sincere, but very short in duration.

While Tului was advancing Ogotai was besieging Ho chung, or Pu chiu, a strong city on the Hoang Ho, in Shan si near its southwestern corner. A pyramidal tower two hundred feet high, immense earth mounds, and tunnels were among the works used in attacking. Soon the towers and wooden works on the walls of the city were ruined. Besieged and besiegers had fought hand to hand fifteen days when the city was taken. Thirty-five days had the place been invested. The governor Tsao ho was captured arms in hand and put to death at direction of Ogotai. Bau tse, the commandant, escaped by the river with three thousand men, and went to Nan king, where the Kin Emperor killed him.

Ogotai received now, through a courier, an account from Tului of the Honan situation and crossed the Hoang Ho without waiting. He ordered Tului to meet him. On hearing of this movement by Ogotai, the Kin Emperor gave orders to cut dikes near the capital, flood the country about it, and thus stop the enemy. Thirty thousand men were sent to guard the great river, but when Kia ku saho, the commander, learned that Ogotai was already on the south side he retreated. In their march forward the Mongols came on the men cutting dikes, attacked them, stopped their work, and slew many thousands.

Tului divided his army into numerous detachments. With these he covered a great stretch of country, and watched the Kin army as it moved northward slowly. Harassed on their march, retarded by wind, rain, and snow, exhausted by marching and hunger, the Kin troops were met finally by a eunuch of the Emperor with an order to move to the capital speedily and succor it. They had hardly touched food for three days, and were mortally weary. While preparing to encamp, they were surrounded on a sudden by Ogotai and Tului, who had just brought their forces together.

The Kin generals charged on the Mongols and strove to cut through them. Many chiefs fell while leading their warriors. Wanien Khada forced his way to Yiu chiu. Tului laid siege to that city immediately; dug a moat round the walls, took the place, and found Wanien Khada. When captured Wanien asked to be brought before Subotai. "Thou hast but a moment to live," remarked Subotai, " why wish to see me ? " " Heaven, not chance, gives us heroes. Now that I have seen thee, I close my eyes without sorrow," replied the Kin general.

When Subotai's fury had calmed somewhat Cheng ho shang, who was also in the city, came out of his hiding and asked to be taken to the chief of the Mongols. " If I had perished in the rush of defeat," said he to Tului, " some men might declare me a traitor; now all will see how I die, and must know that I am honest." He would not submit, though the Mongols tried long to induce him to do so. To make the man kneel they chopped both his feet off, and split his mouth to the ears to force silence; but he ceased not to say in his keen ghastly torment that he would not befoul himself by treason. Struck by his fortitude and elated by kumis (their liquor distilled from mare's milk) the Mongols called out to him: " If thou art ever recalled to this life, splendid warrior, be born in our company ! "

Yra buka was seized on the road to the capital while fleeing. They took him to Ogotai: " Submit and be saved," said the Emperor. To every proposal the answer was: " I am a lord of the Kin Empire, I must be true to my sovereign." Yra buka suffered death like the others. Thus perished the Kin generals, nobly, but without any profit. The best of the army had already perished.

Some days after the capture of Yiu chiu Ogotai visited Tului at his camp ground and listened with delight to his narrative of the march from Fong tsiang, during which immense difficulties had been overcome, especially lack of food, which was such that his men had been forced to eat grass, and the flesh of human beings.

The Grand Khan applauded his brother for skill in that perilous enterprise. Tului replied, that success was due mainly to the

valor and endurance of his warriors, and the fortune attendant on
the sovereign of the Mongols.

When he heard of Tului's achievement, the Kin Emperor summoned to his capital all troops entrusted with defending Honan
on its western border; hence the two generals commanding on that
side, and the governors of Tung kwan, the great fortress, united
their forces, which amounted to one hundred and ten thousand
foot with five thousand horsemen, and moved toward Shan chiu, a
city south of the Hoang Ho. Two hundred barges were to bear
supplies eastward, but the Mongols seized those supplies before
they were laden, and when their forces appeared at Tung kwan
the man left in command there delivered that mighty defence of
Honan to them, and betrayed all the movements about to be made
by his Emperor's army.

The Mongols advanced on Shan chiu, without obstacle. The
Kins retired toward the mountains of Thie ling followed by
vast crowds of people of every age and both sexes, who had
hoped for a shelter in the mountains. As they advanced melt-
ing snow made the roads very difficult and sometimes impassable.
Pursued by the victors, their aged people and children who lagged
behind were cut down without mercy. One Kin general surrendered, but still the captors beheaded him; the others were
overtaken and slain as was also the chief Tung kwan governor.

Defence in the west of Honan collapsed utterly. Fourteen
cities fell; only two held out bravely. One of these, Ho yang, or
Ho nan fu, became famous. This place was defended by three
thousand men who remained from the western army. After a
furious bombardment, continuing some days, the Mongols made a
breach in the walls of Ho yang. The governor deemed the place
lost, and, since he would not survive the disgrace of surrender,
he sprang into the moat and thus drowned himself. The defenders
then chose Kiang chin, a real hero, to lead them. Under him a
most desperate resistance was organized. The place held out for
three months, till the Mongols, still thirty thousand in number,
grown sick and weary of attacking, left that brave city after one
hundred and fifty assaults had been made on it.

Ogotai, now master of nearly all places around the Kin capital,
fixed his camp fourteen leagues to the west of it, and sent
Subotai to finish the struggle.

Nan king (Southern capital) at that time was twelve leagues in circumference. Inside the walls a hundred thousand men were assembled to defend it. Desiring to rouse public feeling to the highest the Emperor gave out a stirring appeal to the people written by Chao wun ping, a great scholar. The siege had begun when Ogotai sent an envoy to persuade the Kin Emperor to submit himself. Ogotai asked that the following people be sent first of all to him as hostages: Chao wun ping, a sage of distinction; Kung yuan tse, a descendant of Confucius, with some other great scholars, and twenty-seven families among the most noted; all families of men who had submitted to the Mongols; the wife and children of Yra buka, the heroic Kin general; young women skilled in embroidery, and also men trained well as falconers. The Kin Emperor accepted every condition and offered Uko, his nephew, besides, as a hostage while Egudeh, his procurator, was discussing final peace with the Khan of the Mongols.

In spite of these marks of submission Subotai continued the siege with great vigor. The command had been given him, he said, to capture the capital and he was obeying it. He had planted long lines of catapults; captive women, young girls, old men, and children were carrying fascines and bundles of straw to fill moats and ditches. Fearing to stop negotiations, the Kin general commanding forbade to reply to attacks of the Mongols. This order roused indignation. The Kin Emperor showed himself in the city to the people, attended by a few horsemen only. A body of officers came to him complaining that they were not allowed to defend themselves, though the moat was already half filled by the enemy: " I am ready to be a mere tributary and a vassal to safeguard my subjects," said the Emperor. " I send my one son this day as a hostage, so be patient till he has gone from me. If the enemy does not retire there will be time then 'for a life and death struggle."

The young prince set out that same day with Li tsi, a state minister, but as the attack was continued, the Kin ruler indignant at Mongol duplicity gave the signal for action.

Subotai had set up an immense line of catapults and hurled large, jagged millstones with dreadful impetus. At the end of some days of ceaseless hurling, stones were piled up at points almost to the top of the ramparts; the towers, though built of

strong timber from old palaces, were broken. To deaden the effect
of these millstones the towers were backed with huge bags filled
with wheat-straw, and horse dung, covered with felt and tied with
cords very firmly, also planks faced with untanned hides of buf-
faloes. The Mongols hurled fire with ballistas to burn the defences.
No projectile, however, could injure those strange massive walls
of the fortress, which were mainly of clay grown as solid as iron.

The besieged made use of inflammable projectiles, that is, iron
pots filled with powder of some kind. These pots hurled out by
ballistas or let down by strong chains burst with great noise,
maiming men or destroying them a hundred feet from the place
of explosion. Attack and defence were original and vigorous.
Some of the Mongols, well shielded by raw hides of buffalo,
approached, dug holes in the walls and remained there at work
safe from all missiles. The besieged hurled spears carrying
fireworks which exploding burned everything within thirty feet
of them. These two kinds of projectiles were greatly feared
by the Mongols.

After assaults which continued sixteen days, almost without
interval, during which time it was said, though of course incorrectly,
that a million of men fell, Subotai sent a message declaring that
as discussions for peace were in progress hostilities would cease
altogether, and he prepared to withdraw to some distance.

The Emperor in answer sent rich parting presents to the Mongol general and his officers. One month after this truce a plague
broke out in the capital, and during fifty days coffins to the
number of nine hundred thousand, as the account runs, were
borne from the city; besides there were corpses of indigent
people which were put in the earth without coffins or boxes.

During discussions for peace, a Mongol envoy, Tang tsing,
with a suite of thirty persons, was slain in Pien king by the populace. This deed went unpunished and unnoted by the Chinese,
hence command was given Subotai to attack the Kin capital a
second time. Ogotai had also another complaint against the Kin
sovereign: Nin kia su had taken into his service, and even rewarded, a general of the Mongols who, not enduring his chief,
had passed to the Kin side and yielded up cities which were
under his control.

When his capital was invested a second time the Kin Emperor

summoned Wu shan, a commander who, after defeat, had
retired on Nan yang, where he had formed a new army. Two
governors were summoned in also by the Emperor, one from the
south, the other from the west. Wu shan advanced to a place
twenty leagues from the capital. He saw Mongol forces at that
point and sent to the governor who was nearest to join him, but the
governor would not come and marched on alone till he also met
Mongols. Then his troops broke and fled without fighting. On
receiving news of this flight Wu shan and his forces fell back on
Nan yang very speedily. Chiga Katrika was sent with a corps
to give aid to Wu shan, but when he learned what had happened
he left all his baggage and fled to Nan king in the night time.

These defeats destroyed in the Emperor every hope of resistance.
Want increased daily, communications were cut for the greater
part, and at last Nin kia su resolved to abandon his capital,
leaving behind the two Empresses and the whole reigning family.
Before going he intrusted command to San ya pu and gave precious
gifts both to officers and soldiers to rouse them to the utmost.

That day the Kong chang commandant marched into the capital
with his army corps, and declared that the country was ruined for
thirty leagues westward, so the Emperor went to the east, — he
could not go elsewhere. When twenty leagues from Nan king
he crossed the Hoang Ho near Tsao hien with the hope of exciting
Shan tung to assist him in saving the capital.

Barely was the Emperor on the northern bank with a part of
his army when such a wind rose that the troops on the south could
not follow. On the southern bank of the river appeared now a
Mongol division sent out by Subotai, and a fierce conflict followed
in which the Kins lost two generals; one was taken captive, the
other surrendered. One thousand men perished, drowned for the
greater part.

When he heard of his lieutenant's victory, Subotai invested the
capital with every possible severity. The Emperor now despatched
Baksan, a prince of the blood, and a descendant of Ho li pu, to
secure the city Wei chiu. Baksan let his men pillage all that they
came on while marching. This enraged the inhabitants who,
instead of assisting the Emperor, fled to Wei chiu and closed its
gates to his warriors. After some days Baksan heard of a hostile
advance and withdrew, but was followed by She tian tse, a

Mongol commander. He himself carried news of his failure to
the Emperor, whom he urged to recross the Hoang Ho, retreat to
Kwe te fu and be safe there. The Emperor crossed in the night
with seven officers, and found refuge in the place pointed out to
him. The troops heard of their Emperor's flight the day following,
and scattered immediately.

The people of Pien king lost courage greatly, but still they
resisted. The Mongols closed in on them; food soon rose to
fabulous prices, people perished of hunger, officials of the Empire
begged on the streets; there were even men who ate their own wives
and children. Houses were torn down for fuel. The Emperor
sent an official to conduct out his consort and the dowager Empress in secret, but he failed in the effort. This attempt roused
the populace: " He has left us to our fate," said they, in despair.

At this evil juncture Tsui li, who commanded the eastern side
of the capital, made himself master of the city in all parts. He
had the governor of the palace, the minister of state and ten other
high dignitaries killed in his presence. Immediately afterward
he proclaimed them as worthy of death for their failure in duty.
He entered the palace with armed hand, held a council and proclaimed Prince Wa nien tsung ko as regent. He sent men in the
name of the Emperor's mother to bring that prince to the city.
He came without delay and was now regent. Tsui li made himself
first minister, chief commander and head of the Imperial Council.
One of his brothers was made city governor, and another one prefect of the palace. All his dependents had places. He judged now
that he needed the Mongols to protect him in office, and he sent
his submission to Subotai. That commander approached the
main gate of the city. Tsui li, arrayed in royal fashion, went out
with a brilliant attendance to the Mongol, as he might to a father.
On returning Tsui li, to prove his submission to Subotai, burned
the outlooks and the wooden towers on the walls of the city. A
little later he had the regent, the Empresses, and all members of
the reigning family assemble in a palace which was guarded by
his confidants. He went himself then to live in the Emperor's
palace. He sent jewels and other precious objects to Subotai
from the treasury; he sent even the state robes of the Emperor
and Empress as gifts to the Mongol commander.

Tsui li summoned now to his palace the daughters and wives

of all those great lords who had gone with the Emperor, and detained those of them who pleased him. Next came an edict compelling the people to bring their silver and gold to the palace. After this came domiciliary visits, and many men perished under torture while striving to save even some of their wealth from Tsui li's endless rapacity. During a visit made by this man and his wife to the Empresses, who recompensed him for services alleged but never rendered, the two helpless women gave Tsui li the most precious effects in their possession. He brought the dowager to write to her son, the Emperor, urging him to submit to the Mongols. This letter was taken to Nin kia su by his nurse, an old woman. Tsui li now seized the two Empresses, the regent, all members of the reigning family, male and female, to the number of five hundred, and sent them to Subotai's camp ground in chariots; he sent Kung yuan tse, a very wise person, a descendant of Confucius; he sent men learned in law and philosophy, and in the Taoist religion; he sent also physicians, artists, actors and embroiderers.

All men of the reigning family were put to death straightway by Subotai. The two Empresses and the princesses were sent to Mongolia; while traveling to Kara Kurum they suffered want and privations of every kind.

Foreseeing the fall of the capital Subotai made a statement to Ogotai, the Grand Khan, substantially as follows: " The city has made such resistance, so many warriors and officers of the Mongols have fallen, that, by the law of Jinghis, we should pillage it." Ye liu chu tsai hurried to the Khan and explained that those people would be his subjects, that among them were many men of great skill and value, that by killing them he would ruin the profit of his conquest. Ogotai hearkened to the wise counsel of Ye liu, and ordered that none should suffer death except members of the Kin family. Thus the kind minister saved many people. He also had the law canceled which ordained death to inhabitants of cities taken by storm, or by siege operations.

And now let us find the Kin sovereign. Soon after his arrival at Kwe te fu the fleeing Emperor, to satisfy his troops, who declared that Baksan had caused the defeats in Shan tung, had the man tried by a council of war and then executed.

Fucha kuan nu, a certain general, seized control of Kwe te fu after killing Li tsi with three hundred mandarins, and also the governor. Kuan nu's mother had been captured after Baksan's defeat. Temutai, a Mongol commander, was besieging a town twenty leagues south of Kwe te fu; the Emperor charged Kuan nu to insinuate to Temutai that if his (Kuan nu's) mother were restored he would bring the Emperor to accept peace conditions. Temutai sent back the woman, and began to negotiate. Kwan nu and Temutai had held many meetings. Meanwhile Kwan nu prepared a secret attack, and surprised the Mongol camp during night hours; arrows with fireworks increased the confusion. Temutai's forces fled, and he lost more than three thousand men in crossing a river. Kwan nu, made chief commander because of this victory, now obtained complete control, and left not a trace of authority to the Emperor.

At this juncture Uku lun hao, governor of districts in Southern Honan, proposed that the Emperor make Tsai chiu his capital. Nin kia su was quite willing, but Kuan nu would not hear of a change which would cost him control of the Emperor's person. There was no outcome now for the Emperor but to be rid of the minister, so one day Kuan nu was killed while entering his sovereign's chamber. The falling monarch had still one hope left in connection with Tsai chiu: Wu shan, a general in the south of Honan, had a force seventy thousand in number. Ogotai the year previous had made a treaty with Li tsong, the Sung Emperor, and the latter, thinking it time to destroy the ancient foe of his dynasty, had agreed to send troops to Honan on condition that after the fall of the Kins that whole region be restored to his Empire. Meng kong, who led the Sung army, now attacked and defeated Wu shan in the Ma teng group of mountains. He captured, moreover, nine forts which that general had held there, receiving besides the surrender of all that was left of his army.

The Kin Emperor had set out for Tsai chiu before this disaster. His escort was nearly three hundred men; of these only fifty were mounted. On arriving he placed at the head of affairs Hu sha hu, a member of his family, a general of skill and a statesman. This minister made every possible effort to form a new army; soon he had ten thousand mounted men, as the nucleus of his forces. It was his plan to convey the Emperor to Kong chang, a safe place in Shen si, and act then with vigor, but the sovereign's intimates

were opposed to this journey, and prevailed on him to stay in
Tsai chiu to the ruin of himself, and his dynasty.

The apparent remoteness of the Mongols gave confidence for
the moment, but the Mongols soon made their appearance. Small
parties came from the army of Tatchar, who was only waiting for
the capture of Lo yang to surround the Kin sovereign's last refuge.
Lo yang had sustained a long siege, and had forced the Mongols
to raise it. Tsi yang shen, who had rendered great service in
regions north of the river, was still in command. His forces, however, were few, and long resistance was this time impossible;
hence he put himself now at the head of a chosen party and
strove to break through the enemy, but was seized arms in hand
fighting valiantly. Tatchar tried to win over so splendid a warrior,
and implored him most earnestly to show homage to Ogotai, to
prostrate himself with face looking northward, but he bowed
toward the south, saluting in this way Nin kia su, his own Emperor, and suffered death for his action.

Tatchar was the son of Boroul, one of Jinghis Khan's four
great heroes, and now being free he moved on Tsai chiu to end the
Kin dynasty. His army was reinforced by twenty thousand good
warriors under Meng kong and Kiang hai, whom the Sung Emperor had sent because of his alliance with Ogotai. The two
commanders brought with them three hundred thousand sacks of
rice for the Mongols. After two months' blockade provisions
were so scarce in the city that human flesh was used as food and
disease ravaged terribly. The defenders armed every man who
could labor. All young women who had strength enough dressed
in men's clothes, and carried fagots and stones to defend the last
refuge of the Emperor. After many attacks the Sung forces and
the Mongols made a fierce assault, and seized a small part of the
bulwarks. To their astonishment they found a new wall in the
rear of the first one, and a broad moat between them.

Nin kia su, when he saw hostile flags on the outer wall, lost
courage, and said as he turned to the friends who were near him,
" I have ruled for ten years and shown no great crimes or failings,
still the fate of wicked princes is ready to strike me. Death has
no terror for me, but to be the last sovereign of a line which
has flourished for more than a century, and to think that
history may confound me with rulers who have ruined their

dynasties by wickedness, — this is the one thing which tortures me. Sovereigns who survive loss of power are kept in confinement, or despised by men generally; I would not survive to be treated in either way. Heaven knows my decision."

Nin kia su, however, made one more attempt to save himself. He gave all his goods to men of the garrison, took a few followers, and sallied forth in disguise during night hours, but he could not elude the keen watch of the enemy, and was forced to return to the city. He yielded to fate then and had his horses all killed to be food for the garrison. On the day of the new year the besieged heard songs and sounds of music; the Mongols were celebrating their festival. In distress and dire need the besieged had boiled and eaten all the hides and leather in the city, also old drums, boots and saddles, and they had left to them a meal of grass and weeds with the pounded bones of dead men and animals — they had eaten already the old and decrepit inhabitants, the captives and the wounded, and now they would eat the crushed bones of those people when the flesh was all stripped from them.

Meng kong, the Sung general, informed by deserters of this terrible hunger, resolved to surprise the failing city. His men with their mouths gagged moved to the storm in safe silence. With ladders they entered through five breaches made in the western walls of the city, and fought with desperation till sunset when they were forced out decisively, but the besieged had lost their first chiefs and best warriors. During the night Nin kia su yielded the throne to Ching lin, brother of Baksan who was put to death for the Shan tung disaster. This prince, descended directly from the Emperor Ho li pu, was charged with defending the Eastern side of the city. Ching lin had no wish to accept the sad gift, and fell prostrate with weeping. " I give thee the throne during terrible need and disaster," said the Emperor. " The size of my body prevents me from fleeing on horseback, but thou mayest save thyself, thou art courageous and swift; thou mayst rescue the dynasty and bring back dominion; this is the real position."

Ching lin took the seal, and was raised to the throne on the morrow. But even while this ceremony was in progress the western gate was broken down and Meng kong rushed into the city. Kiang hai and Tatchar rushed in with him. Hu sha hu fought in the streets at the head of a chosen thousand of warriors.

Nin kia su, seeing no escape possible on any side, announced to his intimates that he was ready to die and charged them to burn his dead body. After that he hanged himself.

Hu sha hu now told his officers that further resistance was useless, and, lest some ignoble hand might take life from him, he sprang into the river and drowned himself. Five officers with five hundred men followed his example, and died in that river. The palace officials burned the Emperor's body immediately. Ching lin, when he learned what had happened, hurried to pay the last tribute to the body; he had barely finished all needful libations when the city was taken.

Meng kong shared with Tatchar everything belonging to the Emperor, besides all the jewels which they could find in the palace. Ching lin was slain that same day by his own warriors. In this way the Kins were deprived of dominion in China May, 1234. Their dynasty of nine sovereigns reigned one century and eighteen years. Excepting Kong chang fu all places which belonged to that dynasty surrendered. The Sung Emperor rejoiced much and gave many festivals while thus rejoicing at the fall of an enemy. He offered the ashes and bones of the last of the Kins to his ancestors. Foolish man, he had given aid to a much greater and more terrible enemy than the one who had vanished, and had assured the near destruction of his own house and dynasty.

Ogotai, the Grand Khan, and Tului, his brother, returned to Kara Kurum two years before the Kin downfall. After Ogotai had crossed the Hoang Ho, and Tului had passed through Honan, the completion of the work was left to the competent Subotai. Tului died in October, 1232, soon after his return to Mongolia. He was forty years of age. Juveïni states that his life was shortened by excessive drinking. He was the favorite son of Jinghis under whom he had learned war in all its phases and details. His campaign in Honan was admired with much reason. When still a boy his father had him married to Siur Kukteni, a niece of Wang Khan, and daughter of Jagambu his brother, a woman noted for wisdom. From this princess Tului had four sons: Mangu, Kubilai, Hulagu and Arik Buga.

CHAPTER XVI

IN 1234 a great Kurultai was summoned by Ogotai at Talantepe, and one at Kara Kurum, his new capital, the year following. At the second Kurultai it was decided to make three great expeditions: One against the Sung Empire; another to bring down Corea, which had shaken off Mongol rule; a third to countries north of the Caspian, the Caucasus and the Black Sea, and westward indefinitely. The Grand Khan wished to march himself with this last expedition, but at the instance of princes of his family he yielded, and appointed Batu, second son of Juchi, to chief command in those regions.

An army under Hukatu was sent to the borders of Cashmir and India. Persia had been reconquered by Chormagun. Jelal ud din had perished in 1231, there was no male descendant of the Kwaresmian Shah, and Iran was governed by Mongol officials.

The attack on Corea was of easy execution, but the expedition against China was difficult, and to it we will turn in advance of the others.

After the destruction of the Kin dynasty the Mongols disregarded their agreement with the Sung sovereign and yielded up merely a small part of Honan, a southeastern bit of that province, joining all the rest to their own immense Empire. Chao fan and Chao kwe, two Imperial princes, were indignant at this perfidy, and explained to their Emperor, that the Hoang Ho was the true northern boundary of the Empire, to which southern Shen si should be added; they urged the need of using force to win that which had been refused them, that which was theirs, both by right and agreement. They must regain their ancient capitals: Pien king, Lo yang, and Si ngan fu. Members of the council declared that this policy would bring back the Mongols, that it would be disastrous to send warriors from afar to hold ruined cities which they would have to provision, moreover the Empire lacked money, trained troops, and good generals. The Emperor Li tsong was deaf to these arguments, and gave command promptly to march on Pien king with a corps of ten thousand.

Meanwhile Tsui li, who had given Pien king to the Mongols, was made master in that capital. The three chiefs, who served under him, were so incensed at his arrogance, that they swore to destroy the vile traitor. The moment these men heard that a Sung general was advancing with an army they declared to him their submission by letter, feigning meanwhile to work in accord with Tsui li the deceiver and tyrant. To carry out their plot better Li po yuan, one of the three, had fire set to a gate of the city, Tsui li hurried to the place and when he arrived there Li po yuan, who had gone with him, plunged a dagger blade into his body so deftly that Tsui li fell from his horse and died near the feet of the animal. Soldiers posted at the gate for the purpose attacked the attendants of the dead man and finished them promptly.

Tsui li's body was tied to the tail of a horse and dragged to the palace, where Li po yuan spoke to the people in these words: " Tsui li was a murderer, a robber, a tyrant, a debauchee, and an infamous traitor. No man so evil as he has lived in old times, or in our day. Did he merit death ? " " To chop such a man into bits while alive would be very small punishment ! " shouted out thousands. His head was exposed to the people and his body was made a burnt offereng to the spirit of Nin kia su, the late Emperor. Tsuan tse tsai, the Sung general, occupied Pien king, and his force was strengthened soon by another of fifty thousand. From these two armies reinforcements were sent to Lo yang without waiting.

On hearing that Li tsong had invaded Honan Ogotai began action immediately. His troops surprised, near Lo yang, a second Sung corps fifteen thousand in number, which marching from Pien king to Lo yang had pitched its camp at the Ho on the bank of that river. The Mongols scattered this corps and camped near the walls of the city. The Chinese issued forth and engaged them. Neither side won, but the Sung troops were forced to abandon Lo yang through a dearth of provisions. Through lack of food also the Sung generals left Pien king and turned southward. The cities of Northern Honan were nearly deserted, and all of them suffered from hunger.

Ogotai recalled Subotai, whom he destined for Europe, and sent to the Sung court an envoy to reproach it with oath breaking. Li tsong sent his envoy to Kara Kurum to allay the coming tempest, but the journey was useless, war had been fixed at the Kurultai. Three army corps were now to attack the Sung Empire, one under command of Prince Kutan, Ogotai's second son, aided by Tagai, a general who was to invade Su chuan, that great western province; a second, under Prince Kutchu, the third son of Ogotai, while the generals Temutai and Chauju were to march on Hu kuang and subject it. In Kiang nan a third army was to act under Chagan and Prince Khon Buga.

Kutan marched through Shen si and, while passing Chung changan, received from the governor the submission of that city, the only one in all the Kin Empire which had not yielded to the Mongols. Kutan left the governor in office, but commanded him to march with his warriors who were placed in the vanguard. Kutan passed through Han chong southwestward, took Mian chiu, whose commandant Gao kia was killed during battle. Chao yan na, the governor of Han chung, hastened to occupy Tsing yen, the key of Su chuan, and was besieged there by Mongols, but Tsao yuan, the commandant of Lu chiu, hurried forward to help him, and drove the Mongol chief northward. Next Tsao threw himself on Ta an, besieged by Wang shi hien, saved that city, at least for a season, and retired, after defeating a large Mongol force in the neighborhood.

These successes were gained over Kutan's advance guard. When his main forces appeared the Chinese, who were greatly inferior in numbers, met them between Su chuan and Shen si, in wild mountain defiles, but had to flee near Yang ping and cease their resistance. After this victory the Mongols entered Su chuan without serious effort. In one month they took many cities, seized the best parts of the province, and massacred multitudes of people. The governor of Wen chau, unable to defend the place, poisoned his family, cremated their bodies, burned up what belonged to the treasury, burned his own property, his diploma of office, and then stabbed himself as the Mongols were bursting into the city. His lieutenant was chopped into bits by the victors, who put to the sword every soul that remained, both of troops and inhabitants.

When he had ruined Su chuan in the west Prince Kutan went back to Shen si, and the Chinese returned to their ruins. In 1237 Ching tu was reoccupied by the Chinese, but in 1239 Tagai, Kutan's assistant, reëntered Su chuan, captured many places, took Ching tu and sacked it a second time. He wished now to enter Hu kuang, the next province, by Kwei chiu, a city on the north bank of the river Yang tse, but Meng kong, the Sung general, had put western Hu kuang into such a good state of defence, that this plan was a failure; he even took Kwei chiu from the Mongols.

Meanwhile Prince Kutchu, whose chief camp was at Teng chu in Honan, entered Hu kuang in 1236. To him the commandants of Siang yang fu surrendered the city with immense stores in it. Kutchu took Tsao yang, he took also Li ngan, but died shortly after.

Prince Kutchu was beloved greatly by Ogotai, and to him he had destined the Empire.

Temutai laid siege now to King chiu, but Meng kong, who was sent by the governor of the province, defeated him at the walls of the city and freed twenty thousand Chinese who were captives.

At the end of 1237 Khon Buga, the Mongol prince, captured three cities abandoned by their commandants, and advanced to Hoang chiu on the river Yang tse and besieged the place, but was forced later on to withdraw from it. He laid siege to another large city the year following but failed to take it.

In 1238 the Mongol general, Chagan, invested Liu chiu, a city of Kiang nan; a sudden and vigorous sortie forced his withdrawal, and he lost some part of his force while retreating. In 1239 Meng kong gained three victories over the Mongols and captured four cities. In February, 1240, Wang tsie, the Mongol envoy, appeared at the Sung court for the fifth time, with offers of peace which were rejected. Wang tsie died before his mission was ended, and the Sung governor delivered his body to the Mongols. In the beginning of 1240 also a number of Mongol army corps marched by various roads into China. No further mention, however, of fighting is made till after Ogotai's death the year following.

While Mongol armies were attacking Corea, ravaging China,

devastating Russia, Hungary, and Poland, and spreading dismay throughout Western Europe, Ogotai was passing his time in delights, enjoying the chase, and his own taste for drinking. At Kara Kurum, where he had built a magnificent palace called the Ordu Balik and by thirty-seven relays of posts connected the city with China, he passed only one month of the springtime, the rest of that season he lived a day's journey from the capital, in a palace called Kertchagan built by Persians, who strove to outdo or to rival those architects from China who at Kara Kurum had shown what their skill was. From Kertchagan he went back to Kara Kurum for some days and then passed the summer at Ormektua where he held court in a white Chinese tent, lined with silk embroidered with gold very deftly. In this tent, known as the Sarai Ordu, or Golden Horde, there was room for one thousand persons. The Grand Khan spent forty days at Lake Kosa. From there he went to Ongki near the Great Gobi desert where he lived all the winter; that was the time of grand hunting and field sports. In this region Ogotai had an enormous corral, or inclosure of earth and stakes called chehik. It was six miles in circuit, and had many doors to it. Troops stationed at long distances on all sides had orders to advance on this central inclosure and urge forward beasts, driving them through the doors into this immense roofless prison. Game was killed first by the Grand Khan and then by his family, permission going down by degrees till common men had their chance finally.

Ogotai drank to excess, for which Jinghis had reprimanded him frequently. Jagatai, to whom he deferred very notably, charged an official to see that he drank only a given number of cups each evening. Ogotai dared not disobey his elder brother, but he eluded the order by using larger cups, and the officer was silent.

One day Ye liu chu tsai brought in an iron ring greatly rusted by wine. " If wine acts on iron in this way, how must it injure the stomach ? " said Chu tsai. This example struck Ogotai greatly, but he could not shake off the habit. One day in March, 1241, he fell ill after hunting. Turakina, his wife, alarmed very seriously, turned to Chu tsai hoping that he might bring Heaven to restore the Grand Khan to her. Chu tsai counseled just deeds and benevolence. " Power has been given by the Khan," said he, " to men who sell places, and traffic in justice. Innocent people are groaning in prison because they have revolted against the wrongs done them. Let an amnesty be issued." Turakina wished to have the amnesty published immediately, but the minister told her that this could be done only at Ogotai's order.

When the Khan came again to his senses all men imprisoned, or exiled, were pardoned. He regained his health that time, but a new attack came some months later. Against Chu tsai's advice he had hunted five days in succession. On the way from the field he sat drinking till midnight. The sixth morning his body was lifeless. This Grand Khan had reigned nearly thirteen years, and was fifty-six years of age at his death hour, December 11, 1241. He was mild for a Mongol of that time, fond of luxury and generous in gift giving. He was tolerant of the various religions, and in general very amiable considering his position. He was fond of hunting and wrestling, often sending to Persia for renowned wrestlers. He was a statesman as well as conqueror, and framed laws which held the Mongol Empire together for a long period.

After Ogotai's death all the roads to his residence were guarded immediately, so that no man might leave the place and couriers were sent off in every direction to stop travelers wherever they might find them, till the members of the Grand Khan's family had officially received the tidings of his death.

Ogotai had appointed Kutchu, his third son, to be his successor, but this young prince died in Hu kuang five years earlier, 1236. Shiramun, son of Kutchu, had been at the court, and Ogotai destined him also to Empire. But Turakina, a self-willed and determined woman, wished Kuyuk, her own eldest son, to be chief of all Mongols. Kuyuk, born in 1206, had served against the Kin Empire; later he had gone to the west with Batu. Ogotai had ordered him back very recently, and he was on the way home when he heard of the death of his father.

Princes of the blood and chiefs of the army received invitations from Ogotai's widow to assemble for the Kurultai; meanwhile at the instance of Jagatai and others the regency was given to Turakina. The regency began by ejecting Ching kai the grand chancellor, an Uigur. A Mohammedan, Abd ur Rahman, who had come some time earlier to Mongolia with merchandise, had won the good-will of Turakina completely; a short time before Ogotai's death he had offered to farm all the revenues of China. Chu tsai had fixed the income of parts lying north of the Hoang Ho at five hundred thousand ounces of silver. After Honan had been conquered the receipts rose to one million one hundred thousand. Abd ur Rahman offered two million two hundred thousand; Chu tsai replied that five millions might be collected, but that sum, he said, would be grievous to tax payers. Turakina, putting aside the advice of Chu tsai, now gave Abd ur Rahman control of the finances of the Empire. It is stated that Chu tsai, foreseeing the destruction of all that he had labored for, grew despondent and died of grief. In any case this remarkable man died June, 1244, at the age of fifty-five years. By his influence over Ogotai he had saved many lives. He had also founded two colleges, one at Yan King, the other at Pin Yan in Shan si, and published a work on astronomy.

Soon after Ogotai's death Temugu, his uncle, who was Jinghis Khan's youngest brother, approached the Khan's residence with his army, and made a faint move toward a seizure of the Empire. Turakina sent to ask why he came to " his daughter " so numerously attended, and sent him his son, who had been living at Ogotai's residence. On hearing that Kuyuk had arrived from the west and had reached the Imil where his yurta was established Temugu dropped his plan, and replied that he wished to condole with his daughter on the loss of her husband; after that he withdrew to his own place.

The assembly to elect a new sovereign was to be at Talantepe, but did not meet till 1246, because of Batu's endless loitering. Batu liked neither Kuyuk, nor the regent, his mother, and feigned to have a sore leg which prevented his traveling. As he was the eldest prince of the family the other members were loath to elect a new sovereign in his absence.

At the prayer of the regent Batu at last gave his word to be present at the Kurultai, but he came not, so the Kurultai was assembled without him, and Kuyuk was elected.

Turakina died two months after Kuyuk was made Grand Khan thereupon the many enemies of Fatima, a Persian woman, the adviser and intimate of Turakina, conspired to destroy her. She was accused by a Samarkand Moslem, named Shira, of having brought on Prince Kutan, Kuyuk's brother, the disease from which he was suffering at that time. Kutan sent an officer to Kuyuk to complain of Fatima, and demand that she be punished should his illness prove fatal. Kutan died, hence Kuyuk commanded the trial of Fatima. She was bastinadoed and tortured till she declared herself guilty. Every opening of her body save her nose was sewed up and closed tightly; after suffering dreadful anguish for a time she was wrapped in felt blankets firmly and thrown into a river; her friends were put to death also. The turn came soon to Shira himself who, accused of bewitching a son of Kuyuk, was put to death with his wife and whole family.

Kuyuk, suffering from gout, the result of drink and dissipation, set out in 1248, during spring, for his own domains to find a more favoring climate. Siur Kukteni, Tului's widow, fearing lest Kuyuk might be hostile to her nephew Batu, who had not come to do homage, warned the latter to be on his guard at all seasons. There was no reason, however, for this caution, since Kuyuk died on the road, being seven days' journey from Bish Balik, the Uigur capital.

After Kuyuk's death, which took place in his forty-third year, the usual precautions were taken to keep back the news till the principal chiefs of the family were informed of it. All ways were stopped and information was sent to Siur Kukteni, and to Batu.

Batu had set out at last from the banks of the Volga to give the new sovereign due homage, and had come to Alaktak when news of Kuyuk's sudden death reached him. He halted at once under pretext of resting his horses and, observing the national usage, gave his consent to the regency to Ogul Gaimish, who held the first place among Kuyuk's consorts. She was the daughter of Kutuk, chief of the Uirats. Meanwhile Batu called a Kurultai at Alaktak. The descendants of Ogotai refused to attend, since the Kurultai should be held, as they said, in the land of the Mongols. They sent, however, Timur Noyon, governor of Kara Kurum, with full powers to act for them, and to confirm the decisions of Batu, and the majority of princes.

At this Kurultai, composed mainly of Juchi's descendants and those of Tului, that is descendants of Jinghis Khan's youngest and eldest sons, Ilchi Kidai of the Jelairs declared that they had engaged to choose no man as sovereign unless a descendant of Ogotai so long as that branch remained living. "Yes," answered Kubilai, son of Tului, "but ye were the first to infringe Jinghis Khan's laws, and disregard Ogotai's will. Ye put Altalun, Jinghis' daughter, to death without reference to Jinghis Khan's statute that no descendant of his may suffer death until judged by an assembly of his or her equals. Ye put Kuyuk on the throne in defiance of Ogotai, who had appointed Shiramun to succeed him."

These two complaints were brought up by those who had determined to take the throne from descendants of Ogotai. Batu, who was also their enemy, had agreed with Siur Kukteni, to elect her eldest son, Mangu. This widow of Tului had an all powerful support in the army. The arrangements by which Jinghis had given the greater part of his troops to Tului assured preponderance to this branch. When the throne held an Emperor the combined army was under the sovereign, but in time of interregnum each part of it recognized the authority of that prince to whom it belonged, and who was its only commander. After the death of Tului his army of one hundred and one thousand out of a total of one hundred and thirty passed to his four sons by his chief wife Siur Kukteni: Mangu, Kubilai, Arik Buga and Hulagu. During the minority of these princes their mother, sure of the commander whom she had bound to her, governed with rare judgment the numerous tribes which were subject to her children. Honored by Batu and many other princes it was easy for her to place one of her sons on the throne, since the candidates among Ogotai's descendants were too young in years yet to be personally considered.

Mangusar, a general, was the first in the assembly to propose Prince Mangu, whose courage and wit he extolled, giving instance of his brilliant career, under Kuyuk, in China, and in western lands under Batu.

But princes offered the throne first of all to Batu, as the eldest of his family. When he refused they begged him to point out a candidate and promised in writing to choose him. Batu refused to do this, but, changing his mind in the night, he deferred the next day to their wishes, and said in the meeting, that to govern the Empire a prince of ability was needed, and one who knew Jinghis Khan's yassa in all points. In view of this he proposed to them Mangu as his candidate.

This prince refused the great honor, and resisted the prayers of the Kurultai for many days in succession, till his brother rose, and said: " We have all promised to follow Prince Batu's decision.

If it be permitted Mangu to break his word now, other princes may follow his example in future." Batu applauded these words, and Mangu ceased resistance. The moment he accepted, the whole assembly saluted him. A new Kurultai was appointed for the following spring to be held in Jinghis Khan's home land near the sources of the Onón and the Kerulon when Mangu was to be recognized by all princes, and by the chiefs of the army.

Ogul Gaimish, Kuyuk's widow, was to be regent in the meanwhile assisted by her two sons: Khodja and Nagu. The only, or at least the main care of this regency was to dispose of tribute by giving orders in advance on the provinces. Ogul Gaimish was given greatly to sorcery and spent much of her time with magicians. The Mongol Empire was thus left to many evil influences.

Khodja and Nagu disavowed the agents who in their names had voted for Mangu. They informed Batu, that they could not hold to decisions of a Kurultai assembled far from the land of Jinghis, and moreover imperfect. Batu enjoined on them to visit the coming Kurultai, and added that the princes had chosen the man whom they held the best fitted to govern the Empire, and that their choice was now made and irrevocable.

The rest of the year passed in fruitless discussions between Mangu's partisans, who strove to bring the malcontents to their way of thinking, and the competitors of Mangu who protested against the election. Batu sent his two brothers, Berkai and Togha Timur, with a strong corps of troops to escort the new Grand Khan to the Kurultai, and seat him on Jinghis Khan's throne. The descendants of Ogotai, and the son and successor of Jagatai refused to appear there, declaring that the election of Mangu was illegal, and that the throne belonged by right to a descendant of Ogotai. Agents sent time after time by Batu and Siur Kukteni implored them not to rend the Empire through factiousness. Batu informed them that children were incompetent to manage Jinghis Khan's great possessions.

The princes persisted, however, in refusing. Berkai, after waiting a year, asked for orders from Batu, who commanded to install Mangu without further discussion, declaring that those who made trouble would pay with their lives for so doing. The princes descended from Juchi and Tului, with the nephews of Jinghis, met at Koitun Ola, the place designated, and made a last effort to bring the heads of the houses of Ogotai and Jagatai to share in the meeting. An officer sent to Ogul Gaimish, and another to Yissu, son of Jagatai, announced that the other princes had assembled, and were waiting. Khodja and Nagu, seeing that opposition was fruitless, gave a promise to come, and fixed the date of arrival. The term passed, but they came not. An order was given to astrologers to name the day and the hour for installation. The installation took place July, 1251, with the ceremonies which were usual and proper. When the princes inside the Imperial pavilion put their girdles on their shoulders and prostrated themselves nine times before Mangu, their example was followed by ten thousand warriors ranged round the tent on the outside.

The Grand Khan commanded that no man should work on that day, that all should forget every quarrel and yield themselves up to rejoicing. He wished to make Nature participate in the festival, and enjoined that no man was to sit on a horse, or put a burden on anything living. No person was to kill an animal, hunt, fish, wound the earth by digging, or otherwise, or trouble the calm of the waters, or their purity.

On the morrow a rich feast was given by Mangu in a tent of rare stuffs and great splendor. At his right sat the princes descended from Jinghis, at his left the princesses. A similar feast was given each day for seven days in succession. Each day every guest wore a dress of new color; each day three hundred horses and bullocks with five thousand sheep were eaten, while two thousand cart loads of wine and kumis were drunk to drive away thirst and console the great company.

In the midst of this feasting and pleasure a man, known as Kishk, made his way to the Grand Khan's pavilion with the statement that he had discovered a plot against Mangu and the princes assembled. He declared that while looking for a mule which had strayed from him he fell in with a body of men going forward with carts, which at first he had thought to be filled with supplies for the Kurultai. He came on a lad and walked for a time with him. The lad mistook Kishk for one of the party, and asked the mule owner to help him in fixing his cart which was injured. Kishk turned to assist; and seeing the cart filled with arms asked the lad why he was taking them. " I have the same as the others," replied he. Kishk was astonished at this, and after some cautious inquiries discovered that the princes Shiramun, Nagu and Khodja were going to the Kurultai to make use of the moment when all would be drunk to finish Mangu and his followers. Kishk declared that through eagerness to tell what he knew at the earliest he had made in one day three days' journey.

The story was received with astonishment at first, and seemed altogether unreal. Kishk was asked to repeat it, so he told all the details again and in such fashion this time that every doubt vanished. Each prince wished to go himself and look into the matter. It was decided to send Mangusar, the chief general, and the first person who in the Kurultai proposed that Mangu should be raised to the throne; with him went two or three thousand men. The princes were not more than two days from the Ordu.

Mangusar reached their camp very early in the morning and, having surrounded it, approached the tent of the princes with one hundred horsemen. He called to them that it had been reported to Mangu that they were coming with evil intentions. If that were false they could clear themselves quickly by going to the Ordu at once. If they would not go, he had orders to take them. The princes came out of their tent, and, seeing that their camp was surrounded, said that they were on the way to give homage to Mangu, and were about to continue their journey. They were forced, however, to follow Mangusar, and were permitted to take only twenty men with them as an escort.

Arriving at the Ordu they offered their presents by nines according to Mongol custom. The first two days they took part in the festival unquestioned, but on the third day the three princes were arrested when ready to enter the Grand Khan's pavilion. Next day Mangu himself questioned them. He began by saying that, though the charges might seem improbable, he was bound to convince himself and thus destroy all suspicions against them, and punish their accusers.

The princes denied the whole story with firmness. Mangu questioned Shiramun's governor, who was forced by the bastinado to avow the conspiracy, but it was made, he declared, by him and his officers without knowledge of the princes; after these words he drew his own sabre and killed himself. A commission of generals under Mangusar was formed to report on the confessions of

the officers of the three princes from whom the avowal of a plot
was at last forced.

Mangu wished to pardon these officers, but his generals and
relatives declared that he should not let slip that chance to be rid
of his enemies. Yielding to this advice he had the officers put in
irons; still he wavered and again asked advice of his chief men.
They advised him one after another, but even then he continued
irresolute. At last seeing Mahmud Yelvadje, the one man who
till then had kept silence, he summoned him and asked why he
said nothing. Yelvadje cited Alexander, who sent a confidant
to ask Aristotle how to treat a detected conspiracy. Aristotle
took the man to a garden; while they were walking he ordered to
pull up some well rooted trees and plant feeble saplings instead of
them. No other answer was given. The man went back and told
Alexander, who understood; he had all the conspirators slain,
and sent their young sons to replace them.

Mangu, struck by the story, put to death seventy officers. Among
them were two sons of Ilchi Kidai then in Persia. Stones were
forced into the mouths of these sons who were stifled in that way;
the father was arrested in Khorassan and conveyed to Batu who
took life from him. The three princes were pardoned through the
intercession of Mangu's mother.

In February, 1252, Mangu lost his mother, Siur Kukteni. She
was a niece of Wang Khan and a Christian; they buried her next
to her husband, Tului. In August, 1252, Mangu went to Kara
Kurum to judge hostile princes and princesses. With Ogul
Gaimish, he was especially angry, since she, when summoned to
render him homage, had answered that Mangu and the other
princes had sworn not to choose a Grand Khan unless from among
the descendants of Ogotai. Both hands and arms of Ogul Gaimish were sewed up in a leather bag, and she with Shiramun's
mother was taken to the residence of Siur Kukteni. Mangusar
stripped her there of all clothing and then proceeded to interrogate.
She reproached him indignantly with exposing her body, which
had never been seen by any man save a sovereign. Both women
were declared guilty of trying to kill Mangu by magic. They
were rolled up in felt rugs and drowned immediately. The sons
of these two women confessed that their mothers had incited them
not to recognize Mangu. Kadak and Chinkai, the chief counsel-

lors of Ogul Gaimish, were put to death also. Buri, the grandson of Jagatai, was delivered to Batu, who had him killed in revenge for words used when in liquor.

The three princes were spared by Mangu in view of their kinship: Khodja was sent to Suligai, east of Kara Kurum; Nagu and Shiramun were ordered to the army. When Kubilai was going, some time later, to China, Mangu as a favor let him take Shiramun on that journey, but when Mangu himself went to China he had Shiramun drowned, through mistrust of this young man, who had been destined to the throne by his grandfather. The greater part of Ogotai's descendants were sent to various places and deprived of the troops which were theirs by inheritance. Mangu gave those troops to other princes devoted to his person. He spared only Kadan Melik and the sons of Prince Kutan, who had come with good grace to give homage. He not only left them their troops, but gave each man one of Ogotai's ordus, and one of his widows.

Not content with punishing the highest, Mangu wished to strike down throughout the empire all who had signified attachment to Ogotai. He had the power to act thus, for his armies formed one immense chain from Eastern Mongolia to Otrar. Belu, a judge, was despatched to discover offenders, and punish them with death, in the countries of Jagatai, while a second inquisitor was sent to the armies in China. Two corps were sent at the same time to the Kirghis and the Kemjuts.

Strong now on his throne through destruction of enemies, Mangu dismissed all the princes and generals who had come to the Kurultai. Berkai and Togha Timur received splendid gifts for themselves, and for Batu, their brother. Kara Hulagu received the inheritance of Jagatai, his grandfather, and was charged to put to death Yissu, his uncle, placed on the throne by Kuyuk, the late sovereign. Kara Hulagu died on the way to his possessions, but Organa, his widow, carried out the sentence on Yissu, and took the inheritance.

Mangu, to reward the mule driver Kishk, made him a Terkhan, and gave him much treasure.

The fate of the Uigur sovereign shows how Mongol Khans treated their vassals. We remember Bardjuk, the Idikut, very well in connection with Jinghis, whom he followed most faithfully. As recompense Jinghis gave the Idikut his daughter Altun Bighi in marriage. This marriage was deferred by the death of the conqueror. Ogotai wished to carry out the desire of his father, but before he could do so Altun Bighi herself died, and Bardjuk died soon after. Bardjuk's son Kishmain went to Ogotai's court and received his father's title of Idikut, or sovereign among the Uigurs. He too died soon after, and Turakina, the regent, appointed her brother Salendi to the Uigur dynasty.

This new Idikut, who was a Buddhist, made haste to give homage to Mangu at the time of his accession, but just after he had started a slave accused him of planning to slay all Mohammedans, not only in the capital, but throughout the whole Uigur kingdom, when assembled in their mosques on a Friday. One of Mangu's officials received the accusation and sent a messenger straightway for the Idikut. Salendi returned without delay to Bish Balik and was confronted with the slave, who told the whole plan minutely. Salendi denied every point with great firmness. The slave demanded to take the affair to Mangu to be judged by him. Seif ud din, the official, sent him to the Grand Khan, and soon after the Idikut was summoned for trial. Questioned and put to torture, he ended by confessing that he was guilty. The Grand Khan sent him back to Bish Balik for execution. On a Friday his head was cut off by his own brother, Okendji. Two of his higher officials, condemned as accomplices, met death by having their bodies cut in four pieces crosswise. A third man, named Bela, was condemned to death also, but Mangu, wishing to win from High Heaven the cure of his mother, reprieved all who were sentenced to death upon that day. Bela was already at the place of execution and stripped of his garments when grace came, but his children and wives and his possessions were taken and he was sent on a mission to Syria and Egypt.

When Mongol princes granted life to a criminal he was either sent to the army, where he might die with some profit to his sovereign, or he was employed on a perilous mission, or was sent to some country with a death-dealing climate.

The slave who had accused Salendi got his recompense and became a Mohammedan. When he returned to Bish Balik after the death of the Idikut, he roused so much terror in the Uigurs who would be endangered by his ill-will that they hastened to pay court to him and offer rich presents.

After Mangu had rid himself of all the Uigurs who might favor Ogotai's descendants he gave the kingdom to Okendji, who had been his own brother's executioner.

After Ogotai's death the Mongol forces, disposed on the southern border of what had been once the Kin Empire, made attacks from time to time on Su chuan, Kiang nan and Hu kuang; they merely ravaged, took cities, and retired then with booty. It might be said that in Mangu's reign the only thing favorable to Mongols was the death of Meng kong, the greatest general of China, the man who had frequently stopped them, and often defeated their forces.

In'1252 Mangu gave Honan to Kubilai, his brother, as an appanage, and a part of Shen si with it also. In the same year, having previously consulted Chinese sages as to all needful and proper details, he made a great sacrifice to Heaven from a mountain top. The year following he directed that a census be taken of the people in Russia. Yun nan was made up at that time of several small kingdoms, independent for the greater part. Toward the end of 1252 Wang te chen, a commander of Mongols, made some advance in Su chuan. He pillaged Ching tu, and took Kia ting fu, thirty leagues to the south of it, thus opening Kubilai's way to him. Kubilai in October, 1253, marched from Lin taow, where he had assembled an army. Under him was Uriang Kadai whose father, Subotai, had done most toward Mangu's elevation. Uriang Kadai was charged by the Grand Khan with the real command of this expedition.

Kubilai traversed all Su chuan, and after a march of great trials, over mountains which seemed quite impassable for an army, he crossed on rafts the Kin sha (Golden Sand), a large river. The king of the Mussu man, the first people beyond the Kin sha, submitted. The sovereign of the next people, the Pe man, made no resistance, but his nephew defended the capital. Kubilai took the city, and put the nephew to death, but he spared the inhabitants.

Tali, the capital of Nan chao, received Mongol rule without fighting. Yao shu, his adviser, told Kubilai how Tsao pin, sent by a Sung Emperor to seize Nan shan, did the work without killing a person, and even without stopping any traffic in the city. Kubilai declared that he would show a like wonder. Shortly after this he mounted his stallion, and arriving at the walls of Tali, he unfurled silk banners, on which it was written in large characters that to kill man or woman was forbidden under penalty of death. In virtue of this statement on the flags, and possibly for some other cause also, Tali opened its gates, and this conquest cost only five lives, those of the city's two commandants, who slew the three officers sent to ask for surrender.

Kubilai did not go beyond Tali; he returned to Mongolia and left Uriang Kadai to master those southern regions. After Nan chao, the Mongol chief attacked and subjected the Tupo or Tibetans, a war-loving people, between one and two millions in number. Many of these entered his army, which was thereby strengthened greatly. Some even served in the vanguard and acted as scouts in attacking.

Towards the end of 1254 Uriang Kadai left his armies in the field, and returned to Mongolia to report to Mangu the work done in the south beyond China. Sent back the next year, he entered through Lower Tibet, and continued his conquests. The kingdom of Ava as well as two others, was either subjected or terrified into yielding. Two years later, in 1257, the Mongol general appeared on the edge of Tung king (Gan nan) and summoned its sovereign, Chen chi kung, a vassal of the Sung Emperor, to own himself tributary to Mangu. Since his envoys did not return to him the general entered Gan nan and marched to the Tha River, which runs through the whole kingdom lengthwise. On the opposite bank he saw the enemy's army with an immense force of elephants in order of battle. The Mongols, disposed in three parts, crossed and routed the enemy. The king hurried into a boat, sailed with the current and fled to an island; a part of his army escaped in boats also.

Uriang Kadai ordered Che she tu to lead a division to the other bank of the river, but not to give battle till the rest of the army had crossed over. Che she tu was to seize all the boats, or take a stand between them and the enemy. Instead of obeying he put the enemy to flight before the other divisions could cross and prevented thereby the capture of the army. Uriang Kadai in his rage gave a biting reproof and threatened a trial, whereupon Che she tu immediately took poison and died.

Kiao chi, the Gan nan capital, surrendered, and now Uriang Kadai found his envoys in prison. They had been bound with bamboo cords so firmly that the bonds had entered their flesh, and one of the men died the same hour in which he was liberated. Uriang Kadai was so enraged at this spectacle, that he gave up the city to be sacked by his warriors.

After his troops had taken nine days of rest, he turned northward for a time to escape the great heat of the region. In 1258 the Gan nan king, Chen chi kung, resigned in favor of his eldest son, Chen kuang ping. The latter now sent his son-in-law and many great lords on an embassy to Mangu, who at that time was marching against the Sung empire.

In 1256 Mangu had assembled a Kurultai at a place called Orbolgetu. During two months he treated the princes of his house with magnificence. All other guests summoned thither he met in the same way, and gave them rich presents. At this time came the submission of Corea, which, since 1247, had ceased to pay tribute. The success of Mongol arms in that country forced the king to render homage in person.

Kubilai's kindness and justice made him very popular in China. Because of this, and of calumny, Mangu became jealous, thinking that his brother wished empire. Hence in 1257 Kubilai was recalled, and replaced straightway by Alemdar. Alemdar arrested a number of Kubilai's fiscal agents and put them to death, saving two, touching whom he was waiting for the Grand Khan's decision. Kubilai suffered keenly, his life was in danger, and he hesitated seriously in action. The sage Yao shu, his adviser, declared that since he was the first subject of his sovereign, he should give an example of obedience. This Chinese sage advised a return to Mongolia with his family as the best way to soften the suspicions of his brother and remove every danger. This advice was regarded and followed. When they met the two brothers could not restrain tears. No reference was made to Chinese matters. Alemdar was recalled, and his commission was ended.

Mongol conquests in the south encircled the Sung Empire; the one question now was to completely subdue that country. There was an old pretext for attacking the Empire: In 1241 Turakina, the regent, had sent an envoy, Yuli massa, to make peace proposals and discuss them. This envoy was arrested as soon as he touched Sung territory, and imprisoned in a fortress with his suite of seventy persons. The envoy died shortly after, but the members of his suite were detained in the fortress until 1254. That year the Mongols besieged Ho chiu, before which they were defeated by Wang kian, the city governor. The Chinese, to show how much peace was desired by them, freed the suite of the late envoy, or at least those who were still living.

In October, 1257, Mangu set out for the Sung Empire, leaving government at home to Arik Buga, his brother, with Alemdar as an assistant. In May of the following year he marched to Shen si and fixed his camp near the Liu pan mountains, made famous by the death of his grandfather. In August, three months later, he advanced to Su chuan, his first field of action.

Mangu had adopted an elaborate plan by which Su chuan, Hu kuang and Kiang nan would be attacked simultaneously. He would march against Su chuan with an army in three divisions; a second army, under Kubilai, would lay siege to Wu chang, where Uriang Kadai was to join him after marching directly from Gan nan (Tung king) through the provinces of Kuang si and Kwei chiu. Togachar, son of the Utchugen, was to strike King shan in the province of Kiang nan with a third army.

Niuli with a strong force, preceding the Emperor, moved on Ching tu, where Adaku, a Mongol commander, was besieged by Liu ching, a Sung general, whom Niuli defeated, thus relieving the city. After that he marched forward, but no sooner had he gone than the place was attacked by Pu ko chi, the Su chuan governor. Adaku was killed in the action which followed, and the city was taken by the governor. Niuli turned back then and thrust in his forces between Ching tu and the Sung army outside it. Through lack of provisions the city surrendered a second time, but now to the Mongols, and the Sung army then retreated. Niuli received the submission of many places in that region and the rank of general-in-chief was conferred on him as reward.

Meanwhile the Grand Khan arrived at Han chung and wished greatly to capture Ku chu yai, a fortress twenty leagues west of Pao ning and commanding the road through the mountains. Niuli left at Ching tu a strong garrison and marched to take this mountain stronghold. Chang shi, a Sung general captured recently, was sent in advance to persuade the commandant of Ku chu yai to surrender. Chang shi entered the city, but, instead of persuading the commandant to surrender, or trying to persuade him and then returning to Niuli, he remained in the stronghold.

Mangu himself now marched against the place and, overcoming all obstacles, brought his army up to it. After ten days of siege work one gate of the city was surrendered by Chao chung, a traitorous officer of the garrison. The Mongols entered in secret, but there was soon a fierce and keen struggle in the streets, during which Yang li, the commandant, was killed and the garrison scattered. The house of Chao chung, the traitor, was spared in the looting and destruction which followed; he himself was rewarded with a rich robe of honor, and the command of a city. Chang shi, the Sung general who did not, or would not persuade the city to surrender, was captured a second time, and next day the Grand Khan had him quartered, that is, his body was cut lengthwise and crosswise. After this, much of Western Su chuan was subjected. The struggle was stubborn and desperate in some parts; in others there was only indifference, or treason. On February 18, 1259, the Mongol New Year, a great feast was given by Mangu, near the mountain Chung kwe. At this feast Togan, a chief of the Jelairs, declared that South China was dangerous through its climate, and that the Grand Khan should go northward for safety. Baritchi of the Erlats called this advice cowardly, and advised the Grand Khan to remain with his army. These words pleased Mangu, who remained, wishing greatly to capture Ho chiu. Tsin ko pao was sent to the city with a summons, but Wang kian had him slain as a traitor immediately.

Now began the siege of Ho chiu, very famous for stubbornness on both sides. Yang ta yuan, the investing commander of the Mongols, began the action, but Mangu himself arrived soon with the bulk of his forces and took his position in front of this city, which stood between the Kia ling and Fiu Rivers. During March and April a number of assaults were delivered. In May there was a dreadful tempest and rain poured down for three weeks without ceasing. Each side tried to cut off supplies from the other and harass it. After desperate struggles a division of the Sung forces destroyed a bridge of boats built on the Fiu by the Emperor. Over this bridge the besiegers were bearing provisions. A Sung corps, ascending the Kia ling on a thousand barges, was attacked from both banks by the Mongols, a hundred barges were sunk and the rest driven back to Chung king, whence they started.

In June assaults were very frequent, but with no profit to either side. One night in July a Mongol general scaled the ramparts with picked warriors and held his position till daybreak. Then, seeing Wang kian, the Sung commander, who was about to begin action again, he shouted: " Wang kian, life is granted to warriors, as well as to citizens; it is better to surrender in season." Barely had he uttered the words when a stone from a catapult killed him. His men on the ramparts were now left unsupported and fled. This was the last attack made on Ho chiu by the Mongols at that time. Their assaults had been many and resolute, and they had lost thousands of men in them; dysentery was raging, Mangu himself had fallen ill of it, and he resolved now to defer all attacks and blockade the position. Leaving three thousand picked men, he led the rest of his troops to Chung king, which he intended to capture, but twelve days later he died (Aug., 1259) at Tiao yu, a mountain one league from Ho chiu, and to the east of it. The chiefs of the army decided to raise the siege and retire toward the north, taking with them the body of their sovereign. Mangu's son Assutai conducted the corpse to Mongolia, where it was buried, near the graves of Jinghis and Tului.

Mangu was generous but stern by nature. He often distributed largess freely among his troops, but insisted that they should be held under severe discipline at all times. In the Su chuan campaign he strictly forbade his men to plunder. On learning that Assutai, while out hunting, had destroyed a wheatfield, he reproved him sternly and had several of his companions punished. He carried discipline so far that once, when a soldier disobeyed orders and forcibly took an onion from a peasant, he was put to death immediately. Though tolerant of all religions he was superstitious, and under the influence of shamans, an influence apparently baneful. A story is told of one of Mangu's wives, who, having given birth to a son, summoned a shaman to read the boy's horoscope. The man predicted long life, but the child died in a few days. Severely censured by the mother, the shaman for self-protection accused a nurse, recently executed for causing by sorcery the death of a princess. The mother, to avenge the death of her child, had the son and daughter of that nurse killed, the first by a man, the latter by a woman. This so angered Mangu that he imprisoned his wife for seven days, and banished her from his presence for a month. He commanded that the man who killed the boy of the nurse should be decapitated and his head hung around the neck of the woman who had killed the girl, then that she should be beaten with blazing firebrands, and put to death.

When Mangu died so unexpectedly, his brothers were far apart. Hulagu was in Syria, Arik Buga was at Kara Kurum, the Mongol capital, and Kubilai, the successor according to the Mongol system, was in China.

Wu chang fu, built along the south bank of the Yang tse directly in front of the Han, must be taken by Kubilai, such was the order which Mangu had given him. In 1258 Kubilai set out for this work from Shang tu, a city which he had founded recently, and which was famed later on as his capital in summer. He advanced slowly, and only in August, 1259, did he halt at the Ju in Honan. He moved thence toward Wu chang fu, and captured strong places near the line of his marching. It was while on this march that he heard of the death of his brother. He made no delay for that reason, however, but crossed the Yang tse in the face of a numerous and active flotilla.

He laid siege at once to Wu chang fu and sent a division of troops to Kiang si, where they captured two cities. These brilliant actions roused fear in Lin ngan (Hang chau), the Sung residence. The Emperor up to this time had not known of the Mongol invasion; for his minister had deceived him systematically, and now he received a vast number of petitions from all sides, declaring the minister a traitor and demanding that death be inflicted for his treason. The Emperor removed the man promptly and replaced him by Kia se tao. Command was given Kia se tao to advance on Wu chang at the head of an army and succor that city. Immense levies were ordered and the Emperor distributed silver and silk to those who took part in making them. The new minister, a man given only to letters, knew nothing of war, or the problem of governing. Moreover, he was desperately reckless, without conscience, and remarkably cunning. His one object was to keep power by all means which his mind could invent. The time favored him greatly, since the Emperor was weak and the court had small honor. The army had no respect for Kia se tao, but he had no thought to save the Sung Empire by fighting, hence disregarded the army. He made offers in secret to Kubilai, who was attacking Wu chang with much vigor. Kia se tao engaged that the Sung Emperor would own himself a vassal of the Grand Khan, the sovereign of the Mongols. Kubilai had received an official account of the death of Mangu, still he rejected the minister's proposal. But when letters came from his partisans, who urged him to hasten and prevent the attempts to be made by Arik Buga, he consulted his generals, and Hao king, one of them, explained very clearly that Arik Buga, master at Kara Kurum, the home capital, and Duredji, governor of Yen king (now Pekin), the capital of China, would act as one man to exclude him, who as first prince of the blood should be regent and preside at the Kurultai; hence the urgent need that he go to Mongolia immediately. Arik Buga wished supreme rule and Kubilai knew that Alemdar and Duredji would help him to win it in every way possible. Because of all this Kubilai decided to accept the conditions just offered by Kia se tao, which, moreover, were favorable. It was agreed then that the Sung Emperor was to own himself a vassal of the Grand Khan, and give two hundred thousand ounces of silver, with two hundred thousand rolls of silk yearly as tribute. The Yang tse was to be the boundary of his lands.

These conditions concluded, Kubilai marched northward with the best of the cavalry, leaving orders with his generals to await Uriang Kadai. Uriang Kadai had been commanded by Mangu to join Kubilai's army at Wu chang, bringing with him the thirteen thousand men furnished by subject nations on the south, beyond China. After he had defeated, on the border, armies more numerous by far than his own, he laid siege to Kwei tiu, the capital of Kiang si, defeated a second Chinese army, and reached Southern Hu kuang, where he laid siege to Chang shi. The treaty now made by Kubilai forced him to desist and cross the Yang tse with his forces.

The two southern generals in command of auxiliaries, reduced now from thirteen to five thousand, led the rear guard of the army, and were crossing the river on a bridge built of boats when Kia se tao broke this bridge by sending barges in full sail against it. One hundred and seventy men left on the southern bank were cut down by the minister.

Kia se tao kept the Sung Emperor in ignorance of the treaty, and attributed the Mongol retreat to his own splendid valor and management. The massacre of Uriang Kadai's rear party was exhibited as a triumph and Kia se tao was summoned to the court to be honored by a brilliant reception.

Kubilai encamped outside the walls of Yen king, and complained to Arik Buga of the levies of men, beasts and money which the latter was making. Arik Buga gave quieting answers; he wished to attract Kubilai and his partisans to the Kurultai which had been summoned. Beyond doubt he either had taken means to assure a majority on his side, or he wished to get Kubilai into his clutches and kill him.

Duredji, who was then at Pekin, urged that Kubilai and the princes in his army proceed to the Kurultai. It was answered, that Kubilai must post his troops first on their cantonments. Duredji sent this answer to Arik Buga, and remained with Kubilai, who went to Shang tu, the place fixed by his adherents for a special election.

Kubilai's party met, and since the position was so serious as to brook no delay, it was impossible for them to wait for Juchi's and Jagatai's descendants or for Hulagu, who was then in Persia. Kubilai was elected immediately and without opposition and placed on the throne with the usual formalities, 1260. — This election was the beginning of a contest which in the sequel destroyed the Mongol Empire. — A deputation of one hundred was now sent to inform Arik Buga of Kubilai's election and enthronement. Duredji tried to flee, but was arrested and forced to reveal the intrigues of Arik Buga; he was then put in prison. Kubilai appointed Apishga, son of Buri, as successor to Jagatai, and sent him home with his brother, but both these princes were seized in Shen si and taken to Arik Buga, who kept them in prison.

Meanwhile at Kara Kurum Arik Buga was not idle. He sent Alemdar to levy troops among tribes in the north, and distribute silk and silver among them; he sent two other men to Shen si, and these two were able to induce certain governors and generals in China to declare for Arik Buga, who, supported in this way, did not hesitate to take the sovereign title. At the head of his party was Kutuktai, once the chief wife of Mangu. With her were associated Mangu's sons: Assutai, Yurungtash and Shireki, also several of Jagatai's grandsons.

The two claimants continued to send envoys to each other all that season without reaching an agreement. In the autumn Arik Buga sent out an army commanded by Karadjar, and by Chumukur, a son of Hulagu. This force was defeated by Kubilai's vanguard. Discouraged by this check, Arik Buga's troops scattered, and he himself sought Kirghis regions for protection after he had put to death Apishga and his brother — those two Jagatai princes friendly to Kubilai — and the deputation of one hundred sent with news of that emperor's election.

In Shen si Arik Buga made no better progress: Straightway after his election Kubilai sent to that province and to Su chuan as governor Lien hi hien, an Uigur by birth, one among the best of his generals. This new governor hastened to Si ngan fu and made Kubilai's authority triumphant very quickly. Arik Buga's agents had arrived two days earlier, and were striving to win all that region for their master. The new governor seized those two men and cast them into prison. Learning meanwhile that Kubilai had issued an amnesty which would arrive very soon, he had the two put to death while in prison, and published the edict after its arrival. Three corps of troops led by Prince Kadan were now sent by the governor against Kundukai, Arik Buga's commander, who, unable to take Si ngan fu and needing reinforcements, withdrew northward to meet Alemdar, who was bringing fresh troops from Mongolia. After these two generals had joined forces, they turned toward the south and were met by Kubilai's army in Middle Shen si, somewhat east of Kin chau. The battle which followed was stubborn to the utmost, and for some time the issue was doubtful, but at last Arik Buga was surrounded and suffered so bloody and crushing a defeat that the campaign was ended. Kundukai and Alemdar were both killed in this battle, and China was secured to Kubilai, who now moved north and, entering Mongolia, established his camp at the river Ungki for that winter. Kara Kurum lacked supplies and, since it received them from China, Kubilai determined to stop every movement to Mongolia and had means to enforce this decision. Want soon appeared in the capital. Arik Buga was in need of arms and provisions; still he persisted, and transferring to Algu, who was with him, the inheritance of Jagatai, he directed the new Khan to send arms and supplies, and to guard the west strictly, so that no aid might reach Kubilai from Hulagu, or from Berkai. Arik Buga was still in the Kem Kemdjut region, and fearing to make an attack in his weakness, he sent a message to Kubilai saying that he repented and acknowledged him as the sovereign, that he would stand before him at once were his horses in condition to travel, though he would prefer to await the arrival of Berkai and Hulagu, whom he had asked with other princes to arrange the affairs of the Empire.

Kubilai answered that he would be glad to see Arik Buga even earlier than other princes. Then, leaving his cousin, Yessugka, in command of the capital to await the arrival of Arik Buga and escort him to the main camp, Kubilai went to Kai ping fu, and sent his army to its cantonments.

CHAPTER XVII

KUBILAI KHAN DESTROYS THE SUNG DYNASTY

THE summer and autumn of 1261 were passed very quietly. Arik Buga's horses recovered; he assembled large forces and set out for Kara Kurum, the chief capital of Mongolia. To put Yessugka off his guard and lull all suspicions, he sent a message announcing his visit and with it submission. After that he appeared on a sudden and fell upon Yessugka's men, whom he crushed. Hurrying southward at once to strike Kubilai, he met him at some distance northeast of Shang tu, on the eastern rim of the great Gobi desert. Arik Buga was beaten and fled northward.

Kubilai, thinking his brother defeated most thoroughly, forbade to pursue him, and turning, marched southward. Arik Buga on hearing of this changed his course, followed quickly, and made a second and more desperate trial. The battle was envenomed and lasted till night put an end to it. Both parties withdrew from the field, and Arik Buga fought no more that year, for just after this battle he learned of Algu's defection.

Algu, made Khan of Jagatai's Horde by Arik Buga, took the government from Organa, Kara Hulagu's widow. His sway then extended from Almalik to the Syr Darya, and soon he had an army of one hundred and fifty thousand. Arik Buga, poor and weak after such numerous reverses, sent three agents to Algu to levy a contribution in cattle, arms, and money. The abundant proceeds of this levy tempted Algu. He seized Arik Buga's men, since, as he stated, they had made offensive discourses against him. After that Algu met his advisers, who hinted that it would have been better to counsel ere he moved against Arik Buga so actively, but since it was late to retrieve the error, he must acknowledge Kubilai as sovereign and take his side openly.

Algu put the three agents to death, seized all the wealth which they had gathered, and gave the greater part of it to his army. Astonished at this act, Arik Buga resolved to march against Algu at the earliest. He went back to Kara Kurum, gave permission to the heads of the various religions to accept Kubilai should the need come, and then he moved westward very quickly.

Kubilai appeared soon after his brothers' departure, received the submission of people, and was about to pursue Arik Buga when couriers brought tidings of trouble in China, hence he turned and marched back to that Empire. Kara Buga, who commanded Arik Buga's advance, met Algu near the city of Pulad, and lost his life in the battle which followed. Algu thought himself safe through this victory. He returned to his home on the Ili and very foolishly dismissed his forces. But Assutai, at the head of a second division, passed the Iron Gate, crossed the Ili, captured Almalik, and seized even the private lands of Algu, who retired toward Khodjend and Kashgar with his right wing, which thus far had been idle. At this time appeared Arik Buga and took up winter quarters on the Ili near Almalik while Algu was retreating toward Samarkand. Arik Buga plundered ruthlessly all winter, and killed every warrior of Algu's whom he captured. When spring came vast numbers perished from hunger. Arik Buga's own officers were furious at his treatment of prisoners and most of them joined Yurungtash. Yurungtash, son of Mangu, the late Emperor, was leading at that time Kubilai's forces in the Altai. Only a handful of men were left Arik Buga, who, knowing that Algu was ready to attack him, tried to make terms with this enemy.

When Arik Buga arrived the year previous, Kara Hulagu's widow, Organa, came to his camp and declared that she had been dispossessed at his order, and was then waiting for recompense. Thereupon Arik Buga sent Organa with Massud Bey to effect an agreement with Algu. When Organa appeared before Algu and told him the cause of her coming he married her; Massud Bey he placed at the head of his finances. This minister levied large contributions on Bokhara and Samarkand. Algu had great need of money at that juncture, since Kaidu, the grandson of Ogotai, aided by Berkai, the successor of Batu, was advancing to seize his possessions. He now had the strength to repel him.

Arik Buga, left without friends, troops or resources, decided in 1264 to appeal to the mercy of his brother, and went to him. On appearing at Kubilai's tent men threw the curtain of the entrance around him; thus covered he made his prostrations. Such was the usage in cases of that kind. Admitted to the interior, he stood in the place given usually to secretaries. Kubilai looked at him long, and, seeing that he wept, could not repress his own tears and emotion. " Ah, my brother," said he at last, " who was right, thou or I ? " " I at first, but to-day the right is on thy side," replied Arik Buga.

At this moment Atchigai, brother of Apishga, approached Assutai and asked: " Is it thou who killed my brother ? " " I killed him at command of Arik Buga, at that time my sovereign. He did not wish that a prince of our house should die by the hand of some common man. Kubilai is my sovereign now; should he command, I would kill even thee in like manner."

Kubilai imposed silence, and added: " This is not the time for such speeches."

Togachar, a nephew of Jinghis, rose then and said: " The Khan desires no mention to-day of the past. He wishes you to feel nothing but pleasantness." Turning to Kubilai then, he added: " Arik Buga is standing; what place dost thou give him ? " He was seated with Kubilai's sons and they passed that day in company. On the morrow, however, Arik Buga's officers were all put in irons, and Kubilai appointed a commission of four princes and three generals to interrogate Arik Buga and his partisans. Arik Buga declared that he alone was responsible, that his officers were not guilty in any way. " How not guilty ? " asked Kubilai. " The generals opposed to Mangu drew no bow against him; still it is known to thee how they were punished, simply for intentions. Ye who have begun civil war and slain so many princes and warriors, what are your deserts ? " The officers made no reply. " My friends," said Tuman Noyon, the most aged among them, " do ye not remember, that in raising Arik Buga to the throne we swore to die for his cause should the need come ? The moment has come to make good that promise."

Kubilai praised this fidelity and asked Arik Buga again, who had roused him to the enterprise. He declared at last that Alemdar and Bolga had said to him: " Hulagu and Kubilai are on distant expeditions, and our late sovereign has left you at the head of the principal ulus of the Mongols. Why hesitate ? Make yourself

Grand Khan immediately." He had consulted with the other officers; all held that opinion together. The officers present confirmed what Arik Buga had stated, and ten of them were sentenced to pay the death penalty. But to judge Arik Buga himself Kubilai wished the presence of Hulagu, Berkai, and Algu. After waiting a long time for them, princes of the blood and generals then present in Mongolia met to determine the fate of Assutai and Arik Buga. Through regard for Kubilai they decided with one mind to grant life to both princes. This decision was taken to Hulagu, Berkai and Algu for their approval. Algu replied, that, since he held power and office with Kubilai's consent, he would give no opinion; the other two confirmed the decision.

Arik Buga and Assutai were set at liberty to render homage to the Khan and move about freely. One month later Arik Buga died of illness and was buried near Jinghis and Tului (1266).

The death of Arik Buga, his brother, did not save the great Emperor from civil war, and a long and terrible contest: Kaidu, a grandson of Ogotai, had his claim to the headship of the Mongols. He brought that claim forward and pushed it with such power, skill and resource that Kubilai had not strength enough to suppress him.

This struggle between the descendants of Ogotai and Tului was the greatest and by far the most striking event in the history of Jinghis Khan's family. Though Kubilai was able to conquer all China and Burma he could not conquer Kaidu. He met him and held him in check, — he had power to do that, and to found at the same time a dynasty in China, but he could not crush him.

We will consider first the subjection of China, and then turn to Kaidu and his exploits.

Kubilai, now Grand Khan, had decided to conquer all China and he began that great work with seriousness. During 1260 he had sent an envoy named Haoking to inform the Sung Emperor of his election. This envoy was to see in addition that the treaty concluded at Wu chang fu with Kia se tao was respected. As soon as the envoy set foot on Sung territory he was cast into prison with all his attendants. This was done at direction of Kia se tao, the real author of the treaty by which the Sung Emperor was made a vassal of Kubilai. Kia se tao had removed from this world every person who knew of that treaty and its various provisions. He was the only man living at that time in China who knew of it. The great point for Kia se tao was that the Sung Emperor must continue in ignorance of his thraldom. This man, whose sacred duty it was to explain the position, used his best power to conceal it, and adhered to his own direful policy at all costs. No one knew the great tragedy of China's position save Kia se tao, first minister of the Empire.

The arrest of his envoy called forth from Kubilai a statement in 1261: "Since my coming to the throne," declared he, "I have striven to secure peace to my subjects, hence I sent an envoy to the court of the Sung Emperor to make a firm agreement of amity. That court, little mindful of the future, has become more incursive and insolent. There is no day in which some of its warriors do not harass our borders. I commanded my generals last spring to be ready, but, remembering the sad fruits of warfare, and trusting that Hao king, my new envoy, would return with the results which I hoped for, I waited. I found myself duped very sorely. My envoy was arrested, against all the rules which exist between sovereigns, and during six months I looked in vain for his coming. Hostilities continue, and thus it is clear, that the Sung government wishes no longer for peace with us. Ought a nation, which for so many years has vaunted its wisdom and observance of the rules of good government, to treat us in this way? Its conduct is little in accord with the laws which it boasts of, and resembles that shade in a picture which, giving contrast, brings out the light with more brilliancy, and causes the shade to seem darker. Thus the beauty of China's laws is in contrast with its government; hence we see the bad faith of the latter more clearly." Then he notified all to prepare horses and weapons for action, and added: "The truth of my intentions, and the justice of my cause assure victory."

But the war which the Grand Khan had to wage with his brother,. forced him to loiter in action against the Sung sovereign. Barely had he come to Yen king after those two stubborn battles with Arik Buga on the eastern edge of the desert when he heard that one of his commanders, Li tan, had revolted. This general in Shan tung, seizing Se tian che and Itu, slew Mongol garrisons in these and other cities, and declared for the Sung Emperor. Kubilai sent Prince Apiche and General Se tian che against Li tan. They invested him closely in Tsi nan, where the defence grew most stubborn. When provisions were exhausted the besieged ate the flesh of the citizens. After four months of bitter struggle Li tan killed his wife and his concubines and then sprang into Ta ning, a shallow lake, from which he was rescued, and immediately Se tian che cut his head off. As was known, this revolt was upheld by the Sungs, although timidly. Notwithstanding Sung action Kubilai delayed serious war for a time.

When he had reigned forty years and lived sixty-two Li tsong, the Sung Emperor, died, November, 1264. Having no son, he left the throne to his nephew, Chao ki, who took the name Tu tsong when made Emperor.

It was only in 1267 that Kubilai moved against Southern China. In planning the campaign he made use of the knowledge of Liu ching, one of China's best officers, who had left the Sung cause and gone over to the Mongols. Liu ching had been governor of Lu chiu in Su chuan some time previous and had been calumniated before Kia se tao, the chief minister, by the Su chuan governor. Fearing for his life, he took service with the Mongols. In 1261 he appeared before Kubilai, who made him governor of Kwei chiu, a city on the Hu kuang and the Su chuan border. War being decided, through his advice it was planned to begin by the siege of Siang yang on the northern bank of the Han; the possession of this city would facilitate the conquest of the great Yang tse region.

Kia se tao, either wishing to win back Liu ching, or to discredit this dignitary with the Mongols, made him prince of Yen, and sent him a gold seal with the diploma and insignia of this office. Liu ching arrested the official who brought the emblems, and went with him to the residence of Kubilai, before whom he renewed his expressions of fidelity. The Emperor treated him with honor and cut off the head of the Chinese official.

At command of Kubilai, Liu ching and At chu, son of Uriang Kadai, went with seventy thousand good men to besiege Siang yang in October, 1268. She tian tse was made commander-in-chief of all forces directed against the Sung Empire, and many men of distinction from various lands of the great Mongol Empire, such as Uigurs, Persians, Arabs, Kipchaks and others, offered their services to this renowned general.

It was decided that the city could sustain a long siege, and that they must reduce it by famine. All communication by land was cut off, but the Chinese had a numerous flotilla and could receive arms and reinforcements by the river. The besiegers constructed fifty great barges on which warriors were exercised daily at warfare on the water; still they could not prevent a well manned flotilla which was laden with arms and provisions from reaching the city in the following autumn (1269) during very high water. At chu punished the Chinese while they were nearing Siang yang, and on their way back he seized five hundred boats from them.

After a blockade of one year the Mongols saw the need of investing Fan ching, on the opposite side of the river. The cities were connected by bridges of boats; both sides of the river were dotted with posts and intrenchments, while the river was barred with strong chains and armed barges. Siang yang seemed abandoned to its fate, for Kia se tao did nothing to succor it, but he took immense pains all this time to hide from his sovereign what was happening in the Empire. Despite his precautions the Emperor heard in 1271 that the Mongols were besieging Siang yang, that being the third year of the investment. He demanded information; the chief minister declared that the siege had been raised, and the enemy was retreating. The minister at first was unable to learn who had enlightened the Emperor, but later on he discovered the man and had him put to death for some other cause. Still the Emperor's questions roused the minister from torpor, and he sent an army under Fan wen hu to relieve the two cities.

On his part Kubilai assembled troops to strengthen the besiegers. He opened the prisons of North China, and thus obtained twenty thousand new warriors. These men gave good service and some of them reached high positions. They marched in three corps and by different routes, and met on the bank of the Han below the point where the flotilla of the Sungs had been stationed. These new troops joined both banks by a boat bridge, and captured nearly all the flotilla. At chu came upon the army of a hundred thousand led by Fan wen hu and sent by the minister. The two vanguards met, and that of the Chinese was cut to pieces, or scattered.

This check spread such a terror among the Sung warriors that the whole army fled, leaving standards and baggage behind it. Still the besieged, whose chiefs were not cast down by reverses, stood firm, and at the end of four years the city was still well supplied with provisions, though salt and a few other articles were needed. The commandant of Ngan lo, a town twenty leagues lower down on the river, undertook to supply what was lacking. He had boats built in a side stream of the Han and he held forth high rewards to all men who would handle them. Three thousand came forward to enter the city of Siang yang, or perish in trying. The boats went in threes; one boat was laden, and a second and a third tied firmly to each side of the laden one. These two were filled with armed warriors, who shot blazing arrows, and with small engines hurled stones and burning coals. They passed both divisions in this manner, breaking through every obstacle by fighting, and entered Siang yang amid endless shouts of delight from the people.

This new flotilla was commanded by Chan shun and Chang kwe, two very brave warriors. Chan shun was killed before reaching the city. Chang kwe in returning to Ngan lo was met by the Mongols, and a desperate hand to hand conflict resulted; every man near Chang kwe was killed, and he was seized. All wounded and blood-covered, he would not acknowledge the Mongols. They slew him immediately and sent four prisoners back to Siang yang with his body. Engineers of great skill in constructing ballistas appeared now in action. These men had been summoned from Persia by Kubilai, and in 1273 they raised engines which breached the walls quickly. The Mongols took the suburbs after terrible slaughter, and then burned the bridge which connected the cities; that done, they turned on Fan ching and stormed it. Fan tien chun, the commander, killed himself, saying that he would die a Sung subject. His colleague, Niu fu, took a company of desperate followers, and fought in the streets against terrible odds, setting fire to the houses, while driven gradually back; the time came when covered with wounds, he threw himself into the flames which his own hands had kindled. The men who fought with him died as he died.

The Mongols master Fedan ching during February, 1273. Kia se tao now offered to lead men himself and give aid to the cities, but, through the Emperor, he commanded himself to remain, declaring his presence at court indispensable. Kao ta, a great enemy of Liu wen hoan, was appointed to lead instead of the wonderfully adroit minister.

The catapults were turned on Siang yang, but the attack began only in November. The machines made a terrible noise; the enormous stone missiles crushed all that they fell upon. The besieged rushed away from exposed spots in terror. Fear spread through the city. Liu ching, who knew Liu wen hoan, the commandant, asked now for parley, and got it, but the two men had barely begun to converse when Chinese warriors sent arrows from the fortress and Liu ching was saved only by the goodness of his armor.

The Mongols, indignant at this action, wished to storm the place straightway, but were stopped by the generals, who informed the besieged that a message had just come to them from Kubilai. It was read in a loud voice and its import was as follows: "A splendid defence, of five years, covers you with great glory. Each faithful subject should serve his own sovereign with his life blood, but to sacrifice thousands of people through stubbornness, only think, is that reasonable or proper, especially for you who are exhausted, without aid, or even hope of it? Submit and no harm will meet any one. We promise to give each of you honorable employment. Ye will be satisfied. We pledge our true word of an Emperor that ye will be satisfied."

Liu wen hoan accepted these promises, and surrendered the city. He went with Alihaiya then to Kubilai, who showed him clear marks of esteem and named him commandant of troops in Siang yang. The officers under him were given good places in the armies of Kubilai.

The defection of Liu wen hoan produced a colossal sensation. His family was one of the best in the Empire, and many of his relatives sent in their resignations since they had the evil fate to be connected by blood with that traitor. Kia se tao, who was a friend of the family, did not present even one resignation to the Emperor.

Kubilai, exercised by the war in his own family, was inclined to cease action on the Yang tse for the present, but his generals explained the great value of the capture of Siang yang in continuing the struggle and urged that he strike his enemies while the advantage was on his side. The Emperor, Tu tsong, had just died, August, 1274, and had left all affairs to Kia se tao, and others as indifferent as that minister to the interests of China. The chief men wished to put on the throne Chao she, eldest son of Tu tsong, but Kia se tao considered that he himself would hold power more completely, and longer, by choosing the second son, Chao hien, a child of four years. This boy was chosen. The new Emperor received the name Kong tsong, and the Empress Siei shi, a widow of Tu tsong's father, was raised to the regency.

While preparing to continue the conquest of China most effectively, Kubilai, to explain and to justify his action, issued a rescript declaring that Jinghis, Ogotai and Mangu had striven to establish firm peace with the Sung Empire, and that he himself when only a prince and commander of armies had made a treaty with the Sung court, but that the court broke every promise as soon as he had withdrawn his forces. On ascending the throne he had sent an envoy to reinforce peace and good feeling, but the envoy had been seized and imprisoned with all his attendants, and was held in confinement till that day.

After this declaration had been made, Kubilai appointed She tian tse and Bayan to command all the armies invading Hu kwang and he gave them as lieutenants At chu, Alihaiya, and Liu wen hoan. Another army was to act in Kiang nan under Polo hwan and four other commanders. These two great groups of warriors reached perhaps two hundred thousand. She tian tse died soon after his appointment and the whole command of that first group was given to Bayan, the best leader among all the Mongols.

Bayan was of the Barin tribe. He had passed his youth in Persian regions, and had come on an embassy from Abaka the Ilkhan. Kubilai was so pleased with Bayan's speech and bearing that in 1265 he took the man into his service, and made him Minister of State very quickly.

From Siang yang, Bayan sailed down the Han toward Ngan lo with a numerous flotilla, but the river was blocked firmly with chains, with piles lashed together, and with barges on which were large forces of warriors well armed and using ballistas. Moreover Ngan lo itself was protected by walls of stone strong and massive in structure. Bayan judged that he could not take such a place without losing much time and many warriors, hence he pondered well over the problem. A Chinese prisoner showed a way out of the trouble, and Bayan took the city. The Mongols made track of strong beams from the river to Lake Teng into which they dragged all their vessels and barges. From this lake they sailed to the Han by an outlet, thus passing Ngan lo without battle. Having taken Sin hing chau and Sha yang, two cities on the right bank of the Han, they sailed down to its mouth, where in command of Hia kwe a strong flotilla was posted to guard the great river. Bayan attacked this line of boats and feigned to force on the left flank a way at all costs through it, but while the battle was raging on that side he seized Sha fu kwe on the other flank, took one hundred war barges, and reached the Yang tse on its north bank, taking nearly all his boats with him. He sent at once a strong fleet across the Yang tse under At chu. Hia kwe, the Chinese general, fearing lest he might be cut off, sailed down with all his flotilla, thus leaving Bayan perfect freedom of action.

Yang lo on the north bank was captured. Han yang surrendered. Bayan crossed the great river with his army, and was preparing a siege for Wu chang fu when Chang yen kien and Ching pong, the commandants of that city, surrendered and passed with their men to the service of Kubilai. Bayan left a strong garrison under Alihaya and moved toward the east with the rest of his forces.

Ching pong had been charged by Bayan with effecting the submission of Chin y, the Hoang chiu commandant. Chin y demanded a good office. Bayan promised to make him chief inspector of lands along the Yang tse. Chin y then opened the gates of Hoang chiu to the Mongols; he induced the governor of Ki chiu to join also and surrender his city. Many commandants along the Yang tse had served under Liu wen hoan, or men of his family, and these surrendered without waiting for a summons. Chin yen, a commandant in Kiang nan, and son of Chin y, followed the example of his father. The governor of Kiu kiang opened his gates to Bayan, who received in this city the surrender of Nan king, Te ngan fu, and Lu ngan. The kindly reception given by Bayan to all Chinese facilitated his conquests immensely.

Kia se tao, now master of the Sung Emperor, had collected meanwhile a great army, and brought to Wu hu, or to a point near it, a great river fleet which was joined by Hia kwe's large flotilla. The first minister sent now to Bayan a Mongol captive as envoy, bearing presents of beautiful fruits and proposals of peace on the basis of his first treaty with Kubilai at Wu chang in 1260. Bayan answered by letter that Kia se tao should have spoken before he (Bayan) had crossed the Yang tse, that if he wished peace with sincerity he should seek it in person. This letter was left without answer.

Chi chiu on the Yang tse had also surrendered to the Mongols, and Kia se tao commissioned Sun hu chin to occupy with large forces an island lower down than that city, and give two thousand five hundred boats to Hia kwe to bar the Yang tse to the Mongols. He chose for himself, and the bulk of his army, a position still nearer the sea.

Bayan moved down both banks of the river with infantry and cavalry, but when he was opposite Sun hu chin's island he opened on the Chinese with ballistas, and ordered an attack by some of his warriors. The Chinese fled in great haste to their vessels, but storms of missiles from both banks sank many of their barges and killed such a large number of men that their blood reddened the river.

This triumph gave immense booty to the Mongols. Kia se tao, informed of the issue by Hia kwe, sailed down the river with all his flotilla. He stopped at the island Kin sha, where he counseled with Sun hu chin and Hai kwe. Nothing could be done, they declared, with warriors who trembled at sight of the Mongols. Kia se tao retired down the river still farther to gather new forces, but in vain; all had lost courage and no man would serve the vile minister. As a result of this last defeat many cities in Kiang nan, whose governors had fled from them, were seized by the Mongols; others were surrendered by the commandants. At the approach of Bayan, Wan li sin, who was governor then of Nan king, despaired of his country, and wishing to die still a Sung subject, invited his relatives and friends to a banquet at which he took poison; the city then fell to the Mongols.

As the time of great heat was approaching, Kubilai wished to spare Mongol forces and instructed Bayan to desist till the autumn. But Bayan expressed his conviction that when one has an enemy by the throat it is not the time to give him a breathing spell. Hao king, Kubilai's envoy, was still in confinement, and the man's brother had been sent to obtain his release from Kia se tao. The mission succeeded; Hao king and his suite were set free, but he fell ill on the road, and died after reaching Yen king (Pekin), the capital of the Empire.

Kubilai sent an embassy soon after this to make new peace proposals. Lien hi kien, the chief of this embassy, stopped at Nan king, Bayan's headquarters, and obtained five hundred men as an escort. Bayan forbade hostile acts on the part of his army, and thus avoided all pretexts for violence to the embassy. In spite of this, Lien hi kien was attacked on the way by Chinese troops, who wounded him and killed his colleague. They took him to Lin ngan, where he died of his injuries. The Sung court sent an officer to Nan king in all haste with a letter declaring that the attack had been made without its knowledge; that the authors of the violence would be discovered and punished; that the Emperor was ready to declare himself Kubilai's vassal.

Bayan was distrustful, and received all these statements very coolly. He sent to Lin ngan with the bearer of this letter Chang yu, his own officer, to treat for peace formally, but really to see the condition of the capital. Chang yu was assassinated on the journey. Bayan, indignant at such treachery, demanded permission of Kubilai to continue hostilities. The Grand Khan, in answer, recalled him at once to the North to take command against Kaidu, who at that time was pressing him sorely.

Kao shi kie, governor of Yu chau in Hu kwang, planned an attack on Wu chang fu. He manned several thousand large boats and seized the straits of King kiang. Alihaiya, the Wu chang commandant, advanced with a fleet against Kao shi kie, who, fearing the risk of a battle, raised anchor and retired to the great Tong ting lake, where he made his boats ready for action. Alihaiya formed his fleet into several squadrons, which put the Chinese to flight with great promptness. They seized Kao shi kie's boat, took him prisoner and then cut his head off. The head was fixed on a lance point and shown beneath the walls of Yu chau, which surrendered when summoned.

Alihaiya now attacked Kiang ling. The governor of this city, Kao ta, was among the best officers in China. Dissatisfied with the court which had put other men above him irregularly, he surrendered his city. After some days he wrote to commandants within his jurisdiction advising surrender, and soon fifteen of them yielded. Alihaiya left all who surrendered in command of their cities. Alihaiya was a favorite of Kubilai, who now sent this general a letter of thanks for his action, and gave Kao ta that same office which the Sung government had refused him.

Southern Su chuan was still unconquered, but now Wang liang chin, the Mongol governor, defeated Tsan wan chiu, the Sung general commanding, and besieged him in Kia ting, his capital. Tsan wan chiu surrendered, giving also an account of every place in his province. He was retained then in office. Still Su chuan did not submit altogether till 1278. The great question now for the government was to be rid of Kia se tao, who had grown odious to all men, and in 1274 the regent deprived him of office. This did not sate public hatred, however. Ten accusations were leveled against this vile minister, but the regent whom he had created could not make up her mind to destroy the man, so she confiscated his property, and assigned Fu kien to him as a place of life exile. An official whose father the minister had banished was given the task of conducting the condemned man. This official made it his pleasure to torment the fallen minister as he traveled, and finished by killing him near the end of the journey. For this act he was put to death straightway.

At chu resolved now to attack Chang shi kie, who had a vast fleet of boats on the river. In front of his own fleet he arranged his largest boats and placed upon them one thousand crossbowmen who discharged blazing arrows to fire the opposing flotilla. He followed closely behind to sustain them.

The Mongol fleet bore down with all force on the Chinese. The thousand bowmen sent burning arrows in every direction, and soon the great river was covered with blazing barges and boats. To avoid being burned or taken captive by Mongols many Chinese hurled themselves into the river and perished. Chang she kie fled, leaving more than seven hundred boats in the hands of the Mongols.

Bayan saw the Grand Khan at Shang tu, and convinced him that harm alone could result from stopping operations in China for even a short time. Bayan was sent back to his office and the plan of campaign was fixed promptly. Bayan was to march straightway (1275), and take the Sung capital. His assistants were to operate on the right and the left in the Hoai nan and Kiang si provinces. His own army was divided into three parts and its

action repeated in some sense the movements of the combined
Mongol forces. The part of this army in which Bayan, the great
chief, was present marched through Chang chan; Liu wen hoan
led its vanguard.

The Sung court sent corps after corps to succor the city. Bayan
crushed all that he met in the field, and then summoned Chang
chau to surrender. When both threats and promises proved useless he destroyed the suburbs, and raising a rampart to the height
of the walls, he then captured the city. Of the four chiefs who
commanded three fell, while the fourth fled and saved himself.
The inhabitants were put to the sword without pity. Bayan's
generals, Argan and Tong wen ping, carried everything before
them; people were fleeing to Lin ngan in thousands; there was
panic in all parts, and terror in the capital. Chin y chong
the first minister forced to the ranks every male above fifteen
years of age. The Empress sent an envoy to Bayan to explain
that the evil done had been done by Kia se tao, whom she had
punished, that the sovereign was still in tender years, and that all
would be remedied.

Bayan answered that Kia se tao had not murdered Lien hi hien,
and bade her remember that when the Sung dynasty won its
dominion, the last of the Cheu line, from which the Sungs had
snatched Empire, was also an infant. " Think it not strange if
your infant is treated as you treated that one."

Bayan advanced farther. The same envoy appeared from
Chin y chong and the Empress to declare that the young Emperor
would agree to call himself the nephew of Kubilai, and pay tribute.
This too was rejected. Now the Empress sent to say that the
Emperor would own himself a subject of Kubilai, and pay yearly
tribute. This offer was made without the knowledge of Chiny y
chong, who wished the court to remove to southern regions and
fight to the end there with valor. The Empress would not hear
of this project. Bayan was approaching the capital irresistibly;
nothing could stop him. The Sung princes advised now to send
Ki wang and Sin wang, the Emperor's half-brothers, to more
remote regions, and preserve in this manner the dynasty. The
Empress consented and, changing the title of Ki wang to Y wang,
and Sin wang to Kwang wang, sent them both to Fu kien, but to
different places in the province.

Bayan was met near Lin ngan by the two other parts of his army. In sign that she submitted the Empress now sent him the grand seal of Empire, which he transmitted to Kubilai immediately. Next he summoned Chin y chong to discuss terms of settlement, but this minister, who was opposed to the Empress, hurried off southward. Chang shi kie retired also with his troops to Ting hai, and when Bayan sent an officer of distinction to invite him to surrender Chang shi kie cut the man's tongue out, and hacked him to pieces. The Empress now made Wen tien siang her first minister, gave him U kien as a colleague, and sent the two men to Bayan on a mission.

The minister told the great general that if the Northern Empire wished China to be on the footing of other kingdoms subdued by the Mongols, he would ask him to retire, at least to Kia hing, where they would settle on the tribute in silver and silk to be paid every year, and on the places to be occupied. " But if your plans," added he, " are farther reaching, and you think to destroy the Sung dynasty, be assured that the road to your object is long, and you will fight many battles ere you reach it. The south is not in your power yet. We shall defend ourselves; the issue of arms is ever changing. Who knows that the whole position will not be reversed utterly ? "

Bayan dismissed U kien and detained Wen tien siang under pretext of arranging a peace with him; the minister protested against this. Seeing Chinese officers who had gone over to the Mongols, he reproached them for their infamy very sharply, not sparing even Liu wen hoan among others. Bayan sent him to Kubilai, but the minister escaped from his guards on the way.

To govern Lin ngan Bayan now appointed a council of Mongols and Chinese, under presidence of Man hu tai and Fan wen hu; he charged also Ching pong to obtain from the Empress an order to all governors of provinces to submit to the Mongols, and, to render this more emphatic, the great functionaries signed it at his instance. All obeyed except one, Kai hiuen hong, whom no threats could intimidate.

Four Mongol officers, at command of Bayan, took the seals of departments, and seized every register book, historical memoir, and map in each archive; these were all carefully placed under seal. Troops were stationed in every part of the capital and exact

order continued. Bayan, whom the Emperor and Empress demanded to see, excused himself under pretext that he knew not
the right ceremonial on such an occasion, and next day he left the
city. Two Chinese dignitaries were charged with watching the
palace, for no reason whatever were they to lose sight of the
Empress. This was done under guise of showing boundless respect
for her.

Very soon after, Atahai, a general, with a large suite of officers,
appeared at the palace. His first act was to abolish all etiquette
observed with the Emperor and Empress. Meanwhile he invited
the Emperor and his mother to set out for Kubilai's court in Shang
tu, without waiting. After this notice had been given, the Empress
with streaming eyes embraced her little boy, lately heir to the Empire: " The son of Heaven spares thy life," said she. " It is proper
to thank him." This heir of seven years, a creation of the dead
Kia se tao, fell on his knees at the side of his mother; their faces
were turned toward the north, toward Shang tu; nine times did
they strike the floor with their foreheads in saluting Kubilai the
Grand Mongol.

The son and mother were then placed in an equipage and left
Lin ngan and their Empire forever. With them went a great
company containing all the princes and princesses of the Sung
family who were in the capital at that time, besides ministers, high
functionaries, men of letters of great note and marked influence.
All these took the road northward, and surely a mournful procession followed the Emperor.

The regent, the Emperor's grandmother, fell ill and was left in
Lin ngan for recovery. A number of Chinamen, desperate at
seeing their Emperor led captive with the chief men of the government and some of the best minds of China, made efforts to save
them. Twice did they rush at the escort of Mongols which was
led by Atahai and Li ting, but the escort was too strong to be
broken; the Mongols repelled the Chinese after a desperate
encounter in each case.

When the young Emperor was reaching Shang tu, Kubilai sent
his first minister to meet him. Orders had been given to treat all
captives properly. The Emperor was reduced to be a kong, or
prince of the third order; Hiao Kong was the title accorded him.
The Empress mother and the regent were stripped of their titles.

Jambui Khatun, the Grand Khan's chief wife, tried to soften the lot of the mother by delicate attention.

Lin ngan, the capital of the Emperor, is said to have been very large and magnificent. It was built amid lagoons and had twelve hundred bridges, some having piers of such great height that vessels of two hundred tons could sail under the bridge. In the city was a beautiful lake surrounded with palaces and mansions. On the islands of this lake were pleasure houses where marriage feasts were held and great banquets given. There were three thousand baths in Lin ngan, each large enough to accommodate one hundred persons at a time. Marco Polo states that the Emperor's palace was the largest in the world. It contained twenty halls, the most capacious of which was used as a state banquet room; aside from these there were one thousand chambers richly decorated in gold and colors. The city contained ten large markets; 1,600,000 houses and seven hundred temples. The inhabitants dressed richly, all, except the lowest class of laborers and coolies, wearing silk.

The Grand Khan had received the gold, silver and other precious objects taken in Lin ngan from the palace. The princes and princesses of Kubilai's court gazed with delight on these spoils of a mighty dynasty, but Jambui Khatun could not keep back her tears as she turned to the Grand Khan and said to him: " It has come to my mind at this moment that the Empire of the Mongols also will finish in this way."

South China remained still unconquered. While Bayan was moving on Lin ngan invincibly, Alihaiya was advancing through Hu kuang and had laid siege to Chang cha. He attacked with such vigor that after some days the city suffered excessively. The Mongols delivered a general assault, won the rampart, and the fate of the place was decided; a part was on fire, and the fall of the whole was a question of hours at the utmost. At this juncture an official from a city of importance, who chanced to be there with two sons who had just come of age, made those sons put hats on their heads (the hat being a symbol of manhood). That done, he cast himself into the flames with them and his household; Li fu, the governor of Chang cha, honored greatly the memory of this visitor, and feeling sure that every official would be true to the dynasty, he summoned a certain Chin tsong and said to him: " I will not dishonor my blood by surrender; I ask you to despatch all my family, and then show to me the same service." In vain did Chin tsong strike the earth with his forehead, in vain did he beg of the governor to relieve him from such a terrible service. Li fu was unbending, and as he insisted, Chin tsong, weeping bitterly, agreed to obey him. Wine was given all who were ready to die, and while under its influence death touched them easily. When Li fu presented his head it was swept from him with one blow of a sabre. Chin tsong set fire to the palace immediately; then he ran to his house, where he slew his own wife and children; that done, he killed himself. All the officials, save two, and a great number of officers and people followed the governor; some sprang into wells, others hanged themselves, or took poison. On entering Chang cha the Mongols were astonished to find the place almost deserted.

Alihaiya then summoned the other cities of Southern Hu kuang; nearly all of them surrendered without raising a weapon to defend themselves. At the same time in Kiang si Sung tu kai made great progress. Eleven cities of this province submitted, and Fu chau also was taken. Bayan had been summoned to appear at Shang tu immediately. Sung tu kai told him at parting, that the Sung princes had assembled many troops in Fu kien and Kuang tung, and that they intended to enter Kiang si. Bayan enjoined on Argan and Tong wen ping, whom he left in command near Lin ngan, to leave those princes no time to strengthen their armies.

When the Sung princes, brothers of the Emperor, came to Wen chau from Lin ngan, the officers who followed or joined them, made Y wang, the elder, chief governor of the Empire, and associated with him his brother Kwang wang. These brothers entered Fu kien, where the two leading cities were on the point of submitting to Hoang wan tau, whom Bayan had made governor of that province very recently. The new governor had guaranteed to reduce the whole province. The Sung partisans seized arms immediately. The Mongol governor was defeated and driven out of the province; his troops deserted and joined the Sung forces.

The two princes arrived at Fu chau, the capital, and Y wang, who was nine years of age, was made Emperor with all needful ceremony. The sovereign had a numerous army divided into four corps, which were to operate in the south and along the Yang tse, on both sides of that river. At this juncture appeared Wen tien siang, who had escaped from the Mongols during the second attack on the men who were taking the young Emperor to Shang tu. To him was now given the conduct of the struggle, and he strove to rally the Chinese, and rouse their love of country. A proclamation of the young Emperor stirred up the nation, and great levies were made, which disquieted the Mongols.

When Bayan obtained a command from the Empress, the Emperor's mother, requiring every Sung subject to submit to the Mongols, At chu sent a copy to Li ting shi, who had tried to rescue the Emperor and who was defending Yang chiu with great stubbornness. Li ting shi answered from the ramparts, that he knew no command save that to defend the place assigned him by the Empress through a document from her own hand. At chu obtained a new command in still stronger language, and addressed to Li ting shi directly. Li ting shi discharged arrows at the man bringing this document.

At chu redoubled his efforts to cut off supplies from his opponent. In despair that he could not conquer one city, while Bayan had reduced a whole province so quickly, and with it the capital of the Empire, he tried other methods. He sent Li ting shi a letter in which Kubilai promised to grant every wish of his. Li ting shi burned this letter, and cut off the head of the man who had brought it. All other cities besieged in those regions had fallen by famine, if not conquered otherwise; hunger was reaching Yang chiu, but how closely was not known to the Mongols at that time.

At At chu's request Kubilai wrote to Li ting shi as follows: " If you will obey even at this hour, I am willing to carry out former promises, and pardon the murder of my envoy." Li ting shi would not receive this new letter, and learning that Y wang was Sung Emperor, he left the defence of Yang chiu to Chu hwan and set out with his colleague, Kiang tsai, and seven thousand men to join his new sovereign. Barely had he gone from the city when Chu hwan surrendered.

At chu sent a strong corps of cavalry to hunt down the two fleeing commanders. One thousand Chinese were slain in this labor, and Li ting shi was forced into Tai chiu, where he was surrounded immediately. Two leading officers in that city betrayed it to the Mongols. Li ting shi, seeing that his last hour was near, sprang into a pond which proved to be very shallow. He was dragged out of it promptly and with Kiang tsai hurried back to Yang chiu. At chu left nothing undone to win these two men to Kubilai, but since both were unbending he killed them.

Tong wen ping and Argan made progress in Che kiang. They won a victory over the Sung army in Chu chiu, and in Fu kien took a fortress, called Sha u. These Mongol successes were followed by Chinese defections and the surrender of cities. This constrained the Sung court to think of its safety. Chin y chong and Chang shi kie assembled a very large fleet, and a considerable army. The Emperor embarked with his court and the army and sailed away southward to Tsuen chiu (the Zaitun of Marco Polo). This port was the seat of much commerce; the harbor was crowded with vessels at all times. The commanders now seized certain ships which they needed. These, as it seemed, belonged mainly to the governor, a very rich merchant. The governor was so greatly enraged at this action that he attacked all who landed, and even forced the fleet to sail out of the harbor; that done, he delivered his city to the Mongols.

Alihaiya had laid siege for three months, with great vigor, to Kwe lin fu, the capital of Kuang si, but failing to conquer the desperate resistance of the governor Ma ki, he tried softer methods. He obtained from Kubilai a diploma appointing Ma ki commander-in-chief of Kuang si, and sent him the document by an officer. Ma ki burned the diploma, and cut down the officer. Kwe lin fu, built at the meeting of two rivers, was exposed at one side alone, where the whole garrison could face any enemy. The Mongol general dug out new beds for the rivers and turned them; the city was assailable now upon every side and he stormed it. His army swept over the walls like a torrent, but Ma ki met the foe worthily. He fought from street to street, from one square to another, till at last, when covered with wounds, and bleeding his life out, that brave man was captured, but died shortly afterward. All the inhabitants were put to the sword without pity.

The capital taken, Alihaiya divided his army into various detachments, which he sent to seize the chief cities of that province.

Ki wang, or Y wang, the young Emperor, sailed to Hweï chiu, not far from the present Hong Kong, and sent one of his officers to Sutu, the Mongol commander, with a letter for Kubilai, in which he offered submission. Sutu sent his son to Shang tu with the bearer of this letter. Meanwhile operations continued, and soon the whole province of Kuang tung, attacked the year previous, had submitted.

At this juncture Kubilai summoned Bayan from South China, directing him to leave there only those who were needed to guard conquered places. Li heng would command troops of that kind. All others were to strike in the North at his enemy Kaidu. After Bayan's departure the Sung party attacked and retook many cities in the four southern provinces. Chang shi kie made great levies in Fu kien, equipped a large fleet and laid siege to Tsuen chiu, but Sutu forced him afterward to raise it. Sutu declared that the Chinese were not to be trusted, and fell back on the old Mongol method of slaughter. City after city was put to the sword without mercy or favor. Since many southern cities had been retaken by Sung forces Kubilai in 1278 sent fresh troops to that part of the Empire, and ordered Ta chu, Li heng, and Liu se kwe to cross the Ta yn ling mountains, while the fleet, under Sutu and others, would attack the Sung squadron.

Sutu now swept all things before him till he reached Chao chiu, where he met firm resistance. Not wishing to delay, lest he be late in the south, he sailed on, and joined the land forces near Canton, which surrendered. After this success he returned to Chao chiu and laid siege to it regularly. The place was built strongly, and Ma fa, the commandant, was so active and resolute that after battering it for twenty days and storming it repeatedly Sutu could show only small progress. Then the commandant made a sortie in which he burned the battering engines of the Mongols, but surrounded at last by greater forces, he perished in a murderous struggle. His men broke and fled to the city; the enemy ran with them, rushed in throngs to the gates, swept through them after the Chinese, took the place, and put all to the sword without exception.

The young Emperor had no port in which to anchor his vessels with safety. Hence he wandered about on the sea without a resting-place, till in May, 1278, at the age of eleven, he died, on Kang chuen, a desert island. Most of the officials and high personages who followed him were averse to this wandering existence, and were ready to submit to Kubilai, but Liu sin fu opposed them with the uttermost vigor. " We have," said he, " a son of Tu tsong with us yet and we must make him the Emperor. We shall find warriors and officers in plenty. If Heaven has not decreed ruin to the Sungs, do ye doubt that it can raise their throne to its former magnificence ? "

These words roused the chiefs; they placed Kuang wang on an earth mound, knelt, and rendered homage. Ti ping was the name given the new Emperor. Liu sin fu and Chang shi kie were his ministers. The Chinese headquarters were mainly on water, their fleet was very great, and carried large forces. This fleet retired to straits in the Gulf of Canton which lay between the mountain Kiche and the island of Ya i. The position, as it seems, was a good one. In every case it was the last refuge and stronghold of the Sung dynasty. Chang shi kie had built on the summit of the island a modern palace for the Emperor, and barracks for the warriors. He worked with great zeal to revictual the vessels and provide all that was needful for every one. Provisions came from Canton and other places, from cities which were subject to the Mongols, as well as the Chinese. Wen tien siang, in spite of his losses, recaptured Canton, and held it, at least for a season.

At this time Chang hong fan explained to Kubilai in a letter that to end the great struggle successfully Kuang wang must be mastered. Kubilai sent him a sword set with jewels, and made him commander-in-chief of the armies appointed to subdue the new Emperor. The first act of the general was to crush the land forces; as these were mainly new levies and the Mongols were veterans, they fled at the earliest onset and their officers were taken captive. Among them were Wen tien siang, chief commander, with Liu tse tsiun and Tsiu fong. The last of these killed himself and the second was burned to death over a slow fire. Wen tien siang begged for death earnestly, but Chang hong fan would not grant it. After asking him in vain to give homage by bowing northward, Chang hong fan sent him to Kubilai, and freed all his friends and relatives who were captive.

The armies of the Sung Emperor were destroyed. The last blow remained, that against the sea forces. Chang hong fan put his army in ships and sailed in past the island called Ya i. The Chinese land troops were intrenched on the island very firmly, and the Chinese fleet seemed secure from attack on the north side, since the water in that part was too shallow, as they thought, for the large Mongol vessels.

Chang hong fan reconnoitred his opponents, and saw that their vessels were unwieldy, so he took a number of his light boats, filled them with straw soaked in oil and ignited them. Favored by a strong southern wind, he sent these burning boats forward to strike on the Chinese. But Chang shi kie had covered all his front barks and their rigging with mud, hence they were not fired and the attack proved fruitless.

Canton had been taken by the Mongols a second time and occupied. Chang hong fan now received thence a reinforcement of men, and also of vessels. These latter he posted north of Ya i, and prepared to attack the Sung fleet, which was west of the island, between it and the mountain. Attacks were made on the north and the south simultaneously. The battle continued all day. The Chinese were unbroken in the evening, but in the fleet there was something approaching a panic; the commanders had lost control for the greater part. Chang shi kie and his colleague determined to reach the open sea under cover of a mist which was present in every place. The Chinese emerged from the straits with sixteen bulky vessels and there formed the front of the squadron. Liu sin fu boarded the Emperor's vessel to save him; that ship was larger than others and more difficult to manage. They sailed on, however, till they came to the mouth of the channel, which was blocked by Mongol barges lashed one to another securely. There was no chance to move forward and to return was impossible.

Liu sin fu, seeing this, had his children and wife hurled into the water. Then, telling Ti ping that a Sung sovereign should prefer death to captivity, he put the boy Emperor on his shoulders and sprang into the sea with him. Most of the dignitaries followed this example, and drowned themselves.

More than eight hundred ships fell into the power of the Mongols. Later on Chinese corpses in thousands were floating on those waters. Among them was that of Ti ping, and on it was found the seal of the Empire. When Chang shi kie heard that his sovereign was dead he went to the ship of the Empress and tried to induce her to aid him in choosing some relative of the Sung family and making him Emperor. But when she learned of the death of her young son she sprang into the sea without further discussion, and was followed by the ladies of her service. Chang shi kie found her body and buried it on the mainland. He then sailed away for Tung king, where he had faithful allies with whom he intended to return and instal a new Emperor if possible. But in crossing the Gulf of Tung king, Chang shi kie was met by a terrible tempest, and perished.

Meanwhile Su liu i, his colleague, fell, slain by his own men. When he was dead all people in China submitted, and Kubilai Khan found himself master of an Empire, for which the Mongols had been fighting for more than five decades. Thus the Sung family vanished after ruling three and one-fifth centuries over China.

CHAPTER XVIII

KUBILAI'S ACTIVITY IN CHINA AND WAR WITH KAIDU

THE struggle of Kubilai Khan against Arik Buga, his brother, has been described in some detail already, as well as the downfall and death of the latter. Next came Kaidu, a more dangerous opponent, who claimed Mongol sovereignty through descent from his grandfather Ogotai. Ogotai had been designated by Jinghis to the khanship of the Mongols, and when this choice was confirmed at the first Kurultai of election the dignity was fixed among Ogotai's descendants. By the election of Mangu, a son of Tului, this pact was rejected and broken. Long and stubborn struggles and ruin were entailed on the Mongols by that change.

The war with Kaidu lasted from the death of Arik Buga to the end of Kubilai's life and somewhat beyond it. Before touching on this bloody conflict it will be perhaps better to show what Kubilai Khan did after conquering China (January 31, 1279).

No sooner had the Grand Khan ended the Sung dynasty than he turned to Japan, which had paid tribute formerly to China. In 1270 he had invited the Japanese monarch, through an envoy, to acknowledge as his suzerain the master of the earth, who was also the son of Heaven, but the envoy was given no audience. Other envoys, sent later, were put to death promptly by the Japanese. Kubilai resolved now to conquer those eastern islands, though his best counsellors tried to dissuade him. They saw the perils of the enterprise and did not believe that success would in any case pay for the outlay, but Kubilai was inflexible, and the order was given to send an army one hundred thousand strong to conquer the islands. The troops embarked at Lin ngan and Tsuen chiu fu toward the end of 1280; the fleet bearing them sailed for Corea to be joined by a contingent of that country composed of nine hundred ships, which carried ten thousand warriors. This immense fleet with its forces was struck near the Japanese coast by a tempest; the ships went ashore for the greater part, and the men were taken prisoners. Sixty thousand Chinese were seized and of Mongols thirty thousand were slain by the Japanese. In the autumn of 1281 a feeble remnant and wreck of this great army made its way back to China.

When the Sung family had fallen the King of Cochin China rendered homage to Kubilai and sent him tribute. Not content with the tribute thus brought him, Kubilai sent to that country a ruling council composed of his own officers. After two years the heir of Cochin China, indignant at the sight of foreign men ruling his country, moved his father to arrest them. To punish this rebellion, as he called it, Kubilai sent a fleet from South China with an army under General Sutu, who landed in 1281 at the capital, which he captured. The king's son retired toward the mountains, and occupied Sutu with phrases of submission. Meanwhile he was preparing to defeat him if possible. Sutu learned shortly after that men were advancing from many directions to cut him off from his vessels. He found it well for this reason to return to Canton.

Western Yun nan was formed of two princedoms, Laï liu and Yung chang, which must be brought to obedience, such was the order of the Emperor. The King of Mien tien, the Burma of our day, to whom, as it seems, the two princedoms paid tribute, set out in 1277 to drive back the Mongols. He advanced with a force sixty thousand in number formed of horsemen and infantry. His first line was of elephants bearing towers which held archers.

At approach of this Burmese army, the Mongols, whose flank was protected by a forest, rode out from behind their intrenchments to charge on the enemy then advancing, but their horses ran in terror from the elephants, and for some minutes no man could check the beast under him. When the panic was over Nassir ud din commanded his men to dismount, put their beasts in the forest, and, advancing on foot, attack the first line of elephants with arrows. The elephants, unprotected by armor of any kind, were covered with wounds very quickly. Maddened by pain, they turned and rushed through the ranks just behind them. Many fled to the forest, where they broke the towers on their backs and hurled down the men who were in them.

Free of the elephants, the Mongols remounted, attacked the Burmese with arrows, and next with their swords at close quarters. The unarmored Burmese were put to flight promptly. Two hundred elephants were seized by the Mongols, who pursued the enemy until intense heat drove them back. After this brief and striking campaign Kubilai retained elephants in his army. In 1283 Kubilai sent a large army under command of Sian kur to force the king of Mien tien to submission, that is to become tributary and permit Mongol officials to reside in the country. After a short siege Tai Kung, the capital, was taken and the whole kingdom agreed to pay tribute to Kubilai. The Kin shi, a people of Yun nan, who till that time had been kept by the king from submission to the Mongols, declared obedience.

The great Emperor planned now a second attack on the Japanese islands, to repair the disaster which happened to the first one. Atagai was named chief of the expedition. The Corean king was to give five hundred ships to it. In Kiang nan, Che kiang and Fu kien, ships were built, and new levies made, to the great harm of commerce in those places. Workmen in the docks, and also sailors, forcibly levied, deserted in crowds, and robbed on the highway, or became pirates along the coast regions. The army was dissatisfied and most men in the Emperor's own council opposed the expedition, but Kubilai's attention was soon drawn elsewhere. The King of Cochin China after the withdrawal of Sutu in 1281 had sent ambassadors to appease Kubilai, but the Emperor refused them an audience, and commanded Togan, his son, then governing Yun nan of the East, to march through Tung king, and attack Cochin China; Sutu was to aid in planning this action. Tung king had submitted to Kubilai on his advent to power, and Ching koan ping, its ruler, had engaged to pay once in three years a given quantity of gold, silver, precious stones, and drugs useful in medicine, also horns of rhinoceros, and ivory. At the same time an agent from Kubilai came to reside at the capital. Ching koan ping had for successor in 1277 his son, Chin ge suan, who hated the Mongols and was waiting to attack them. When Togan on his way to Cochin China demanded provisions, Chin ge suan raised false objections, and Togan, seeing his active hostility, knew that he must first of all bring Tung king down to obedience. He entered the coun-

try in 1285 during January and on rafts crossed the Fu liang
River. At the other bank stood the enemy in order of battle, but
they fled, and their hostile King vanished. Togan thought the
war ended, but the enemy rallied and harassed his marches. The
great heat of summer and the rains brought disease to his northern
warriors. The army was forced to fall back on Yun nan and was
harassed continually while retreating. Li heng, who commanded
under Togan's direction, was wounded with an arrow, and died
very soon, for the arrow had been poisoned.

Sutu, who was twenty leagues distant from this army and had no
account of its trouble, was cut off by Tung king men, and perished
in a battle at the Kien moan River. Kubilai grieved much for the
loss of so gifted a general. To this loss was added the death of
Chingkin, that son whom he had declared his successor, a man
of great wisdom, instructed in all Chinese learning, esteemed for
his probity and his love of justice. Chingkin was forty-three
years of age when he died. He left three sons: Kamala, Dharma
Bala, and Timur of whom we shall hear much hereafter.

In 1286 the Japanese expedition was still pending. All forces
were ready, however, and the ships were to meet in September at
Hupu, the great rendezvous. Meanwhile the president of the
tribunal of mandarins dissuaded the Emperor from so hazardous a
project. He left Japan in peace, but a new expedition was sent to
Cochin China. Alihaiya was to take troops from South China
garrisons, and fall on Tung king with the uttermost vigor. Prince
Togan, who had command of this army, entered Tung king in
1287 during February; he had under him the generals Ching
pong fei and Fan tsie. Meanwhile a fleet from Kuang tung bore
a second good army under Situr, a great Kipchak leader who
brought with him officers and warriors of his people.

Kubilai's forces beat the Tung king men in seventeen engagements, ravaged a part of the country, pillaged the capital,
seized immense wealth, and retired on Yun nan with rejoicing. The King, Chin ge suan, had sailed away, no one knew
whither, but now, when the Mongols had gone, he appeared with
large forces a second time.

Togan reëntered the country in 1288, and found the inhabitants
armed and ready for action. The campaign was continued till
summer, which brought much disease, and forced Togan to fall back

on Kuang si for a period. Chin ge suan now attacked him and strove to stop his retreat altogether. Togan lost many men in various battles, among others the generals Fan tsie and Apatchi, and was saved only by the valor of Situr, who put himself at the head of the vanguard and opened a way for the army.

Notwithstanding his victory the king thought it wise now to offer submission; he begged Kubilai to forget past events and with his prayers sent a gold statue. Kubilai, in punishment for defeat, took Yun nan rule from Prince Togan, forbade him the palace, and assigned him Yang chiu as a residence.

In 1285 Kubilai had charged Yang ting pie to visit the islands south of China and inform himself secretly of the forces and the wealth on them. The mission was successful, for in October of 1286 the ships of ten kingdoms sailed into Tsuen chiu, a port of the Fu kien province, bearing tribute, as was stated. It is quite likely, however, that these ships brought simply presents.

The chief and perhaps the one reason why Kubilai dropped his campaign against the Japanese islands was the menacing action of Kaidu, who had struggled two decades to win headship in the Empire. Kaidu, the grandson of Ogotai, claimed the Mongol throne as a right which no man might question, or venture to take from him, since it came from the will of Jinghis, and also from the solemn decision of the first Mongol Kurultai. For many years, and under varying pretexts, Kaidu had avoided appearing at Kubilai's court and now he declared himself openly hostile. The Emperor reckoned on the support of Borak, whom he had made Khan of Jagatai, and whose dominions touched those of Kaidu on the western border.

These two rulers did, in fact, begin war by a battle on the Syr Darya or Yaxartes. Borak gained the victory through an ambush. He made many prisoners, and took rich booty. Later on Kaidu got assistance from Mangu Timur of the Golden Horde, a descendant of Juchi, who sent an army commanded by Bergatchar, his uncle. With his own and these forces Kaidu met Borak and defeated him in a murderous battle. The defeated man then withdrew to Transoxiana and recruited his army, which he welded together again through treasures obtained from Bokhara and Samarkand, those famous old cities between the two rivers. He was preparing for a second struggle when peace proposals were brought him from Kaidu by Kipchak Ogul, a grandson of Ogotai, and friendly to both these opponents. The proposals were agreeable to Borak, who immediately accepted them. He formed an alliance then with Kaidu and each man became to the other a sworn friend or " anda."

This union gave control to Kaidu of the Jagatai country made up of Turkistan and Transoxiana. Borak died in 1270, and his successor, Nikbey, son of Sarban, and grandson of Jagatai, having taken arms against Kaidu was attacked in 1272, and killed in a battle. Next came Toga Timur; after his death Kaidu put on the throne Dua, son of Borak, his own " anda." In 1275 Kaidu and Dua invaded the country of the Uigurs with an army a hundred thousand in number and laid siege to the capital. These allies wished to force the Idikut to join in the war against Kubilai, but at this juncture the Idikut received aid from the Emperor's troops, which appeared in that region.

That same year Kubilai sent westward a numerous army commanded by his son Numugan, who had under him as general Hantum, a minister of State, and a descendant of Mukuli, Jinghis Khan's most beloved and perhaps his most gifted commander. Guekji, Numugan's brother, and Shireki, son of Mangu, went also with his army, as well as Tok Timur and other princes with their warriors. Numugan was appointed chief governor of Almalik at the outset.

In 1277 Tok Timur, dissatisfied with Kubilai, proposed to put Shireki, son of Mangu, on the throne of the Mongols. Shireki accepted the offer; Kubilai's two sons and the general, Hantum, were seized in the night time. Both princes were delivered to Mangu Timur, the sovereign of Kipchak; Hantum was given to Kaidu. Sarban, son of Jagatai, was won for the cause somewhat later, and other princes of this branch as well as that of Ogotai. At this juncture Kubilai summoned Bayan from South China and put him at the head of an army to crush the above combination. Bayan found his foes well entrenched on the Orgun. He cut off their supplies and they, dreading hunger, accepted the wager of battle. The conflict on which such great interests depended was stubborn to the utmost. For hours it raged with equal chances, till Bayan's skill turned the scale finally. Shireki was defeated and withdrew toward the Irtish. Tok Timur fled to the land of the Kirghis, where Kubilai's forces surprised him and seized all his camp goods. He sent to Shireki for succor, but Shireki failed to give it. Tok Timur took revenge for this by offering the throne of the Mongols to Sarban. Shireki tried to conciliate him, but Tok Timur gave answer as follows: " Thou hast not the courage for this dignity, Sarban is more worthy." Shireki was forced to give way, and had even to send his own envoys with those of other princes to Mangu Timur and to Kaidu to declare that Sarban had been chosen.

Tok Timur now wished to force Yubukur to acknowledge the sovereign just created. Yubukur assembled his forces to oppose, but before he had a chance to begin battle Tok Timur's warriors deserted to his enemy. Tok Timur, thus abandoned, took to flight, but was seized and given to Shireki, who had him killed at Yubukur's order. Tok Timur was renowned for splendid bravery and for skill as a bowman; he always rode a white horse during battle, and said that men choose dark horses lest blood from wounds might be apparent on their bodies, but to his mind the blood of the horse and the rider ornamented the latter, as rouge does the cheeks of a woman.

Sarban, who was now without effective aid, went to Shireki, and begged to be forgiven for letting Tok Timur wheedle him. Shireki took Sarban's troops and soon after sent the man under an escort of fifty warriors to Kotchi Ogul, a grandson of Juchi, but while passing the district of Jend and Ozkend he was rescued by his own men, who were quartered just then in those places. Putting himself at the head of them, he advanced on Shireki. When the two forces met Shireki's men deserted to Sarban, who captured him. Yubukur, who had come to give aid to Shireki, was also abandoned by his own troops and captured by Sarban, who, giving each of these princes to a guard of five hundred, set out on a visit to Kubilai. Yubukur, while passing near the Utchugen's land, sent gifts of silver and jewels to the prince who was ruling at that time and begged for deliverance. Sarban was attacked on a sudden by the Utchugen's descendants and his force taken captive. He himself escaped unattended, and made his way to the Emperor, who gave him both lands and warriors in sufficience, but Shireki, when taken to Kubilai, was sent to an island where the climate was pestiferous and he died in due season. Yubukur, after serving a time with Kaidu, made his peace with the Emperor and later on Kubilai's son, Numugan, who had been seized by Shireki was set free.

Ten years after these struggles Kaidu formed a new league against the Emperor. This time he drew to his side men descended from Jinghis Khan's brothers, namely: Nayan, fifth in descent from the Utchugen, youngest brother of Jinghis Khan; Singtur, descended from Juchi Kassar; and Kadan, who was fourth in descent from Kadjiun, also a brother of Jinghis. These princes were all in the present Manchuria. Nayan had forty thousand men under him and was waiting for Kaidu, who had promised to bring one hundred thousand picked warriors. To prevent the meeting of these forces the Emperor sent Bayan to the west, where he was to hold Kaidu in check while Kubilai himself was crushing Nayan and the others.

Kubilai, who had sent forward provisions by sea to the mouth of the river Liao, moved on Nayan by forced marches, and found him near that same river, at some distance south of Mukden in Manchuria. The Emperor had sent scouts far ahead of his forces so that no knowledge of his movements might reach the man against whom he was marching. Kubilai divided his army into two parts, one composed of Chinese, under Li ting, a Manchu, the other of Mongols, under Yissu Timur, a grandson of Boörchu, one of Jinghis Khan's four great heroes.

After consulting his astrologers, who promised a victory, the Emperor gave the signal for action. He had thirty regiments of cavalry, in three divisions. Before each regiment were five hundred infantry with pikes and sabres. These foot-soldiers were trained to mount behind horsemen and thus advance swiftly; when near the enemy they slipped down, used their pikes and next their sabres. If the cavalry retreated, or moved to another part those footmen sprang up behind them. Kubilai's place was in a wooden tower borne by four elephants; these beasts were covered with cloth of gold put on above strong leather armor. The Imperial standard with the sun and the moon on it waved over this tower, which was manned and surrounded by crossbowmen and archers.

When the two armies were drawn up in order of battle the whole space which they occupied, and a broad belt around it, was filled with a great blare of trumpets and the music of many wind-instruments. This was followed by songs from the warriors on both sides, and then the great kettledrum sounded the onset. The air was filled with clouds of arrows; when the opponents drew nearer spears were used deftly, and they closed finally with sabres and hand to hand weapons. Nayan's army showed great resolution, fighting from dawn until midday, but at last numbers triumphed. Nayan, when almost surrounded, strove to escape, but was captured. Kubilai had him killed on the field without waiting; he was wrapped in a pair of felt blankets and beaten to death without bloodshed. It is said that he was a Christian and bore on his standard a cross in contrast to the sun and moon of the standards of Kubilai.

The Emperor returned to Shang tu after this great encounter and triumph. The princes Singtur and Kadan were still in arms, hence Kubilai sent his grandson, Timur, against both with the generals Polo khwan, Tutuka, Yissu Timur and Li ting shi. After a toilsome campaign, which took place in the following summer, Timur defeated Singtur and Kadan, and received the submission of Southern Manchuria.

The chief enemy who had raised the whole conflict remained in the West, and against him the Emperor now turned his efforts. To guard western frontiers most surely, Kubilai gave Kara Kurum to Bayan as headquarters. This great commander received power without limit, since he was to watch all home regions and hold them securely. Before Bayan had arrived at the army Kamala, a son of Chingkin, led a corps in advance and tried to stop Kaidu from crossing the mountains of Kang kai. Kamala, Kubilai's favorite grandson, was defeated and surrounded near the river Selinga. He was barely rescued by Tutuka and his Kipchak warriors.

Affairs now seemed so serious that the Emperor, despite advanced age, thought it best to march forward in person. He sent for Tutuka to act with him, and praised the recent exploit of that general. Kubilai left Shang tu for the West July, 1289, but returned without meeting Kaidu, or coming near him.

For four years now Bayan held Kaidu in check, till at length being accused of inaction, and even of connivance with the Emperor's rival, Kubilai recalled the great general, and gave command to Timur, his own grandson. But before Timur came to take over the office Bayan had gone forth to meet Kaidu and had defeated his army. On returning to headquarters he yielded command and gave Timur a banquet at which he made him rich presents. Bayan then departed for Tai tung fu, assigned him already as a residence. On arriving he found there an order to stand before Kubilai. The Emperor, who had shaken off all his prejudice in the meanwhile, received the famed leader with every distinction, praised him in public, exalted his zeal and his services, made him first minister and commander of the guards and other troops in both capitals (Shang tu and Ta tu).

Kubilai liked to send envoys to various countries south of China whence ships came in large numbers bearing rare objects as presents. He sent once a Chinese minister to visit the sovereign of a land called Kuava (Java). This ruler for some unknown reason had the minister branded on the face, and sent him home with great insult. Kubilai felt the outrage, and all his officers demanded sharp vengeance. In 1293 a thousand ships with thirty thousand men on them and provisions for a twelvemonth set sail for Kuava. Chepi, a Chinese, who knew the language of Java, commanded this squadron. The King of Kuava gave pretended submission and persuaded Chepi to conquer Kolang, a near kingdom at war then with Kuava. Chepi won a great victory over the King of Kolang whom he seized and killed straightway. The King of Kuava tried now to get rid of the Chinese, and strove to cut them off from their vessels. Chepi reached the fleet, thirty leagues distant, with difficulty, after some serious encounters in which he lost three thousand warriors, though he brought away much gold and many jewels. On arriving at court he gave these to the Emperor, but Kubilai, enraged because Chepi had not conquered the kingdom of Kuava, condemned him to seventy blows of a stick, and took one third of his property.

On coming to the throne Kubilai had confided his finances to Seyid Edjell, a Bukhariote, and an adherent of Islam, a man who had a great reputation for probity. This minister died in 1270. Next came Ahmed, a native of Fenaket, a city on the Syr Darya. Ahmed's good fortune came from his intimacy with Jambui Khatun, the first and favorite wife of the Emperor; this intimacy began when Jumbui was still in the house of her father, Iltchi Noyon, a chief of the Kunkurats. Ahmed became attached to the court of the Empress, and adroit, insinuating, rich in expedients, he had the chance of winning favor from Kubilai, who after the death of Seyid Edjell put the wealth of the Empire into his keeping.

Kubilai needed money at all times, he needed much of it, and Ahmed found means to get money. Invincible through the Emperor's favor, he exercised power without limit; at his will he disposed of the highest offices in the Empire. He brought down to death whomsoever he accounted an enemy, and no man, whatever his rank or position, had the courage to brave Ahmed's hatred. He amassed boundless wealth by abuses of all sorts; no man obtained any office without giving great presents to this minister. He had twenty-five sons, all holding high places. No woman of beauty was safe from his passion; he left no means unused to satisfy his greed and ambition and lust.

For twelve years this man proved invincible, though his secret enemies were an army in number, and he was hated by the people for his endless abuses. Those learned Chinese who were intimate with the Emperor strove in vain to open his eyes to the real character of Ahmed. At last they were able to expose him to Chingkin well and clearly and Chingkin became Ahmed's most resolute enemy. This son of Kubilai was so angry one day at the minister, that he struck him on the face with his bow, and laid his cheek open. Kubilai, seeing the minister wounded, inquired what the cause was. "I have been kicked by a horse," replied Ahmed. "Art thou ashamed to tell who struck thee?" asked Chingkin, who was present. Another time Chingkin pummeled him with his fists before the eyes of the Emperor.

At last, in 1282, appeared Wang chu, a Chinese, a man of high office in the ministry. Wang chu resolved to deliver the Empire from this greatest of miscreants. To carry out his plan he chose the time when Kubilai and Chingkin were at Shang tu, their residence in summer. As Ahmed had remained in the capital for business of his ministry Wang chu brought in one day the false news that Chingkin was coming. All the great functionaries hastened to the palace to greet him. Ahmed went at the head of the mandarins; just as he was passing the gate Wang chu struck him down with a club and thus killed him. At news of this deed Kubilai was terribly enraged. He had Wang chu and his associates seized, judged, and executed. A large sum of money was assigned for a funeral of great splendor, and Kubilai commanded all his most distinguished officers to be present. But grief at the tragic death of his favorite was followed soon by furious anger. Seeking to find a large diamond for his own use, as an ornament, he discovered that some time before two merchants had brought him a stone of rare size and quality which they had left for delivery with Ahmed. This same stone was now found in possession of the principal wife of the late minister. The Emperor's wrath was so excited by this and by other disclosures, and intensified by Chingkin's strong speeches, that he ordered that Ahmed's body be dug up immediately, and the head cut from it and exposed as a spectacle. When all this was done the body was hurled to the dogs to be eaten. That one of Ahmed's widows who had worn the diamond was put to death with her two sons; his forty other wives and four hundred concubines were distributed as gifts to various people. Ahmed's property was confiscated, and his clients to the number of seven hundred suffered variously in proportion as they had shared in his abuses, and assisted him in deceiving the Emperor.

The ministry of finance was given now to an Uigur named Sanga, whose brother was the principal Lama. Sanga had occupied his dignity eight years, following closely the example of Ahmed, when one of Kubilai's officers undertook to expose the evil deeds of the minister. In time of a hunt he spoke with the Emperor about Sanga. Kubilai thought him a vilifier and had the man beaten. Later on the Emperor tried to force from this officer a confession that he was serving the hatred of men who were envious of Sanga. The officer declared that he was in no way opposed to the minister and was only trying to render service to his sovereign, and benefit the country. Kubilai found on inquiry that the officer had spoken the truth, and if no one before him had reported the evil doings of Sanga, it was because people dreaded the merciless revenge of that minister. At last Sanga was destroyed in the mind of the Emperor.

One day Kubilai asked pearls of the minister; the latter declared that he had none. A Persian who was favored by Kubilai, and who detested the minister, made haste to declare that he had seen a great quantity of pearls and precious stones in possession of Sanga, and if the Emperor would deign to occupy Sanga some moments he would bring those same pearls from that minister's mansion. The Emperor agreed, and in a short time the Persian returned, bringing with him two caskets filled with pearls of great value. "How is this?" cried the Emperor to Sanga; "thou hast all these pearls and art unwilling to give me even a few of them? Where didst thou find such great riches?" The minister answered that he got them from various Mohammedans who were governors of provinces in China. "Why have these men brought me nothing?" asked Kubilai. "Thou bringest me trifles and for thyself keepest all that is most precious." "They were given me," said the minister. "If it is thy wish I will return them to the donors."

Kubilai in his rage had Sanga's mouth filled with excrement and condemned him to death without waiting for further inquiry. His immense fortune was seized and the Emperor, incensed at those functionaries whose duty it had been to expose the excesses of the minister, demanded of the censors of the Empire what punishment they had merited. By decision of the censors they were stripped of office. Two Mohammedan governors lost their lives, as did many others involved in the recent abuses.

Thus after the death of Seyid Edjell, for about one fifth of a century the chiefs of finance in China were men from other countries, as were most of their agents. These persons kept themselves in power by revolting exactions. Kubilai, ever greedy of money since he needed endless sums of it, chose as agents in finance men who were ready to increase the state income if physically possible, and gave power to persons who stopped before nothing. Extortion, false witness, confiscation, and even murder were means used by them frequently. Oldjai followed Sanga as minister.

Kubilai died in 1294 during February, in Ta tu, the Pekin of the present day. He was eighty years old at the time of his death and sovereign over the largest domain ever ruled by one person.

Besides building his beautiful city Kubilai did much to improve the general condition of China. Among other great public works which he carried out was the building of the Grand Canal which joined his capital with the more fertile districts of the country. He also extended an excellent post system. According to Marco Polo all the principal roads met at Ta tu. Along those roads at intervals of twenty-five or thirty miles were well equipped post houses, at some of which four hundred horses were kept, two hundred for immediate use and two hundred at pasture. Three hundred thousand horses were engaged in this service, and there were ten thousand post stations.

Two systems of carriers were maintained by the government. The foot messengers wore belts with bells attached and were stationed at intervals of three miles apart. When the bells announced the approach of a runner a fresh man prepared to take his place at once. Each man ran at his greatest speed. The mounted couriers by a similar system of relief could travel four hundred miles in twenty-four hours, the distance covered at night being much less than that during day, for at night footmen with torches accompanied the mounted courier.

Kubilai built his capital near the ancient capital of the Kin Emperors. Marco Polo states that it was twenty-four miles in circuit. Its ramparts were fifty feet in width and fifty feet high; at each corner was an immense bastion and on each side were three gates, each gate garrisoned by one thousand men. The palace itself was surrounded by two walls, the outer one being a mile square and ornamented with battle scenes painted in bright colors. Between the two walls were parks and pleasure grounds through which were paved roads raised two cubits above the level of the ground. In the center of the enclosure rose the magnificent palace.

His summer palace was at Shang tu and was similar to the one in Ta tu. In a grove not far from the palace was a beautiful bamboo dwelling supported by gilt and lacquered columns, a resort for the Emperor during the warmer days. This bamboo palace was stayed by two hundred silk ropes and could very easily be put up and taken down.

Kubilai enjoyed hunting. In March of each year a great hunt was organized. Marco Polo says that there were two masters of the hunt, each having under him ten thousand men, five thousand dressed in red and five thousand in blue. These men surrounded an immense space and drove in the animals. When everything was ready the Khan set out with his ten thousand falconers. He traveled in a palanquin carried by four elephants. This palanquin was lined with gold and covered with lion skins. Ten thousand tents were erected near the hunting ground. The Emperor's great tent where receptions were held accommodated one thousand persons. Near by was his private tent and the tent in which he slept. Each one of these Imperial tents was covered with lion skins and lined with ermine and sable. There were many ropes to these tents and all were of silk.

The magnificence and luxury of the Mongol court would be remarkable even in our time. On his name-day Kubilai held a reception and received many presents. On New Year's Day also was held a festival when gifts were presented to the Grand Khan. If possible a multiple of nine, the sacred number, was chosen for the number of the articles given. On one of these great feast days Kubilai was presented with a hundred thousand horses with rich coverings. During the day his five thousand elephants were exhibited in their housings of bright colored cloth on which birds and beasts were represented. These elephants bore caskets containing the Imperial plate and furniture and were followed by camels laden with things needful for the feast.

Only the princes and higher officers assembled in the hall, other people remained outside. When every one was seated an official rose and cried: " Bow and pay homage ! " All then touched the ground with their foreheads. This was repeated four times. A similar obeisance was made before an altar on which was a tablet bearing the great Khan's name.

At the banquet the table of the Khan was raised above the others and so placed that he sat facing the south. At his left hand sat his chief wife and on his right princes of the Imperial family, but lower down, so that their heads would not be above the level of the Emperor's feet. Lower still sat the chief officers. Ordinary guests and warriors seated themselves on the carpet. Two large men stood at the entrance of the hall to punish those who were so unfortunate as to step on the threshold, such offenders were immediately stripped and beaten severely with rods. Various household officials moved about to see that the guests were properly served. Near the Khan's table was a magnificently carved stand in which was inserted a golden vessel holding an enormous quantity of spiced wine. Besides this there were many golden vessels, each holding wine for ten persons. There were large wine bowls on the tables with handled cups from which to drink. One of these bowls was placed between every two persons. The men who served the Khan had their mouths and noses covered with delicate napkins of silk and gold, that their breath might not offend him. Whenever he raised the wine cup to his lips the musicians began to play, and princes and officials went down on one knee.

Kubilai had five principal wives the chief of whom was Jambui Khatun. Each wife had her own court and was attended by not fewer than three hundred damsels as well as by many pages and eunuchs. The Kunkurats were celebrated for the beauty of their women and supplied most of the wives and concubines of the Khan. Officials were often sent to select several hundred girls and pay their parents for them, estimating their value according to their beauty. The girls were sent to the court and examined by a number of matrons. Polo states: "These women make the girls sleep with them in turn to ascertain that they have a sweet breath and are strong of limb." The few who passed this examination attended the Khan, the rejected married officers or became palace employees.

It is stated by chroniclers of that time that Kubilai became, through the influence of Jambui Khatun, a Lamaist. Still, to secure good fortune, he prayed to Christ, Mohammed, Moses and Buddha, whom he revered as the four great prophets of the world.

Kubilai was a man of medium stature. He had a fair complexion and keen black eyes, and was of a kindly disposition. He had designated as heir his fourth son, Numugan, but while that prince was a prisoner in the war with Kaidu he chose Chingkin, his second son, as successor. Some time after this Numugan was set free, and as he criticized the appointment of his brother he incurred Kubilai's wrath, and was banished. He died soon after. Chingkin died also before his father.

In 1293, eight years after the death of Chingkin, his widow, Guekjin, urged the great general, Bayan, to remark to the Emperor that he had not named a successor. Thereupon Kubilai appointed his grandson, Timur, whom he had sent to Kara Kurum as its governor, and charged Bayan to announce to that prince his appointment, and instal him as heir with due festivals and ceremonies.

After Kubilai's death, February, 1294, a Kurultai of election was held at Shang tu, the summer capital. Timur went to that city from his army and, though he was formally heir, his elder brother, Kamala, aspired to the Empire. The princes of the family wavered for a time, but the generals and the Chinese officials gave Timur their adherence. At last Bayan, who by character and office had the greatest influence in that meeting, took his sabre and declared that he would suffer no man on the throne save him whom Kubilai had selected. This ended debate, and Kamala knelt to his brother; the other princes followed his example, and Timur was proclaimed then Grand Khan of the Mongols.

The first work of Timur was to give Imperial rank to his parents, and next to rear a monument to Kubilai, Jambui, the late Empress, and Chingkin, his own father. Kamala was made the chief governor of Mongolia with Kara Kurum as his residence. Guekdju and Kurguez, Timur's brothers-in-law, received command over troops opposed to Kaidu and Dua on the northwestern border. Timur's cousin, Prince Ananda, was made governor of Tangut, that region west of the Yellow River. Bayan Fentchan kept the ministry.

Bayan, the chief commander and greatest general of Kubilai's reign, died early in 1295, at the age of fifty-nine years. He and Ye liu chu tsai, Ogotai's faithful adviser, were renowned for lofty character and justice beyond all men in the history of Mongols. Both tried to spare human blood, and both were endowed with rare modesty.

Only two events of note came to pass in Timur's time: a war in the regions which lie between China and India, and a war in the west against Kaidu.

Once on the throne, Timur made peace with the King of Ngan nan and opened communication with India, which had been stopped by the war and operations against Java. For several years Titiya, King of Mien tien (Burma), had failed to send tribute, and Timur was preparing large forces against him when Titiya's son, Sinhobati, came with both homage and tribute in the name of his father. Through a patent Timur then declared Titiya king, with his son Sinhobati as successor, and gave to the prince a square seal with the figure of a tiger. Mongol generals on the borders of Burma received the command to respect that vassal State and protect commerce between it and the Empire.

Three years later on Titiya was dethroned, and then killed by Asankoye, his brother. His son went to beg the assistance of China. Timur sent this command to Seitchaur, then governing in Yun nan for the Empire: "March into Mien tien; seize and bring me Asankoye." Seitchaur met many checks and returned to Yun nan, spreading meanwhile the statement that he had quelled all rebellion, but a number of his officers were punished with death because they had been bribed by the rebels; this had been proven. The Emperor degraded Seitchaur and seized all his property.

While the war in Mien tien was progressing Timur learned that Pape si fu, which lies west of Yun nan, had refused China's calendar, and would not obey that great Empire. He took the advice of Li yu chin, whom he sent with a force of thirty thousand to bring all to obedience. This army was reduced very soon to one third of its numbers by difficult marches and the tropical climate. Demands in Yun nan for provisions and horses roused revolt among hill tribes, whom the Chinese called barbarous. Song long tsi, a chief among these people, put himself at the head of their forces, surrounded Li yu chin, the Imperial commander, and would have cut his whole army to pieces had not the viceroy Hugatchi, Timur's uncle, marched very quickly from Yun nan and saved him.

The Emperor at this juncture commanded his generals Liu kwe kie and Yang sai yu pwa to assemble all troops available in Su chuan, Yun nan and Hu kuang and advance to support Li yu chin, who, pressed by Song long tsi most unsparingly, was retreating, or rather, fleeing to a place of protection. He had abandoned his baggage and lost many warriors.

The revolt spread now on all sides, and many new tribes joined it. Detached bands plundered towns, and ravaged loyal places. Liu kwe kie held his own till fresh men came by swift marches to strengthen him; with these new forces and his own he pushed into the country of the rebels, and defeated them. Large numbers were captured, and among them Che tsi we, a woman who had led mountain men from the first in that struggle. She was killed without hesitation or pity.

In the North the long war continued. The Imperial troops led by Chohaugur, who in 1297 succeeded his father Tutuka, won advantages over Kaidu and Dua, who in their turn gained a victory, thanks to neglect on the other side. A division of Dua's army attacked the cordon which stood against him and his ally. This cordon was of cavalry placed on a line from southwest stretching northeastward; contact between the groups was kept up by couriers. When an enemy was sighted mounted men dashed away to notify the next group. One night the commanders of three posts met for a drinking feast. News came at midnight that the enemy was approaching, but they were too drunk to mount, rush away, and give notice. Kurguez, the general in charge, did not know of this and marshalled his warriors, six thousand in number. The attack was a fierce one, Kurguez fought as best he was able, but waited in vain for assistance; he fled at last, was pursued and taken captive. " I am the Emperor's brother-in-law," said he. With these words he saved his life, for they spared him. Timur had the three men, who had failed through their drinking, put in irons, but the loss caused by their feasting soon found a recompense. Wishing, as they said, to serve the Emperor, two princes, Yubukur and Ulus Buga, with one general, Durduka, taking twelve hundred men with them, abandoned Dua. These same three had deserted the Empire in Kubilai's day, hence Timur, distrusting such persons, sent troops, who arrested them.

Ulus Buga from Kara Kurum sent his men out to pillage and was seized for such action. Friends saved him, however, from punishment, but Timur would not give him employment. Yubukur, on the contrary, was treated with kindness by the Emperor. Durduka, who had deserted twice before, received this time a death sentence. He wept while defending his action, and declared in reply to this sentence, that fear had forced him to go from the service of Kubilai, that he had never raised arms against that sovereign, that seeing Timur on the throne he had persuaded the two others who were with him to rally to the Emperor, that he had brought back more troops than he had taken, and had brought them to march against Timur's opponents.

Timur pardoned Durduka and sent him with an army against Dua. Yubukur was permitted to go with him, These two men, who knew Dua's strength well, wished to win distinction by crushing it. After his recent triumph Dua was marching home by slow stages. He intended to fall on the troops of Ananda, Achiki and Chobai when he came to them, disposed as they were along Tangut on the border as far as Kara Kodja toward Uigur regions. But while Dua's troops were preparing to pass a certain river,

Durduka, coming up on a sudden, defeated them and slew or drowned a great number.

In 1301 Kaidu was leading the largest army that he had ever assembled. With him went Dua and forty princes descended from his grandfather and from his grand-uncle Jagatai. Khaishan, Timur's nephew, who had come a short time before to learn war under Yuetchar and Chohaugur, summoned promptly the five army corps stationed in that region and gave battle between Kara Kurum and the Tamir River. The historian Vassaf describes the battle as resulting in victory for Kaidu, who died while his troops were marching homeward, but this westward march seems to prove that the victory, if there was one, could not have been on his side decisively.

Kaidu had assumed the title Grand Khan, thus claiming the headship of the Mongols, which belonged to him by the will of Jinghis, and the solemn oath of the earliest Kurultai. Could he have lived some years longer he might have obtained the great primacy, since after Timur the Mongol sovereigns of China deteriorated and became not merely paltry but pitiful and wretched, while Kaidu was a genius and also a hero. He was loved in the West very greatly, and his veterans were renowned even among Mongols. Kaidu was exalted by his people for magnanimity and kindness. His boundless bravery and strength of body roused admiration and wonder. He had forty sons and one daughter, named Aiyaruk (Shining Moon), whom Marco Polo states was famous for beauty and still more famous for the strength of her body; she surpassed every warrior of that day, not only among Mongols, but all surrounding nations. This young princess declared that she would marry no man save him who could conquer her in wrestling. When the time came notice was given to every one that Kaidu's only daughter would marry the man who could throw her in wrestling, but if he were thrown by the princess he would lose a hundred horses. Man after man came till the princess had thrown a hundred suitors and won ten thousand horses. After this hundred came the best man of all, a young hero from a rich remote kingdom, a man who had never met an equal in any land. He felt sure of victory, and brought with him a forfeit of not one hundred, but one thousand horses. Kaidu and the young lady's mother were charmed with this suitor when they saw him, and, being the son of a great and famous sovereign, begged their daughter to yield in case she were winning in the struggle, but she answered: " I will not yield unless he can throw me. If he throws me, I will marry him." A day was appointed for the meeting, and an immense audience came to witness the trial. When all the great company was ready the strong maid and the young man came into the courtyard and closed in the struggle. They wrestled with great skill and energy and it seemed for a long time that neither could conquer the other, but at last the damsel threw the young hero. Immense was the suitor's confusion as he lay in the courtyard, but he rose and hurried off with all his attendants, leaving the one thousand horses behind him as forfeit.

Kaidu's warriors mourned the death of their ruler with loud intense wailing. Dua, to whom he had told his last wishes, proposed to the princes who stood round the bier of the sovereign to choose as successor the eldest among the dead man's forty sons, namely, Chabar, who was then absent. Dua on his part owed much to Chabar. When, after the death of Borak, the members of his family repaired to the court of Kaidu, as custom commanded, Dua, though not the eldest of Jagatai's descendants, obtained his succession through the influence of Chabar. All present agreed with Dua, and each of the princes sent officers to attend Kaidu's body to its resting-place.

Chabar arrived very soon, and the princes, with Dua at the head of them, rendered him homage as Kaidu's successor. When Chabar was installed in Ogotai's dominion, Dua proposed to acknowledge overlordship of Timur, grandson of Kubilai, and thus end the strife which had raged for three decades in Jinghis Khan's family. This advice was accepted by Chabar and all other princes, and they sent envoys immediately to offer submission. This pledge of peace was received with great gladness by Timur, who now saw his authority recognized by every member of his family.

But this agreement was short-lived. In the year following, disputes burst forth between Chabar and Dua which involved the two sides of Jinghis Khan's family. In 1306, at Dua's persuasion, Timur, who was watchful, of course, and suspicious, attacked Chabar, the son of Kaidu his recent opponent. Chabar was deserted immediately by most of his adherents. He turned in distress then to Dua to support him. Dua treated his guest with distinction, but took that guest's states from him, and joined Turkistan to Transoxiana. He thus reëstablished well-nigh in completeness the dominions of Jagatai, which Kaidu had dismembered.

So Chabar, the successor of Kaidu of Kuyuk and of Ogotai, was the last real sovereign descended from Ogotai, son of Jinghis; that Ogotai to whom the great conqueror had given supreme rule in the world of the Mongols; Ogotai, whose descendants, despoiled by Batu, son of Juchi, had won for themselves immense regions through the fruitful activity and genius of Kaidu.

Dua, son of Borak, died in 1306; his son, Gundjuk, who succeeded him, held power one year and a half only. After Gundjuk's death supreme power was next captured by Taliku, who through Moatagan was descended from Jagatai. Taliku had grown old in combats; a Mohammedan by religion, he strove to spread his belief among Mongols.

Meanwhile two princes, descended from Jagatai, insisted, weapons in hand, that the throne belonged by right to a son of Dua; these two were vanquished. Many others were preparing to avenge the defeat which these men had suffered when Taliku was killed at a banquet by officers who wished to raise a son of their former sovereign, Dua, to dominion. The conspirators then proclaimed Dua's youngest son, Gebek (1308). This prince was barely installed when Chabar, leagued with other princes descended from Kaidu, attacked him. Chabar being vanquished in this struggle, crossed the Ili. Only a few followers went with him, and he and they found a refuge in the lands of the Emperor. After this victory over Chabar, which destroyed every hope among Ogotai's descendants, the Jagatai branch held a Kurultai at which they chose Issen Buga, a brother of Gebek, as their ruler. This prince, who was then in the territory of the Grand Khan, came for the sovereignty, which Gebek gave him with willingness. After Issen Buga's death, — we know not when it happened, — Gebek received power and used it.

Bloody quarrels of this kind brought ruin to Turkistan regions and to Transoxiana. Prosperity could not exist long with such sovereigns. When the fruit of any labor grew evident it was

pounced upon straightway. The whole life of that land was
passed in confusion, bloodshed and anarchy.

Timur, the Grand Khan at Ta tu, was forty-two years of age when
he died in 1307, after a reign of thirteen years. During his last illness a decree was issued forbidding the killing of any animal for
forty-two days; still he died. He was a sovereign well liked by
the Chinese, who praised his humanity and prudence. Humane
he seems to have been to some extent. Princes and princesses of
the Jinghis Khan line had held boundless power over vassals and
people who served them till Timur declared that no prince whatever should put to death any one without his confirmation. He
founded an Imperial College at Ta tu and built a magnificent
palace in honor of Confucius.

Before he mounted the throne Timur, like so many men of his
family and race, had been an unrestrained, boundless drinker;
his grandfather, Kubilai, reprimanded him frequently and bastinadoed him thrice for his conduct. At last physicians were sent
to see that he ate and drank within reason, but an alchemist, whose
duty it was to attend him in the bathing house, filled his bath tub
with wine or other liquor instead of water. Kubilai heard of this
trick, and when Timur clung to his favorite, Kubilai had the man
exiled and then killed on the journey. But Timur, when made
Emperor, forsook his intemperance and became as abstemious as
he had been irrestrainable aforetime.

CHAPTER XIX

EXPULSION OF THE MONGOLS FROM CHINA

THE late Emperor was childless. His widow, Bulagan, who toward the end of her husband's reign had great influence, wished to put on the throne Ananda, a son of Mangkala and grandson of Kubilai. He was living at that time in Tangut as its viceroy. Tangut in those days included Shen si, with Tibet and Su chuan also in some part. While Timur lay on his death-bed Bulagan warned Ananda in secret to hasten to the capital. She wished to keep the throne from Khaishan and Ayurbali Batra, the two sons of Chingkin's son Tarmabala; she had had the mother of these two princes sent to Corea as an exile. Khaishan was on the northwestern border at that time, commanding an army of observation, and had won high repute through discretion and bravery in the struggle with Kaidu. Batra was with his mother in exile.

Bulagan, now the regent, was sustained in supporting Ananda by Agutai, the first minister, and by others. She disposed troops along the roads of Mongolia to hinder Khaishan in reaching Ta tu. There was, however, a party which favored the sons of Tarmabala. Karakhass, who was chief of this party, sent secretly to hurry Khaishan on his journey and mentioned the route by which he should travel to avoid meeting enemies. He urged Batra also to be in Ta tu, and Batra did not fail to come promptly with his mother. Meanwhile Ananda's adherents had settled the day on which to instal him.

Khaishan's party saw that there was no time for loitering. They could not wait for their candidate; he was too far from the capital. So Prince Tulu brought in a large army corps which he was commanding, and acted. Melik Timur, a son of Arik Buga, was one of Ananda's chief partisans. He had served in the army of Chabar, had revolted, and then fled to China; this Melik Timur was put in chains, conveyed to Shang tu, and immured there securely. Agutai and other partisans of Ananda were arrested and condemned to die for endeavoring to dispose of the throne arbitrarily, but the execution was deferred till Khaishan's arrival. Bulagan and Ananda were guarded in the palace. The princes of the blood asked Batra to proclaim himself Emperor, but he refused, saying that the throne belonged to his elder brother. Batra now sent the seal of the Empire to that brother, and took the title of regent till Khaishan's arrival, holding down meanwhile the partisans of the Empress.

Khaishan hurried to Kara Kurum, where he took counsel with princes and generals. The army, in which he was a great favorite, desired to proclaim him in the homeland. Khaishan refused and started for Shang tu with a picked force thirty thousand in number. He sent a message to his mother and brother inviting them to assist at his installation. Batra set out at once for Shang tu, where Khaishan was saluted as sovereign by the princes and generals assembled in a Kurultai. He took the name Kuluk Khan, raised his mother to be Empress and gave his dead father the title of Emperor. He acknowledged at the same time the services of his brother by making him heir, though he had heirs in his own sons.

Khaishan's first act was to give homage to his ancestors in the temple devoted to their service. Next he carried out the judgment passed by Batra against the adherents of Ananda. Ananda himself, with Melik Timur, his close intimate, and Bulagan, the Empress had to die according to sentence. They had broken the laws of the Yassa by their efforts to dispose of the throne without winning consent from Jinghis Khan's family.

Khaishan's acts as a ruler were not merely paltry, they were harmful, except this, that he had one work of Confucius translated into Mongol, and also many sacred texts of the Buddhists. He angered the Chinese by favoring Lamas beyond measure. A law was passed that whosoever struck a Lama his hand should be cut off, and whoso spoke against a Lama should have his tongue cut out. Given to women and wine, Khaishan died at the age of thirty-one, in the year 1311. His brother Batra was then proclaimed Emperor, but with the condition that a son of Khaishan should be his heir. The feast of installation lasted for a week. At an hour designated by astrologers he ascended the throne and was saluted under the name Bayantu. The first act of this sovereign was to punish those ministers who, taking advantage of Khaishan's incompetence, had acquired wealth for themselves through injustice; he put to death some of these, and sent others to exile.

Notwithstanding an ordinance made by Kubilai, examinations of scholars had not been reëstablished. Bayantu brought them now into use, thus winning good will from the learned. He prohibited the employment of eunuchs in every office, though he infringed his own law the year following (1315), by making a eunuch Grand Mandarin. Bayantu was himself a scholar and encouraged learned men. Among many who are mentioned as being guests at his court is Chahan, one of the most celebrated scholars of his time.

Now comes the great cause, and beginning of ruin for the ruling line of the Mongols in China: the struggle among members of that line for dominion. Though Bayantu was made heir on condition that he appoint to that dignity one of his nephews, he removed his nephew, Kushala, the eldest son of Kuluk Khan (Kaishan) the late Emperor, and sent him to live in Yun nan as its governor. The officers of Kushala's household looked upon this as exile, and in crossing Shen si they persuaded many Mongol commanders in those parts to take arms in Kushala's favor. But when Kushala saw himself abandoned soon after by those very officers, he fled to the Altai for refuge among the Khans of Jagatai. Thereupon the Emperor appointed as heir his own son Shudi Bala.

Bayantu died in February, 1320, his age being somewhat beyond thirty years.

His first minister was a Mongol named Temudar, who made himself odious by countless deeds of injustice. Accused by the censors of the Empire, he was driven from office, and given a death sentence, but the Empress delayed the execution. While the case was still pending Bayantu died, and the Empress reinstated her favorite in all former dignities. Shudi Bala, or Gheghen Khan, the new Emperor, mourned sincerely for his father, fasted long and gave large sums in charity. Through regard for his mother he did not act against Temudar, but he gave his confidence to Baidju, a descendant of Mukuli, Jinghis Khan's great commander. Temudar took revenge on many of his enemies, but after his death which took place in 1322 a host of accusers attacked this oppressor. Fear restrained them no longer, hence they called loudly for justice and obtained it as far as was possible at that time. The Emperor degraded the dead minister by cancelling his titles, destroying his tomb, and seizing his property. Those who had shared in Temudar's crimes, among others his adopted son Tekchi, formed a plan to assassinate Shudi Bala and Baidju, his first minister, and give the throne then to Yissun Timur, a son of Kamala, brother of Kuluk Khan.

Tekchi, being military inspector, had immense power in the army, and he sent off in secret to Yissun Timur, who was then at the Tula, an officer named Walus. This man bore a letter with sixteen names affixed to it. In this letter the plan was explained, and Yissun invited to be Emperor. The prince had Walus arrested and sent at once an account to the Emperor of the plot against his person. The couriers were late in arriving. The conspirators, fearing lest the plot be discovered, resolved to finish all without waiting for an answer. Shudi Bala had set out from Shang tu, his summer residence, for Ta tu, the chief capital, and while he was spending the night at Nanpo, the conspirators killed Baidju in his tent to begin with, and then forced the guard of the Emperor's pavilion. Tekchi himself slew his sovereign. Shudi Bala was only twenty-one years of age when his death came. This was the first death by assassination that there had ever been in the Imperial family of the Mongols. Two princes, Antai Buga and Yesien Timur, seized the great seal, with other insignia of dominion, and bore them to Yissun Timur, son of Kamala, who proclaimed himself Emperor at the Kerulon River, and granted a pardon to all men.

At first he intended to place at the head of affairs those who had brought him dominion through their murders; but when experienced advisers explained to the new sovereign clearly that if this were done the whole nation might suspect him of complicity, he had Yesien Timur with two other conspirators arrested and executed in the place where the Emperor and his minister had been murdered. He then sent two officers bearing an order to put to death Tekchi with his accomplices, also their families, and then to confiscate their property.

Sonan, son of Temudar, had been condemned simply to exile,

but when the ministers remarked that he had cut off Baidju's
shoulder with a sabre stroke, Sonan suffered death with the others.
Those princes of the blood who had joined the conspiracy were
sent to various places of exile.

Yissun Timur entered Ta tu in December, 1323, and early the
following year he appointed as heir his son Asukeba. This paltry
monarch did nothing of note while in power, and died when thirty-
six years of age. Though Asukeba, who was eldest among the
four sons of the Emperor, was heir by appointment, his right to
the Empire was challenged. It will be remembered that when
Bayantu had succeeded Kuluk Khan he did so on condition that
he make a son of the latter his heir. Instead of doing that he
kept the place for his own son and removed to a distance Kuluk's
sons, Tob Timur and Kushala. When the conspiracy against
Shudi Bala, or Gheghen Khan, had succeeded, the second of
Kuluk's sons was in Southern China, the first in the west far
beyond the Altai.

It was easy for Yissun Timur to seize power in their absence,
and he did so. Five years later he died in Shang tu, where he had
gone to pass the summer.

The Empress now sent Upetala, a minister of State, to Ta tu to
seize each department seal. Her son Asukeba, at that time nine
years of age, had been declared heir when in his fifth year, but
Yang Timur, governor of the capital, was the chief of a party which
wished a son of Kuluk Khan to be Emperor. Yang Timur, son
of Choahugur, was distinguished as a warrior, while his position
was strengthened by the fame of his father and grandfather.
Raised to high dignities through Kuluk Khan, by whom he was
favored, this governor felt himself bound to the sons of that Emperor by gratitude, as well as self-interest. When setting out for
Shang tu some months earlier Yissun Timur had given him power
in the capital. Yang Timur now summoned high officials to the
palace and proposed the elevation of one of Kuluk's sons to Empire, threatening with death all who showed opposition. After
this declaration he arrested Upetala, and other high functionaries;
these men he replaced by others in whom he had confidence.
The troops, who had no knowledge yet of his intentions, were
ordered to kneel, looking southward, and touch the earth with
their foreheads. This was to indicate that through them Yang

Timur had proclaimed Tob Timur Emperor. That prince was then in Nan king. The minister had urged him to hasten, and now announced his early arrival.

Three descendants of Jinghis with fourteen high officials conspired to slay the first minister for his unparalleled daring. Yang Timur, learning of their plot, seized the seventeen and put to death every man of them.

Meanwhile the Empress had Asukeba proclaimed at Shang tu, and chose Prince Wan tsin, a grandson of Kamala, as first minister. She chose as commander of the army Taché Timur, a son of the minister Toto, a Kankali, and gave him the word to attack Yang Timur, who was trying to cut off Shang tu by seizing other places of importance.

Tob Timur appeared now in Ta tu, assumed power and made appointments to office. He put to death Upetala, the minister, and sent Toto to exile with other persons whom Yang Timur had imprisoned. The governor urged the prince to proclaim himself Emperor, but he insisted that power belonged by right to his elder brother, Kushala, who besides had more merit because of his services. At last, however, he agreed to the installation, and promised to act till the coming of Kushala, but he declared that he would yield up the throne on his arrival.

The Empire once established, Yang Timur marched toward Liao tung to meet an army moving in the interest of Asukeba, but learning that Wan tsin had seized a fortress on the way from Shang tu to the capital, he wheeled about quickly, fell on Wan tsin, and forced him to retreat toward Mongolia. Other generals in the interior declared for Asukeba. Temuku advanced from the south on Honan with considerable forces, while Prince Kokohoa, leading troops from Shen si, took possession of Tung Kwan, the great fortress. Yessen Timur proclaimed Asukeba in that same province, and advanced on the capital. Yang Timur faced all these enemies and conquered. He met Yessen Timur when four leagues from Ta tu and vanquished his army completely.

Buka Timur, uncle of Yang Timur and commander-in-chief of all forces at the Liao tung border, on hearing of Tob Timur's accession invited Prince Yuelu Timur to join forces and march on Shang tu with him. Tao la chu, who commanded at the summer palace, sallied forth repeatedly with partisans of Asukeba, to battle with besiegers, but reduced finally, he yielded. He surrendered the seal of the Empire and gave up also the rich jewels belonging to Asukeba. The young Emperor died shortly after, no one knows in what manner. Temuku, the Liao tung governor, was killed during battle, weapons in hand. Yuelu Timur, now master of Shang tu, and possessing the seal of dominion, conducted the Empress mother to the capital. The minister Tao la chu traveled with her. Yessen Timur and many other titled prisoners went also. The Empress was exiled to a place in Pe che li, and Tao la chu, Wan tsin, Yessen Timur and other lords of their party suffered death at the capital.

News of this tragedy at Shang tu spread soon throughout China, and caused the partisans of Asukeba to cease all resistance.

Tob Timur sent officers now to Kushala beyond the Gobi desert, to declare what had happened and urge him to hasten. Kushala, as if distrusting his brother, and feeling that danger was before him, advanced very slowly, but when near the Mongol capital he proclaimed himself sovereign. Tob Timur sent his first minister to Kara Kurum to Kushala with the great seal of State, as well as the robes and regalia of Empire. Kushala was courteous and genial in meeting his brother's first minister, and charged him at parting to tell Tob Timur that he would confirm his appointments. At the same time the new Emperor named his own ministers, and sent one of them to inform Tob Timur that the throne was made his in succession.

Tob Timur and his first minister set out for Shang tu now without loitering, and met the new sovereign a little north of the city. That same evening, while at a feast, Kushala became ill on a sudden and died some days later (1329). A report went abroad that he had been poisoned; suspicion touched Yang Timur, the first minister. Kushala was thirty years old when he died, and was entitled Ming tsong in Chinese.

Eight days after the death of Kushala, Tob Timur was made Emperor the second time.

Tob Timur's reign, however, was brief, and during his day nothing happened of importance, except the personal plotting and treason of Tukien, a prince of the blood, and governor in the Yun nan province, who in 1330 took the title of King of Yun nan, and revolted. He was put down by force the year following this

action, 1331.   Like Yissun Timur and Kuluk, who preceded him,
Tob Timur favored Buddhism greatly.   He appointed large sums
to build temples, and brought from Uigur regions a renowned
Lama, Nien chin kilas, whom he called " Instructor of the Emperor."   Tob Timur commanded the highest personages to advance to meet this great Lama.   All persons whom he addressed
bent the knee to him, by order, and served wine to the Lama,
who received it without any answering civility.   Shocked at his
haughtiness, the chief of the great Chinese college in presenting
wine spoke thus to him: " You are a follower of Buddha and
chief of all the Ho Chang.   I am a follower of Confucius, and
chief of all scholars.   Confucius is not less illustrious than Buddha,
and there is no need of this ceremony between us."   The Lama
smiled, rose and received as he stood there the cup which the chief
held before him.   Notwithstanding these marks of the Emperor's
favor Lamas and Uigurs conspired with powerful Mongols to put
on the throne Yuelu Timur, a son of Ananda.   The plot was
discovered and the conspirators died for their treason.   Yuelu
Timur died with the others.

The Emperor was anxious to please learned men and thus win
the Chinese; hence he decreed new honors to the father and
mother of Confucius, as well as to some of his disciples.   Having
ordered the college of Han lin, in which were found the best
scholars of the Empire, to describe Mongol history and manners,
he visited that body one day, and conferred long on history; he
commanded to bring then the memoirs of his own reign.   The
officers of his suite went to bring them.   No opposition was offered
till Liu sse ching, a subaltern in the college, fell at Tob Timur's
feet and explained that that tribunal was bound in all sacredness
to write down exactly the good and bad deeds of Emperors, princes
and great men, and write them down without favor, that these
records were not to be seen by any one save high officials of the
College of Historians until after the death of the Emperor.   During time immemorial no sovereign had violated the annals of his
dynasty, much less those of his own reign, and he hoped that the
Emperor would not be the first to infringe on this sacred and long
honored usage.   Tob Timur yielded, and even praised the official
for his courage and honesty.

Occupied with his own pleasures mainly, and leaving State cares to his minister, Tob Timur became a nonentity. He died in 1332 at Shang tu, being twenty-nine years of age when his life ended.

Though the throne had been appointed to a son of Kushala, Yang Timur proposed to the Empress Putacheli to inaugurate a son of the late Emperor. Tob Timur had so loved the first minister that he gave him his one son to educate, bestowing on the youth the new name Yang Tekus, and took Targai, the minister's son, to be reared in the palace. The Empress wished to enthrone a boy of seven years, Ylechebe, second son of Kushala, who had been named heir by the late sovereign. She had this boy proclaimed, and then became regent, but the health of Ylechebe was feeble, and he died some months afterward. The Chinese name Ning tsong was bestowed on him.

Yang Timur now made fresh efforts in favor of Yang Tekus, but the Empress objected that this prince was too young; Tob Timur, she declared, had promised Kushala to leave the throne to a son of his, and she informed the ex-minister that she had sent an officer to visit Kuang si and bring Togan Timur, Kushala's eldest son, to Ta tu at the earliest.

The prince was thirteen years of age at that period. At the beginning of Tob Timur's reign, Putacheli had put to death the Empress Papucha, wife of Kushala, and sent her son, Togan Timur, to an island off the coast of Corea with the command to let no man whatever approach him. When a year had passed the report ran that Togan Timur had been exiled because he was the true and rightful heir to the Empire. Tob Timur declared in reply, that Kushala had had no children in Mongolia, hence Togan Timur was no son of his. But he brought the boy back and sent him to live at Kuang si in South China

When Togan Timur was some leagues from the capital, Yang Timur, with princes and persons of distinction, set out to meet him. But, little satisfied with the reception given him by Togan and the persons accompanying him, Yang Timur delayed the enthronement. The coming Emperor saw his fault, and tried to repair it by marrying Peyao, Yang Timur's daughter. While discussing this matter, and settling its details, death struck the minister. Since Tob Timur's advent to authority this minister had been all-powerful; no person or combination of persons however mighty had been able to successfully oppose him; he had done what he wished in all cases; he had forced the widow of Yissun Timur, an Empress, to marry him, and had dared to take forty princesses descended from Jinghis, the great conqueror, and make them his concubines; some of them he retained for three days only. His death, hastened by incontinence and drink, assured the throne to the son of Kushala. The Empress published the last will of the late Emperor, and Togan Timur was made sovereign immediately, with the promise to demand of the Empress that Yang Tekus, her son, would succeed him.

The new Emperor's bent was toward luxury and pleasure, and he did nothing of service to any one. Peyen became minister, and Satun chief commander of the army. Satun, Yang Timur's eldest brother, died soon after he had entered on his office, and was succeeded by Tang Kichi, the eldest son of that renowned minister, and therefore brother of Peyao, the young Empress. Togan Timur, wishing now to win Yang Timur's powerful family, had raised Peyao to the highest rank possible to a woman. Tang Kichi, fiery and envious by nature, was enraged at seeing Peyen decide by himself the highest questions, hence he formed a plot to raise to the throne Hoan ho Timur, a grandson of Mangu the Emperor and a son of Shireki.

The conspirators, among whom with Tang Kichi were Targai, his brother, and Talientali, Tang Kichi's uncle, planned to secrete troops and seize the Shang tu summer palace. Peyen, informed of this plot by a prince of the blood, gave command to arrest Tang Kichi and Targai in the palace. Tang Kichi, who strove to defend himself, was cut down and killed where they found him. Targai fled to the apartment of his sister, the Empress, who tried to conceal him with her garments; but she failed for the men hunting Targai cared not for her modesty, hence he was discovered and sabred to death in her presence. Peyao herself fared no better, for Peyen obtained from the Emperor an order to kill her, and charged himself with the office of headsman.

When Peyao saw him enter her apartments she divined what he wanted, and rushing to the Emperor's chamber, begged life of him. Little touched by the tears of his consort, Togan Timur replied very coolly that her uncle and her brothers had plotted against him, and he would do nothing to save her. She was taken

from the palace to some house where Peyen himself killed her.
Talientali defended his life arms in hand till he fled to Hoan ho
Timur's mansion, where the blood hunters slew him. Hoan ho was
forced to raise hands on himself, and be his own executioner.
Thus the great family of Yang Timur, the late minister, was
extinguished.

Emperors of a day, palace tragedies, murders, civil war, and
weakness roused up the Chinese at last, and they began to cast off
the Mongol yoke. Revolts broke out in Honan, Su chuan, and
Kuang tung simultaneously; they were stifled at the very inception.
The Mongol court became thoroughly suspicious of the Chinese.
In 1336 it prohibited them from having horses and arms and forbade them to use the language of the Mongols, their masters.

Peyen, the all-powerful minister, had reached now the acme of
his influence, and was approaching his ruin and his doom. This
man had the boldness to put to death without the Emperor's
knowledge a prince of the blood of Jinghis, and to exile two others.
Ambitious and merciless, greedy and insolent to the utmost, he had
drawn to his person the hatred of all save the Emperor and his
own tools and creatures. Togan Timur knew nothing whatever of
Peyen's activity, being guarded most strictly by that minister's
servants, who owed all they had to their master. The blow came
in 1340 from Peyen's own nephew, Toktagha. This man, a mere
officer of the guards, undertook to explain to the Emperor the
real condition of the country and succeeded. Measures taken in
secret secured Peyen's downfall. The moment was chosen when
the minister was absent on a hunting trip; when he returned he
was not permitted to reënter the capital. He was driven to an
exile in South China, and died, as exiles usually died, while on
the way. His brother, Machartai, took his place as first minister.

This same year, 1340, the Emperor removed from the hall of
Imperial ancestors Tob Timur's tablet, and excluded from his
court the Empress widow. He exiled also, to Corea, Yang Tekus,
treated as heir up to that time. This action was explained by an
edict which was worded thuswise in substance: "At the death
of Kuluk Khan the Empress, yielding to intrigues, excluded from
court Kushala Khan, my own father, and made him prince of
Yun nan to be rid of him. When Shudi Bala (Gheghen Khan)
was slain, the throne was given to Kushala, who for safety had

withdrawn beyond the Gobi desert. While my father was returning rule was tendered Tob Timur, who accepted on condition of
yielding to Kushala on the latter's arrival. Meanwhile he sent the
seal of Empire to the coming Emperor, who was journeying toward
his capital. My father, to reward his brother's apparent zeal,
appointed him successor. In pay for this Tob Timur and his
adherents went to meet the Emperor, and caused his death, while
showing him great marks of kindness. Then my uncle took the
throne a second time. False to the word which he had given my
father, he appointed his own son successor. He put to death the
Empress Papucha, and sent me as an exile to distant regions. He
even tried to prove that I was not Kushala's son. Heaven punished
well this man for so many offenses by taking his life from him.
Putacheli, through abuse of authority, placed on the throne to
my prejudice a child of seven years, my own brother. When he
died the great men and princes gave me that dominion which was
due me as eldest son of the Emperor Kushala. My first care has
been to purge the court of those intriguers, who breathe only murder
and dissensions. Filled with gratitude for Heaven's favor I cannot
uphold those whom its justice has abandoned. Let the right
tribunal repair to the hall of Imperial ancestors and remove thence
Tob Timur's tablet; let Putacheli be deprived of her title and
appanage of an Empress, and be conveyed to Tong ngan chiu;
let Yang Tekus go to Corea as an exile; let all others who have
shared this mystery of crime and are still living get the punishment
befitting their offenses."

Yang Tekus was sent to Corea under Yue Kusar, a mandarin,
who took his life on the journey. Putacheli was sent to the exile
appointed, and died there soon after. Fearing lest people might
impute these cruel acts to his counsels, Machartai the minister,
who disapproved them, resigned, and his place was taken by
Toktagha, his son, and by Timur Buga.

At this time were completed annals of the Liao, the Kin, and
the Sung dynasties. Kubilai at beginning his reign had commanded to write memoirs of the first and second of these dynasties,
the memoirs being officially established, and after its fall memoirs
of the Sung dynasty also. He wished too that the data on which
they were founded should form a part of those annals. These labors,
neglected, notwithstanding his orders and those of his immediate

successors, were but slightly advanced when Togan Timur became Emperor. To finish them he established, under Toktagha, a commission of the most eminent scholars in the Empire. These men produced annals of those three dynasties. Besides there were in these works calendars; methods of astronomical research; lists of great men and their biographies; lists of books published by scholars; and in the Sung history a library of books on all subjects. There were also statistics touching several foreign countries, and detailed description of States paying tribute to the dynasties.

At the end of three years Toktagha, disgusted with court life, retired from office. When consulted about a successor he recommended Alutu, a descendant in the fourth generation from Boörchu, the first man of Jinghis Khan's comrades and one of his four bravest warriors. Alutu when in office exiled Machartai and Toktagha. In 1347 his place was taken by Pierkie Buga, son of the minister Agutai, who had been put to death by Kuluk Khan's order. This last man held the place only a few months. Turchi, his successor, demanded as colleague Tai ping who obtained the recall of Toktagha, whose father, Machartai, had died while in exile. Toktagha was not slow in regaining the Emperor's favor, which he made use of to send Tai ping of whom he was jealous into exile.

All this time the insurrection was spreading rapidly in Southern China. In 1341 two private persons had raised troops in Hu kuang, and seized many cities. Discontent had grown rife in Shan tung, while robber bands ravaged other regions. A pirate chief, Fang kwe chin, harried the coasts of Che kiang and Kiang nan. This man sailed up southern rivers, plundered cities, and ruined commerce, turning specially to vessels filled with grain, rice and various provisions intended for the capital. The Mongols seemed to disregard these the earliest attacks, and disorders increased very rapidly. Those who raised them made use of the great public works undertaken in 1351 by the government.

The damage wrought by Hoang Ho floods caused the plan of opening a new bed for a part of the river. An embankment eighty leagues long was undertaken. More than seventy thousand men were employed at this labor, either warriors, or men who lived on both banks of the river, or near them. The insurgents enrolled some impressed laborers, as well as men whose lands had been taken for the new river bed, and who were to find land in other places. Fresh taxes imposed to carry out those works increased dissatisfaction.

Han chan tong, an obscure private person, seeing the ferment of minds, raised the report that Fohi (Buddha) had now appeared to deliver the Chinese from Mongol oppression. He roused rebellion in Honan, Kiang nan, and Shan tung, but the chief leaders, knowing that this story would not be accepted unless strengthened, gave out to the world that Han chan tong was of the Sung dynasty, and eighth in descent from Hwei tsung. They took an oath to him, sacrificing a black bull, and a white stallion. They chose then a red cap as ensign. This pretender to Sung blood had very poor fortune, however. Attacked by the Mongols, he was captured and killed by them, but his wife, and his son, Han lin ulh, fled and continued the struggle.

The first reverse did not cast down those rebels. Their principal chief, Liau fu tong, captured cities in Kiang nan and passed over then to Honan with a numerous army. Other chiefs enrolled malcontents in Kiang nan and Hu kuang and gave them the red cap as ensign. One rebel chief, Siu chiu hwei, was proclaimed Emperor at Ki chiu, a city in Hu kuang, and he gave the title Tien wan to the dynasty which he was seeking to establish.

After a feeble resistance the Mongols abandoned the whole Yang tse region. A comet appeared now, and a report was spread widely by the rebels that this heralded Togan Timur's early downfall. The Mongol Government to conciliate men who had the most influence over people admitted to offices of all kinds those Chinese scholars in the south, who till then had been able to act only in matters touching literature and commerce, and were wholly unfitted for military command.

The government despatched to Honan an army commanded by Yessen Timur, a brother of Toktagha, the prime minister, and exiled to the distant north Yng kwe, a true descendant of the Sung family, with an order not to let him communicate with any man. This was done since most rebel chiefs hid their plans of ambition under pretext of putting the prince on the throne of his fathers.

Siu chiu hwei continued his triumphs, and to attach men to his fortunes more surely, he let them pillage all cities which he captured. He took Han yang, and Wu chang in Hu kuang, as well as

Kiu kiang in the north of Kiang si.   He defeated Fan chi king and
mastered Hang chau, which the Sung dynasty had once made its
capital, but the Mongol general, Tong pu siao, crossed the Yang
tse, and laying siege to Hang chau, regained it after desperate carnage.   Yessen Timur, who had been sent to put down rebellion
in Honan, defeated by Li fu tong, retired to Kai fong fu, and thus
left the field to the rebels.   This incompetent general was reprimanded and soon after the increase of the uprising caused the
Emperor to replace him by his brother Toktagha.   Toktagha, leading Honan forces, defeated the insurgents near Pe sui chiu, but
Sing ki, who commanded all Imperial troops in Yang tse regions,
was defeated and lost his life in a battle against a new rebel army.

Fang kwe chin, the pirate chieftain, was very active.   He continued to capture ships sailing northward, and thus deprived Ta tu
of supplies from South China, and also of tribute.   Besides this, he
killed most perfidiously Tai Buga, a general.   Hence the government, greatly anxious to win the bold, active pirate, charged Tie
li Timur to confer with him.   The pirate gave assurance that he
would submit and disband his forces if he, with his brothers, two
in number, were made mandarins of the fifth class.   Tie li Timur,
delighted at this offer, gave the three brothers Hiu chin, Kuang te,
and Siu chiu in the Che kiang province.   The pirate, however, for
reasons which he alone knew, refused the places when the time
came to take them, raised sail, and disappeared with his ship and
his cutthroats.

In 1354, Chang se ching, a new rebel, appeared in Kiang nan and
though his troops were all levies he routed Tachi Timur, who had
been sent out to crush him.   At this juncture, the first minister,
Toktagha, fell on Chang se ching, beat him thoroughly, and retook
the cities which he had captured.   But while Toktagha was
retrieving the losses of his sovereign, his own colleague at the capital
was working his ruin.   Hama and Sue sue, two brothers, notorious
for dissolute conduct, had become mighty in the Emperor's councils.   They were Kankali Turks, adventurers in the worst sense,
hardened profligates, and thoroughly perfidious.   When he had
reached power Toktagha gave Hama occupation, and then appointed him minister.   Very soon this new minister made himself
independent of Toktagha and rose every day to greater influence.
In due time he found support in Ki, the Empress, a Corean princess

by origin. She was Togan Timur's favorite wife, and mother of the heir apparent. Hama applied himself quickly also to serving the worst inclinations of his sovereign, and peopled the palace with his creatures, youthful debauchees given to every disorder, and Tibetan Lamas, who practised all sorts of magic, and held immensely grotesque superstitions. At this man's instigation the censors of the Empire accused Toktagha of taking for his own use, or giving to his favorites, funds intended for war and public service. Toktagha, the victor, so greatly needed at this crisis, was stripped of his dignities and ordered to Hoai nan into exile, and before going was forced to yield his command to the generals Yué yué and Yué Kutchar.

Meanwhile Siu chiu hwei, who called himself Emperor, was master of Wu chang, the chief city of the great Hu kwang province. Wishing also to capture Mien yang, he charged with this service Ni wen tsiun, one of his best leaders. The prince of Weï chun, who commanded that region, sent his son, Poan nu, to oppose that rebel chieftain, but Poan nu's barks being weighty were stranded in the Han chuen shallows, where the rebels burned the flotilla with fire bearing arrows. Poan nu perished with a number of his warriors — and Mien yang was lost to the Mongols.

The year following (1356), Ni wen tsiun took Siang yang and conquered the region of Tchong ling, after he had beaten Tur chi pan, a Mongol general.

Because of great distance these reverses in the South roused at first slight attention in Ta tu, or any other place, but when Honan rebels raided regions north of the Hoang Ho there was lively dread at the capital. Troops were sent to Honan, Shen si and Shan tung at the earliest. Liau fu tong, chief of Honan red caps, thought that he was increasing his partisans by proclaiming Han lin ulh, son of Han chan tong, the first pretender, as the legal Sung Emperor. This prince took the designation Ming wang, and established his court at Po chiu in Honan.

The Mongol court, fearing lest the name Sung, so dear to the Chinese, might rouse them, hurried off an army under Taché Bahadur, against the pretender. This general met Liau fu tong and was defeated. Liu hala Buga, who had been sent with a second corps to support the defeated man, attacked the rebel leader and vanquished him. He received chief command now because of his victory, and marching directly toward Po chiu, he overtook and again defeated Liau fu tong, who fled for relief toward Ngan fong and took his Emperor with him.

After Toktagha's disgrace Hama was created first minister and Sue sue, his brother, chief censor of the Empire. All power now was in those two brothers. Since Hama had nothing to fear, as he thought, save the return of Toktagha, he had the late minister killed at the place of his banishment. But noting soon that the Empire was decaying very swiftly, and the sovereign was depraved beyond repentance, a result to which Hama himself had contributed immensely, he thought of means to cure the evils around him, and decided to raise to the throne the heir apparent, a person of some wit and a self seeker. This design was discovered and Hama was sentenced to exile and in 1356 his enemies had him strangled.

In 1355 appeared the man destined to destroy Mongol rule in China and found the Ming dynasty.—Chu yuan chang, a Buddhist, and also a priest who cast off his habit in Kiang nan to become a simple warrior under Ko tse ling, a rebel chieftain. This Chu was not slow in creating a party. Continual success, with moderation, brought him many supporters, and his renown increased daily. Advancing to the river Yang tse he was met by the people in Tai ping as their saviour. After he had captured Nan king, Yang chiu and Chin kiang he laid siege to Chang chiu near the mouth of the river. This city was held by the troops of Chang se ching, who himself was not present. This rebel leader, though defeated by Toktagha, had recovered through Mongol remissness, and made himself master of many cities. Chang se ching sent his brother Chang se te to succor Chang chiu, but this brother was defeated and captured.

Chang se ching wrote now to the future Emperor of China and entreated him to cease his siege labor and liberate Chang se te, promising in return to become his vassal and pay a large yearly tribute in grain, gold and silver. Chu, convinced of Chang se ching's thorough perfidy, held firmly to his prisoner and captured the city.

In the North the adherents of Ming wang, the pseudo Sung Emperor who desolated Shen si and Honan, were beaten in Shen si by Chagan Timur, the Mongol general. Liau fu tong, Ming wang's first minister, had mastered Honan for the greater part, and now wished to capture Kai fong fu, the capital of Honan, and

establish in that place the court of his sovereign. Two army
corps which he had sent to Shan tung committed great ravages.
Pe pu sin, chief of one corps of these warriors, entered Shen si
somewhat later, captured Tsin long with Kong chang, and laid
siege to Fong tsiang. Chagan Timur, who hastened to rescue this
city, surprised Pe pu sin and captured his baggage. Pe pu sin fled
to Su chuan and thus saved himself. The rebel force which had
burst into Shan tung and taken many cities defeated Talima che li
and laid siege to Tsi nan, the chief city of Shan tung and its capital.

When Tong toan siao arrived from Honan with a Mongol division he defeated the rebels at the walls of Tsi nan and then left the
place; but barely had he gone when Mao kwe, who commanded the
pseudo Sung forces, attacked this central city of Shan tung and captured it. Then he pursued Tong toan siao, closed with his forces,
and killed him in battle. After this victory in 1357 Mao kwe seized
the city of Ho kien and made raids to the very edge of Ta tu, the
capital of the Mongol Empire. It was thought by some members of the council, that the Emperor should immediately
withdraw from Ta tu, but the minister, Tai ping, opposed this,
and summoned Liu kara Buga, a good general, who defeated
Maok we, and forced him back on Tsi nan, which he had
taken. While one of his detachments was threatening the
capital in this way Liau fu tong seized Kai fong fu, from
which the governor had withdrawn on a sudden. Liau fu
tong then established his Emperor in that city, which had been a
residence of the Kin dynasty just previous to its downfall. Then
he sent north of the Hoang Ho two divisions of warriors under
Kwan sien seng and Po te u pan, who had ravaged Shan si for the
greater part. The first of these leaders took a long turn northward
to Liao tung, whose capital, Liao yang, he plundered, and even
touched the border of Corea while ravaging. Doubling back, he
made the long march to the Emperor's great summer residence,
Shang tu, which he captured and pillaged; and his warriors burned
Kubilai Khan's splendid palace in that city.

In the South Siu chiu hwei had made himself master of most
of Hu kwang and a part of Kiang si. Chu yuan chang, the coming
Emperor, strengthened his position in Kiang nan, and set about
conquering Che kiang in its Eastern division. He received the submission of the pirate, Fang kwe chin, who, threatened in the West by

Chang se ching and in the south by Chin yiu ting, master in Fu kien, preferred to be vassal of a man whom he trusted. The pirate agreed to surrender Wen chau, Tai chu, and King yuen in southern Che kiang when they came to him; he sent also his son Fang kwan as a hostage. Chu, believing the word of this pirate, sent his son back to him, and on receiving the above mentioned districts he returned to Nan king, where he formed a strong council to govern those newly won places.

While Chu yuan chang was thus increasing and strengthening his power, division was rapidly weakening the other two parties. The life of Mao kwe, the Sung general, was taken by his colleague, Chao kiun yong. To avenge Mao kwe, Siu ki tsu set out at once from Liao yang and overtook Chao kiun yong at Y tu, where he struck him down straightway and killed him. Dissensions were still more rife among Siu chiu hwei's partisans. Chin yiu liang, a general of this founder of the Tien wan would-be dynasty, had just captured Sin chiu (Kuang sin) on the eastern border of Kiang si after a siege which was famous for desperate resistance (1358). The defenders were led by Ta chin nu of the blood of Jinghis, and by Beyen Buga, a descendant of the Idikut of the Uigurs. Both these men perished in the deadly encounter. The provisions in the garrison became so reduced that the warriors ate the flesh of those of their comrades who had perished. At last they killed all of the inhabitants who through age or weakness could not aid in the defence and used them for food. The place was finally captured by means of an underground passage. At this juncture Siu chiu hwei wished to transfer his capital from Han yang to Nan chang fu, a recent conquest, though the general who was with him opposed it lest his influence might be lessened.

The pretender went by way of Kiu kiang. Chin yiu liang went out to meet him under pretext of showing great honor, but when Siu chiu hwei had entered Kiu kiang, the gates were closed quickly behind him, and troops, waiting silently in ambush, cut down his attendants. Chin, master now of the Emperor's person, spared his life and his title, but he confined him, and called himself Prince of Han. Somewhat later he marched on Tai ping, with his prisoner, and when he had captured that city he beat the Sin chiu to death in his barge, with a crowbar.

Chin now proclaimed himself Emperor, named his dynasty the

Han, and returned to Kiu kiang, whence he had set out on his enterprise.

Chagan Timur, the Mongol general, seeing the Sung party divided, planned now to capture Nan king with Liau fu tong and his Emperor. He so arranged the march of his three army divisions that they arrived over different roads simultaneously. Nan king thus found itself invested on a sudden. He cut off all provisions, intending to weaken the city, or perhaps take it by famine. When he saw that provisions in Nan king were exhausted, he delivered a general assault in the night time, scaled the walls, and took the place. Liau fu tong escaped to Ngan fong with his Emperor.

In 1353 Togan Timur had made Aiyuchelitala his heir, and published a general amnesty. Seven years later the heir in accord with Ki, the Empress, his mother, wished that Tai ping, the first minister, should prevail on Togan to resign and leave him dominion. The minister would not try this experiment, hence they strove to destroy him. The heir had poisoned a number of the minister's partisans to weaken him. Tai ping, exposed then to every blow and attack of a daring conspiracy, retired from his office. Power passed after that to a eunuch, Pa pu hwa, and to Cho se kien, two infamous men who had no thought except to increase their own wealth and authority, and who kept the weak and debauched Emperor in complete ignorance of all things around him.

A quarrel between two Mongol military chiefs at this critical moment is of interest: Chagan Timur, acting in Shan si, had retaken Tsin ki from the rebels. Polo Timur, the Tai tung fu governor, declared that this district belonged to his province, and should not be detached from it. He advanced with troops therefore to take the place. Chagan protested. The Emperor settled the boundaries and the generals withdrew, each man to the region assigned him. Hardly had they obeyed when the Emperor commanded Chagan to yield up Ki ning to his rival, but Chagan replied that Ki ning was needed to defend Kai fong fu, and reassembling his warriors he moved now against Polo. Again orders came from the Emperor; the movement was stopped, and the governors laid down their weapons, though unwillingly.

This same year (1360) a storm rose in the North, which at first seemed more dangerous by far than the rebellion in China. More than once had the Emperor ordered princes of his family to aid him with troops in defending his dominions; but now one of these princes, Ali hwei Timur, seventh in descent from Ogotai, tried to seize the throne for his own use, instead of helping its occupant. This prince was advancing with aid, but when some days march from the Great Wall of China, he declared that Togan Timur the Emperor was powerless to preserve that which he had received from his ancestors; that he had lost more than half of it already. Ali hwei then invited the Emperor to yield what remained of the inheritance. Tukien Timur, whom the Emperor sent to crush this bold rebel, was beaten and withdrew on Shang tu to find refuge. The Mongol court was in terror and hurried on forces, but at this juncture the rebel prince was betrayed by his own men, and delivered to the Emperor's general who commanded him to be put to death immediately.

Chagan Timur, having won back Honan, put garrisons in the principal cities and passed over then to Shan tung to restore it to the Mongols. On reaching this province he received the submission of Tien fong and Wang se ching, two chiefs of the rebels. He divided his army into several corps and sent these into action on all sides. He himself went to Tsi nan, the chief city, or capital, to besiege it, and took the place after three months' investment. After that he attacked Y tu, the only place left those insurgents at that time, 1362. Tien fong and Wang se ching repented now of having aided this shrewd leader of the Mongols, so they plotted death to him. Tien fong invited the general to a review of his army, and Chagan Timur, who accounted Tien fong as the best among all of his intimates, took with him only a dozen attendants. Barely had he entered the tent of his host when Wang se ching gave him a death blow. The two friends hurried then with their forces and entered Y tu as had been agreed with the governor. Kuku Timur, the murdered man's son by adoption, inherited his dignities and title, and continued the siege of Y tu in obedience to the Emperor. He attacked the place eagerly, and finding resistance as brave as the onset, he turned to dig tunnels, and dug till he worked himself into that city and took it. The chief of the rebels he sent to the Emperor, but Tien fong and Wang se chin he reserved for his personal and exquisite vengeance. He brought them bound and alive to the coffin of Chagan Timur, and there tore their hearts out, those hearts he then offered to the spirit of his father. All the troops of these men who had followed them into the city were put to the sword without exception.

A new Emperor appeared now in Su chuan, an officer named Ming yu chin, who had been sent to conquer this province by Siu chiu hwei just before he was beaten to death with a crowbar. Ming yu chin, having learned of the murder of his master, made conquests for himself and finished by capturing the Su chuan capital, where he proclaimed himself Emperor and called his dynasty the Hia.

Now began war between Chu yuan chang, the coming Emperor of China, and Chin yiu liang, that seeker for Empire who, when a general, had beaten to death with a crowbar his own would-be Emperor, Siu chiu hwei. Chin had taken Tai ping and advanced to the lands of Nan king. Chu yuan marched against him, and when he had taken Nan king he found Chin near Kiu kiang and cut his army to pieces. Chin fled to Wu chang. Chu yuan captured Kiu kiang, and then Nan chang fu. Master of this capital, he received submission from the principal cities of Kiang si. Chin, wishing to win back Nan chang fu at all hazards, equipped a vast number of vessels and laid siege to the city, which he pressed cruelly, hoping to take the place before Chu yuan chang could appear with relief for it; but those in command made a gallant defence and were able to notify Chu yuan of their peril. Chu yuan sailed away from Nan king to assist them with his flotilla, bearing on it a numerous army. To cut off retreat from his enemy he ranged all his craft near Hu kiu, where Lake Poyang joins the Kiang si through a channel. Chin, who had besieged Nan chang eighty-five days in succession, raised the siege straightway, and entered the lake, where he met Chu's flotilla. The battle raged for three days, when Chin, who had lost most of his vessels, was killed by an arrow. Chin chan ulh, his eldest son, named by him successor, was captured, and his principal officers yielded to the victor. Chin li, the second son, fled to Wu chang and proclaimed himself Emperor; but besieged, and seeing his cause in utter chaos, he yielded without asking conditions. The surrender of this capital of Hu kuang was followed by that of the province. Conquest was made easy now by Chu yuan chang's reputation for leniency, and the discipline of his army.

Before this campaign which destroyed the would-be new dynasty

of Han, Chu yuan, learning that Chang se ching and Liu chin had
captured Ngan fong, where the Sung Emperor was living, and
that they had slain Liau fu tong, his commander in that city,
advanced toward it and defeated Liu chin. Giving up command
of his army then to his general, Su ta, Chu charged him in 1366
with the investing of Hiu chiu. The Mongols recaptured Ngan
fong after Chu yuan chang had departed.

Now new troubles burst forth among the Mongols, and first
that which seemed most serious: After the murder of Chagan
Timur, the one man who might have restored Mongol authority
in China, Polo Timur, his opponent, strove to capture Tsin
ki, and, in spite of repeated commands from the Emperor,
he sent troops to take the place. These troops were defeated by
Kuku Timur, son of Chagan. Polo Timur then desisted, but
another event armed him soon against even the Emperor. The
weakness of the sovereign favored factions, and the heir, who
was unprincipled and ambitious, took active part in the struggles
of rivals. Cho se kien, the first minister, persuaded the heir that
many great persons, whom he named, were ready to rise in
rebellion; he then induced him to ruin them. The prince
accused these men to his father, and through his power of insistence brought death to two leading persons.

Cho se kien and the eunuch, Pa pu hwa, bound to each other
by criminal plotting, now feared lest Tukien Timur, a friend of the
two men just done to death without reason, might avenge them,
hence they decided to destroy Tukien also. They brought a
criminal action against him. Polo Timur roused a defender to
act for him. The heir, enraged by this daring, accused Polo himself of complicity with Tukien and had him stripped of his office.
Polo refused to yield up command and his enemy Kuku Timur
was sent to constrain him. Polo knew that this order had been
given without the Emperor's knowledge, and induced Tukien to
make a feint on the capital, hence he seized the Kiu yong kwan
fortress. They wished to bring the Emperor to banish the man
who had taken possession of him. Ye su, who commanded the
place next that fortress, attacked Tukien Timur, but his forces
were utterly broken. Thereupon the heir, not feeling secure in
the capital, fled northward for safety. Tukien now advanced
to the river Tsing ho, where he halted to wait for the Emperor's

decision. He declared that Polo Timur, by whose orders he was acting, had no dream of failing in duty to the Emperor, he merely desired to deliver his sovereign from Cho se kien and Pa pu hwa the two traitors; he would retire the moment these direst foes of the Emperor were given to him. They meditated long at the court over this proposition, counter proposals were made, but Tukien remained firm and retired only when the two ministers were put in his possession and Polo Timur was reinstated in office.

Mongol dominion had fallen in China and civil war was raging around Shang tu. The heir, a rebel also, was ordered back to Ta tu by the Emperor. He obeyed, but if he did it was simply to assemble an army and send it under Kuku Timur to fall upon Polo at Tai tung fu, his headquarters. Polo, leaving men to defend the place, hastened on to Ta tu with the bulk of his army. The heir advanced to the river Tsing ho, but at sight of Polo's large army his forces fled to Ta tu, and not feeling safe even in that place, went out through the western gate to join Kuku Timur, then near Tai yuen fu, the Shan si capital. The heir followed them. When they had gone Polo entered Ta tu, and going with a party of his generals to the palace fell at the feet of the Emperor and received pardon for those acts to which, as he said, he had been driven.

Togan Timur made him commander-in-chief and first minister. Polo now, 1364, put to death Tolo Timur, the Emperor's favorite and companion in debauchery; he drove from the palace a legion of parasites, among others a real cohort of eunuchs and the whole throng of Lamas. At his request the Emperor sent courier after courier to the heir demanding his return to the palace. The heir, far from obeying, resolved to try arms against Polo, his now all-powerful opponent. The recent example of Tukien Timur was in this case most apposite.

When Polo learned that the heir was advancing he arrested Ki, the Empress, and forced her to send in her own hand an order by which she recalled her son to the capital. This done he sent Tukien toward Shang tu to oppose the heir's Mongol partisans on that side. He sent Ye su, a general, to attack Kuku Timur and the heir, who was with him. Ye su had not marched seven leagues to the south beyond Ta tu when he saw that the officers in his army were dissatisfied with Polo, so he assembled the chief ones, and in counsel it was resolved to obey that first minister no longer. They therefore turned back toward Yong ping a short distance, from which point Ye su informed Kuku Timur and the princes in Mongolia of the resolve they had taken.

Polo Timur in despair at this defection sent against Ye su Yao pe yen Buga, his best general. Ye su surprised this man, cut his army to pieces, took him prisoner, and killed him. Polo Timur took the field now himself, but a rain storm which lasted three days and nights prevented all immediate action, and he returned to the capital. The opposition which he met rendered him so distrustful that he put several officers to death on suspicion. Seeking to drown in wine his sad humor, and the grief which had seized him, he grew both ferocious and pitiless. More than once, while in those moods he killed men with his own hand, and he soon became odious to every one.

Ho chang, son of the Prince of Wei chun, got a secret order from the Emperor to put an end to Polo and his partisans, and soon he found the occasion to do so.

Polo receiving news of the capture of Shang tu, a victory over Mongol adherents of the heir, hurried on to inform the Emperor, but just as he was entering the palace he was stopped by Ho chang's men who opened his skull with a sabre stroke. When news of this death reached Tukien's army the officers deserted their general. Tukien was arrested, and put to death straightway. The Emperor sent Polo's head to the heir at Ki ning and an order for him to appear at the palace. The prince returned now with Kuku Timur, who became commander-in-chief and first minister. The heir strove to force Kuku Timur to persuade the Emperor to resign in his favor, and not finding the minister compliant grew enraged at him. The Emperor was unwilling to abdicate, but he gave his son power almost equal to that which he himself had, making him lieutenant in the Empire. Kuku Timur tried to prevent this, but failed, and was stripped of his dignities. Thereupon, he retired to Shang si, where he lived in a stronghold.

While the Mongol court was thus torn asunder by dissension Chu yuan chang was extending his Empire continually. He lived at Nan king, working always to establish a government on justice and order, as recommended by ancient philosophers of China. Mean-

while his generals Su ta and Chang yu chun attacked Chang si
ching, who was master yet of a part of Che kiang and Kiang nan.
In 1366 these two distinguished chiefs won a great victory over
Chang si ching, took Hiu chiu, one of the wealthiest cities in Che
kiang, and also Hang chau, the capital of that province. The next
year they captured Chang si ching in Ping liang, and took him
to Nan king directly. Chu yuan gave the man liberty in return
for his word that he would not go from the city in any case.
Chang gave his word to remain in it, and then hanged himself.

Ming yu chin, who had declared himself Emperor of the Hia
dynasty, died in 1366. Min ching, his son, who was ten years of
age, succeeded, with his mother as regent. This same year Han
lin ulh, who claimed to be of the Sung dynasty, vanished, and with
him went his adherents.

Fang kwe chin submitted at last. This faith-breaking pirate
had refused not only to appear before Chu yuan chang, and send
tribute, but he had acted against him in the North in alliance with
Kuku Timur, and in the South with Chin yiu ting, who held a part
of the Fu kien province. Chu then sent his general, Tang ho, to
take the cities Wen chau, Tai chu and King yuen. At the approach
of his forces the pirate retired to an island in the sea. When all
those cities soon after opened their gates to Tang ho the pirate
sent his son with submission, and put himself also at command
of the general, who sent him off to Nan king under escort.

Chu yuan chang undertook now the liberation of all China. Su
ta, his great general, and Chang yu chun marched northward with
an army which numbered one fourth of a million. While Hu
ting shui, a third general, reduced Fu kien and Kuang tung, Yang
king took Kwang si and held it. These southern provinces, tired
of oppression from strangers, made no resistance whatever. First
of all Su ta and his colleague took the country between the Hoai
and Hoang Ho, then they crossed the latter river and entered Shan
tung, proclaiming that barbarians, like the Mongols, were unfitted to
rule a polished people from whom they themselves should receive
law and order; that the Mongols had conquered the Empire, not by
their merit, but through Heaven's aid given purposely to punish the
Chinese. Heaven, roused now by the crimes of the Mongols, had
taken power from them to give it to a warrior filled with virtue and
greatness, a warrior loved and respected by all men who knew him.

The generals met no resistance in any place. When all Shan tung had submitted they passed to Honan, where they had success of the same kind — the gates of every city were opened to their standards.

Togan Timur, who was terrified at the swiftness of these conquests, sent courier after courier for Kuku Timur, but that general did nothing to rescue the capital; he held aloof and marched away toward Tai yuen.

Master of China, Chu yuan chang proclaimed himself Emperor at Nan king on the first day of the Chinese year, February, 1368. He gave the name Ming to his dynasty, which means light, and to the years of his reign Hung wu (lucky war), a term applied also to this emperor himself, who after his death received the title Tai tsu, founder or great ancestor, which in China is usually given to the founder of a dynasty.

Chu yuan chang, the new Emperor, left Nan king in August, 1368, crossed the Hoang Ho at Ping lien, and marched on the capital; all cities submitted to him willingly. At the same time his two generals entered Pe che li from Shan tung. At this juncture Che li nien, one of Togan Timur's ministers, took from the temple of ancestors all tablets of the Mongol Emperors and fled to the north, the heir fleeing with him. Togan Timur decided to follow immediately, and naming Timur Buga his lieutenant, he appointed King tong as defender of the capital. Then, assembling the princes, princesses and high officials, he declared his resolve to retire to Mongolia. He set out that same night for Shang tu with his family. The new Emperor of China was soon at the gates of Ta tu, which he entered after a very slight struggle. Mongol dominion in China was ended.

Nearly all China now received the Ming Emperor, and he set about winning what was still under control of the Mongols. That done he intended to follow them to their birthland and take it. The fleeing Mongol Emperor, Togan Timur, did not think himself safe in Shang tu, hence he hurried northward to Ing chang on the bank of Lake Tal, where in 1370 his life came to its end. He had reigned thirty-five years, and was fifty-one years of age.

The Ming forces seized Ing chang and captured Maitilipala, Togan Timur's grandson, as well as many princes and princesses and distinguished persons who were all taken back to

China. The heir escaped safely to Kara Kurum, which now became the one capital of the Mongols. On learning that this prince had mustered troops in his homeland and was about to invade China the Ming Emperor in 1372 sent a strong force, under Su ta, to stop him. Su ta marched to the Kerulon River and the Tula, but gained no decided advantage. Kuku Timur, the great Mongol general, died in 1375.

The Mongol heir who died in 1378 had taken the title of Kha kan, White khan, that is Grand Khan. He was followed by his son Tukus Timur, who was complimented by the Ming Emperors on his accession to the sovereignty of the Mongols now driven back to their original home. In succeeding years the troops of this Khan advanced frequently to violate Chinese borders, but in 1388 the new Emperor sent an army against Tukus Timur which defeated him at Buyur lake very thoroughly. His wives, his second son and more than three thousand officers were captured. Tukus Timur was assassinated near the Tula while seeking safety in flight. Yissudar, who did the deed, was a prince of the Emperor's family, and seized the throne left by him. The ambition of others roused civil war which seemed permanent. After long quarrels and short reigns a prince named Goltsi gained supreme power in 1403. His reign was brief also, for he fell by an assassin and Buin Shara was made Khan to succeed him.

When in 1408 the Emperor of China invited Buin Shara to declare himself a vassal, he refused. A Chinese army now invaded Mongolia, but was defeated near the Tula. Yung lo, the third Emperor of the Ming dynasty, advanced with a large army in 1410 to the Kerulon River. Prince Olotai, Buin Shara's lieutenant, deserted him through ambition, retiring eastward to the Hailar River. Yung lo defeated both the prince and his lieutenant, the first on the Onon, the second on the eastern boundary of Mongolia.

Buin Shara was killed in 1412 by Mahmud, prince of the Uriats, who put Dalbek on the throne of the Mongols.

During two centuries Mongol princes strove unceasingly to regain lost dominion; yielding to China when sufficient force was sent against them, or attacking border provinces of the Empire when those provinces were left unguarded.

Toward the middle of the seventeenth century, when the Ming dynasty was nearing its downfall, the Mongols were divided into groups under various small chieftains, each of whom bore the title Khan.

The Kalkas were in the North in the birthland of the Mongols. West of them the lands of the former Naimans and the Uigurs were occupied by the Eleuts; the Chakars, and the Ordos lived in the country between the Great Wall and the Gobi desert. The Manchu dynasty which during 1644 won dominion in China took under its protection first the easternmost Mongols and the Kalkas. Strengthened by them, it conquered the Chakars, and later the Ordos. The Kalkas had preserved thus far independence, but attacked by the Eleuts they found themselves forced to seek aid from the Manchu sovereign of China. In 1691 the Emperor Kang hi received homage from the three Kalka Khans forty leagues north of the Great Wall. At last toward 1760 the Eleuts themselves were reduced, so that most of the Mongols proper are to-day subject to China, while the rest are under the control of Russia.

Remarkable as has been the part played by the Mongols in history the part to be played by them yet may be far greater. How great and how varied it may be and of what character is the secret of the future.

INDEX

Abaka, Hulagu's eldest son and heir, 294.

Abbasid Kalifs, 97, 199, 202, 206, 223; Rashid killed, 224, 231, 238, 247, 258.

Abdallah, son of Kaddah, plans to establish ancient faith of Persia, 204.

Abu Abdallah, sent to Africa; announces a Mahdi; assassinated by Obedallah, 205.

Abu Ali Mansur, tenth Kalif of the Fatimid line, assassinated, 223.

Abu Bekr, the first Kalif, 197.

Abul Fettah, nephew of Hassan Sabah, 215.

Abul Wefa, an Assassin from Persia, makes a treaty with the King of Jerusalem, 220.

Abu Mohammed, Grand Prior of the Assassins of Syria, 216.

Adhad the Kalif, asks aid of Nur ed din; his death, 231.

Aguta, subdues the Kitans; his death, 80.

Aiké Charan, reveals a plot to kill Temudjin, 52.

Aiyaruk, daughter of Kaidu, 380.

Aiyuchelitala, heir of Togan Timur, 403, 404.

Alai ed din, Kei Kubad, Sultan of Rûm, makes an alliance with Ashraf, 161, 162.

Ala Kush, Ongut envoy, 62; makes invasion easy, 83.

Alamut, Seljuk fortress, seized by Hassan Sabah, 210, 239, 240, 241, 244.

Alan Goa, daughter of Bargudai, 4; her death, 6; descendants, 7.

Aleppo, added to the Fatimid Empire, 264; Saladin's great-grandson rules the principality, 258; besieged by Hulagu, 264; captured by assault, 265.

Algu, deserts Arik Buga, 336.

Alihaiya, Mongol officer, attacks Kiang ling; city surrenders, 348; favorite of Kubilai, 349; lays siege to Chang cha, 353; captures the city, 354; ordered to Tung king, 364.

Ali hwei Timur tries to seize power, 404.

Ali Shir, brother of Kwaresm Shah, 95.

Ali ul Mulk, acknowledged as Kalif by Shah Mohammed, 98.

Aly, son-in-law of Mohammed, elected; rules at Kufa; assassinated, 197, 198, 201, 202.

Amalric, King of Jerusalem, raises the siege of Alexandria, 229; violates his promise, 230.

Ambagai, descendant of Taidjuts, 9; seized by Tartars, 12; nailed to wooden ass, 13; his widows, 18.

Amid, Kubilai Khan's Minister of Finance, killed by Wang chu, 371.

Amid ul Mulk, vizir, favors retreat of Shah Mohammed, 113.

Ananda, attempts to seize power, 384; murdered, 385.

Antchin, sent to conclude an alliance with Lyuko, 84.

Argun, sent to capture Kurguz, 191; becomes governor, 192; visits Mangu's court, 193.

Arik Buga, brother of Hulagu, wishes to be Grand Khan, 283; left in command by Mangu, 328; begins a struggle for Empire, 332; puts Apishga in prison; takes sovereign title, 333; defeated, 334; sends message to Kubilai, 335; defeated, 336; resolves to march against

Algu; returns to China, 337; his death, 339.

Arslan, Khan of the Karluks, 77; marries Altun Bighi, daughter of Jinghis, 78.

Ashraf, acts against Kwaresmians, 153; sends a commander to the West, 154; sets out for Harran; joins Kei Kubad, 163, 168; sends message to Jelal; makes a journey to Egypt, 169.

Assassins, see Hassan Sabah, Kia Mohammed, Hassan II, etc.

Assutai, one of the Arik Buga's commanders, passes the " Iron Gate," 337.

Asukeba, heir of Yissu Timur, 388; proclaimed at Shang tu, 389.

Ata ul Mulk Juveini, vizir and historian, 243, 244.

At chu, Mongol commander of fleet, captures seven hundred boats, 349.

Aziz, grandson of Saladin, 258.

Babek, A. D. 816, defeated and captured, 203.

Badai, discovers a plot to kill Temudjin, 53; rewarded by the Grand Khan, 60.

Baibuga, Naiman chief, makes Wang Khan's skull into a drinking-cup, 61; alarmed at Temudjin's growing power, 62; defeat and death, 63.

Baidju, succeeds Chormagun in Persia, 177; demands mother of Kei Korsu, 178; trouble with Queen Rusudan, 179.

Baiktar, killed by Temudjin, his half-brother, 19, 20.

Baisutai clan, origin of, 9.

Baitulu, chief of Tumats, withdraws from obedience, 88.

Banias, a castle in Syria, 219.

Barans, defeated by Temudjin, 41.

Bardjuk, chief of the Uigurs, receives Jinghis Khan's envoy, 76; about to marry the daughter of Jinghis, 323.

Bartan, grandfather of Temudjin, 10; his death, 15.

Batra, grandson of Chingkin, 384; sets out for Shang tu, 385; proclaimed Emperor; takes the title Byantu; appoints his son; his death, 386.

Batu, son of Juchi; Khan of the Golden Horde; loiters, 316; calls a Kurultai, 317; sends troops to escort Mangu to the Kurultai, 318; his death, 282.

Bar Hebraeus, a historian, 273.

Bayan, receives command, 345; captures Yang lo, 346; sends Chang yu to make peace; demands permission to continue hostilities, 348; visits the Grand Khan, 349; captures Chang chau, 350; sends Empress and Emperor to Kubilai; summoned to move on Kaidu, 352; headquarters at Kara Kurum, 369; declares for Timur; his death, 377.

Bedr ud din Lulu, Prince of Mosul, arranges for Syria to pay a tax, 179; summoned by Hulagu; his origin, 256.

Bedr ud din of Otrar, his hatred for Shah Mohammed, 105.

Beibars Bundukdar, minister of Nassir of Damascus; strikes the vizir; goes to Gaza; sends his oath of fidelity to the Sultan of Egypt, 262; declares for war, 268; commands the Egyptian vanguard, 269; sent to pursue the Mongols, 271; asks for government of Aleppo; plots to assassinate Kutuz; murders the Sultan; is made Sultan; arrives in Cairo; a Polovtsi by origin, 272; gives his former owner the government of Damascus, 273; sends for Abul Ahmed, 274; invested with sovereignty; orders the provinces to receive Ahmed as Kalif, 275; sends troops to the boundary of Persia, 285; sends envoys to the Khan of the Golden Horde, 286, 287; hangs Hulagu's envoys, 288.

Berkai, son of Juchi; Khan of the Golden Horde; converted to Islam, 282; desires the election of Arik Buga, 283; sends an army against Hulagu, 284, 285, 287; begins a new campaign; dies while marching against Abaka, Hulagu's successor, 294.

Ben Amran, a traitor, 254-255.

Belgutai, half-brother of Temudjin, 19; goes with Temudjin for his bride, 25; wounded at a feast, 36; kills Bura Buga; is excluded from council, 48; made master of horse training, 43.

Beglu Ali, mother of Jelal ud din, 158.

Boduanchar, son of Alan Goa, 5; leaves home, 6; finds a wife, 7.

Boörchu, 24; becomes Temudjin's comrade, 25, 27, 31, 32; sends troops against the Naimans; saves Sengun, 42; escapes from Keraits, 55; made commander of ten thousand, 67, 68, 69; saves Chepé Noyon, 92.

Borak, commander in Jelal ud din's army, 146; gives his daughter to Jelal; master of Kerman; nine of his family keep rule for eighty-six years, 147; revolts, 152; marries Beglu Ali, Ghiath's mother; strangles Ghiath, 158; asks the Kalif for title of Sultan; takes the name Kutlug Khan; his death; succeeded by Rokn ud din, 195.

Bortai, chosen by Yessugai as bride for Temudjin, 17; captured by Merkits, 25, 26, 27, 28; birth of Juchi, 29; counsels Temudjin, 30, 73; always held the first place, 138; Jinghis speaks of her when dying, 139.

Boroul, found in the Churki camp and given to Hoelun, 39, 42, 53; saves the life of Ogotai, 55; sent to aid Wang Khan, 56; released from nine death sentences, 70, 71; his death, 88, 307.

Boshin, great-great-grandfather of Temudjin, 10.

Bugundai, fourth son of Alan Goa, 4.

Buhadur Yessugai, father of Jinghis Khan, 15. See Yessugai.

Buin Shara, succeeds Goltsi on the Mongol throne; assassinated, 411.

Bulagan, partisan of Ananda, strives to put him on the throne, 384; killed, 385.

Burma, struggles to drive back the Mongols, 362; defeated, 363, 377.

Burshi, first victim of the second Grand Prior of the Assassins, 223.

Busi, Prince of Damascus, 219, 220; slaughters many Assassins, 221; marked for destruction, 222.

Chabar, son of Timur, 381; last real sovereign descended from Ogotai, 382, 385.

Changan Timur, Mongol general, 312, 400; takes Nan king; quarrels with Polo Timur; wins back Honan, 403, 404, 406.

Chang hong fan, made commander by Kubilai, 358; attacks Sung fleet, 359.

Chang se ching, a Chinese rebel, 398, 400, 401, 405, 408, 409.

Chang se te, brother of Chang se ching; defeated and captured, 400.

Chang shi kie, 349; assembles a fleet, 356; makes levies in Fu kien, 357; builds a palace, 358, 359; loses his life in a storm, 360.

Chao wun ping, a distinguished scholar, 301.

Charaha, son of Kaidu, 9; father of Munlik, stepfather of Temudjin, 18, 35.

Charchiutai, gives his son Chelmai to Temudjin, 25, 26.

Chelmai, son of Charchiutai, given to Temudjin, 26, 27, 32; saves the life of Temudjin, 46, 53; released from nine death sentences, 70, 71.

Cheng ho shang, a Kin hero, 299.

Chepé Noyon, aids in winning the land of the Kitans, 84, 85; sent against the Kara Kitan usurper; Jinghis warns him not to be proud, 91; kills Gutchluk; carries Mongol arms into Armenia; his origin, 92; sent to capture Shah Mohammed, 114; takes Nishapur, 115; sacks Rayi, 116; plunders Persian Irak, 132; commanded to conquer Polovtsi, 133.

Chepi, a Chinese general, sent against Java; wins a victory for Java; condemned; receives seventy blows, 370.

Chilaidu, a Merkit; Yessugai seizes his wife Hoelun, 16; Merkits attack Temudjin to take vengeance, 28, 29.

Chiluku, ruler of Kara Kitai, grandson of Yeliu Tashi, 89, 90.

Ching ling, made Kin Emperor, 308; slain, 309.

Chin ge suan, ruler of Tung king, refuses to furnish Togan with war supplies, 363, 364, 365.

Chingkin, Kubilai's intended successor; his death, 364; his exposure of Ahmed, 371, 372.

Chin Timur, left as governor of Kwaresm, 184; attacks Kankalis; deprived of power; sends Kelilat to Grand Khan, 185; made governor by Ogotai, 186; his death, 187.

Chin yiu liang, a general of the, founder of the would-be Tien

dynasty, captures Sin chiu; beats
the Emperor to death with a crowbar, 402, 405.
Chin y, commandant of Hoang chiu,
surrenders the city, 346.
Chohaugur, leader of the Imperial
troops, succeeds Tutuka; defeats
Kaidu, 378, 380; his son, 388.
Chong hei, Emperor of China, 81, 82,
83.
Chormagun, leader of army sent in
pursuit of Jelal ud din, 164, 166,
174, 175, 176, 177.
Cho se kien, minister of Togan Timur,
403, 406, 407.
Churchadai, leader of the Uruts, 33,
54; offers to lead the vanguard,
56, 59, 68; rewarded, 69.
Chu yuan chang, a Buddhist priest
destined to destroy Mongol rule,
400, 401; gains power, 402, 405,
406, 409; proclaims himself Emperor, names his dynasty Ming,
410.
Crusaders, 220, 221, 230.

Dair Usun, chief of Hoasi Merkits, 28,
63.
Dargham, a commander in Egypt,
228, 229.
Desaichan, father of Bortai, 17, 34.
Dalbek put on the Mongol throne,
411.
Doben, ninth in descent from Batachi, 4; boy received in exchange
for venison, 5; descendants of
Doben and Alan Goa, 7.
Dokuz Khatun, granddaughter of
Wang Khan and wife of Hulagu,
255; her death, 256.
Dua, put on the Jagatai throne by
Kaidu, 366; deserted by his
troops, 379; proposes Chabar
as Timur's successor; proposes
to acknowledge overlordship of
Timur, Kubilai's son; his death,
381.

Egypt, scene of great struggles between Kalifs of Bagdad and
Cairo, 223. See Saladin, Nur ed
din, Kutuz.
Eibeg, a Mameluk chief, marries
concubine of Sultan Salih, rules
Egypt, 257; restores lands belonging to Nassir of Syria, 258,
259; slain by his wife, 262, 263.
Euzbeg, a general, watches India for

Jelal ud din, 146; his neglect, 151,
152.
Eyub, commandant of Tenkrit castle,
father of Saladin, 227, 228, 238.

Fakhr ud din Saki, last commandant
of Aleppo, 266, 267.
Fang kwe chin, a pirate, 396; shows
great activity, 398; submits, 409.
Faris ud din Aktai, a celebrated
Mameluk chief, 258; makes Beibars Sultan, 272.
Fatimids, first Kalif, Obeidallah,
205; their territory; declared
spurious by Bagdad; struggle to
supplant the Abbasids, 206; trained
in the House of Science, 211; doctrine, 212; agents in Persia and
Syria, 214, 231, 233. See Assassins.

Georgians, make a league against
Jelal ud din, 159; defeated by
Jelal, 160.
Ghiath ud din, son of Shah Mohammed, retires to Karun; marches
against Ispahan, 145; quarrels
with his brother, 146, 148, 151;
arrests Jelal's envoys; betrays
Jelal, 155; retires to the mountains; kills Mohammed at a feast;
goes to the Assassins, 157; goes
to Kerman; strangled by Borak,
head sent to Ogotai, 158, 194.
Goltsi, gains power in Mongolia, 411.
Gumushtegin, a eunuch, guardian
of Salih, son of Nur ed din, 237;
hires Assassins to kill Saladin, 238.
Gutchluk, given as title to son-in-
law of the Kara Kitai ruler, 90;
makes war on his father-in-law,
91, 92.
Gutchluk, son of Baibuga of the
Naimans, 103, 104.

Hayton, King of Cilicia, 178, 180;
decides to visit Mangu the Grand
Khan, 183; sets out, 287; aids the
Mongols, 288.
Hakim, 276; claims to be fourth in
descent from Mostershed; goes
to Egypt, 277; is Kalif, 285.
Hama, has an evil influence in councils
of the Emperor, 398, 399, 400.
Han lin ulh, son of Sung pretender,
396; disappears, 409.
Herat, summoned to surrender, 125,
128, 129, 131; repeopled, 190, 194.

Hoan ho Timur, grandson of Mangu, 393, 394.

Hoelun, captured by Yessugai, 16; gives birth to Temudjin, 17, 18, 19, 20, 39; warns Temudjin against Jamuka, 32; saves her son Kassar; her death, 73.

Horchi, describes a vision, 30; given thirty beautiful women, 68.

Huildar, leader of the Manhuts; plants Temudjin's standard on Gubtan, 54, 55; his death, 56.

Hulagu marches into Asia Minor, 184, 195; advances to exterminate the Assassins, 241; sends envoys to Grand Prior, 242, 243; surrender of Alamut, 244; gives a great feast, 245; kills all the Ismailians; sets out to destroy the Kalifat, 247; seduces commandant of Daritang, 249, 250, 251; slaughters the inhabitants of Bagdad, 252; kills the Kalif, 254; warns Nassir of Syria, 259, 260, 261; summons Aleppo to surrender, 264; sacks Aleppo; receives keys of Damascus, 265; receives news of Mangu's death, 266; promises to reinstate Nassir, 267; kills Nassir, 273; trouble with Berkai, son of Juchi, 282; defeated near Shemaki; victorious at Shirvan, 287; builds a palace at Alatag, 288; extent of rule, 289; places Uns Khatun on the Far's throne, 291; quells an uprising, 292; his death, 293.

Hassan Ben Sabah, son of Ali, sent to the Nishapur school, 206; classmate of Omar Khayyam, 207; gains influence over Melik Shah, 208; favors the second son of the Sultan of Egypt; gets possession of Alamut, 209; wins followers, secures power, 210; causes the death of Nizam ul Mulk and of Melik Shah, 211; his secret doctrines, 212; selects victims, 215; warns Sindjar, Sultan of the Seljuks, 217; makes Kia Busurgomid his successor; his death, 218.

Hassan, son of Kia Mohammed, Grand Prior of the Assassins, spreads report that he is the promised Iman, 226; becomes Grand Prior; determines to expose the secrets of the Order, 231; proclaims himself the Iman; celebrates the 17th Ramadan, 232; driven to prove himself a descendant of Fatimid Kalifs, 233; teaches atheism and immorality; assassinated, 234.

Hussein, son of Aly, 198; offers of support from Kufa, 199; leaves Mecca, 200; attacked by the troops of the governor of Kufa; his death, 201, 202.

Hussein Kaini, an active Dayis, 204, 210.

Ismailians, 154, 196, 211; Ismailian doctrine, 225, 234, 236, 240, 245. See Assassins.

Ibn al Athir, the historian, 172, 173.

Ibn Yunus, steals a letter from Salih of Mosul, 278; first governor of Mosul, 281.

Jagatai, marches to China with Jinghis, his father, 83; receives command at Otrar, 105, 119; quarrels with Juchi, his brother, 120; returns to Jinghis, 126, 138; his dominion, 141, 314, 315; his son, 333, 334, 336, 366, 380.

Jamuka, chief of the Juriats; descended from Kabul Khan, 27, 29, 30; forms a party, 31; his brother Taichar, 32; allies himself with Temudjin's enemies, 33, 34, 36; influences Sengun, 43; attacks Wang Khan and Jamuka, 46; his forces scatter, 47; fills Sengun's heart with fear, 50, 51; conspires to kill Temudjin, 52; battle with Temudjin, 53; message from Temudjin, 57; betrayed and surrendered to Temudjin, 63; words from Temudjin, 66; his death, 67.

Jambui Khatun, wife of Kubilai, 353, 370, 376, 377.

Jelairs, a clan; origin, 7; kill Monalun, 8; crushed by Nachin, 9; oath taken to destroy Temudjin and Wang Khan, 9, 44.

Jelal ud din, son of Shah Mohammed, saves his father, 104; joined by Timur Melik, 108; opposes retreat, 113; with his two brothers he reaches Urgendj; attacked by Kankali Turks, 119; defeats the Mongols at Ghazni, 121; defends himself at the Indus, 127; springs into the Indus, 128; pursued to India, marries the daughter of the Sultan of Delhi, 146; feigns ignorance of his father-in-law's

treason, 147; marries daughter of
Sád of Fars, 148; campaign
against Nassir the Kalif; sends
letter to Prince of Damascus, 149;
marches to Azerbaidjan, 150; captures Tovin; learns of plot against
him in Tebriz, 151; abandons
siege of Khalat; sets out for Kerman, 152; marches against the
Assassins of Persia; repulses Mongols, 154; betrayed by his brother;
defeated by Mongols, 155; learns
that Ghiath has gone to the Assassins, 157; secures the district
of Gushtasfi, 158; fines his vizir
for giving advice, 159; besieges
Khalat a second time; commands
Moslems to pray for Mostansir,
160; takes Khalat, 162; falls ill;
defeated, 163; goes to Mugan to
obtain warriors, 165; surprised
by Mongols; discovers the treason
of his vizir, 166; sets out for Jaraper, 167; surrounded by Mongols,
169; captured by Kurds; is killed;
appearance as described by Nessa,
171.
Jelal ud din Hassan of Alamut, son
of Mohammed II, 239; opposed
to the doctrines taught at Alamut;
poisoned, 240.
Jinghis Khan (see early life under
Temudjin), rewards his Empire
builders, 68, 69; jealous of his
brother; reproved by his mother,
73; angry at Munlik, 75; sends
envoy to Idikut of the Uigurs, 76;
intrenched in Kara Kitai, 78;
seeks co-operation of the Kitans,
81; informed of the succession
of Chong hei, 81; sends message
to the Chinese Emperor, 82; moves
from the Kerulon to conquer
China; crosses Gobi; invests Tai
tong fu, 84; resumes activity in
China, 85; marries a daughter
of Utubu, 86; marches on Tangut;
receives submission of Corea, 89;
Kalif requests his aid; sends
message to Shah Mohammed, 100;
resolves to extinguish Gutchluk,
101; ends Gutchluk and his kingdom; marches westward; places
his sons in command, 105; moves
again to Bokhara, 106. 108; enters
mosque on horseback; marches
against Samarkand; cuts off Jelal's
retreat, 119; camps on the Nak-

sheb steppes; besieges Termend;
destroys Kerduan; takes Bamian;
grandson killed, 126; attacks
Jelal at the Indus, 127; cuts down
men faithful to Jelal ud din, 129;
passes winter near the Indus;
resolves to return to China; gives
command to kill prisoners; leaves
Samarkand; back in homeland
1225; enters Tangut, 137; his
death; remains taken to birthplace, 138; funeral chant, 139,
140.
Juchi, son of Temudjin, his birth, 29,
50, 52; goes to China with Jinghis,
83; tries to save Kultuk, 88; sent
to act against cities from Jend to
Lake Aral; gives orders to attack
the city of Jend, 106, 107, 108, 119;
quarrels with Jagatai, 120; goes
north of Lake Aral and establishes
the Golden Horde, 126; Juchi's
heirs inherit from Jinghis, 141, 144;
his grandson, 367.

Kabul, son of Tumbinai, visits China;
taken prisoner, 11, 12, 15; rivalry
between descendants of Kabul and
Ambagai, 16.
Kaidan, meets Taidjut in single
combat, 12, 13.
Kaidu, saved by his nurse, 8; from
him are descended the greatest
historical men of the Mongols, 9;
grandfather of Tumbinai, 10, 16.
Kaidu, great-grandson of Jinghis
Khan, advances to attack Algu,
337, 339, 361; makes war on
Kubilai, 365; gets control of the
Jagatai country, 366; forms a new
league, 368; held in check by
Bayan, 369, 376; assumes the
title of Grand Khan; his death,
380, 381, 382.
Kamala, Kubilai's grandson, 369;
aspires to Empire, 376, 377, 387.
Kamil, Prince of Mayafarkin, 273,
274.
Kamil. Sultan of Egypt, 163, 174.
Kankalis, 101, 107; expect to be
treated as kinsmen, 111; are
slaughtered, 112; dissatisfied with
Jelal ud din. 119; move westward;
form nucleus of Ottoman Empire,
126; closely connected with Kwaresmian rulers, 158.
Kara Buga, Mongol commander, 276,
277.

Kara Kitai, its extent, 75, 78; its origin, 89, 90, 91, 93, 94, 100.

Kara Hulagu, grandson of Jagatai; dies on the way to his possessions, 323.

Karmath, agent of Abdallah, 204; captures Mecca; his followers rage for a century, 205.

Kassar (Juchi), brother of Temudjin, 17; together with Temudjin kills his half-brother, 19, 20, 21, 27, 35; victory over the Naimans, 44, 45; disobeys Temudjin, 59; saved by his mother, 72, 73, 74.

Kassin Almed, uncle of Mostassim, made Kalif, 275; lost in a battle against Kara Buga, 277.

Katchi Kyuluk, eldest son of Monalun, 7; his descendants, 8.

Kei Kosru, ruler of Rūm in 1238, 177, 178; marries the daughter of Queen Rusudan, 179; his death, 181.

Kei Kubad, Sultan of Rūm, 161, 162, 163, 164, 165, 168, 169.

Kentei Khan mountains, have two water systems, 3; body of Jinghis carried to the Kentei Khan region, 139.

Khaishan, son of Chingkin, aspires to power, 384; saluted as sovereign; takes the name Kuluk Khan, 385; his death, 385.

Ki, wife of Togan Timur, 398.

Kia Busurgomid, second Grand Prior, 218, 219, 225.

Kia Mohammed, third Grand Prior of the Assassins, 225, 226.

Kia se tao, Chinese official, makes secret treaty proposals to Kubilai, 332, 343, 344; master of Sung Emperor, 346, 347; exiled and murdered, 349.

Kitans, succeeded by the Golden Khans, 2; a part of the Manchu stock, 78, 79; Aguta subdues the Empire, 80, 81; insurrection, 84, 85, 90.

Kokochu, a shaman, son of Munlik, Jinghis Khan's stepfather, 72; called also Taibtengeri, gathers followers, 73; is killed, 74.

Kotyan, a Polovtsi Khan whose daughter married Mystislav of Russia, 133.

Kubilai Khan, favored by Hulagu, 283; son of Tului, 309, 318; receives Honan from Mangu, 325; returns to Mongolia, 326; popular in China, 327; accepts conditions offered by Kia se tao, 332; urged to proceed to Kurultai, 333; meets Arik Buga's army in Middle Shen si, 334; goes to Kai ping fu, 335; attacked by Arik Buga, 336, 337, 338; decides to conquer all China, 339; his envoys imprisoned, 340; delays war, 341; assembles troops, 342; exercised by war in his own family, 344; issues a rescript, 345; sends an embassy, 348; writes to Li ting shi, 355; summons Bayan from South China, 357, 358; resolves to subdue China, 361; forces Burma to pay tribute, 363; plans second attack on Japan; conquers Tung king, 364; drops his campaign against Java, 365; surprises the army of Tob Timur, 366; crushes Nayan, 368; leaves Shang tu, 369; needs money, 371, 372; his death, 373; his capital and palace, 374.

Kuichu, found in the Udut camp and given to Hoelun, 29; Jinghis Khan rewards him, 70.

Kuku Timur, son of Chagan, 404, 406, 407, 408, 409, 410, 411.

Kuluk Khan, see Khaishan, 385.

Kutula, fourth son of Kabul, 12; assembles warriors, 13; attacked by Durbans, 14; blood feud, 15.

Kuku Timur, besieges Y tu, 404; opposes the heir, 408, 409; his death, 411.

Kung yuan tse, descendant of Confucius, 301; sent to Subotai, 305.

Kurguz, Chin Timur's chancellor, 186; summoned to Mongolia, 187; sent to make a census; explains accusations made against him, 187; causes the death of Ongu; rules west of the Oxus, 189; protects Persians against Mongols; is killed by Kara Hulagu, 191.

Kushala, son of Tob Timur, 386, 388, 389; distrusts his brother; poisoned at a feast, 390, 392, 394, 395.

Kutb ud din, nephew of Borak, tries to usurp power; goes to Kurultai; obtains throne of Kerman; kills Rokn ud din, 195, 196.

Kuridai, warns Temudjin of a plot to kill him, 45.

Kurja Kuz, father of Wang Khan (Togrul), 40.
Kush Timur leads Bagdad forces, 149; killed, 150.
Kutuz, general of Eibeg, ruler of Egypt, 259, 262; his origin; becomes master in Egypt, 263; calls a council; decides on war, 268; sends envoy to Syria, 269; addresses his generals, 270; wins a great victory; names his lieutenants in Syria; leaves for Egypt; assassinated by Beibars, 272.
Kuyuk, installed Grand Khan, 180, 181, 182; his death, 182.
Kwaresmian Shah, see Shah Mohammed and Shah Jelal ud din.
Kwan sien seng, captures Shang tu, 104.

Liau fu tong, chief of the Sung pretender. 397; proclaims Han lin ulh, 399, 400; seizes Kai fong fu, 401; escapes to Ngan fong, 403; slain, 406.
Lien hi hien, a Uigur, Arik Buga's best general, 334.
Li ting shi, tries to rescue his Emperor, 355; rescued from drowning, and slain, 356.
Li tsong, Sung Emperor, 311, 312; his death, 341, 358.
Liu kara Buga, a Mongol general, 401.
Liu sin fu, minister of the Sung Emperor, 357, 358, 359.
Liu wen hoan, minister of Sung Emperor, 343; surrenders Siang yang, 344, 345, 346, 348, 351.
Lyuko, prince of Kitan dynasty, joins Jinghis, 84, 85.

Mahmud, successor of Sindjar, 219.
Ma ki, governor of Kuang si, resists the Mongols, 356.
Mamun, son of Harun al Rashid, makes an effort to unite the Alyites and Abbasids, 202.
Mangu, son of Tului; his brothers, 318; election declared illegal, 319; feast of installation; plot against his life, 320; death of his mother, 322; goes to Kara Kurum; kills his cousin, 323; has Ogotai's grandson drowned. 323; gives Honan to Kubilai Khan, 325; makes ready to march against the Sung Empire, 327; sets out

for the Sung Empire, 328; gives a great feast, 329; his death, 330, 331; wife and sons, 333.
Mangu Timur of the Golden Horde, descendant of Juchi, 365; sovereign of Kipchak, 366, 367.
Mansur, son of Eibeg of Egypt, 262; imprisoned by Kutuz, 263.
Mao kwe, commander of the Sung forces, 401; his death, 402.
Massud, Seljuk Sultan, takes authority from Abbasid Kalifs, 223.
Melik Salih Ismail, son of Bedr ud din Lulu; marries the daughter of Jelal ud din, last Shah of Kwaresm, 260.
Melik Shah, Seljuk Sultan, 93; gives an office to Hassan Ben Sabah, 207, 208, 209; alarmed by the defeat of his troops, 210; murdered by Hassan Ben Sabah's Assassins, 211.
Melik Timur, son of Arik Buga, partisan of Ananda, 384; murdered, 385.
Merkit, clan, the people from whom Hoelun, the mother of Temudjin, was stolen, 16; avenge the kidnapping, 27; hunted by Wang Khan and Temudjin, 28. 29, 30, 49, 56, 58, 62, 63, 64, 65.
Merv, attacked by Tului's army, 122; invested; surrenders; slaughter of its citizens, 123; repeopled, 128; again destroyed, 129.
Mien yang, taken by Siu chiu hwei, lost to the Mongols, 399.
Mingan, a distinguished Chinese general, 84; praised for siege work, 87.
Ming yu chin, a new Emperor, appears in Su chuan, 405; his death, 409.
Moazzam, Prince of Aleppo, refuses to surrender the city, 264; Aleppo destroyed, 265.
Mohammed, Shah of Kwaresm. withdraws from subjection to Chiluku ruler in Kara Kitai, 90, 91; invades the lands of the Gurkhan, 94; is defeated, 95; kills his brother. 96; resolves to destroy the Abbasid Kalifat, 97; moves toward Bagdad, 98; receives envoys from Jinghis, 100; his mother, 101; assembles a large army at Samarkand, 103; alarmed at the approach of the Mongol army, 104,

105; chased by thirty thousand men, 112, 113, 114, 115; suffering from pleurisy and weakness, takes refuge on an island, 117; his death, 117.

Mohammed of Nessa, the historian, 161; describes appearance of Jelal ud din, 171.

Mohammed II of Alamut, son of Hassan II, avenges the death of his father; preaches the doctrine of license, crime, and vice, 234; death from poison, 239.

Monalun, mother of Katchi Kyuluk and Nachin, 7; quarrels with the Jelairs; is murdered by them, 8.

Mongith, Prince of Karak, 288; murdered by Hulagu, 288.

Mostansir, Fatimid Kalif at Cairo, 160, 161, 206, 208, 209.

Mostassim, Kalif in Bagdad in 1257; his answer to Hulagu's summons to level the walls, 247; advised to send gifts to the Mongols, 248, 249; refuses to visit Mongol camp, 250; bound to his destiny, 252; begs for the lives of his family, 253; murdered by Hulagu, 254, 274.

Mostershed, the twenty-ninth Abbasid Kalif, 223; marches against Seljuk Sultan, 224; killed by the Assassins, 224.

Mozaffer, son of Bedr ud din Lulu, given Aleppo, 271.

Mozaffer, son of Säid of Mardin, rewarded by Hulagu, 275.

Muavia, governor of Syria, made Kalif to overthrow Aly; wins Egypt as first Ommayad Kalif, 197; sole Kalif of Islam, 198; forces the election of Yezid; his death, 199; exile of his descendants, 202.

Mukuli, a Jelair, given to Temudjin by his (Mukuli's) father, 39; rewarded by Jinghis, 67, 68; rewarded beyond all other generals, 88; reënters China, 136; his death, 136.

Munlik, son of Charaha, goes after Temudjin when Yessugai is dying, 18, 33; marries Temudjin's mother, 35; gives Temudjin advice which saves his life, 52; is rewarded by Jinghis, 72; one of his seven sons killed by Jinghis, 74, 75.

Mystislav, Russian prince, defeated at the Kalka, 135.

Nachin, uncle of Kaidu, 7, 8, 9.

Nassir, Kalif of Bagdad, ascends the throne, 96, 97; strengthens Bagdad, 149; his death, 160.

Nassir Salah ud din Yusseif, descendant of Saladin, 180, 257; rules Syria; undertakes to drive Eibeg from the Egyptian throne, 258; envoys received by Hulagu, 259; concludes a treaty with Mogith, 260, 261; alarmed by the approach of the Mongols, 262; receives a letter from Kutuz, 263; hears of the sack of Aleppo, 265; betrayed, and seized by the Mongols, 267, 269, 273.

Nassir ud din, vizir of Turkan Khatun, mother of Shah Mohammed, exercises authority in spite of Mohammed, 103.

Nassir ud din, famous astronomer, 244.

Naur, murders the grandfather of Wang Khan (Togrul), 40.

Nin kai su, Kin Emperor, 295, 300; accepts every condition, 301; abandons the capital, 303; sets out to make Tsai chiu his capital, 306; loses courage, 307; makes one more attempt to save himself, 308; yields the throne to Ching lin; hangs himself, 309.

Nishapur, twelve days' journey from Merv, attacked by Tului, 124; city occupied, 125.

Nizam ul Mulk, student at the Nishapur school of Movaffik, 206; first statesman of his period, 207; Nizam's own statement; killed by Hassan Ben Sabah, 211.

Nogai, Berkai's commander, 283, surprises Hulagu's men, 284; forced to retreat; is wounded, 294.

Nur ed din, Prince of Damascus, receives command from the Assassins, 217; son of Zenky, 226; rules the Syrian province, 228; conquers Haram; receives news of the advance of Amalric, King of Jerusalem, 229; sends Shirkuh to Egypt, 230; wishes to abolish the Fatimid Kalifat, 231; sees with alarm the growing influence of Saladin, 236; his death, 237.

Nusrat i kuh, in the Talekan district, defends itself for six weeks, 121; no living soul is spared, 122.

Obeidallah, governs in Bussorah; kills Muslim, 200; insists on absolute surrender of Hussein, 201; slays Hussein and his followers, 202.

Obeidallah, son of Mohammed Alhabib, summoned to Africa by Abdallah; imprisoned; rescued by Abdallah; made the first Fatimid Kalif, 205.

Ogotai, is wounded, 55; is given the wife of Tukta Bijhi, 64, 71; goes with Jinghis, his father, to China, 83; placed in command at Otrar, 105; given command at Urgendj, 120; sent to take Ghazni, 128; receives his inheritance, 141, 143, 144; Borak sends him the head of Ghiath, 158; receives the body of Shah Mohammed, 161, 164; Tamara of Georgia visits his court, 176; receives Kelilat, 185; gratified by a visit from the princes of Iran, 186, 187; receives presents from Kutuz, 188; commands to raise up Khorassan, 190, 191, 193; gives command over Chinese troops to three generals of that race, 295; master of Shen si, 296, 297; receives a message from Tului in Honan, 298; visits Tului, 299; master of all places around Kin capital, 300; asks for hostages, 301; alliance with Sung Emperor, 307; returns to Kara Kurum, 309; holds a great Kurultai, 310; recalls Subotai, 312; death of Kutchu, his favorite son, 312; passes his time in hunting and drinking, 314; falls ill; his death, 315; his widow assembles a Kurultai; the influence of Ye liu chu tsai, 314, 316.

Ogul Gaimish, Kuyuk's widow, 319; put to death, 323.

Okin Barka, son of Kabul, 13, 14.

Onguts, a tribe living near the Great Wall of China, 62.

Onon River, its source, 2, 4.

Order of Templars, 220.

Osman, ruler of Samarkand, makes an attack on the Gurkhan of Kara Kitai; wins a victory; kills Kwaresmians; death caused by his wife, 95.

Pa pu hwa, a eunuch, keeps Togan Timur under his evil influence, 403, 406; Tu kien delivers his sovereign from the traitor, 407.

Peyao, daughter of Yang Timur, marries Togan Timur, 392; murdered by Peyen, 393, 394.

Peyen, first minister of Togan Timur, discovers a plot to assassinate the Grand Khan, 393; kills the Empress Peyao, 394; his downfall and exile, 394.

Polo Timur, governor of Tai tung, quarrels with Chagan Timur, 403; strives to capture Tsin ki; refuses to yield up command, 406; reinstated in office, 407; puts to death Tolo Timur; despair over the defection of his best general, 408; his head sent to the heir of Togan Timur, 408.

Polovtsi, a tribe akin to the Mongols; befriend the Mongols; are betrayed and slaughtered, 133; seized with terror, they desert their allies at the Kalka, 134, 135.

Risvan, Prince of Aleppo, a friend of the Assassins, 214; loses Apaméa; reproached by Syrian princes; his death, 215.

Rokn ud din, son of Shah Mohammed, holds Persian Irak, 113; slain by Mongols, 145.

Rokn ud din Kelidj Arslan, son of Kei Kosru, sovereign of Rûm, 181; his partisans, 182; receives the land west of the Sivas; installed as Sultan, 183; receives news of his father's death; visits Ogotai; asks asylum of the Kalif; his death, 195.

Rokn ud din, son of Alai ed din, Grand Prior of the Assassins, 240; made heir; opposes his father; causes the assassination of his father, 241; demolishes castles and gives the Mongols assurance of obedience, 242; is given five days for surrender, 243; visits Hulagu; marries a Mongol woman; goes to Mongolia; his death, 245.

Rusudan, Queen of Georgia, 159; finds an asylum in Imeretia, 175; refuses to leave Usaneth; sends her son as hostage to Batu, 179; attacked by King David; recommends her son to Batu, Khan of the Golden Horde; takes poison and dies, 180.